The Crises of Civilization

'*The Crises of Civilization* is a marvelous feast. It is, first, a wide-ranging collection of fascinating essays, including a beautiful autobiographical meditation that illuminates Chakrabarty's thought through witty and moving narration of his Marxist youth, his discovery of history, and his encounter with both natural beauty and natural disaster in Australia. Later, I particularly loved the essay on Tagore's visit to Chicago, which opens up a reflection on the possibility of cross-cultural friendship. But the book is not simply a collection of individual gems: it has a challenging overall architecture, moving from reflections on postcolonial historiography in the first part to exciting new material on climate change in the second. Here Chakrabarty reflects on what can become of the practice of history, a practice long understood in terms of human subjectivity, when we recognize that the human being is also a geophysical force. Historians now, he argues, must take on the "difficult, if not impossible, task of making available to human experience a cascade of events that unfold on a non-human scale". Challenging, moving, wise, and witty, this work by one of our leading historians is a major event.'

—Martha C. Nussbaum,
Ernst Freund Distinguished Service Professor of Law and Ethics,
The University of Chicago, USA

'This is arguably the first serious effort to push the subaltern school of history, of which the author is a distinguished member, beyond its familiar world of global theoretical and empirical concerns, to open a conversation with planetary history, which in turn is concerned with human and planetary survival. The result is a marvellous exchange that transcends the self-imposed limits of Indian historiography. *The Crises of Civilization* is not merely a new, revised manifesto of the subaltern historians; it is a call for the emancipation of the discipline of history in India.'

—Ashis Nandy, Senior Honorary Fellow,
Centre for the Study of Developing Societies, New Delhi, India

The Crises of Civilization

Exploring
Global and Planetary Histories

DIPESH CHAKRABARTY

OXFORD
UNIVERSITY PRESS

OXFORD
UNIVERSITY PRESS

Oxford University Press is a department of the University of Oxford.
It furthers the University's objective of excellence in research, scholarship,
and education by publishing worldwide. Oxford is a registered trademark of
Oxford University Press in the UK and in certain other countries.

Published in India by
Oxford University Press
2/11 Ground Floor, Ansari Road, Daryaganj, New Delhi 110 002, India

ISBN-13 (print edition): 978-0-19-948673-1
ISBN-10 (print edition): 0-19-948673-5

ISBN-13 (eBook): 978-0-19-909602-2
ISBN-10 (eBook): 0-19-909602-3

Typeset in Berling LT Std 9.5/13
by Tranistics Data Technologies, New Delhi 110 044
Printed in India by Nutech Print Services India

To

Raju and Sanjay,
with affection

CONTENTS

Contents

II THE PLANETARY HUMAN

PREFACE

As many readers will immediately know, the title of this book is a riff on the title of a famous essay that Rabindranath Tagore penned in 1941—the year he died—to describe the sense of sadness with which he seemed to be nearing the end of his life. Entitled 'The Crisis of Civilization', that prophetic essay captured how many Indians felt about the blighting of what they also regarded as the most sublime ideal that Europe, for all the dark sides of her imperial aggression, had gifted to humanity—the idea of a civilized, modern collective existence based on the exercise of reason in the public sphere.[1] What clouded the evening of Tagore's life were the irrational passions and barbarities that marked the Second World War, of which, mercifully, he saw only the beginnings.

The crisis that Tagore spoke of in his essay on civilization had to do with his own disappointment with Europe. He was deeply sad to see European nations go to war with one another again even before the wounds of the Great War had fully healed. Aware that imperial acts of domination often betrayed the self-congratulatory premises of what Europeans regarded as their 'civilizing mission' outside of Europe, Tagore had nonetheless welcomed—as indeed had Gandhi—

---

[1] Rabindranath Tagore, 'The Crisis in Civilization' ['Sabhyatar Shankat'], in *The Collected Works of Rabindranath* [*Rabindrarachanabali*], vol. 13 (Calcutta: Government of West Bengal, 1961, centenary edition), p. 407. An English version of the essay appears in *The English Writings of Rabindranath Tagore*, vol. 3, ed. Sisir Kumar Das (Delhi: Sahitya Akademi, 1999), pp. 724–6.

the very idea of civility that lay at the core of the ideal of civilization. He had always acknowledged what India owed to British rule: modern ideas of equality, justice, and freedom. He saw these ideas as constitutive of a free and civilized society. Yet the two massively violent world wars of the twentieth century had profoundly tarnished the image of Europe in his eyes. He refused to surrender his 'faith in humans' but could not avoid the feeling that Europe had failed to put into practice some of her best and universal ideas. More than twenty years after Tagore's death, Frantz Fanon, another anti-colonial thinker, expressed an idea very similar to Tagore's. European thought, he noted, had created all the ingredients needed for the imagination of a world free of the oppression of humans by humans, but racism and empire prevented them from using these ideas effectively. It was up to the colonized, thought Fanon, to use these very same ideas to give humanity another chance.

In borrowing from the title of Tagore's essay, I have used the word 'crises' in its plural form, for I think the idea of civilization now suffers multiple forms of crisis and that these different crises may contribute, in their own ways, to a growing number of conflicts in the world. The essays in the first part of this book relate directly to some of Tagore's concerns (looked at from today's perspective). They track the rise and fall of the idea of civilization and its cognate forms of humanism—mostly, though not always, with reference to the history of colonial India. The Bengali word for civilization, *sabhyata*, as Tagore noted in his essay, was a neologism of the nineteenth century, for Bengali did not have either the concept or the word before the advent of British rule. The same is perhaps true of most other Indian languages. Early generations of Indian nationalists found the word useful, though today the material and textual evidence that nationalists cited to defend the idea of an 'Indian civilization' would be open to criticisms based on their colonial, nationalist, elitist, and often upper-caste if not Brahminical character. Certainly, 'civilization' and 'humanism' are now tainted words. They have been under attack from many directions, both political and theoretical. Conceptually, 'humanism' has been in crisis ever since Althusser's critique of 'humanist Marxism' became well known in the late 1960s. The word 'civilization', similarly, cannot be used in India today without being aware of its elitist provenance or without paying heed to Dalit criticisms of the many upper-caste prejudices that the word may actually hide.

While acknowledging these dark sides to the histories of the idea of civilization or humanity, the essays collected here do argue, however, for the continuing relevance of the ideas of civility and humanism in social and political relationships and suggest that there is something to be retrieved from these concepts for use in the writing of global history today. These words have suffered crises in different ways, no doubt, and we need to remain vigilant about how they are used, but the undeniable crises in the global careers of these words do not exhaust their appeal, since questions of civility—a cognate of the word 'civilization'—still trouble emergent forms of public life in democracies such as India's where, with the rise of a culture of intolerance of dissident voices, powerful forces often seek to resolve disagreements through violent and authoritarian means.

The book is organized in two parts preceded by an introductory chapter, which gives a somewhat autobiographical account of the evolution of my work. I first drafted this autobiographical essay in response to an invitation from a group of young Australian historians who requested a short piece on 'my life in history' for their journal, *History Australia*. I apologize for the autobiographical nature of this chapter, but I thought it could help the reader by underlining two points about this book: that the essays included here arose from the itinerant nature of my global-academic life, now stretched—sometimes uncomfortably—over three continents; and that they emerge from a perspective that considers Indian or South Asian history simultaneously from within and without.

I have called the first part of the book 'Global Worlds'. The essays collected here highlight not only the role that ideas about civilization and humanism have played in worlding the global, but also emphasize the necessarily contested, 'translated', and crisis-ridden nature of this global as seen from within a broadly postcolonial perspective. Of course, the instances, texts, and lives I draw upon to elucidate my points are limited for a variety of reasons including my own shortcomings. But I remain acutely aware that a word like 'civilization' exercised many gifted minds in South Asia within multiple traditions of thinking—I think particularly of personalities such as Muhammad Iqbal and Maulana Abul Kalam Azad—and that close studies of their texts and lives would help enrich and complicate the thoughts I develop here.

The second part of the book, 'The Planetary Human', tracks yet another sense of crisis—potentially graver than that elaborated in the first part—that now haunts the contemporary use of words like 'civilization' and 'humanism'. This is the crisis triggered by what is called global warming or climate change. Many climate scientists acknowledge that the warming atmosphere and the rising and acidifying seas pose a grave threat to the world's urban life and agriculture, and thus to all that we think of as the achievements of human civilization, including the division of labour that has made increasingly complex urban societies possible. This crisis, moreover, has come at a time when, ironically, more and more humans are choosing to live in cities, not only making this gravely iniquitous world resemble what Mike Davis has aptly christened 'the planet of slums', but also transforming humanity, for the first time in history, into a predominantly urban-dwelling species. Furthermore, most scientists predict a serious rise in the likelihood of conflict within and between nations as the world warms. If global warming, rising and acidifying seas in an increasingly urbanized world, and the loss of species represent the most recent crisis of civilization that we have begun to suffer, the phenomenon of climate change has also brought into focus the question of the relationship between capital and the history of biological life on the planet—a point most aptly expressed in the title of the sociologist Jason Moore's book *Capitalism in the Web of Life*[2]—thus raising the further issue of whether or not thoughts on human welfare and justice now require us to go beyond their usual and obsessive focus on the human flourishing that has been such a detriment to many other forms of life. Climate change has rekindled many fascinating debates on post-humanism or the need to supplement the usual anthropocentrism of the humanities.

I need to prepare the reader, however, for what may seem like a disjuncture between the two parts of the book. There is indeed a fault line running between them. In leaving this fault line open for future investigation, I have eschewed a popular argument that many—especially friends on the left—now make in connecting global warming and globalization. Proceeding in one continuous arc from the time of European imperialism through to the recent history of a capitalist

---

[2] Jason Moore, *Capitalism in the Web of Life: Ecology and the Accumulation of Capital* (New York: Verso, 2015).

globalization that has exploited the planet's resources—in particular fossil fuels—these scholars would squarely blame profit-hungry capitalist forces and the developed nations for precipitating global warming and the consequent changes in planetary climate. For them, it is the world system of capitalism that explains all. I certainly do not deny that the expanding use of fossil fuel—in both capitalist and the formerly 'socialist' bloc—has increased the share of greenhouse gases in the atmosphere. Nor do I deny—as my essay 'The Climate of History' will show—the historical responsibility of industrialized nations for accumulating an excess of greenhouses gases in the atmosphere that the planet's natural 'sinks' can no longer absorb. But the problem of 'planetary climate change' could not have been formulated by using only the variables we take into account while analysing the history of capitalist institutions. The scientific construction of a 'hyper-object', to borrow a term from Timothy Morton, like 'planetary climate system', entailed the bringing together of observational data of many different sciences, ranging from climate modelling to satellite observations of land, oceans, and atmosphere, to the geobiological history of the earth, to ice-core samples (obtained by drilling) of old air that go back several hundreds of thousands of years, and so on. In short, it has entailed the emergence of the new interdisciplinary field now called earth system science and has placed the human story within a horizon of time that is much, much larger than the 200 or 500 years—depending on how one defines 'capital'—that we credit capitalism with. Besides, this new science also allows for the agency of many planetary processes—such as the planet's glacial–interglacial, carbon, and nitrogen cycles—in explaining the phenomenon of 'planetary climate change' that can take place with or without human intervention. Humans are not necessarily at the centre of this very large-scale story the sciences tell, though it is true that, as humans, we can only ever think of what humans can do to avoid—as far as practicable—the worst impacts of global warming. And because humans are divided into privileged and underprivileged humans, and because climate change—if it does not lead to runaway global warming—impacts adversely the lives of the poor more than those of the rich, debates about issues of 'climate justice' are entirely legitimate and valid. I do not deny or dispute issues of justice between humans that the climate crisis poses.

But even if we thought of 'capitalism' (an imprecise word) as the system responsible for the emission of greenhouse gases, which today act as the one of the main drivers for planetary climate change, there would still remain an argument for seeing 'climate change' as a 'capitalism plus' problem. Take the question of the exponential increase in human population around the world since the 1950s, something to be factored in all future scenarios of the world. Increased use of fossil fuel in raising agricultural productivity and in improving medicine and public health—modernization, in other words—has facilitated this, no doubt. Thanks to all this, even the poor have longer—not necessarily better, but longer—lives. I am not convinced that the population question can be reduced to something like 'the logic of capital' alone, especially when population growth since 1950 has taken place principally in poorer or less capitalist countries such as India and China—and now in Africa—while countries that would be seen as more 'properly' capitalist (or at least, rich) have experienced slow or even negative rates of demographic growth! The history of population, it has seemed to me for quite some time now, belongs to two different narratives at once. The spread of humans all over the planet belongs to the story of *Homo sapiens*; never before did one biological species so dominate the entire land surface of this planet until we came along and flourished after the last ice age. The rise in the number of humans is surely part of a more recent story of modernization and the pursuit of modernization in different nations, but the dispersion of humans all over the world belongs to an older history of *Homo sapiens*, our species. And, taken together, the two histories show how our numbers and justifiable desire for human flourishing are intricately tied up with the history of the availability of cheap and plentiful energy that has been supplied primarily by fossil fuels of different kinds.

Earth systems scientists' emphasis on the 'agency' of planetary processes has in some ways reinvigorated discussions of the actor-network theories of Bruno Latour and views of the post-human put forward by a range of scholars including Jane Bennett, Isabelle Stengers, Rosi Braidotti, Donna Haraway, Anna Tsing, and—from related but different points of view—Eduardo Vivieros de Castro, Dana Danowski, and Eduardo Kohn. There was a time when the words 'global' and 'planetary' were used as synonyms in the human sciences. But with the emergence of earth system science, it has seemed to me for some time now, the word 'planet' has increasingly hived itself off from any absolute association with the word 'globe'. The adjective 'global' refers to this planet, our earth, with humans as the protagonist of the stories we tell. But when we think of planetary processes, it is not only the earth that we have in mind—other planets swim into view as well, humans or no humans. The fault line separating the two parts of the book is meant to symbolize this veering away of the two categories of the global and the planetary from each other. The global is human-centric in construction; the planetary involves many other actors and thus elicits the thorny question of how we go beyond the anthropocentric to discuss and conceptualize the agency of the non-human. The global and the planetary thus refer us to very different takes on human history.

My work on the implications of climate change and earth system science is still in the process of evolution. My reference to and use of the biological concept of species has been subjected to criticisms both appreciative and adversarial. I have had opportunities elsewhere to respond to some of those criticisms.[3] There is a whole field to be opened up here—particularly in South Asia. Discussions on climate change and the Anthropocene have not featured much in humanistic literature in or on India. The topic has mainly been the preserve of policy and science specialists. The publication of Amitav Ghosh's timely and much-discussed volume *The Great Derangement* and a special issue of *Humanities Circle*, edited by Prasad Pannian, have made a welcome beginning, however.[4] My hope for these essays is that they will contribute to further opening up of the field in the wake of these two pioneering publications.

The essays presented here were written over the last fifteen or so years. I have benefited from discussions with various scholars who read or heard these essays as lectures, and am grateful to the institutions that hosted me. Many of these debts are acknowledged in the individual essays. A version

[3] See the discussion in the special issue of the journal of the Rachel Carson Centre, Munich, 'Whose Anthropocene? Revisiting Dipesh Chakrabarty's "Four Theses"', special issue of *RCC Perspectives*, no. 2 (2016), and my interview with the French journal *Actuel Marx* reproduced in this collection.

[4] Amitav Ghosh, *The Great Derangement: Climate Change and the Unthinkable* (Chicago: University of Chicago Press, 2016); 'The Anthropocene and the Human Sciences', special issue of *Humanities Circle* 3, no. 2 (Winter 2015), published by the Central University of Kerala.

of Chapter 3 was previously published as 'An Anti-colonial History of the Postcolonial Turn: An Essay in Memory of Greg Dening', *Melbourne Journal of History*, vol. 37, no. 1 (2009): 1–23. The chapter also draws on material previously published as 'The Legacies of Bandung: Decolonization and the Politics of Culture', in *Making a World after Empire: The Bandung Moment and Its Political Afterlives*, ed. Christopher J. Lee (Athens: Ohio University Press, 2010). This material is used by permission of Ohio University Press, www.ohioswallow.com.

In putting this book together I have received sterling help from Mr Gerard (Gerry) Siarny, a friend who has also assisted me with my research in the last few years. Gerry's criticisms and suggestions have helped me to improve my research, presentation, and prose. It is also a pleasure to acknowledge the generous and constructive criticisms and suggestions I received from two anonymous scholars who read the manuscript for the Press. I am also deeply grateful to the editors, designers, and staff of Oxford University Press, India, for their help in the preparation of the volume, and to the artist Anna Madeleine for allowing me to use her absorbing and thought-provoking artwork on the cover of the book.

Rochona Majumdar has been the first reader of many if not all of these essays. My debt to her just keeps accumulating!

Dipesh Chakrabarty
Chicago, 20 July 2017

INTRODUCTION
Communing with Magpies*

An Indian Prelude

I never had the thought in school that I would be a historian. I was a student of science in my school years in Calcutta though my first love was Bengali literature. And perhaps my even deeper love—but somewhat unbeknown to myself—was philosophy. I used to wonder to myself about such questions as why artistic compositions needed an element of 'balance' in them or if the proverbial act of a drowning person clutching at straws could be taken as proof that she or he actually believed that the straws could save her or him from drowning. But there was no one at school to discuss these things with. The questions only had a silent existence in my school-day diaries. I persevered with science education and went on to do an honours degree in physics (with minors in geology and mathematics) from Presidency College, then affiliated to the University of Calcutta. But I was always more interested in the philosophical or conceptual aspects of physics than in the more applied or practical sides of the discipline. The de Broglie wave–particle hypothesis, for instance, fascinated me much more than finding out how exactly a DC motor worked. But that was not what got me into history. If India had had a more flexible education system or better educational counselling when I was an undergraduate student, I would have probably switched to philosophy.

What aroused my interests in the social sciences—though I did not know them then as such—was my youthful desire for an India that

* Edited from 'My Life in History: Communing with Magpies', *History Australia* 11, no. 3 (December 2014): 194–206, and from 'From Civilization to Globalization: The "West" as a Shifting Signifier in Indian Modernity', *Inter-Asia Cultural Studies* 13, no. 1 (2012): 138–52.

was less corrupt and more just. I was born and raised in the colonial
city of Calcutta (Kolkata) within a few years of Indian independence.
True, the British were gone, but there was still a lot of anti-British sentiment around. Growing up, we imbibed the nationalism of our parents.
But this incipient interest in politics was shadowed by a sense that the
nationalism that had energized our parents' generation had failed us.
By the time I was in high school, Mahatma Gandhi's party, the Indian
National Congress that dominated the political scene, appeared to be
in the hands of corrupt and self-serving politicians—though they were
actually much less corrupt in comparison to the average Indian politi-
cian today.

Our adolescence found India in all kinds of crises. There was a
humiliating border war with China in 1962, which produced much discussion and debate in our community. One group, the majority, blamed
China. At the same time, I had some cousins who were communists and
thought that a Communist country would never start wars. Because, as
they believed, Nehru represented the bourgeois classes and his government was controlled by the rich, India, they argued, must have started
the conflict. By the time I entered high school, I was convinced India
was at fault. So a lot of my friends and I used to argue with other
Indians and supported China in that war.

Crisis also haunted India at home. Food scarcity racked the country and exposed the weaknesses of the Indian agricultural system—
weaknesses that were later 'corrected' through the so-called Green
Revolution. In the world I knew in Calcutta, I witnessed widespread
unemployment and abysmal poverty. I had some very indigent close
relatives whose condition, for me, acted as a mirror of the country.

I was born in a Brahmin family. Brahmins are known as *dvija*, or
twice-born, for young Brahmin men undergo a sacred religious ceremony to become fully Brahmin—a coming-of-age ceremony like the
Jewish bar mitzvah. Yet upon my induction into Brahminhood, friends
from my college gave me a Moscow-published edition of the first volume of *Das Kapital* and four volumes of the *Selected Works of Mao*.
Thus, on my 'second birth', I was born a Maoist. This intermingling
of Brahminical tradition and leftist politics is only an example of how
tradition and modernity spoke to each other in the India of my youth.

I came of age, intellectually and politically, in a time of upheaval in
the left. It was around 1959 that the USSR started having difficulties

with China and began withdrawing its economic, technical, and diplomatic support. By 1962, the differences between the two countries were out in the open. In 1964, the global split in the Communist movement widened fractures within Indian communism: the parent Communist Party of India—or CPI—supported the USSR, while a breakaway party, the Communist Party of India (Marxist)—or CPI(M)—advocated neutrality. CPI(M) certainly had members whose sympathies lay with the Chinese, but the party did not quite declare for one side or the other.

Like many Bengalis of my generation, I got caught up in the enthusiasm that generally surrounded the formation of this party in 1964 and its subsequent rise. My friends and I were young people angry about poverty and injustice in our country. In a lot of ways, we were similar to the students at Tiananmen Square in 1989. We thought that India's real problem was that an exploitative class—and politicians beholden to that exploitative class—ran the country. We believed that India needed a revolution of the Chinese type—and we believed that a revolution, as the Chinese Communist Party said in its polemics with the Soviets, had to be a violent one. We were drawn to Mao's teachings, and we read Mao saying that just like you need a broom to clear away the dust, you need violence to clear away the exploiters of the people.

A general sense of political and social disaffection saw a combination of leftist parties elected to office in West Bengal—my home state—in 1967. Dominant among the new coalition governing from Calcutta was the new CPI(M) that had split away from the parent CPI. Just after the leftists and their Communist allies had been elected to office, however, the CPI(M) faced a challenge from within its own ranks. A Maoist peasant uprising broke out in a village called Naxalbari in North Bengal. The leaders of the insurgency were members of the CPI(M), but they believed in the Maoist theory of a violent peasant-based armed revolution. The CPI(M) was formally neither pro-Moscow nor pro-Beijing, but nevertheless opposed the peasants and attempted to put down their rebellion by force.

My friends and I morally supported both this uprising and the broader international Maoist movement of which it was a part. Many of my friends in college joined this new Maoist 'Naxalite' movement—soon to result in 1969 in a new party called the Communist Party of India (Marxist–Leninist), or CPI(ML), which was to be the Maoist party in India. From the start, the international connections were clear.

Because India and China were already enemies, *People's Daily* published an essay in 1967 entitled 'Spring Thunder Breaks Out over India' giving us moral support. Young Maoists would go around Calcutta writing slogans such as 'China's path is our path' and 'China's chairman is our chairman'. These slogans would often offend nationalist sentiments and lead to arguments with my friends and relatives. When this Maoist party was formed, some of its leaders reportedly—so at least the story went—snuck into China and offered the chairmanship to Mao, which Mao had the good sense to decline. I do not know if this story is true, but it is true that the CPI(ML) left the position of the chairman vacant. The highest position ever occupied by an Indian in that party was that of the vice-chairman, for the chairmanship, it was said, could only be Mao's. This was our anti-nationalism, or our internationalism.

China's Great Proletarian Cultural Revolution broke out in 1966. As it gathered momentum, the Maoists in India came quite seriously under its influence. The vice-chairman of the CPI(ML) called on India's urban youth to kindle the revolution in the villages. Many of my friends went to the countryside, braving police oppression. Haversacks on their backs and the little Red Book in their hands, these romantic revolutionaries left for the countryside to organize a peasant army that they thought would liberate India by 1975! Their first struggle in the countryside was with diarrhoea; several of them returned to the city for treatment, and then went back again to launch their violent revolution by killing oppressive landlords, assuming that such acts of violence would start a Maoist 'prairie fire'. Eventually, the police moved into the villages and flushed them out, so they came back to the city and made ordinary, poorly paid traffic constables the targets of their violence. Yet in the cities as in the countryside, the movement was slowly crushed by the government. Around 4,000 young Indians died, by Amnesty International's calculations.

I did not leave my city life behind to join my friends in the countryside—not because I did not share their beliefs, but because I was genuinely scared to be hounded by the police, who I knew could be brutally cruel. My courage failed me. Ashamed of myself, at one of our 'self-criticism' meetings—à la the Red Guards—I denounced myself. My friends, understandably, condemned what they called my 'petty bourgeois attitude' and began to shun my company. In my own heart, I agreed with their moral judgement.

As it happened, the Government of India had just set up two busi- ness schools in collaboration with American universities. Since my life suddenly seemed to have no revolutionary significance, I thought I must simply earn money. On graduation, I decided—perhaps out of self-hatred and as a morbid measure of self-punishment—to apply for admission to business school, and in 1969, I entered the Indian Institute of Management Calcutta (IIMC) as a postgraduate student. The insti- tute was in the sixth year of its existence. A deep irony of postcolonial development in India lent this business school some unique features. I owe my career as a historian to that irony.

Let me explain. It may sound strange but Marxist history was something I formally learned in my business school years. This was because of the kind of curriculum the institute had developed. Spurred by the belief that India could industrialize only by produc- ing a professional class of engineers and managers, Prime Minister Nehru's government had encouraged the setting up, first, of the Indian Institutes of Technology (IITs) and then of the Indian Institutes of Management (IIMs). There were only two IIMs in the beginning, one in Ahmedabad in the state of Gujarat and one in Calcutta in West Bengal. The Ahmedabad one had been actively helped in its early years by the Harvard Business School, while the institute in Calcutta had benefited from the cooperation of the Sloan School of Management at the Massachusetts Institute of Technology (MIT). The IIMs were modelled on American business schools but with one critical differ- ence: history was made a compulsory subject for all business school students. Because the future of India lay with capitalism, Nehru's government had decided that Indian business managers must have capitalistic economics, but Nehru also wanted to ensure that India's sense of the past was anti-colonial. Thus, the IIMs were perhaps the only business schools in the world that made history a compulsory subject (for students who were mostly of science and engineering backgrounds). And the IIMC had recruited a well-regarded Marxist historian, Barun De, who taught courses on how British colonial rule underdeveloped India. But, at the same time, the key economist we read was the very neo-classical Paul Samuelson. It was as if the Indian manager was meant to look forward to a capitalist future but carry a deep anti-colonial, anti-capitalist memory! (It is this second legacy that globalizing India struggles with today.)

This split symbolized Nehru's India: an aspiration to be a modern market economy combined with a deep distrust of the West's predatory history and thus a conflicted relationship to (Western) capitalism. But for me the discovery of Marxist social history was a godsend. Here I was, learning about large-scale socioeconomic forces that dwarfed the ambitions and foibles of individual humans. Suddenly, my morbid obsession with my own failure to be a revolutionary seemed overly narcissistic! I took all the courses my professor offered, courses that the more practical-minded business school students normally would not take. And when I graduated and got a job as a trainee personnel manager with a Scottish company in India and my professor asked me if I would rather be a historian, my choice was easy: life seemed meaningless without the study of history. I opted to be a historian.

I knew nothing about the subject but my professor was extremely generous. He taught me much, often on a one-on-one basis, and sent me off to the archives after showing me a big, fat book called *The Making of the English Working Class*. He asked: 'Do you think you could do something like this for our country?' There was, of course, no question of doing what one of the greatest historians of the twentieth century had achieved. I was a person of much more limited capabilities. Doing working-class history itself, however, was a concept I was to engage with critically in my first book, but more of that later. For now, let me just underscore the further irony of the fact that without the Nehruvian legacy—a legacy we would later on challenge in the pages of Subaltern Studies—there would be no question of business schools appointing Marxist historians on their faculty, and without my encounter with Barun De, I would have probably been a standard, run-of-the-mill business school professor, ignorant of the ways in which the past mattered in human affairs.

Australian Lessons

Practical and personal considerations eventually brought me to Australia to study for a doctoral degree in history. The University of Calcutta was too conservative an institution to admit as a PhD student someone who had never done any formal degrees in history (even though I had managed to publish half a dozen research articles in Indian journals of history). Fortunately, I met a professor from the

Australian National University (ANU) visiting Calcutta in late 1974 or early 1975. This was Professor D. A. Low, a gifted and generous historian of the British Empire in Africa and India, who came to speak at a social science centre that the Government of India had just set up with my Indian professor, Barun De, as its director. Professor Low had had a series of students work with him on Indian history; they were all established historians by this time. We in India knew of the work that was being done in Canberra on colonial Indian history under his leadership. At our meeting, Professor Low expressed interest in having me as a student. Thanks to his interest, the ANU eventually offered me a scholarship to study with him as one of his doctoral students.

After weathering many arguments and debates with friends and teachers in Calcutta who did not want me to leave the country, I came to Canberra in December 1976. Anthony Low, as he was more generally known, had become the vice chancellor of the university in 1975, soon after we met in India. It was a real privilege to have Anthony as my supervisor. However busy his schedule, he always made time to attend to his students. Importantly, he encouraged me to study South East Asian history in my first year, which opened up for me a completely new world of historiography. Some of the most well-known practitioners of this historiography were at the ANU itself: Anthony Reid, David Marr, and later Craig Reynolds and Rey Ileto. Even though I was formally Anthony Low's student and he conscientiously saw me every two weeks in my first year of study, it was Robin Jeffrey, then a post-doctoral fellow in the vice chancellor's section of the Research School of Pacific Studies (as it was called), who took great care of the everyday intellectual and material concerns of Anthony's 'sepoys' as the latter affectionately called us. Along with others pursuing South Asian studies at ANU, ours was a happy family that effectively was a branch of a larger group of historians in Australia and New Zealand who worked hard to keep alive a shared sense of South Asian studies.

But there was a larger element to the education I received in Australia. Being out of India and being in a liberal–democratic 'Western' country was itself a great source of learning. Perhaps I should recount here in some detail what Australia taught me, for much of what I learned in this new country moulded my intellectual life in quite fundamental ways.

'Which Indian city does Canberra remind you of?', Ken Gillion, the noted historian of Ahmedabad (but also of Fiji), asked me on our first meeting in Canberra in 1974 in the famous Coombs Building at ANU where he was then a research fellow. I was visiting Australia for a few days at personal expense to explore the possibilities for graduate studies at ANU and other Australian universities. I gave him an obvious and unoriginal answer, thinking of the similarities between the Civic in the then Canberra and Connaught Place in Lutyens' Delhi: 'Delhi, of course'. Ken's eyes twinkled mischievously through his thick glasses as he shook his head for an instant as if to both disagree and supply the right answer. 'No', he said, 'it's Fatehpur Sikri!' The village of Sikri near Agra was where the emperor Akbar (1542–1605) once shifted his capital to celebrate a military victory (hence the name Fatehpur, from the Persian *fath*, denoting victory)— only to abandon the place for lack of water. Canberra was dead and uninhabitable—that was Ken's judgement. This was a good 30 years before the recent water restrictions in the city came into force. And to think I would return to the place in December of 1976 to stay for the next several years as a doctoral student!

Ken Gillion's ironical description of Canberra was a good and friendly warning to someone coming into the city from Calcutta. Indeed you could not have two cities more different from each other. I was a Calcutta boy, used to all the pleasures and follies of that city: used to the crowds on the streets, to the hot and humid Calcutta summers, to the torrential rains and political demonstrations that now and again brought the city to a standstill, to the rickety trams and buses that plied its streets, to Bengali Marxism and hours of arguments and convivial fun in *addas* (palavers) over unending cups of tea and cheap cigarettes, and to the tradition of plays, literature, and cinema that enlivened the otherwise miserable existence the city offered to those not rich. Canberra, on the other hand, was squeaky clean, hot in summer and (for a Bengali) unbearably cold in winter, picture-postcard beautiful, and, above all, empty—there was not a person to be seen walking on the streets! In Calcutta, I would walk miles; but in Canberra taking a walking trip from the university to the National Library in the summer sun—a half-hour walk—would be considered sheer madness. Everyone looked at you! For several years, I pined for the crowds, the addas, and for conversations and arguments with boon companions that actually sometimes hurt you, but that nevertheless filled up all the existential blanks of human life and kept you, for both good and bad, from being with yourself and yourself alone. Being with yourself was something that stared you in the face in Canberra. There was no escaping it.

Yet Ken's unforgettable introduction to Canberra, while true in many respects, did not quite catch what the city and the experience of studying there were to offer me in the years to come. Canberra was the first city I lived in after living and growing up in Calcutta for 26 or 27 years. All my experiences there were deeply influential for the rest of my life. Australia came into my life through Canberra. It is not a representative Australian city by any means—many Australians love to hate it. But the Australia that I came to love was also the place I found in that city. There were things I had never known to be possible in Calcutta. I had not known what it meant to study in serene, bucolic surroundings. Presidency College, Calcutta, where I had done my undergraduate studies, was exciting for the bright students and famous teachers who walked its corridors and enlivened the classroom. But the consuming and divisive passions of my time had to do with the Maoist movement of the day, and the college was a mini battleground not just for ideas, political or otherwise, but also for the warring groups of different political organizations of students. Violence was in the air. One breathed in politics and with it the smell of gunpowder. The business school I went to for my master's degree was liberating in many respects after the colonial and bureaucratic rigidities of the University of Calcutta, but its campus then—on the north side of the city—was rather uninviting. The ANU had what they used to call a 'bush' campus (much destroyed now, regrettably, by the building boom of the last decade). Nature in Calcutta often meant looking up at the sky. You barely saw the horizon. In Canberra, the sky was all around you—a bright deep blue you felt you could drink. Nature would come your way while you were walking between buildings. I remember once being distracted by a great magpie commotion up on a gum tree as I was on my way from the Chancelry Building to my office in Coombs. The time must have been October or November-ish. Alerted by bird noise, I looked up and down and figured out what was going on: a mother magpie poked among the grass for worms while her little baby impatiently fluttered and squawked on a branch above, watching her every movement with nervous anticipation—leaning eagerly forward,

furiously flapping its two small wings to keep balance, and making an
awful ruckus! Every day, kookaburras would sit on trees inside the
hexagonal compounds of Coombs, and mock academics with loud and
utterly irreverent laughter; every day, they would remind us what a
joke all our work was. But my most funny experience was when I found
myself one day on one side of Fellows Road waiting for cars to pass
by—and who should be standing next to me, also waiting to cross the
street it seemed, but a big kangaroo!

There were other ways to discover nature in Canberra, and I must
make it clear that it was not always an 'Australian nature' that I discovered in the university's surroundings. I often found the nature I had
read about in Bengali literature and sometimes seen in Bengali films. A
creek ran through the ANU, Sullivan's Creek, and joined Lake Burley
Griffin. There was a dirt track (it has been sealed now, sadly)—near the
students' dormitories and satellite antennas of the Research School of
Physical Sciences—that followed the creek as it made its way to the
lake. If you walked along that path towards the lake, the land on your
right would quickly fall away into the creek, into a long line of reeds
that skirted the bank, among which wild ducks and geese would paddle
with their fuzzy little families. The scene always reminded me of lines
written by the immortal Bengali poet Jibanananda Das:

> If I were a wild duck,
> If you were my mate,
> On some faraway Jalsiri river bank
> Beside a paddy field
> Among the slender reeds
> In a secluded nest.[1]

I knew intellectually that the Bangladeshi district of Barisal celebrated
in Das's poetry would have had nothing in common with the landscape
of Canberra, but the creek comforted me by giving me the illusion of
being somewhere near a home that I had actually never even had. I had
not yet been to Bangladesh from where my parents' families migrated
when India was partitioned in 1947. My nostalgia was really nostalgia
for Das's nostalgia for another time. But that is perhaps how nostalgia

[1] Translated by Clinton B. Seely in his *A Poet Apart: A Literary Biography
of the Bengali Poet Jibanananda Das (1889–1954)* (Newark: University of
Delaware Press, 1990), p. 216.

works. I fell in love with the bush in and around Canberra through the mediation of Bengali literature. This was to prove rather important for my historical work in the long run. For it was my intensely personal sense of grief at the loss of this 'nature' when devastating fires broke out in Canberra in 2003 that got me interested in the history of bush fires in Australia and eventually led to my current work on climate change.

On the academic front, one of my biggest initial and pleasant surprises in Australia was to discover that intelligent people could be genuinely kind as well. An academic joust in Calcutta was like a duel; success was measured by how much blood was left on the floor. You bayed for the heads of your rivals in argument. The aim of an argument was to win—as though Indian history was not big enough to sustain two competing arguments about it—and the sign of conquest was that your rival was humiliated. A young man—and this was mainly a male game—showed off his intelligence as so much muscle power of the mind. It is possible that Australians display a similarly competitive attitude towards one another in the arena of physical sports. But such competitiveness was not socially acceptable in the academic domain. This was not always a good thing. Sometimes, in the Australian context, there was too much toleration even for arguments that were obviously weak and I did experience some negative sides of the Australian academic world later in life. But for me, it was liberating to learn that being kind in an academic exchange or to listen to one's opponent with openness and humility was not necessarily to concede defeat in an argument; that, in fact, being able to sustain an ongoing conversation was often more stimulating than aiming for an argument that would vanquish all rivals. Australia liberated me from a Kshatriya—the old warrior castes in the fourfold imagination of Hindu society—mode of thinking.

The biggest intellectual change that took place within me, however, was a very deep and slow one. This was learning to look at India from the outside. I had grown up in India into my early adult life. I was not born to a family that dreamt of sending its children overseas. I had many poor and indigent relatives. And there were all the contradictions of the Indian middle class that Edward Shils once wrote about. I was a Marxist but was also vaguely aware of having been born into a poor Brahmin family that valued education above all. My friends in India and I argued about Indian history but we were all insiders. Our passions about our histories came out of the literature we read, the soccer teams we supported, our relation to cricket, the songs we sang, and the films we watched. Nothing was separated from the immediacy of life. The plane that brought me to Canberra as a student broke my connection to that immediacy in a matter of hours. But the reality of this change took years, perhaps decades, to sink in. For a long time to come, I argued in my head with my friends back home. For a long time to come, I would secretly—and sometimes not so secretly—seek their approbation for what I wrote. At the same time, I was becoming an anthropologist of my own history and culture. Most of my work, until very recently, has both gained and suffered from this process. My first book, *Rethinking Working-Class History: Bengal 1890–1940*,[2] which was published more than a decade after I left India, was caught between the debates I had been a part of in Calcutta and what I learned about my people and their pasts after leaving my country. I perhaps got criticisms from both sides. 'Why is he so obsessed with Marxism?', asked South Asian studies scholars in the West, while friends at home did not at all like the Marxism they found in my writing—it was not revolutionary enough. And it was always hard to explain to one point of view the other one, though I could see both points of view and was not in full agreement with either.

Another subterranean influence of Australia on my thinking and work on India came from my exposure to debates that broke out in the 1980s and 1990s over Aboriginal history and cultural studies. I was then teaching at the University of Melbourne. Henry Reynolds was producing in these years his path-breaking books on the history of the black people and race relations in Australia, using with new vigour Frederick Jackson Turner's idea of the frontier. Stephen Muecke was producing exciting ways of 'reading' the country. In my generation of Australian historians, Bain Attwood, Patrick Wolfe, and others were raising new questions about the place and the past of Aboriginal people in Australia. Meaghan Morris, Simon During, and others had become world leaders in the new field of cultural studies. Greg Dening and Donna Merwick, historians at Melbourne University, along with Inga Clendinnen and Rhys Isaac at La Trobe, were bringing together anthropology and history in their work to raise fundamental questions about

---

[2] Dipesh Chakrabarty, *Rethinking Working-Class History: Bengal 1890–1940* (Princeton, NJ: Princeton University Press, 1989).

the nature of the historian's craft. And the environment of Australian history was changing radically in the hands of younger scholars such as Christopher Healy, Tony Birch, Klaus Neumann, and others. My list is very incomplete and probably unfair to many. But my point is that confronting in Australian and Pacific studies those peoples whom Eric Wolf had once described memorably as 'people without history' could not but have a profound effect on my thinking. Besides, as I came from a nation that valued its ancient texts, encountering in Aboriginal history problems of orality, memory, and deep human pasts that could only be rendered academic through the disciplines of pre-history and archaeology was a strange but absolutely enriching experience.

Looking back, today, I cannot separate the effect on me of that intellectual ferment in Australia from the equally powerful influence of the many insurgent questions that Ranajit Guha—who joined the ANU around 1980—raised in the field of Indian history. Subaltern Studies, Guha's brainchild, occupied much of my time and identity in the 1980s and 1990s. The project is associated with arguments in Indian history. But the deep presence of Australia in my work of the period is something I have become increasingly aware of in the last decade. I do not think I could have written the chapter called 'Minority Histories, Subaltern Pasts' in my book *Provincializing Europe*[3] without having been exposed to the debates and questions on methods that Aboriginal history, Pacific history, and cultural studies necessarily provoked.

The American Chapter

There were many reasons for moving to the United States—to the University of Chicago—in 1995. One important reason was the decline of teaching and research in South Asian history in Australia. At the University of Melbourne, where I taught from 1985 to 1995, there was nobody teaching Indian or South Asian history by the time I left. (Yet Melbourne once boasted a department devoted to Indian Studies.) I was teaching social theory. This was an exciting field, in which one read classical social theorists alongside the modern gurus of post-structuralism, feminism, environmentalism, and deconstruction; but I

---

[3] Dipesh Chakrabarty, *Provincializing Europe: Postcolonial Thought and Historical Difference* (Princeton, NJ: Princeton University Press, 2000).

missed my bread and butter—South Asian history. The second reason, I
suppose, was the rise of postcolonial theory and criticism and the place
my work—and that of scholars associated with Subaltern Studies—
gradually found within it, particularly in the American academy.

I got my position in the faculty of the University of Chicago in the
pleasantest of ways: no applications, no interviews, no nothing. Sheldon
Pollock, the famous Sanskritist then at Chicago, called me one day
in 1994 in my office in Melbourne and said that they had a position
for me should I be interested. Later on, after joining them in 1995, I
learned that what got them interested was an article I wrote in 1990
while visiting the Department of History at Berkeley for a semester
(at the invitation of Thomas Metcalf). It was eventually published in
the California journal *Representations* in 1992. In it, I had first broached
the idea of 'provincializing Europe', an idea I elaborated on later in my
book of that name published in 2000.[4]

I should say a few words about this essay. Its fundamental idea—
the unease I expressed about using 'indispensable and yet inadequate'
European categories in writing modern histories of South Asia—came
really from basic methodological and philosophy-of-history problems
discussed in my first book, which was based on my 1984 ANU thesis.
I often think of the last chapter of this book as really the first chapter
of *Provincializing Europe* (*PE*). The two books—and the companion to
PE, *Habitations of Modernity: Essays in the Wake of Subaltern Studies*
(2002)[5]—constituted a long process of my coming to terms with and
finally exorcizing the ghost of Calcutta Marxism that both formed and
troubled me over many long years. The project of *PE* was something I
began to work on while still at the University of Melbourne and I completed it at the University of Chicago. But the movement from Melbourne
to Chicago changed my interlocutors to some degree. The two colleagues
I was very close to at Melbourne were Simon During and Chris Healy,
both working—Chris as a historian and Simon as a literary scholar—at
the intersection of postcolonial criticism and cultural history/studies. In
Chicago, I similarly found three close colleagues with whom I had sig-

---

[4] Dipesh Chakrabarty, 'Postcoloniality and the Artifice of History: Who
Speaks for "Indian" Pasts?', *Representations*, no. 37 (Winter 1992): 1–26.
[5] Dipesh Chakrabarty, *Habitations of Modernity: Essays in the Wake of Subaltern Studies* (Chicago: University of Chicago Press, 2002).

nificant everyday conversations that profoundly influenced my thinking in my first decade at the university. Sheldon Pollock, Homi Bhabha, and Arjun Appadurai—all of them in different ways and from very different disciplinary backgrounds were students and theorists of global processes and histories. *PE* carries the stamp of all these different periods of my development: the enriching and mind-expanding arguments with friends in Subaltern Studies; the 'theory', 'cultural studies', and Aboriginal Studies ferment at the University of Melbourne; and conversations I joined at the University of Chicago, which ranged across premodern philology, area studies, the postcolonial world, and globalization.

The ANU was extremely kind to me after I left Australia, welcoming me back every year for a part of the North American summer. Friends at the University of Technology Sydney have made possible a collaboration on an Australian Research Council-funded project on climate change. These summer visits have also allowed me to run workshops with Bain Attwood (whom I regard as one of my teachers of indigenous histories) and with my very dear friends and mentors, the late Greg Dening and Donna Merwick. These conversations led to an increased interest in the whole issue of the relationship between history and memory, an issue that came out of Subaltern Studies as well (especially in the work of Shahid Amin). Along with Claudio Lomnitz (now at Columbia), Bain and I put together a whole volume of *Public Culture* on the topic of what we called 'the public life of history'. I became interested in the question of how one might distinguish the 'public' life of a discipline like history—always open to the pressures of public discussions of the past—from its institutional or 'cloistered' life as it were, and that started me on a project I recently completed. This was a monographic study of private letters and other documents pertaining to the life and work of Sir Jadunath Sarkar (1870–1958), easily the most famous of historians writing in colonial India in the first part of the twentieth century and also the first to seriously import into Indian history Rankean ideas of truth and source criticism.[6]

My continuing Australian connections, however, also enabled me to keep in regular touch with generations of South Asianists in Australia. Equally important, it gave rise to another project: the research and

---

[6] Dipesh Chakrabarty, *The Calling of History: Sir Jadunath Sarkar and His Empire of Truth* (Chicago: University of Chicago Press, 2015).

investigations that I am currently conducting into the implications of (the science of) climate change or global warming for humanist histories. As I said before, I would not have fallen into this project without the saddening experience of the most recent and long-lasting drought in Australia. It was this experience that led me to write an essay that has now travelled a fair bit and been translated into many languages: 'The Climate of History: Four Theses', published in *Critical Inquiry* in the winter of 2009.[7] I find it amusing to think that when I first wrote this essay in Bengali for a Calcutta magazine, it sank without a trace.[8] Though friends made admiring comments, they were not fundamentally interested in the topic, as though 'climate change' could not be a matter of concern for historians and social scientists of South Asia. The English version of the article, on the other hand, has opened up a completely new set of conversations for me in the United States, Australia, Latin America, the United Kingdom, China, South Africa, and, very importantly, Europe. In my home institution, friends and colleagues around the journal *Critical Inquiry*, along with colleagues in the Chicago Center for Contemporary Theory and colleagues throughout the university have helped me to renew and reinvigorate my long-standing interest in philosophies of history. One of the problems I started to work on was how one might think of the human after climate change, particularly in an era when many climate and other knowledgeable scientists say that humans collectively have become a geophysical force capable of changing the planet's climate to the detriment of humanity. Yet I am fascinated by how empty the category 'humanity' remains and how difficult it is to operationalize it even when we know that there are planetary problems affecting us all, though not equally or in the same way.

I now live and work in the United States. India and Australia are two countries I visit every year. I feel I am made of bits and pieces of all of these three countries but put together in a haphazard and incoherent fashion. To each of these countries, I have now an insider/outsider relationship. This is not always a good or comfortable place to be in. But over time I have come to appreciate its worth.

---

[7] Dipesh Chakrabarty, 'The Climate of History: Four Theses', *Critical Inquiry* 35, no. 2 (Winter 2009): 197–222.

[8] The original essay in Bengali has been reprinted in my book *Itihaser jana-jibon o onyanyo probondho* (Calcutta: Ananda, 2011).

PART I

GLOBAL WORLDS

I

BELATEDNESS AS POSSIBILITY
The Subaltern Subject and the Problem of
Repetition in World History*

A ubiquitous theme of modern history—indeed a theme that often
makes a particular piece of history belong to the so-called modern
period—is how and why different parts of the world come to embrace
capitalist relations. This is the process that in the past has given rise to
debates about the 'transition to capitalism' in the history of the modern
West. It has its echoes in the history of the non-West. The narratives of
transition have usually concerned themselves with sociological questions: Was trade the real motor of capitalist growth in Europe? Or was
it class struggle? Was it proto-industrialization? What weakened the
social bonds of pre-capitalist societies? And so on. But this series of
sociological questions have their cultural correlates. If modernity in the
colony comes late, sometime after the emergence of modernity in the
metropolis, how do we understand this belatedness of modernity in
the colony? Is the difference here a mark of residual backwardness or

* This essay draws on my articles 'Place and Displaced Categories, or How
We Translate Ourselves into Global Histories of the Modern', in *The Trans/
national Study of Culture: A Translational Perspective*, ed. Doris Bachmann-
Medick (Berlin: De Gruyter, 2014), pp. 53–68, and 'Belatedness as Possibility:
Subaltern Histories, Once More', in *The Indian Postcolonial: A Critical Reader*,
ed. Elleke Boehmer and Rosinka Chaudhuri (London: Routledge, 2011),
pp. 163–76. I am grateful to Doris Bachmann-Medick for helpful comments
on an earlier draft.

does it represent something 'new' created by the very temporal structure that marks the global history of the modern? Homi Bhabha made
this a pressing question in his book *The Location of Culture*: 'How does
newness enter the world?'[1] The problem of belatedness speaks to a
problem of repetition and recognition in history. If something happens that resembles something else within a field that is conceptually
structured by before–after relationships, then that which comes later
is seen as belated. How do we know what is new in what seems like a
repetition? In the rest of this essay, I wish to address that question with
the help of the example of the Indian series Subaltern Studies.

I want to submit to you two propositions that may initially seem a
little paradoxical. My first proposition is that newness enters the world
through acts of displacement. My second proposition is that newness
confounds judgement because judgement tends to see the new as repetition and therefore deficient. Newness is hard to distinguish from a
simulacrum, a fake that is neither a copy nor original. To be open to
the new is to engage in a Heideggerian struggle: it is like straining to
hear that which I do not already understand. Judgement, and I mean
political judgement, makes this a very difficult task.

The Subaltern as a Modern Political Subject

It may be helpful at the outset to take a page out of Gilles Deleuze,
someone who, in our times, has thought more than most about difference and repetition. Deleuze makes a primary distinction between
'repetition' and 'generality' in order to make a further distinction
between 'repetition' and 'resemblance'. 'Repetition is not generality',
he says and adds: 'Repetition and resemblances are different in kind—
extremely so.' Generality, according to Deleuze, 'presents two major
orders: the qualitative order of resemblances and the quantitative order
of equivalences. Cycles and equalities are their respective symbols.'
Repetition, on the other hand, stands for 'non-exchangeable and non-
substitutable singularities'. To repeat 'is to behave in a certain manner,
but in relation to something unique or singular that has no equal or
equivalent'.[2] He writes:

[1] Homi K. Bhabha, 'How Does Newness Enter the World?', in his *The Location of Culture* (London and New York: Routledge, 1994).
[2] Gilles Deleuze, *Difference and Repetition*, trans. Paul Patton (New York:
Columbia University Press, 1994), p. 1.

It is not the Federation Day which commemorates or represents the fall of the Bastille, but the fall of the Bastille which celebrates and repeats in advance all the Federation Days; or Monet's first water lily which repeats all the others. Generality, as generality of the particular, thus stands opposed to repetition as universality of the singular. The repetition of a work of art is like singularity without a concept, and it is not by chance that a poem must be learned by heart.[3]

The distinction hinted at in this passage between law and poetry, history and memory, is what gives repetition its power to transgress. 'The theatre of repetition is opposed to the theatre of representation, just as movement is opposed to the concept and to representation which refers it back to the concept.'[4] Deleuze makes it clear that repetition is how newness enters the world but it does so in disguise and through displacement—'disguise no less than displacement forms part of repetition'—for repetition (this is Deleuze's reading of Kierkegaard and Nietzsche) is 'the double condemnation of habit and memory' both of which, as we shall see, underlie political judgement.[5] Repetition thus constitutes a crisis of political judgement.

Let me now elaborate these themes of displacement and disguise, the two aspects of Deleuzian repetition, through the example of Subaltern Studies, the Indian series with which I was involved since its inception in 1982. Subaltern Studies was an instance of politically motivated historiography. Political judgement was central to this project. It came out of a Marxist tradition of history writing in South Asia and was markedly indebted to Mao and Gramsci in the initial formulations that guided the series. Given this background, it was not surprising that right from the moment of its birth, Subaltern Studies should be greeted by several commentators as a 'belated' project, carrying out in the subcontinent what British 'history from below' had accomplished a long time ago.[6] Belatedness was not a new problem in historiography. Alexander Gerschenkron, the reputed Harvard historian who wrote a book in the early 1960s entitled *Economic Backwardness in Historical Perspective*, saw the problem of Russian modernization through the prism of belat-

[3] Deleuze, *Difference and Repetition*, pp. 1–2.
[4] Deleuze, *Difference and Repetition*, p. 10.
[5] Deleuze, *Difference and Repetition*, pp. xvi, 7.
[6] I discuss this point in more detail in my essay 'A Small History of Subaltern Studies', in *Habitations of Modernity: Essays in the Wake of Subaltern Studies* (Chicago: University of Chicago Press, 2002).

edness and the politics of having to 'catch up' with the more 'modern' nations.[7] Belatedness, as I tried to argue in *Provincializing Europe*, was an integral part of a certain kind of historicist outlook that was born in the nineteenth century.[8]

It is, of course, true that the tradition of history writing on the Left in India was deeply influenced by English Marxist or socialist historiography, the 'history from below' tradition pioneered by the likes of Edward Thompson, Eric Hobsbawm, and others. Subaltern Studies inherited this tradition but there were very important differences. English Marxist narratives of popular histories were moulded on developmental ideas of time and consciousness: the peasant, in that story, either became extinct or was superseded to give rise to the worker who, through machine-breaking, Chartism, and other struggles for rights, one day metamorphosed into the figure of the citizen or the revolutionary proletariat. The situation in the colony was different. The peasant or tribal of the Third World—as if through a process of telescoping of the centuries—suddenly had the colonial state and its modern bureaucratic and repressive apparatus thrust in his face. To someone like Hobsbawm, this peasant remained a 'pre-political' person: someone who did not, as it were, understand the operative languages of modern governing institutions while forced to deal with them. Subaltern Studies, on the other hand, began by repudiating this developmental idea of 'becoming political'. The peasant or the subaltern, it was claimed, was *political* from the very instance they rose up in rebellion against the institutions of the Raj.[9] Their actions were political in the sense that they responded to and impacted on the institutional bases of colonial governance: the Raj, the moneylender, and the landlord.

We did not then think much about the implications of our claim that the subaltern could be political without undergoing a process of 'political development'. Yet the implications of that claim were writ large on our historiography. I should explain that the legacies of both imperialism and anti-colonialism speak to each other in this

[7] Alexander Gerschenkron, *Economic Backwardness in Historical Perspective—A Book of Essays* (Cambridge, MA: Belknap Harvard, 1962).

[8] See Dipesh Chakrabarty, *Provincializing Europe: Postcolonial Thought and Historical Difference* (Princeton, NJ: Princeton University Press, 2007 [2000]).

[9] See Chakrabarty, 'A Small History of *Subaltern Studies*'.

implicit debate about whether the subaltern became political over time (through some kind of pedagogic practice) or whether the figure of the subaltern was constitutionally political. Developmental time, or the sense of time underlying a stadial view of history, was indeed a legacy bequeathed by the imperial rule in India. This is the time of the 'not yet', as I called it *Provincializing Europe*. European political thinkers such as Mill (or even Marx) employed this temporal structure in the way they thought about history. Nationalists and anti-colonialists, on the other hand, repudiated this imagination of time in the twentieth century in asking for self-rule to be granted right away, without a period of waiting or preparation, without delay, 'now'. What replaced the structure of the 'not yet' in their imagination was the horizon of the 'now'.[10]

What underwrote this anti-colonial and nationalist (though populist) faith in the modern–political capacity of the masses was another European inheritance, a certain kind of poetics of history: romanticism. It is, of course, true that the middle-class leaders of anti-colonial movements involving peasants and workers never quite abandoned the idea of developmental time and a pedagogical project of educating the peasant. Gandhi's writings and those of other nationalist leaders often express a fear of the lawless mob and see education as a solution to the problem.[11] But this fear was qualified by its opposite, a political faith in the masses. In the 1920s and the 1930s, this romanticism marked Indian nationalism generally—many nationalists who were not Communist or of the Left, for instance, would express this faith.

One should note that this romantic–political faith in the masses was populist as well in a classical sense of the term. Like Russian populism of the late nineteenth century, this mode of thought not only sought a 'good' political quality in the peasant but also, by that step, worked to convert the so-called backwardness of the peasant into a historical advantage. The peasant, 'uncorrupted' by self-tending individualism of the bourgeois and oriented to the needs of his or her community, was imagined as already endowed with the capacity to create a modern

[10] See the discussion in the 'Introduction' to *Provincializing Europe*.

[11] See Gyanendra Pandey, 'Peasant Revolt and Indian Nationalism: The Peasant Movement in Awadh, 1919–22', in *Selected Subaltern Studies*, ed. Ranajit Guha and Gayatri Chakravorty Spivak (New York: Oxford University Press, 1988), pp. 233–87.

society different from and more communitarian than what was prevalent in the West.[12]

The inauguration of the age of mass politics in India was thus enabled
by ideologies that displayed some of the key global characteristics of
populist thought. There was, first, the tendency to see a certain political
goodness in the peasant or in the masses. And there was, in addition, also
the tendency to see historical advantage where, by colonial judgement,
there was only backwardness and disadvantage. To see 'advantage' in
'backwardness'—that is, to see belatedness as an opportunity—was also
to challenge the time that was assumed by stadial views about history;
it was to twist the time of the colonial 'not yet' into the structure of the
democratic and anti-colonial 'now'.

I give this potted history of the romantic–populist origins of Indian
democratic thought—though not of Indian democracy as such and the
distinction is important—to suggest a point fundamental to my exposition. The insistence, in the early volumes of Subaltern Studies (first
published in 1982) and in Ranajit Guha's *Elementary Aspects of Peasant
Insurgency in Colonial India* (1983), that the peasant or the subaltern
was always already political—and not 'pre-political' in any develop-
mentalist sense—was in some ways a recapitulation of a populist premise that was implicit in any case in the anti-colonial mass movements in
British India.[13] But there was, in my sense, a displacement as well of this
term. The populism in Subaltern Studies was more intense and explicit
than in the traditions of nationalism or even official Maoism. There was,
first of all, no 'fear of the masses' in Subaltern Studies analysis. Absent
also—and this went against the grain of classically Marxist or Leninist
or Maoist analysis—was any discussion of the need for organization or
a party. Guha and his colleagues drew inspiration from Mao (particularly his 1927 report on the peasant movement in the Hunan district)
and Gramsci (mainly his *Prison Notebooks*). But their use of Mao and
Gramsci speaks of the times when Subaltern Studies was born. This
was, after all, the 1970s: a period of global Maoism that Althusser and

[12] For an excellent discussion of this point, see Andrzej Walicki, *The
Controversy over Capitalism: Studies in the Social Philosophy of the Russian Populists* (Notre Dame, IN: University of Notre Dame Press, 1989), Chapters 1 and
2, in particular the section 'The Privilege of Backwardness'.

[13] Ranajit Guha, *Elementary Aspects of Peasant Insurgency in Colonial India*
(Delhi: Oxford University Press, 1983), Chapter 1.

others had made respectable. Excerpts from Gramsci's notebooks had come out in English in 1971. Both Gramsci and Mao were celebrated as a way out of Stalinist or Soviet Marxism after Czechoslovakia of 1968. Many of the historians in Subaltern Studies were participants in or sympathizers with the Maoist movement that shook parts of India between 1969 and 1971.[14]

Yet, significantly, neither Mao's references to the need for 'leadership of the Party' nor Gramsci's strictures against 'spontaneity' featured with any degree of prominence in *Elementary Aspects* or Subaltern Studies. Guha's focus remained firmly on understanding the nature of the practices that made up peasant revolts in a period that was part of the colonial rule but that preceded the times when the peasants were inducted by middle-class leaders into the politics of nationalism. Guha wanted to understand the peasant as a collective author of these uprisings by doing a structuralist analysis of the space- and time-creating practices of mobilization, communication, and public violence that constituted peasant rebellions (and thus, for Guha, a subaltern domain of politics). There were limitations, from Guha's socialist point of view, to what the peasants could achieve on their own but these limitations did not call for the mediation of a party. But a cult of rebellion marked the early efforts of Subaltern Studies, reminiscent of one of Mao's sayings popular during the Cultural Revolution: 'to rebel is justified'. Rebellion was not a technique for achieving something; it was its own end. Indeed, from a global perspective, one may say that Subaltern Studies was perhaps the last—or the latest—instance of a long global history of the Left: the romantic–popular search for a non-industrial revolutionary subject that was initiated in Russia, among other places, in the second half of the nineteenth century. This romantic populism shaped much of Maoism in the twentieth century and left its imprint on the antinomies and ambiguities of Antonio Gramsci's thoughts on the party as the modern prince.

The political potential of this romanticism is exhausted today. But looking back one can see the twin problems of naming and belatedness

---

[14] Shahid Amin, 'De-Ghettoising the Histories of the Non-West'; Gyan Prakash, 'The Location of Scholarship'; and Dipesh Chakrabarty, 'Globalization, Democracy, and the Evacuation of History?', in *At Home in Diaspora: South Asian Scholars and the West*, ed. Jackie Assayag and Veronique Benei (Bloomington: Indiana University Press, 2003).

that plagued this search for a revolutionary subject in the relatively non-industrialized countries of the world. Such a subject by definition could not be the proletariat. Yet it was difficult to define a world-historical subject that would take the place of the industrial working classes that did not exist, not in great numbers anyway, in the peasant-based economies drawn into the orbit of the capitalist world. Would the revolution, as Trotsky said, be an act of substitutionism? Would the party stand in for the working classes? Could the peasantry, under the guidance of the party, be the revolutionary class? Would it fall under the category 'subaltern' or Fanon's 'the wretched of the earth'?

When the young, left-Hegelian Marx thought up the category of the proletariat as the new revolutionary subject of history that would replace the bourgeoisie—and he did this before Engels wrote his book on the Manchester working class in 1844—there was a philosophical precision to the category. It also seemed to find a sociological correlate in working classes born of the industrial revolution. But names such as 'peasants' (Mao), 'subaltern' (Gramsci), 'the wretched of the earth' (Fanon), and 'the party as the subject' (Lenin/Lukács) have neither philosophical nor sociological precision. It was as if the search for a revolutionary subject that was *not-the-proletariat* (in the absence of a large working class) was itself an exercise in a series of displacements of the original term. A telling case in point is Fanon himself. The expression 'the wretched of the earth', as Fanon's biographer David Macey has pointed out, alludes to the Communist Internationale, the song— 'Debout, les damnés de la terre'/'Arise, ye wretched of the earth'— where it clearly refers to the proletariat.[15] Yet Fanon uses it to mean precisely a new and unnamed revolutionary subject. This other subject he cannot quite define but he is clear that in the colony it cannot be the proletariat. One only has to recall how quite early on in his book he cautions: 'Marxist analysis should always be slightly stretched every time we have to do with the colonial problem.'[16]

A collective subject with no proper name, a subject who can be named only through a series of displacements of the original European

[15] David Macey, *Frantz Fanon: A Biography* (New York: Picador, 2000), p. 177.

[16] Frantz Fanon, *The Wretched of the Earth*, trans. Constance Farrington (New York: Grove Press, 1963), p. 40.

term 'the proletariat'—this is a condition both of failure and of a new beginning. The failure is easy to see. It lies in the lack of specificity or definition. But where is the beginning? First of all, the very imprecision is a pointer to the inadequacy of Eurocentric thought in the context of a global striving for a socialist transformation of the world. Outside of the industrialized countries, the revolutionary subject was even theoretically undefined. The history of this imprecision amounts to the acknowledgement that if we want to understand the nature of popular political practices globally with names of subjects invented in Europe, we can only resort to a series of stand-ins (never mind the fact that the original may have been a simulacrum as well). Why? Because we are working at and on the limits of European political thought even as we admit an affiliation to nineteenth-century European revolutionary romanticism. Recognizing the stand-in nature of categories such as 'the masses', 'the subaltern', or 'the peasant' is, I suggest, the first step towards writing histories of democracies that have emerged through the mass politics of anti-colonial nationalism. There is a mass subject here, no doubt. But it can only be apprehended by consciously working through the limits of European thought. A straightforward search for a revolutionary world-historical subject only leads to stand-ins. The global and theoretical failure to find a proper name for the revolutionary subject that is not-the-proletariat thus inaugurates the need for new thought and research outside the West, resulting in a series of displacements of the once European category, the proletariat.

The Problem of Political Judgement

To sum up, then, much socialist political thought has been made possible outside of the West by a continual process of working through European categories in order to displace them from the locus of their original signification. So much for the theme of displacement that, as Deleuze reminded us, was a critical part of the transgressive power of repetition. But what about the theme of disguise?

The theme of disguise pertains to our capacity to name and recognize the new. It is here that the tension (to speak with Deleuze) between generality and repetition, between law and poetry, and between history/sociology and memory reveals itself at its most intense and demonstrates how political judgement seeks to tame the new. Consider once again the foundational text of Subaltern Studies, Ranajit Guha's *Elementary Aspects of Peasant Insurgency in Colonial India*. What is the status of the category 'political' in Guha's (and our) polemic with Hobsbawm that the peasants and the tribals were not 'pre-political', that they were in fact as political as the British or the middle classes?[17] The status is ambiguous: the peasants were political in the already understood sense of the term—in that they dealt with the institutions of colonial rule—but they were also 'political' in some other sense about which we were not clear at all. But the political claim that nineteenth-century peasant rebellions were political could only be made on the assumption—and this remains an assumption—that we already knew completely what being political meant. What was new about peasant resistance in nineteenth-century India could only be expressed in the guise of an old category: 'politics'.

Something very similar happens—just to cite a distant example that will show that the problem is more than historiographical or merely Indian—in the Australian historian Henry Reynold's path-breaking work on Aboriginal resistance to white occupation in nineteenth-century Australia. Take his book *Fate of a Free People*, analysing Aboriginal resistance in nineteenth-century Tasmania. Reynolds is aware of the European roots of the modern idea of the political. He writes how some European settlers were astonished to find among Aboriginals 'ideas of their natural rights', which Reynolds regards, rightly, as European attempts at interpreting 'in European terms' the world-making they encountered among the Aboriginals. Yet in resisting prejudiced histories written by earlier white historians and chroniclers, Reynolds, much like Guha, insists on the applicability of the category 'political' in describing Aboriginal resistance. He challenges 'the clear assumption that the Tasmanians were incapable of taking political action' and describes the nineteenth-century Aboriginal leader Walter Arthur as 'the first Aboriginal nationalist', thus tearing the idea of 'nationalism' from all its anchorage in the history of modern institutions.[18] Clearly, 'politics' and 'nationalism' are underdetermined, part-sociological and part-rhetorical categories here, not completely open to the demand for

---

[17] Guha, *Elementary Aspects*, Chapter 1.

[18] Henry Reynolds, *Fate of a Free People* (Ringwood, Victoria: Penguin, 1995), pp. 11, 23, 69.

clarification. And it is in their rhetorical imprecision that the disguising of the new happens.

Or take Partha Chatterjee's category of 'the governed'—again, a term in the series of displacements of the revolutionary subject that I have already traced before. Having documented the struggle for survival (entailing such practices as the stealing of electricity) that goes on every day in lives of the slum-dwellers in the city of Calcutta, he suddenly, towards the end of his analysis, makes 'the governed' the creators of something that he claims even Aristotle might recognize: democracy. 'What I have tried to show', he writes, 'is that alongside the abstract promise of popular sovereignty, people in most of the world are devising new ways in which they can choose how they should be governed'. He recognizes that 'many of the forms of the political society' and their unlawful activities that he describes perhaps would not meet with 'Aristotle's approval'. Yet he believes that the 'wise Greek', if he could see Chatterjee's evidence, might actually recognize an 'ethical justification' for democracy in popular action that he might otherwise disapprove.[19] My point is, again, the ambiguity of this move, the claim that while popular action in everyday Calcutta does not always look democratic, it still heralds a democracy to come. It is, of course, entirely possible that everyday life in Calcutta looks forward to a different future for which we do not have a name yet. The question has to be left open—the future is like the shorthand often used in incomplete descriptions of academic conferences—'TBA', or 'to be announced'.[20] Thus, it is in the flickering light and shadow of our classical concepts of democracy and the practices of slum-dwellers that get legitimized by the rhetoric of those conceptions that the actual 'newness' of what goes on in Calcutta hides itself. Now we see it, now we do not.

My last example of disguise of the new is Hardt and Negri's well-known category of the 'multitude', once again a candidate for inclusion in my list of terms that displace the original revolutionary subject of Europe. The disguise is ironical for a book that, in its first half, struggles—in a Deleuzian vein—to capture that which is new about

---

[19] Partha Chatterjee, *The Politics of the Governed: Reflections on Popular Politics in Most of the World* (New York: Columbia University Press, 2004), pp. 77–8.

[20] This sentence faintly echoes what the Thai historian Thongchai Winichakul has said in another context.

domination in the world: empire. Yet their revolutionary agency 'the multitude', while conceived of as immanent in a Spinozist way, has to acquire an 'adequate consciousness' in order to be political. 'How can the actions of the multitude become political?', they ask. Their answer: 'The only response we can give ... is that the action of the multitude becomes primarily political when it begins to confront directly and with an adequate consciousness the central repressive operations of Empire.'[21] There is here a return to—or a resonance of—Hegelian Marxism that cannot be overlooked.

I am then left to ask my final question: why does displacement combine with disguise to create the very structure of repetition? It goes back, I think, to a problem that Marx referred to a long time ago. Newness enters the world as a challenge to judgement and law. That is why Deleuze refers to it through the figure of poetry. Political judgement is tied to the old. Even Bhabha once began his journey as a postcolonial theorist with a gesture towards connecting with socialist politics as it was known in Britain in the 1980s.[22] I think Marx, in a moment of reflection on the problem of repetition and resemblance in history—and thus on the question of the belated—put his finger on the necessary disguise of the new. The lines are very well known indeed but may bear repetition in the context of this discussion:

> Men make their own history, but they do not make it just as they please.... The tradition of all the dead generations weighs like a nightmare on the brain of the living. And just when they seem ... engaged in creating something that has never yet existed, ... they anxiously conjure up the spirits of the past to their service and borrow from them names, battle cries and costumes in order to present the new scene of world history in this time-honoured disguise and this borrowed language.[23]

Clearly, Marx expected this process to have a Hegelian ending. He, as you know, compared it to a person's experience of learning a new

[21] Michael Hardt and Antonio Negri, *Empire* (Cambridge, MA: Harvard University Press, 2000), p. 399.

[22] Homi Bhabha, 'The Commitment to Theory', in his *Locations of Culture* (London and New York: Routledge, 1994).

[23] Karl Marx, 'The Eighteenth Brumaire of Louis Bonaparte', in Karl Marx and Frederick Engels, *Selected Works*, vol. 1 (Moscow: Progress Publishers, 1969), p. 398.

language: 'A beginner who has learnt a new language always translates it back into his mother tongue, but he has assimilated the spirit of the new language and can freely express himself in it only when he finds his way in it without recalling the old and forgets his native tongue in the use of the new.'[24] Marx did not see this process of translation to be problematic. The Hegelian in him expected such worldly translation to do the job of Hegelian mediation and successfully deliver the desired political good. This is where we may have to part with Marx and his progenies in contemplating the problem of repetition and belatedness in our time. The idea that that we wait for the proper names of subaltern or postcolonial history constitutes, I think, wise counsel.

---

[24] Marx, 'The Eighteenth Brumaire of Louis Bonaparte', p. 398.

2

CAN POLITICAL ECONOMY BE POSTCOLONIAL?

A Note*

Postcolonial criticism of the 1980s and 1990s arose from the left field—there is no right-wing postcolonial theorist to my knowledge—and was, therefore, often subject to a particular kind of criticism from Marxist or other left-leaning intellectuals who complained that postcolonial thinking emphasized textual criticism at the expense of political–economic analysis. The charge was never entirely true—Gayatri Spivak, for instance, always remained interested in questions to do with 'international division of labour' and in many other issues of development.[1] Katherine Gibson and Julie Graham, writing under the name J. K. Gibson-Graham, have produced economic analyses incorporating post-modern/postcolonial insights. Recently, Vinay Gidwani has also made significant new contributions to this body of literature.[2]

* Edited from 'Can Political Economy Be Postcolonial? A Note', in *Postcolonial Economies*, ed. Jane Pollard, Cheryl McEwan, and Alex Hughes (London: Zed Books, 2011), pp. 23–35.

[1] Her famous essay 'Can the Subaltern Speak?' demonstrates the truth of this proposition. Gayatri Spivak, 'Can the Subaltern Speak?', in *Can the Subaltern Speak? Reflections on the History of an Idea*, ed. R. C. Morris (New York: Columbia University Press, 2010 [1988]), pp. 21–78.

[2] J. K. Gibson-Graham, S. Resnick, and R. D. Wolff, eds, *Re/presenting Class: Essays in Postmodern Marxism* (Durham, NC: Duke University Press, 2001); J. K. Gibson-Graham, *A Postcapitalist Politics* (Minneapolis: University of Minnesota Press, 2006); J. K. Gibson-Graham and Gerda Roelvink, 'An Economic

I claim no expertise in economics or political economy. But since my early training as a historian in India took place in the 1970s when a certain kind of Marxist political economy ruled the day and when economic history had the pride of place in all discussions of colonial rule, I too began my career subscribing to the opinion—common among Marxists those days—that economic facts constituted a kind of limit for human freedom, that the economy was the 'base', and everything else about any social structure followed from it. There were, of course, quite sophisticated debates about the extent to which economic factors were determining of other factors in history, discussions about what Engels may have meant in his famous 1890 letter in which he spoke of the economy being determining only 'in the last instance', and many speculations about how one would recognize 'the last instance' if one ever ran into it. But however sophisticated the discussions may have been, they were all about saving the primacy of the economic in historical explanations. Much of our historiographical revolt in the series Subaltern Studies was against this primacy given to the economic in radical historians' explanations of rebellions by subaltern classes. With Mao as our inspiration, we rejected what we saw as the 'economism' of the usual Marxist explanations and gave primacy to the political instead. Peasant insurgencies, we argued, always began by destroying the usual social and material symbols of domination possessed by the oppressive classes and these acts were about how power worked in Indian rural society.[3] Capitalist and colonial rule in India, we further argued, worked by acting on these levers of power in Indian society.[4] This rejection of 'economism' was also reflected in the interest many Subaltern Studies scholars developed in post-structuralism and deconstruction. In

---

Ethics for the Anthropocene', *Antipode: A Radical Journal of Geography* 41, supplement 1 (2010): 320–46; Vinay Gidwani, *Capital, Interrupted: Agrarian Development and the Politics of Work in India* (Minneapolis: University of Minnesota Press, 2008).

[3] Ranajit Guha, *Elementary Aspects of Peasant Insurgency in Colonial India* (Delhi: Oxford University Press, 1983).

[4] Some of these arguments are rehearsed in the essay 'A Small History of Subaltern Studies' in Dipesh Chakrabarty, *Habitations of Modernity: Essays in the Wake of Subaltern Studies* (Chicago: University of Chicago Press, 2002); see also Partha Chatterjee, 'Reflections on "Can the Subaltern Speak"', in *Can the Subaltern Speak? Reflections on the History of an Idea*, ed. R. C. Morris (New York: Columbia University Press, 2010).

my book *Provincializing Europe*, I tried to advance the proposition that the question of transition to capitalism in any setting was a question of translation as well, of a group of people being able to translate their life-worlds into the categories of capitalism.[5]

Our turn towards the political and the cultural/textual gave rise to the general criticism among historians of India that Subaltern Studies neglected economic history. I do not know if we did. But it is true that while we wrote much on historico-philosophical problems of modernity and capitalism, we never did much to revitalize economic history as such. The 'new' economic history that developed in India in the 1990s thereafter adopted, implicitly or explicitly, rational choice frameworks for analysis.[6] This delivered the subject from the shibboleths and tyrannies of a stultified nationalist Marxism that dominated before but the price of the liberation was the debunking of leftist historiography in general.

I have since wondered about what it might mean to incorporate insights from postcolonial criticism into the writing of economic history. Unfortunately, I do not consider myself best suited for the task. But reading Kenneth Pomeranz's widely acclaimed book, *The Great Divergence: China, Europe, and the Making of the Modern World Economy*,[7] afforded me an opportunity to think about the problem and in this short chapter I want to share with the reader some of my preliminary thoughts.

* * *

Let me begin by acknowledging how much I learnt from Pomeranz's superb and revolutionary book *The Great Divergence*. Pomeranz's scholarship is extraordinary, his intellect vigorous, his judgements astute and brave, and his heart—if one may speak of such things in an academic context—is absolutely in the right place insofar as the project of 'de-centring Europe' is concerned. This book deserves every bit of

[5] Dipesh Chakrabarty, *Provincializing Europe: Postcolonial Thought and Historical Difference* (Princeton, NJ: Princeton University Press, 2000 [2007]).

[6] One of the most prominent Indian historians of this school is Tirthankar Roy.

[7] Kenneth Pomeranz, *The Great Divergence: China, Europe, and the Making of the Modern World Economy* (Princeton, NJ: Princeton University Press, 2000).

the praise that has been heaped on it. There is one more characteristic of Pomeranz's scholarship that I appreciated on reading both this book and his reply to his critics in a debate that followed in the pages of *The Journal of Asian Studies*. Even where he has the better of his opponents in terms of facts and arguments, Pomeranz is remarkably gracious and generous in his response to opposition. This is not a small merit in the academic world I know.

Much of Pomeranz's argument in *The Great Divergence* I find at least provocative and challenging even when my agreement with the book is not total. The overall project seems entirely laudable. Studies of transition to capitalism in various parts of the world often become Eurocentric through the deployment, conscious or unconscious, of the assumption that patterns of economic growth in Western Europe provide some kind of a unique model by which to judge the performance of other economies and societies. Pomeranz challenges this tendency of thought. He does so by seeking to demonstrate empirically that up until the eighteenth century there was very little to distinguish between the economic and institutional features of Western European societies and some areas of the Asian world: Japan, the Yangzi delta in China, and the Gujarat region of western India. This attempt at empirical demonstration is no mean feat involving, as it did, research on many different literatures and sites at once. As subsequent debates have shown, Pomeranz is able to hold his ground in the face of criticism by scholars who are specialists on areas where Pomeranz does not claim expertise. As a student of South Asian history, I can only admire the care with which Pomeranz sifts the sands of the economic history of the subcontinent in the Mughal and 'early modern' period. The book demonstrates in an exemplary manner the power of 'historical facts' in reversing habits of thought.

Pomeranz also mounts a challenge to those practitioners of history who see the present as the culmination of a process of historical becoming. Scholars have often written long and continuous histories of industrialization in Europe reinforcing the commonplace idea that gradual and unique transformations over a long period prepared (Western) European societies and economies for the industrial and capitalist domination of the world that they were to enjoy from the nineteenth century onwards. Pomeranz throws the developmental narrative into disarray by highlighting the largely contingent nature of the

discovery of fossil fuel (coal) and the forced opening up of the New
World. These, in his view, were the two contingent factors that enabled
Europe to remove the bottleneck of 'land constraint' that choked the
possibilities for industrialization in non-European societies that were
otherwise on a par with Europe until about the eighteenth century.

Pomeranz thus succeeds in two of his aims: de-centring Europe
and challenging historicism (or at least a certain popular version of
it). By showing that industrial Europe becomes itself by dint of factors external to its geography or any perceptible, immanent logic to
its historical evolution, Pomeranz avoids the problems of immanentist,
internalist accounts of European becoming. These are definitely the
three major methodological achievements of the book apart from the
many substantial contributions it makes to its own field of early modern economic history (these I am not able to evaluate critically though
I find them thought-provoking to say the least). These gains are the
dividends yielded by Pomeranz's consciously chosen method of writing
comparative, connected histories.

Pomeranz begins the book with a somewhat polemical swipe at
some unnamed, 'current "postmodern" scholars'. These scholars, he
writes, 'make it impossible even to approach many of the most important questions in history (and in contemporary life)' by 'abandoning
cross-cultural comparison altogether and focusing almost exclusively
on exposing the contingency, particularity, and perhaps unknowability
of historical moments'.[8] I have no intention of defending these scholars
who, after all, go unnamed in Pomeranz's book. Besides, I also value
comparisons. Even more than that, I think comparison is unavoidable in
the social sciences. Some scholars explicitly set out to compare. Others
do not. But our conceptions and theories, to the extent that they are
social measures as well, provide scales and yardsticks whose use-value
lies in their enabling us to compare. I have no quarrels therefore with
comparative methods as such. But comparisons and the questions of
unknowability or indeterminacy in history may not be as mutually
exclusive as the quotation from Pomeranz suggests.

The problem of comparison is about the scale or the measure that
helps us to compare. I want to use this opportunity to think about this
question of the measuring scale as it comes up in Pomeranz's work.

8 Pomeranz, *The Great Divergence*, p. 8.

What I say is not as such a criticism of Pomeranz. I am not asking for a different book from him. He has written the book he wanted to write, and he has done so superbly. I have no significant criticisms to offer on his own terms. This is more a reflection on these terms themselves with a view to exploring what we all may collectively learn from thinking about the comparative method as it is employed in this book. What I have to say may also connect with Pomeranz's polemic with 'postmodernism' (the scare quotes are, advisedly, his).

My point of entry is a couple of moments in the text where Pomeranz discusses some of his own preferences in social theory and particularly in areas where he explicitly negotiates some anthropological theory. Pomeranz begins the book by acknowledging that most available comparisons between 'West and the rest' are biased in favour of the West. But it is preferable, he writes, 'to confront biased comparisons by trying to produce better ones'. What is important is to view 'both sides of the comparison as "deviations" when seen through the expectations of the other, rather than leaving one as always the norm'. This, he adds, 'will be much of his procedure' in *The Great Divergence*.[9] Later, Pomeranz takes to task, rightly I think, texts that create a dichotomy

> between societies in which 'commodities' and 'markets' determine social relations, and exchange is conceived as the individualistic pursuit of gain, on the one hand, and those in which social relations regulate the economy, status governs consumption, and people are concerned with reciprocity, on the other. When these dichotomies are applied to history, the result tends to be a division between a Europe that became 'materialist' first and the rest of the planet, which because it has not yet crossed the divide, had to have 'commodities', 'materialism', and 'economic man' introduced from the outside.[10]

Instead he prefers, after Arjun Appadurai, the idea of 'a continuum that runs from "fashion systems" on the one hand to "coupon" or "license" systems on the other'. 'This formulation', writes Pomeranz, 'avoids placing societies in one camp or another ... and so makes it clear that we have both "economy" and "culture" in all societies'.[11]

---

[9] Pomeranz, *The Great Divergence*, p. 8.

[10] Pomeranz, *The Great Divergence*, p. 128.

[11] Pomeranz, *The Great Divergence*, p. 129.

Pomeranz thus carefully avoids having to rank societies on any evolutionary scale culminating in the coming of capitalism. But the idea of a culture/economy continuum is not unproblematic. We may have 'economy' and 'culture' in all societies but they may be present in different degrees (otherwise the continuum would shrink to a single point). The *homo economicus* (economic man) may have been present from the beginning of human history but it seems reasonable to suggest that some societies value it more actively as a way of being than others. More importantly, surely not all societies—at least up until the eighteenth and early nineteenth centuries—explicitly made this conscious analytical distinction between 'culture' and 'economy'. Nor did all societies create abstract objects of intellectual investigation such as 'economy' and 'culture'. In fact, it could be safely said that only societies with more 'economy' created intellectual tools for studying something called the 'economy'. I obviously have in mind the history of political economy, an academic subject without which an exercise such as Pomeranz's would be unthinkable.

The question is, are these knowledge protocols or abstract categories such as 'land', 'labour', and 'capital' still European/Western or Eurocentric in any sense since we all use them now and since they seem applicable to all societies? Or does their use, however unavoidable, also devolve on us the responsibility of remembering their histories as part of the politics of knowledge today? Or are they just analytical/descriptive categories giving us access to social realities that we would otherwise miss? In Pomeranz's text, categories such as 'free' and 'unfree' labour or 'land' work as simple analytical and descriptive terms, shorn of whatever philosophical or theological associations these words may have had even as late as the seventeenth century.

That the categories of political economy are peculiarly European in origin seems less questionable. Also, it is well known that at their origin these categories were often possessed of certain moral and/or theological import (not surprising if one remembers that economics emerges from moral philosophy in the eighteenth century).[12] And since such import could never be completely rational, we would be

---

[12] Amartya Sen has made this point time and again, reminding economists of the continuing relationship between economics and ethics. See, for example, *On Ethics and Economics* (Oxford, Basil Blackwell, 1987).

justified in saying that these categories contained a certain degree of prejudice—that is to say, a certain element of that which was particular, prejudicial, and not universal—built into them even as they emerged as academic, analytical categories. Consider, for instance, the question of the price of commodities. Analytically, price is the point where the supply and demand curves meet on paper. Historically, however, as Michael Perelman has shown in his book *The Invention of Capitalism*, classical political economic thought was in part an intellectual war on the habits of the poor. Adam Smith's teacher Frances Hutcheson had this to say on the issue of price in his *System of Moral Philosophy* (1755): 'If people have not acquired the habit of industry, the cheapness of all the necessities of life encourages sloth. The best remedy is to raise the demand for all necessities.... Sloth should be punished by temporary servitude at least.'[13]

Now, do we need to know about Hutcheson and his contemporaries in using categories such as price or labour today? Books on physics—as distinct from those on the history of science—seldom teach the history of thought in the physical sciences. So why should the practitioners of political economy be concerned about the murky origins of their analytical categories? Has not the dross of all particularistic thought been drained away as they have morphed into effective analytical tools? Here, I think the answer is both yes and no. To the extent that political economy (or social science categories) can speak the language of mathematics, that is to say, to the extent that it does not speak prose, political economy can indeed claim to have become something like the universal languages of the physical and mathematical sciences. But I think that the social sciences also share in the fate of the other sciences—such as the biological or medical ones—which are mired in the prose (and hence the prejudices) of the world. Here, origins do matter because they are never completely transcended. Prose brings with it the history of its own idiomaticity and that is always a matter of a particular rather than universal history.

Take the category of 'labour efficiency'. By definition, efficiency is measured by the ratio of output over input (of labour). However, as any

---

[13] Quoted in M. Perelman, *The Invention of Capitalism: Classical Political Economy and the Secret History of Primitive Accumulation* (Durham, NC: Duke University Press, 2000), p. 16.

labour historian of colonial Asia would know, records in nineteenth-
century South and South East Asia—well after classical political economy had evolved as a recognized intellectual endeavour—demonstrate
tellingly how themes of race were indissolubly implicated in this
category. The Europeans in devising local, regional, or global schemes
of migration of labour always asked themselves: 'Do the Chinese
make better workers than the Indians, or the Indians better than the
Malays?'[14] In other words, colonial or even contemporary discussions
of an issue such as 'labour efficiency' could easily slide into its opposite,
that of sloth or laziness. This issue seldom enters academic analyses in
a straightforward way today as there cannot be an objective, analytical
category of 'laziness' shorn of all suggestions of interest, power, and
domination. The prejudicial aspect of the category 'labour efficiency'
now has unnamed, shadowy, spectral presence—built into the recommendations of the International Monetary Fund (IMF) and the World
Bank, I imagine. Origins let us invoke this spectre and see the category
'efficiency' for what it is—both an analytical tool as well as a piece of
technology of power.

A better example yet is the category of 'land'. Let me conclude this
section with a brief discussion of it. The indigenous people of Australia
in the eighteenth and for a large part of the nineteenth century constituted societies that, in Pomeranz's terms, probably had more 'culture' than 'economy'. 'Land' was critical to their ways of being, but a
sentence such as this one would not have been translatable into their
languages, as a reified, objectified, and abstract category of 'land' simply
would not have made sense to them. Yet European colonization proceeded on the basis of an imagination that took the political–economic
category of 'land' for granted. Eventually, the Aborigines had to deal
with this category as they learned to make 'land' claims over time. In
the push and pull of politics in everyday life in Australia, 'land' has
become a hybridized category—the courts routinely listen to both
political–economic understandings and 'Aboriginal' understandings
(now mediated by anthropologists and historians). Soon, I hope, we
will have political economists of Aboriginal origin making perfectly

---

[14] The classic book on this theme is Syed Hussein Alatas, *The Myth of the
Lazy Native: A Study of the Image of the Malays, Filipinos and Javanese from the
16th to the 20th Century and Its Function in the Ideology of Colonial Capitalism*
(London: Routledge, 1977).

legible and effective political claims or writing economic analyses on behalf of their people. But that does not deny the fact this is a contested category. It is both a tool of disinterested analysis and at the same time a tool of ideological and material domination if not also of epistemic violence.

✿ ✿ ✿

If, then, the categories of political economy or social science analysis are in varying degrees both analytical and prejudicial in their content, it follows that incorporating this insight into their treatment in classrooms would entail, at least, three steps that will need to be taken simultaneously:

1. acknowledging this dual nature of our analytical categories;
2. raising and, wherever possible, dealing with the problems of categorial translation as part of the narrative of transition to capitalism; and
3. returning to questions of analysis and knowledge.

In bringing this note to a close, let me briefly explain these steps using Pomeranz's book only as an example (that is, without the implication that Pomeranz himself should have taken these steps). Taking the first step—point 1 in our aforementioned schema—would mean accepting that words that feature in both ordinary words and analytical prose are always caught up in the strife-ridden nature of the world that exists outside the classroom. In distilling them out of their worldly uses and in giving them special or specialized meanings in our disciplines, we cut off or disable many of their usual semantic connections. Thus, we 'forget' that 'price' is part of class struggle when we represent it simply as a point on a two-dimensional graph. The process is not always successful. Sometimes the clamour of our conflicts in everyday world enters the classroom and students or colleagues refuse to accept the disinterested quality our disciplines attribute to these words. Nurtured in an academic way, this may very well give rise to critiques of disciplines from inside themselves (as indeed happened with anthropology in the 1970s and 1980s). Another way to handle this problem may be to include, in a Foucault-like manner, intellectual and social histories of our analytical categories—this would require some philological expertise—into our discussion of these words in the classroom. But this has to be done carefully, without reducing the analytical categories to their strife-torn lives in our daily worlds or expunging such pasts altogether. This exercise calls for the achievement of a delicate balance and that may be a difficult task. But the difficulty does not invalidate my point.

The second point is an extension of the first but now set in a cross-cultural context. For instance, one could ask of Pomeranz's book: What were the different words in Chinese, Japanese, and Gujarati sources that Pomeranz implicitly translates as 'land?' Do these words look to horizons of meaning that the English word never looked to? In translating all of them back into the single English word 'land'—with very specific etymological meanings—do we not work with the unthought assumption that the meanings that fall through the cracks of this translation do not matter? This, incidentally, was often the structure of British colonial glossaries in India that assimilated many Indian expressions to only one English word. Or should economists or comparative economic historians be, ideally, multilingual philologists too? Of course, this is an extreme demand, unreasonable to expect of any one scholar. But I am speaking of ideals here. And I am also making the point that it is through such implicit rough translations of categories that we make our way into the world that global capital makes. A postcolonial political economy will try to make such translational processes visible.

My third point relates to an idea of defending academic knowledge as a special way of knowing. I am not a relativist. And I do not believe that all knowledge systems or ways of knowing the world are equally open to *reasonable* criticism. For example, knowledge claims that are based on the position 'we have the experience, so we know and you do not' are not open to such criticism. The disciplines we teach in universities have their blind spots, no doubt, but they all, in their own ways, teach us certain methods for argumentation and for the marshalling of evidence in support of our arguments. Whether such evidence be archival, textual, literary, filmic does not matter for my point—we all have ideas about what constitutes the relevant archive for the discipline at issue. We argue in everyday life too and present 'evidence' but the rules for such disputation are different. Often the rules are more implicit than explicit and may include all kinds of social claims to privilege, ranging from 'we have the experience, so we know' to 'I am old and/ or rich, so I must be granted authority', and so on. The classroom or the seminar represents an abstract Kantian space that is also abstracted from society. Once we know this, we also know that it is absurd to ask of society that it behave like a classroom and solve all its conflicts on the basis of procedures and protocols of argumentation developed for the classroom or the seminar only (reasonable argumentation, the furnishing of acceptable proofs, and so on). By the same token, we cannot expect the classroom to become like society where all issues are decided through actual participation in strife. Here I am defending the status of 'knowledge' as knowledge. This does not mean, as I have said earlier, that social strife does not enter the classroom or the seminar from time to time. Of course, it does, for the abstraction of the classroom is never complete. But we need to understand the classroom for what it ideally is: an abstract place for the pursuit of knowledge that actually becomes 'knowledge' only because it seeks to abstract itself from the hurly-burly of everyday world. That is what the disciplinary aspects of a discipline are: procedures for abstracting data from our life and then so arranging this abstract data—conscious models to narrations—that the world can become an object of our study. If, in the name of politics, we do not teach ourselves (or our students) these procedures, we maim our own—or their—analytical abilities. That, to my mind, would be a regrettable consequence.

A postcolonial approach to political economy will, therefore, entail taking all these three steps at once.

3

AN ANTI-COLONIAL HISTORY OF POSTCOLONIAL THOUGHT
A Tribute to Greg Dening

Long before there was any talk of the hybrid, the third space, and the in-between in the corridors of postcolonial theorizing and a couple of years after Edward Said's *Orientalism* was published, we saw the publication of a book called *Islands and Beaches* that spoke—creatively, evocatively, passionately, and philosophically—of the importance of the in-between in the history of contact between Europeans and 'natives' in the human worlds of the modern Pacific.[1] Greg Dening was a 'natural' ancestor of postcolonial scholarship. The allegory of the beach as an in-between space in life, as the theatre of cross-cultural exchanges, runs through his entire oeuvre.[2]

The in-between was not necessarily a peaceful place. It contained the play of power just as much as it acted as the theatre of cross-cultural performances. Blood was spilled. A William Gooch or a Captain Cook died as the 'natives' vented their passions. Dening knew that the in-between in human affairs cannot be separated from the play of power

[1] Greg Dening, *Islands and Beaches: Discussions on a Silent Land—Marquesas, 1774–1880* (Honolulu: University of Hawaii Press, 1980).

[2] See, in particular, Greg Dening, *The Death of William Gooch: History's Anthropology* (Lanham, MD: University Press of America, 1988; second edition, 1995) and *Beach-Crossings: Voyages across Times, Cultures, and Self* (Philadelphia: University of Pennsylvania Press, 2004).

or from the conflicts that divide us. The in-between is not necessarily an argument against the binary of the European and the 'native' or the colonizer and the colonized. Rather, it is the binary that—one could argue—acts as the condition of possibility for the existence of the in-between.

It is this insight that I derive from Dening's writings that I want to illustrate by discussing the relationship between anti-colonial and postcolonial thought in this chapter.

Postcolonial and Anti-Colonial

Scholars usually draw several distinctions to distinguish between postcolonial and anti-colonial thinking. They appear to be mutually opposed currents of thought. Anti-colonial thought, it is said with good reason, saw the colonizer and the colonized locked in a binary of total opposition to each other. The urge to be rid of the colonizer in every possible way, to see sovereignty as a win-or-lose game between the colonizer and the colonized, was internal to all anti-colonial criticism that flourished from about the end of the First World War and lasted till the period of decolonization after 1945. Postcolonial critics of our times, on the other hand, are wary of binaries. They have emphasized instead how colonial situations produced forms of hybridity or mimicry—a condition of identity that in Homi Bhabha's language is predicated on 'difference within'—something that necessarily escaped the Manichean logic of the colonial encounter.[3]

It is not only this intellectual shift that separates anti-colonial and postcolonial criticism. The two genres have been separated also by the political geographies and histories of their origins. After all, the demand for political and intellectual sovereignty arose mainly in the colonized countries and among the intellectuals of anti-colonial movements. Postcolonial writing and criticism, on the other hand, was born in the West, and initially in the English-speaking part of it. They were influenced by anti-colonial criticisms but their early target audiences were in the West itself, for if anti-colonialism spoke to the project of decolonization, postcolonial writings have been an essential part

---

[3] Homi Bhabha, *The Location of Culture* (London and New York: Routledge, 1994).

of the struggle to make the liberal–capitalist (and, in the beginning, Anglo-American) Western democracies more democratic with respect to their immigrant, minority, and indigenous populations (though there have been tensions among these groups). Race and the politics of recognition have thus featured centrally in postcolonial criticism while their position in anti-colonial discourse varies. Race is crucial to the formulations of Fanon, Césaire, or C. L. R. James, for example, but it is not as central to how a Gandhi or a Tagore thought about colonial domination.[4]

And finally there is the question of globalization. Some have posited a periodizing schema working along the following lines. Decolonization was a process that ended more or less with the Vietnam War in 1975. Or maybe one could extend the date to the South African scene. The anti-apartheid struggle, it can be claimed, was the last instance of a successful battle against the world that European colonizers made. Anti-colonial sentiments were displaced by postcolonial discourse in the closing decades of the twentieth century. More recent commentators on postcolonial theory argue that even the postcolonial moment is now behind us, its critical clamour having been drowned, in turn, by the mighty tide of globalization.[5]

This linear periodizing schema—anti-colonialism → postcolonial criticism → globalization—that suggests itself all too easily as a way of dividing up the twentieth century is, however, unsettled once we notice with some care not just the discrepant chronologies in which non-Western peoples have found themselves in the twentieth century but also the actual debates that attended the process of decolonization. Postcolonial theory and criticism, I would argue, are more deeply rooted in the debates over decolonization than is usually recognized. Anti-colonial thinkers, on certain registers of thinking, were as interested in the hybrid and the in-between as postcolonial critics are today.

---

[4] See the discussion in my *L'Humanisme en Una Era Global/Humanism in an Age of Globalization* (Barcelona: Center for Contemporary Culture, 2008), reprinted in *Alltag, Erfahrung, Eigensinn: Historisch-anthropologische Erkundungen*, ed. Belinda Davis, Thomas Lindenberger, and Michael Wildt (Frankfurt and New York: Campus Verlag, 2008), pp. 74–90.

[5] See the discussion in my preface to the second edition of *Provincializing Europe: Postcolonial Thought and Historical Difference* (Princeton, NJ: Princeton University Press, 2007 [2000]).

So what were the debates that consumed the anti-colonial leaders of the 1950s? One quick way to answer this may be to look in some detail at the historic conference in Bandung, Indonesia, where some 600 leaders and delegates of 29 newly independent countries from Asia and Africa met between 18 and 24 April 1955 to exchange views of the world at a time when the Cold War and a new United Nations (UN) regime were already important factors in international relations.[6] This conference also acts as a timely reminder of a relatively recent moment in human history when the idea of empire wielded absolutely no moral force. Today the opposite rules: the theme of the empire has made a triumphant return in historiography while the nation state has fallen out of favour. Historians of Niall Ferguson's ilk even seem to recommend a return to imperial arrangements in the interest of a decent global future for mankind.[7] It may be salutary to revisit a time when both the category 'empire' and actual historical European empires truly seemed to have seen the sun set over them.

Bandung, April 1955

In 1955 when Richard Wright—the noted African-American writer then resident in Paris—decided to attend the Bandung Conference,

[6] The countries that sponsored the conference were Burma, India, Ceylon, Indonesia, Pakistan, and Sri Lanka. In addition, 24 other countries joined the conference. They were: Afghanistan, Cambodia, People's Republic of China, Egypt, Ethiopia, Gold Coast, Iran, Iraq, Japan, Jordan, Laos, Lebanon, Liberia, Libya, Nepal, the Philippines, Saudi Arabia, Sudan, Syria, Thailand, Turkey, Democratic Republic of (North) Vietnam, State of Vietnam, and Yemen. See *Selected Documents of the Bandung Conference* (New York: Institute of Pacific Relations, 1955), p. 29. It should be noted that Israel was invited to participate in the Asian Relations Conference of 1947 but the delegation was called the 'Jewish delegation from Palestine'. See *Asian Relations: Report of the Proceedings and Documentation of the First Asian Relations Conference, New Delhi, March–April, 1947*, introduced by Professor D. Gopal (Delhi: Authorspress, 2003). Bandung, however, excluded Israel, mainly because of 'strong opposition' from Arab countries. See Jawaharlal Nehru, *Selected Works of Jawaharlal Nehru*, second series, vol. 27, ed. Ravinder Kumar and H. Y. Sharada Prasad (Delhi: JN Memorial Fund, 2000), pp. 109, 566.

[7] Niall Ferguson, *Empire: How Britain Made the Modern World* (London: Penguin, 2003). See in particular the 'Conclusion'.

many of his European friends thought that this would be an occasion simply for criticizing the West. Even the economist Gunnar Myrdal, in composing his foreword to the book that Wright wrote on his experience of the conference, ended up penning an indictment of what happened in Bandung: 'His [Wright's] interest was focused on the two powerful urges far beyond Left and Right which he found at work there: Religion and Race.... Asia and Africa thus carry the irrationalism of both East and West.'[8] Both Myrdal and Wright's Parisian friends appear to have misjudged what decolonization was all about. It was not a simple project of disengaging from the West. Nor was there any reverse racism at work in Bandung. If anything, the aspiration for political and economic freedom that the conference stood for entailed a long and troubled conversation with an imagined Europe or the West. 'I was discovering', wrote Wright, 'that this Asian elite was, in many ways, more Western than the West, their Westernness consisting in their having been made to break with the past in a manner that but few Westerners could possibly do'.[9] It was, in fact, the newsmen from his own country who attended the conference who, Wright felt, 'had no philosophy of history with which to understand Bandung'.[10]

I will shortly come to this question of the philosophy of history that marked the discourse of decolonization. For now let me simply note the historical context in which the conference met. The Bandung Conference was held at time when currents of deep and widespread sympathy with the newly independent nations—or with those struggling to be independent (such as Algeria, Tunisia, Morocco, Central Africa, and so on)—met those of the Cold War. Treaties, unsatisfactory to the United States, had been signed in Vietnam, Laos, and Cambodia. The French had lost in Dien Bien Phu and the Korean War had ended. Some of the Asian nations had joined defence pacts with the United

---

[8] Gunnar Myrdal, 'Foreword', to Richard Wright, *The Color Curtain: A Report on the Bandung Conference* (Cleveland and New York: The World Publishing Company, 1956), p. 7.

[9] Wright, *The Color Curtain*, p. 71. This point is underlined in a review of Wright's book by Merze Tate of Howard University in *The Journal of Negro History* 41, no. 3 (July 1956): 263–5. Tate quotes the following lines from Wright: 'Bandung was the last call of Westernized Asians to the moral conscience of the West' (265).

[10] Wright, *The Color Curtain*, p. 82.

States: Pakistan, Thailand, and the Philippines. Some others belonged to the Socialist Bloc.

Bandung was an attempt to sustain a sense of Asian–African affinity. This was not easy, as there was pressure from the Western countries to influence the course of the conversation at Bandung by excluding China, for example. Nehru's correspondence with the UN makes it obvious that sometimes he had to stand his ground on the question of neutrality in the Cold War. A letter he wrote to the secretary general of the UN dated 18 December 1954, on the subject of Bandung, reads:

> We have no desire to create a bad impression about anything in the US and the UK. But the world is somewhat larger than the US and the UK and we have to take into account what impressions we create in the rest of the world.... For us to be told, therefore, that the US and the UK will not like the inclusion of China in the Afro-Asian Conference is not very helpful. In fact, it is somewhat irritating. There are many things that the US and the UK have done which we do not like at all.[11]

The leaders who got together in Bandung, however, were divided also among themselves. They were not of the same mind on questions of international politics, nor did they have the same understanding of what constituted imperialism. They did not even necessarily like each other. The representative of the Philippines, Carlos Romulo, for example, found Nehru to be a 'highly cultivated intellect' but full of 'pedantry' (and also, one might add, opposed—as a believer in non-alignment—to the Manila Pact of which the Philippines were a member). 'His pronounced propensity to be dogmatic, impatient, irascible, and unyielding ... alienated the goodwill of many delegates', wrote Romulo. Nehru 'typified' for him 'the affectations of cultural superiority induced by a conscious identification with an ancient civilization which has come to be the hallmark of Indian representatives to international conferences. He also showed an anti-American complex, which is characteristic of Indian representations at international diplomatic meetings'.[12] The memoirs of Roeslan Abdulgani, once Jakarta's ambassador to the

---

[11] Nehru, *Selected Works*, second series, vol. 27, p. 106.

[12] Carlos P. Romulo, *The Meaning of Bandung* (Chapel Hill: University of North Carolina Press, 1956), pp. 11–12. This book was published as the Weil Lectures on American Citizenship delivered at the University of North Carolina, Chapel Hill.

United States and an organizer of the conference, reflect some of the competitive currents that characterized the relationship between the Indian and the Indonesian leadership and officials. 'The cleverness of the Indian delegation', he wrote, 'lay in the fact that they had thoroughly mastered the English language, and had very much experience in negotiations with the British.... Some of them were even arrogant as for instance ... Krishna Menon, and, at times, Prime Minister Nehru himself'.[13]

Nehru, in turn, had trouble trusting the Indonesians with the responsibility for organizing the conference. He wrote to B. Tyabji, the Indian ambassador to Indonesia, on 20 February 1955:

> I am rather anxious about this Asian-African Conference and, more especially, about the arrangements. I wonder if the people in Indonesia have any full realization of what this Conference is going to be. All the world's eyes will be turned upon it.... Because of all this, we cannot take the slightest risk of lack of adequate arrangements.... You have been pointing out that the Indonesians are sensitive. We should respect their sensitiveness. But we cannot afford to have anything messed up because they are sensitive.[14]

His particular concern, it turns out, were the arrangements for bathrooms and lavatories. It is hard to know whether he was being merely anxious or expressing a peculiar Brahminical obsession with ritual purity and cleanliness when he went on to say:

---

[13] Roeslan Abdulgani, *The Bandung Connection: The Asia-Africa Conference in Bandung in 1955* (Singapore: Gunung Agung, 1981), p. 26. To be fair to Abdulgani, however, it needs to be said that he also expressed much admiration for Nehru's speech at a closed meeting of the Political Committee of the conference on 22 April 1955: 'The influence of that speech was very great indeed. [Nehru] was a fighter, well-on in years, his hair going white, his voice strong, speaking in fluent English, without pretence, full of idealism and valuable ideas.... I can never forget those moments. Everyone present listened spellbound' (Abdulgani, *The Bandung Connection*, p. 143). Abdulgani also presented the following evaluation of Nehru: 'He was very wealthy, but he lived simply full of discipline. Every morning, he did physical exercises, in the form of yoga. For a dozen minutes, he stood on his hand, with two feet in the air. In order to guard [*sic*] the easy coursing of blood in his veins. And in this way to clear his thoughts, he said' (Abdulgani, *The Bandung Connection*, p. 143).

[14] Jawaharlal Nehru, *Selected Works of Jawaharlal Nehru*, second series, vol. 28, ed. Ravinder Kumar and H. Y. Sharada Prasad (Delhi: Jawaharlal Nehru Memorial Fund, 2001), p. 98.

I have learnt that it is proposed to crowd numbers of people in single rooms.... Your Joint Secretariat will not get much praise from anybody if delegates are herded up like cattle.... Above all, one fact should be remembered, and this is usually forgotten in Indonesia. This fact is an adequate provision for bathrooms and lavatories. People can do without drawing rooms, but they cannot do without bathrooms and lavatories.[15]

Apart from such lack of mutual trust and respect, the conference, so opposed to imperialism, had no operative definition of the term. This was so mainly because there were deep and irreconcilable differences among the nations represented. The prime minister of Ceylon (Sri Lanka), Sir John Kotelawala, caused a stir in the Political Committee of the conference when on the afternoon of Thursday, 21 April 1955, he referred to the Eastern European countries and asked: 'Are not these colonies as much as any of the colonial territories in Africa or Asia?... Should it not be our duty openly to declare opposition to Soviet colonialism as much as Western imperialism?'[16] The compromise prose drafted by the conference in trying to accommodate the spirit of Sir John's question clearly reveals the shallow intellectual unity on which the conference was based. Rather than refer directly to 'the form of the colonialism of the Soviet Union', the Founding Committee eventually agreed on a statement that called for an end to 'colonialism in all its manifestations'.[17]

What then held the conference together? Appadorai, the Indian member of the joint secretariat set up for the conference, was right in saying that 'not much that is significantly new can be found in the Bandung Declaration. Most of the points of the historical declaration are found in the United Nations Charter'.[18] Bandung surely helped the newly independent states become parts of the UN system. But

[15] Nehru, *Selected Works*, second series, vol. 28, p. 99.

[16] Abdulgani, *Bandung Connection*, pp. 115, 117. See also John Kotelawala, *An Asian Prime Minister's Story* (London: George G. Harrap and Co., 1956).

[17] Abdulgani, *Bandung Connection*, p. 119. It should be noted that Bandung Conference was not to make any 'majority' decisions or raise divisive, controversial issues. See Nehru, *Selected Works*, second series, vol. 28, pp. 97–8.

[18] A. Appadorai, *The Bandung Conference* (New Delhi: The Indian Council of World Affairs, 1955, reprinted from *India Quarterly*), p. 29. See also A. W. Stargardt, 'The Emergence of the Asian Systems of Power', *Modern Asian Studies* 23, no. 3 (1989): 561–95.

it brought into the imagination of that system a shared anti-imperial ethic. Whatever the meaning of the term 'imperialism', there was an absolute unanimity among the participants of the conference that they were all opposed to 'it'. From Nehru to Romulo, the message was clear. As Romulo put it in his statement to the conference: 'The age of empire is being helped into oblivion by the aroused will and action of the people determined to be masters of their own fate.' He was confident that 'the old structure of Western empire will and must pass from the scene'.[19] A pictorial album produced soon after the conference from the Netherlands on the theme nationalism and colonialism in Africa and Asia thus characterized the meeting at Bandung: 'The end of Western supremacy has never been demonstrated more clearly.'[20] This was indeed a time when, whatever its meaning, any conscious project labelled 'empire' had no takers. The pro-empire historians of today would have found few readers then.

The organizers went to some trouble to make sure that the anti-imperialist sentiments undergirding the conference were open to the most expansive definition of anti-imperialism. The American War of Independence was deliberately made a point of reference for the conference. The planning conference at Bogor had decided that the conference would be held in the last week of April in 1955. In the meanwhile, says Abdulgani, news was received from America indicating that the Americans feared 'that Western colonialism would be subjected to attack [at Bandung] and would be the main target. Especially so with the attendance of the People's Republic of China'. Abdulgani writes:

> I and my staff thought and puzzled for a long time about how to get rid of, or how to neutralize American fears. Suddenly, we recalled the date of 18 April in the history of the American Revolution; exactly what it was, we didn't remember.... I telephoned American Ambassador Hugh Cummings [and] ... asked him for data about the American revolution around the month of April. On the following day, Ambassador Cummings sent several

[19] Romulo, *The Meaning of Bandung*, p. 66; Appadorai, *The Bandung Conference*, p. 30.

[20] *A World on the Move: A History of Colonialism and Nationalism in Asia and North Africa from the Turn of the Century to the Bandung Conference* (Amsterdam: Djambaten, 1956), p. 246. A review of this book in *The Bulletin of the School of Oriental and African Studies, University of London* 22, no. 1/3 (1959): 198–9, remarked: 'The real value of this book lies in the clear picture it will give to the Western students of the way Asian thinkers feel about "colonialism".'

books of reference.... It turned out that ... [o]n 18 April 1775, ... amidst the upheaval of the American revolution for independence against British colonialism, a young patriot named Paul Revere rode at midnight from Boston harbour to the town of Concord, arousing the spirit of opposition to British troops, who were landing at that time.... It was clear that 18 April 1775 was an historic day for the American nation in their struggle against colonialism. Why should we not simply link these two events, the date of which was the same, the spirit of which was the same, only the years were different?[21]

Indeed, President Sukarno made this American connection in his opening speech on the very first day of the conference.[22]

The Pedagogical Style of Developmental Politics

For the generation of leaders who spoke at Bandung, colonial domination produced two opposed kinds of discourses about decolonization. One related to the idea of economic development. It produced what I will call a 'pedagogical style' of politics between dominant groups and the dominated, both within and between nations. But colonial contact also produced curiosity about the West and a desire to explore and enjoy human differences without putting them in a hierarchy. It is clearly the latter that in many ways anticipated our contemporary debates on the 'in-between' and the hybrid.

The idea that colonial rule hindered economic development and that decolonization should free up nations to pursue that goal often entailed an uncritical emphasis on modernization. Sustaining this attitude was a clear and conscious desire to 'catch up' with the West. As Nehru would often say in the 1950s: 'What Europe did in a hundred or a hundred and fifty years, we must do in ten or fifteen years'—or, as it was put in the very title of a 1971 biography of the Tanzanian leader Julius Nyerere: *We Must Run While They Walk*.[23]

---

[21] Abdulgani, *Bandung Connection*, pp. 46–8.

[22] *Selected Documents*, p. 3.

[23] Jawaharlal Nehru, 'Speech Inaugurating the New Building of the Punjab High Court, Chandigarh, 19 March 1955', in *Selected Works of Jawaharlal Nehru*, vol. 28, ed. Ravinder Kumar and H. Y. Sharada Prasad (Delhi: Jawaharlal Nehru Memorial Fund, 2001) , p. 30; William Edgett Smith, *We Must Run While They Walk: A Portrait of Africa's Julius Nyerere* (New York: Random House, 1971).

This emphasis on development as catching up with the West produced a particular split that marked both the relationship between the
West and the rest as well as that between elites and subalterns within
national boundaries. Just as the emergent nations demanded *political*
equality with Euro-American nations while wanting to catch up with
them on the economic front, so did their leaders think of their peasants
and workers not only as people who were *already* full citizens or at
least full members of the nation—in that they had the associated rights
or were fully present in national representations—but also as people
who were not quite full citizens in that they needed to be educated in
the habits and manners of the citizen. This produced a style of politics
on the part of the leaders that could only be called pedagogical. From
Nasser and Nyerere to Sukarno and Nehru, decolonization produced
a crop of leaders who saw themselves, fundamentally, as teachers to
their nations.[24] Nyerere actually was known in his country by the
name 'Mwalimu', a Swahili word for teacher. There are two remarkably similar incidents in Nehru's and Nyerere's lives that illustrate this
pedagogical style of leadership. Both incidents involve them speaking
to their countrymen on the subject of singing the national anthem. The
similarities are striking.

Here is Nehru speaking at a public meeting in Dibrugarh on 29
August 1955. Mark the teacherly voice and a disciplinarian's insistence
on military bodily postures that citizens were urged to assume when
singing the national anthem. Nehru could have been speaking at a school
assembly: 'Now we shall have the national anthem. Please listen carefully
to what I have to say. One, nobody should start singing until the word
is given. I have found that in Dibrugarh people start singing even while
I am speaking. It is all wrong, you must start only when I say so, not
until then.' It also appears that some people had closed their eyes while
singing the anthem, overcome perhaps by their feelings of devotion to
the nation. It was, for instance, a familiar practice in traditions of Indian
devotional singing for people to sing with their eyes shut. So Nehru felt
compelled to add: 'Two, *Jana gana mana* is our national anthem. So it

[24] Wright, *The Color Curtain*, p. 132 (emphasis added). Christopher Lee
tells me of a fictionalized film about Nasser, *Nasser 56*, in which Nasser, trying to gather support and expertise for nationalizing the Suez, exhorts two
engineers who question his judgement, by saying 'You are engineers, not poets'.
Personal communication from Christopher Lee, 20 May 2005.

must be sung in loud and clear voices, with eyes open.' He was at some pains to remind them that the national anthem was more about military discipline than about being overwhelmed by nationalist emotions:

> You must stand erect like soldiers and sing, not hum it under your breath. Thirdly, you must remember that *Jana gana mana* ... has been selected to be our national anthem.... It is given great honour abroad. So ... everybody must stand up when the national anthem is sung because it is the voice of the nation, of *Bharat Mata*. We must stand erect like soldiers and not shuffle around while it is being sung. I would like to tell you that everyone must learn to sing the national anthem.

And, finally, he himself took charge of conducting the singing: 'When the girls sing just now all of you must join in. It does not matter if you do not know the words. The girls will sing one line at a time and you will repeat it. Have you understood? All right, stand up, everybody. Let us start.'[25]

Compare this with what Nyerere said at a mass rally on 7 July 1963 explaining the vice of 'pomposity' in his own 'new' nation. The similarities are striking and it is not difficult to hear the same teacherly voice of the leader trying to instil in his audience the proper habits of citizenship: 'When we became independent', Nyerere said,

> we started by singing the national anthem every time the Prime Minister arrived anywhere, even at supposedly informal dinner parties.... This, already, was rather unnecessary; but, as a little over-enthusiasm was understandable just at first. I had hoped that in time we should learn to reserve the anthem for the really ceremonial functions at which its playing is appropriate. It seems I was too hopeful; for now we sing it whenever a Minister, a Parliamentary Secretary, a regional Commissioner or an Area Commissioner arrives at a gathering of any kind anywhere in Tanganyika! Nothing could be more disrespectful to our national anthem than to treat it as a popular song-hit, or a 'signature-tune' to be 'plugged' the moment any member of the Government appears on the scene.... It is customary in every country in the world for visiting foreigners, as well as the local public, to show their respect by standing to attention while the anthem is being played. But it is not customary in other countries to play or sing their national anthem without any warning, just because some official of the government happens to

---

[25] Jawaharlal Nehru, *Selected Works of Jawaharlal Nehru*, vol. 29, ed. H. Y. Sharada Prasad and A. K. Damodaran (Delhi: Jawaharlal Nehru Memorial Fund, 2001), p. 67.

have dropped in unexpectedly at a small gathering, or landed at an airstrip on a visit to his mother-in-law![26]

Even as these two excerpts from Nehru's and Nyerere's speeches confirm, the pedagogical aspect of their politics had to do with their desire to see their respective nations take their pride of place in the global order of nations. This is why the reference to 'abroad' or 'every country in the world' in these speeches. The 'voice' of Bharat Mata (Mother India) had the 'inter-national' world as its audience. Behind the idea of pedagogical politics was the idea that the nation was more about development than diversity. More than that, leaders often assumed that development was the answer to the question of diversity. The politics of recognition of various identities that flourished in the 1980s and 1990s and later were yet to come.

The Death of Pedagogical Politics

This pedagogical model of political development, so intimately tied to anti-colonial projects of modernization, died in the 1960s and later as an expression of the political will of the elite in the ex-colonial countries. Why? There were many reasons, but one surely was a rising level of disillusionment with the performance of the nation. One has to remember that the very exclusion of large sections of the colonized from the institutions of governance during colonial rule ensured that the nation, until the attainment of independence, was in the main an emotional and utopian experience achieved through mobilization on the streets and with the aid of cultural artefacts such as literature, music, films (from the thirties onwards), and rituals. Once the generation of the teacher-like, anti-colonial leaders was gone—Nehru died in 1964; Nasser in 1970; Sukarno died in 1970 but was out of power by 1965; Mao's authority was so under challenge by the mid-1960s that he had to launch the Cultural Revolution; Nyerere, the youngest of the lot and the leader of a country that became independent later, stayed on in power till 1985 but his *ujaama* (communitarian, lit. 'familyhood') socialism was in crisis by the late 1970s—once these

---

[26] Julius K. Nyerere, *Freedom and Unity* (London: Oxford University Press, 1967), lecture on 'Pomposity' on 7 July 1963 at a mass rally to celebrate the formation of his political party, TANU (7 July 1954), pp. 223–4.

leaders died or were removed, the pedagogical spirit became an empty shell of a rhetoric for projects of modernization that had clearly failed to meet the raised expectations of the masses. The charisma of the teacherly leaders kept people's faith alive in the organs of the state in the face of massive administrative failures. Once they were gone, there was nothing to stop the process of popular alienation from the state. It was as if these leaders embodied a certain compact between the general population and the state that unravelled with the departure of these unifying figures.

At the same time, that is to say, by the late sixties to early seventies, immigration rules in the United States, Canada, Australia, and the United Kingdom changed allowing for the migration of professionals from the ex-colonial countries to the metropolitan centres. This was a crucial development in the rise of postcolonialism. There had, of course, been working-class migration for years. Britain actually sought labourers from the West Indies immediately after the war for demographic reasons, and there had been much older diasporas of working-class population spread throughout the world through the history of slavery and what followed its abolition in the early nineteenth century. But working-class migration would not have, by itself, given rise to postcolonial thinking. There is no postcolonialism in a Western country without the chattering classes—the classes that read and write in newspapers or are present in the media—being continually supplied by streams of professionals from the ex-colonial countries who then make this group, literally, multicoloured and thus multicultural as well.

Also significant was the fact that 'the West' in which these intellectuals and professionals from the ex-colonies landed was a post-imperial West—challenged internally not only through new social movements such as feminism or the student movements and the Hippie protests of the 1960s, but also by the decline of imperialism and by the fact that in the settler colonial nations such as the United States, Canada, Australia, New Zealand, or South Africa, the indigenous peoples and minority groups in search of recognition and autonomy had begun to devour anti-colonial writings for their own ends. Even the racism that the coloured or black population often confronted in post-war Britain or France was partly a result of the experience not only of the loss of empire but also the return, from the formerly colonial countries, of white populations who had settled there. Hence the popularity of a Fanon among indigenous leaders or of a Gandhi in the civil rights movement in America or in the struggle against apartheid.[27]

In some ways, then, the global space for the white man's sense of supremacy and the pedagogical spirit of anti-colonial modernization died at about the same time, the time from when scholars date the beginnings of the contemporary forms of globalization: the late 1970s.[28] If decolonization was thus generally predicated on a worldwide urge on the part of the formerly colonized countries to catch up with Europe (or more broadly the West), one could say that decolonization was a discourse that saw an imaginary Europe as the most important agentive force in the world. Decolonization thus may be thought of as the last phase in the history of what Martin Heidegger once called 'the Europeanization' of the earth.[29] Vietnam was perhaps the last war for 'national liberation' that was seen as delivering a blow to a weak link in the imperial chain that was the West. Other long-term struggles—such as those of the Kurds, the Kashmiris, the Palestinians, the Nagas, the

[27] For an interesting reading of the sixties in the West that seeks to connect the developments of this era to the later emergence of postmodernism, see Julie Stephens, *Anti-Disciplinary Politics: Sixties Radicalism and Postmodernism* (Cambridge: Cambridge University Press, 1998). Rochona Majumdar's *Writing Postcolonial History* (London: Bloomsbury, 2010) has an excellent discussion of post-imperial racism in metropolitan nations.

[28] Chapter 2 of Arjun Appadurai's *Modernity at Large: Cultural Dimensions of Globalization* (Minneapolis: University of Minnesota Press, 1996) dates contemporary globalization from the 1970s. David Harvey, in Chapter 9 of *The Condition of Postmodernity* (Oxford: Blackwell, 2000), dates what he calls 'flexible accumulation' from the same period. For a transnational history of white supremacist ideologies and struggles against them, see Marilyn Lake and Henry Reynolds, *Drawing the Global Color Line: White Men's Countries and the International Challenge of Racial Equality* (New York: Cambridge University Press, 2008).

[29] This, roughly, was the argument of my essay 'Postcoloniality and the Artifice of History: Who Speaks for 'Indian' Pasts?', first published in 1992 and then incorporated with modifications in my book *Provincializing Europe: Postcolonial Thought and Historical Difference* (Princeton, NJ: Princeton University Press, 2000). For Heidegger's statement, see 'A Dialogue on Language' in Martin Heidegger, *On the Way to Language*, trans. Peter D. Hertz (New York: Harper and Row, 1982), p. 15. Aimé Césaire, *Discourse on Colonialism* (New York and London: Monthy Review Press, 1972), also discusses the world in terms of its 'Europeanization'.

Tibetans—for self-determination that occurred in a 'national' context would never produce the upsurge of anti-colonial and cross-cultural sentiments in the world of the kind that was evoked by the struggle in Vietnam.

Postcolonial theory emerges from re-circulation of anti-colonial texts within what I have called the post-imperial West. It could not have been an insignificant fact that Homi Bhabha from India, and Stuart Hall and Isaac Julien from the Caribbean, for instance, came together to read and organize conferences on Fanon in England of the 1980s under the sponsorship of the Institute of Contemporary Art and with funding from the Greater London Council, a municipal govern-ment left wing in its traditions but a part of the British state neverthe-less. Isaac Julien would go on to make a noted film on Fanon. It is also significant that the immediate context for their readings would be furnished by their participation in a shared struggle against British racism—Stuart Hall described in his reminiscences how they would go on anti-racist marches together (interesting to remember that the phi-losopher Charles Taylor was a fellow traveller in these years—it could not have been a coincidence that he would go on to write a seminal text on the politics of recognition). But the racism they fought was itself of post-imperial origins: it was born of cultural adjustments neces-sitated by the loss of empire and rise in migration of both the formerly colonized and groups of those who were once colonial settlers.[30]

Stuart Hall's intellectual journey, which culminated in his leader-ship of the Birmingham Centre for Cultural Studies, may be seen as an allegory of the *social* changes that brought about certain *academic* changes in Britain. There had been a push towards greater working-class literacy with the enactment of the 1944 Education Act, which raised the school leaving age to 15.[31] The Birmingham Centre for Cultural Studies was set up in the late 1950s. Richard Hoggart, its

---

[30] See David Morley and Kuan-Hsing Chen, eds, *Stuart Hall: Critical Dia-logue and Cultural Studies* (London and New York: Routledge, 1996), p. 477; Alan Read, ed., *The Fact of Blackness: Frantz Fanon and Visual Representation* (Seattle: Bay Press, 1996).

[31] I am grateful to Catherine Robson for discussions on these points. Her forthcoming book on the role of literature in working-class education in late nineteenth-century and early twentieth-century Britain will have much to say on this history.

founding director, wrote about his own working-class upbringing in
the justly famous book, *The Uses of Literacy* (1957).[32] Hoggart established the centre as he and his colleagues felt that the established
departments and disciplines in the university remained invested
in studying the elite—it was no surprise that a major critique of
E. P. Thompson's classic book, *The Making of the English Working
Class*, would be launched from this centre in the 1970s by Richard
Johnson.[33] The centre was to study popular culture—sub-cultures, to
be precise, such as the formation of punks and other rebels in British
society. Intellectuals associated with this movement took a deep
interest in contemporary French structuralism and post-structuralism
and brought out a series of booklets under the title *New Accents*.[34]
Gramsci, popular in English translation since the publication in
1972 of selections from his *Prison Notebooks*, became a theoretical patron-saint of this intellectual move. Stuart Hall, who stepped
into the shoes of Hoggart on the latter's retirement, had engaged
with Hoggart's writings as early as the fifties. His essay 'A Sense of
Classlessness' published in *Universities and Left Review*, Autumn
1958, was a response to Hoggart.[35] Grant Farred has reminded us
how this movement of ideas stemming from a general democratization of British political culture took on the question of racism as
Asian nationals arrived in Britain from places such as Uganda and
Kenya from where they were expelled after 1972.[36] As he says, it
was the racialized muggings in the 1970s that led to the centre in
Birmingham publishing—under the editorship of Stuart Hall, Chris
Critcher, Tony Jefferson, John Clarke, and Brian Roberts—the book

[32] Richard Hoggart, *The Uses of Literacy* (London: Chatto and Windus,
1957).

[33] See the essays in J. Clarke, C. Critcher, and R. Johnson, eds, *Working-Class
Culture: Studies in Theory and History* (New York: St Martin's Press, 1979).

[34] Terrence Hawkes, Christopher Norris, Dick Hebdidge, and others published some significant books under this series title.

[35] Stuart Hall, 'A Sense of Classlessness', *Universities and Left Review*
(Autumn 1958): 26–32. I owe this reference to Catherine Robson.

[36] Grant Farred, 'Out of Context: Rethinking Cultural Studies Diasporically', *Cultural Studies Review* 15, no. 1 (March 2009): 130–50.

Policing the Crisis: Mugging, the State, and Law and Order.[37] About the same time or soon after, intellectuals such as Salman Rushdie and Homi Bhabha began to question the received litanies of both British and Indian nationalisms and formulating their understandings of identities that were 'in-between' and interstitial.

These struggles around low culture/high culture in the context of capitalism, decolonization, and immigration of non-Western intellectuals into the West inspired debates in English universities about questioning the canonical texts that had until then represented the nation or the West, leading, in turn, to a search for more inclusive syllabi and resulting in the emergence of new fields that the Australian academic Kenneth Ruthven once called 'the new humanities'—a list that included, of course, postcolonial and cultural studies.[38] Universities in different Anglo countries took different paths to this juncture but debates about academic canons and about what constituted cultural education were common to them all. Universities in the United States saw the kind of 'culture wars' that went on at Stanford and elsewhere in the 1980s about the content of common core courses on Western civilization, debates propelled by identity politics that had come out of the civil liberties and other movements for recognition. I lived in Australia in those years and witnessed the beginnings of a national process of recognizing the 'historical wounds' that the Aboriginal people carried as a result, or so it was claimed, of the colonization of the country by Europeans. The Canadian debates on indigenous peoples and their rights often acted as precedents for debates in Australia. New Zealand was already further down this path than the Australians were. These debates were also fuelled by the sociological fact of the growing importance of the media in defining youth cultures. The argument for cultural and postcolonial studies rested on the fact that an idea of high culture, fashioned after the theories of Matthew Arnold or Thomas Carlyle, was no longer feasible. I participated in the debate that accompanied the name change of the English department at

[37] Stuart Hall, Chris Critcher, Tony Jefferson, John Clarke, and Brian Roberts, eds, *Policing the Crisis: Mugging, the State, and Law and Order* (London: Macmillan, 1978), cited in Farred, 'Out of Context', p. 131.

[38] Kenneth Ruthven, ed., *Beyond the Disciplines: The New Humanities* (Canberra: Australian Academy of Humanities, 1992).

the University of Melbourne (a process in which Kenneth Ruthven, Stephen Knight, Simon During, and David Bennett played leading roles). The department was to be henceforth called the Department of English and Cultural Studies. As this brief history will have suggested, cultural studies was born as a close cognate of postcolonial studies in British, Australian, and Canadian universities.

The Dialogical Side of Decolonization

Since postcolonial criticism and cultural studies were fundamentally about making the West embrace a degree of cultural pluralism, their primary polemical targets were modes of thinking that tended to understand identities as frozen in eternal essentials: black, white, indigenous, and so on. Yet at the same time they had to reject the universal in whose name the call of immigrant, indigenous, and minority communities for recognition of their identities were usually ignored. The suspicion of a particular form of the universal that, on examination, always turned out to be white and male was inherited from anti-colonial and feminist thought.

However, the answer to racism could not be reverse racism. Nor could it be a shallow universalism or humanism that did not know how to deal with difference. Surely, the lesson from Fanon was that the colour of the colonized had to be both critical and ephemeral at the same time. Postcolonial criticism was an attempt to read the colonial archive to develop a politics of difference that avoided the two kinds of politics of sameness—an uncritical humanism that often underlay both the imperial stance of civilizing the 'natives' as well as the anti-colonial leader's modernization programme and his pedagogical relationship to his people. How would one then think of difference as a real but inherently unstable object, so unstable that it would defeat all attempts, academic or otherwise, to objectify it?[39]

It is then not surprising that postcolonial critics should accumulate a huge intellectual debt to the so-called philosophers of

---

[39] It could not have been a mere coincidence that all major disciplines of the social sciences developed in this period substantial critiques of their key foundational concepts: thus, anthropology came to critique the idea of 'culture', history those of historical time and facts, geography that of 'space', and economics that of the 'market'.

difference—Lacan's distinction between the subject of enunciation and subject of utterance, Derrida's ideas of *différance*, and Foucault's challenge to all foundationalist thinking in his *Order of Things* were deployed to new ends by Bhabha and Spivak. Think of Bhabha's formulations of mimicry—his expression 'not quite, not white'— and Spivak's question 'can the subaltern speak?' that had much in common, say, with Luce Irigaray's project in *This Sex Which is Not One*.

But that only brings me back to my point about how important the 1960s and its antecedents are in any genealogy of postcolonialism, a point that Julie Stephens made in her Melbourne PhD thesis, which resulted in the book *Anti-Disciplinary Protest: Sixties Politics and Postmodernism*.[40] The so-called post-structuralist thinkers all came from the Left—there is no right-wing post-structuralism or postcolonialism—searching for principles of democratic life that could go beyond the verities of Marxism.[41] However, we would fall short in our historical understanding of the world if we see postcolonial thought as a simple case of some non-Western scholars applying the tools of post-structuralism to the colonial archive. My argument is this: just as the nineteenth century belonged to a world created by centuries of European expansion and colonial domination, postcolonial criticism belongs to the world fashioned by anti-colonial struggles even though the politics of decolonization were significantly different from those of postcolonial writing.

Nowhere is this connection between the postcolonial and the anti-colonial seen more clearly than in what I call the dialogical side of decolonization to distinguish it from its pedagogical side. Contrary to what they said when they thought of catching up with the West, anti-colonial thinkers often devoted a great deal of time to a question that eventually became a postcolonial question as well: how could a global conversation of humanity genuinely acknowledge and communicate across cultural diversity without distributing such diversity over a hierarchical scale of civilization—that is to say, how could one express an urge towards cross-cultural dialogue without the baggage of

[40] Stephens, *Anti-Disciplinary Politics*.
[41] One has to remember that Foucault read Deleuze and Guattari's *Anti-Oedipus* as a guide to non-fascist forms of living.

imperialism? A utopian question but one that is critical to anti-colonial imaginations of freedom, a point I take up later.

There are clear anticipations of postcolonial positions in what the anti-colonialist thinkers said in these dialogical moments. Take, for instance, the question of 'global English'. Bandung brought Richard Wright a premonition of the global future of this language that was once, as Gauri Viswanathan and others have shown, very much a part of the colonizing mission.[42] 'I felt while at Bandung', wrote Wright,

> that the English language was about to undergo one of the most severe tests in its long and glorious history. Not only was English becoming the common, dominant tongue of the globe, but it was evident that soon there would be more people speaking English than there were people whose native tongue was English.... What will happen when millions upon millions of new people in the tropics begin to speak English? Alien pressures and structures of thought and feeling will be brought to bear upon this mother tongue and we shall be hearing some strange and twisted expressions.... But this is all to the good; a language is useless unless it can be used for the vital purposes of life, and to use a language in new situations is, inevitably, to change it.[43]

The Nigerian writer Chinua Achebe would echo this vision in ten years after Wright:

> Is it right that a man should abandon his mother tongue for someone else's? It looks like a dreadful betrayal and produces a guilty feeling. But for me there is no other choice. I have been given the [English] language and I intend to use it.... I felt that the English language will be able to carry the weight of my African experience. But it will have to a new English, still in full communication with its ancestral home but altered to suit new African surroundings.[44]

Or listen to Aimé Césaire, Fanon's one-time teacher, speaking, in 1978, in opposition to Sartre and others who thought the French language

---

[42] Gauri Viswanathan, *Masks of Conquest: Literary Studies and British Rule in India* (New York: Columbia University Press, 1989).

[43] Wright, *The Color Curtain*, p. 200.

[44] Chinua Achebe's 1964 lecture 'The African Writer and the English Language', cited in Ngũgĩ wa Thiong'o, *Decolonising the Mind: The Politics of Language in African Literature* (London: James Curry, 1986), p. 7.

could not be an effective vehicle for the expression of Africanness or blackness. Césaire said:

> I am not a prisoner of the French language. I try and have always wanted to *bend* French. That's why I have had a strong affection for Mallarmé, because he has shown me ... that language at bottom is arbitrary. It is not a natural phenomenon.... I re-create a language that is not French. If the French rediscover their language in mine, well, that's their affair.[45]

It is striking to notice how much these positions anticipate what critics would marvel at later in the postcolonial novels of Salman Rushdie: his capacity to make his Urdu or Hindustani speak through his English.

Yet delivering the Robb lectures—later published as *Decolonising the Mind: The Politics of Language in African Literature*—at the University of Auckland in New Zealand as recently as 1984, Ngũgĩ wa Thiong'o, the Kenyan writer, adopted a position exactly the opposite of that spelt out by Wright, Césaire, and Achebe. An essay by the Nigerian writer Gabriel Okara in the Africanist journal *Transition* illustrated for Ngũgĩ the 'lengths to which we were prepared to go in our mission of enriching foreign languages by injecting Senghorian "black blood" into their rusty joints'. Okara had written:

> In order to capture the vivid images of African speech, I had to eschew the habit of expressing my thoughts first in English. It was difficult at first, but I had to learn. I had to study each jaw expression I used and to discover the probable situation in which it was used in order to bring out their nearest meaning in English. I found it a fascinating exercise.

Ngũgĩ disagreed. 'Why', he asks,

> should an African writer, or any writer, become so obsessed with taking from his mother-tongue to enrich other tongues? ... What seemed to worry us more was this: after all this literary gymnastics of preying on our languages to add life and vigour to English and other foreign languages, would the result still be accepted as good English or good French?[46]

He for one experienced this as a 'neo-colonial situation' and went on to describe the book resulting from his lectures as his 'farewell to English

---

[45] See Aimé Césaire, *Non-vicious Circle: Twenty Poems of Aimé Césaire*, trans. and introduced by Gregson Davis (Stanford, CA: Stanford University Press, 1984), p. 14.

[46] Cited in Ngũgĩ, *Decolonising the Mind*, pp. 7–8.

as a vehicle for any of [his] writing': 'From now on it is Gikuyu and Kiswahili all the way'.[47]

It is not my purpose to use the positions of Wright and Ngũgĩ to cancel each other out. I just wanted to show the degree to which the debates about globalization and postcolonialism had been anticipated in the discourses of many an anti-colonial thinker. Take the question of place and its relationship to culture difference. Some theorists of globalization—such as Michael Hardt and Antonio Negri in their widely discussed book, *Empire*, or David Harvey in his many writings—take the position that how a place is produced is really a more important question rather than how it is lived. They think that our sense of spatio-temporal difference is actually only an effect of the ultimately placeless logic of capital. The critical question, according to them, is how capital generalizes itself by turning 'anthropological difference' into consumer preferences.[48] Yet see how Leopold Senghor—of whose love of French, you will remember, Ngũgĩ was no fan—both anticipated and argued against the position occupied by these thinkers. Senghor's thoughts—even in what he wrote on the (somewhat unpopular) topic of 'assimilation' to French culture in 1945—have much to say to us about what it might mean to inflect our global conversation by a genuine appreciation of human diversity. Senghor reminds us of the fact that simply acquiring the rights of global passage by following the placeless logic of capital may not define the ends of life for many. We may indeed all want the same rights—and this may very well include the right of global passage—but we may want these rights in order to pursue precisely those diverse 'meanings of life' that make the history of one part of the world debate issues that may not resonate in another corner of humanity.

Clearly, Senghor was not for nativist isolation. He wrote, for instance: 'Mathematics and the exact sciences … by definition have no frontiers and appeal to a faculty of reason which is found in all peoples.' This, he thought, was true for even 'History and Geography' which had 'attained a universal value'. But what about languages such as 'Greek, Latin and French?' He wrote: 'I know the advantages of these languages because I was brought up on them.' But 'the teaching of the

---

[47] Ngũgĩ, *Decolonising the Mind*, pp. xii, xiv.

[48] I owe the expression 'anthropological difference' to Etienne Balibar.

classical languages is not an end in itself. It is a tool for discovering human truths in oneself and for expressing them under their various aspects'. However, this could work only if there were subjects such as 'African' and other 'humanities'.[49]

Senghor's thoughts received an even sharper focus when, writing in 1961 on the question of Marxism, he made a passionate plea against overlooking the always situated human being—man in his concrete affiliations to the past—in favour of the figure of the abstract and place-less human, so much the favourite of the nationalist modernizers or of some globalizers of today, from both the Left and the Right. 'Man is not without a homeland', wrote Senghor, as if arguing directly against the Hardts and Negris of his times:

> He is not a man without colour or history or country or civilization. He is West African man, our neighbour, precisely determined by his time and his place: the Malian, the Mauritian, the Ivory-Coaster; the Wolof, the Tuareg, the Hausa, the Fon, the Mossi, a man of flesh and bone and blood, who feeds on milk and millet and rice and yam, a man humiliated for centuries less perhaps in his hunger and nakedness than in his colour and civilization, in his dignity as incarnate man.[50]

'Incarnate man'—or man as always already incarnate—was how Senghor imagined the world's heritage of historical and cultural diversity. It was not a diversity that got in the way of cross-cultural communication but nor was it a diversity that did not matter. For Senghor, one way that diversity could be harnessed in the cause of development was by deliberately creating a plural and yet thriving tradition of humanities in the teaching institutions of the world. The vision was different from those of Wright or Ngũgĩ. Neither 'global' English (or French) nor a return to one's 'native' language was the option Senghor outlined. The way forward was a world of multi-lingual individuals who would appreciate language both as means

---

[49] See the 1945 essay on 'assimilation' '*Vues sur l'Afrique noire, ou Assimiler, non être assimilés*. Léopold Sédar Senghor, *Prose and Poetry*, selected and translated by John Reed and Clive Wake (London: Oxford University Press, 1965), pp. 53–5.

[50] Senghor, *Prose and Poetry*, p. 59. See also the discussion of Senghor and other African thinkers in Paulin J. Hountondji, *African Philosophy: Myth and Reality*, trans. Henri Evans and Jonathan Rée (Bloomington: Indiana University Press, 1983 [1976]).

of communication and as repositories of difference. A philologist's utopia perhaps, but how far from the vision of anti-colonial modernizers such as Nehru or Nasser who, in their single-minded pursuit of science and technology in order to catch up with the West, ended up leaving to the West itself the task of preserving and nurturing the world's plural heritage of the humanities.

Returning to Dening, in Conclusion

Here then is what I see as the quintessential difference between post-colonial thought and recent theories of globalization, particularly of the Marxist variety. Globalization theorists do not share the deep fascination of postcolonial thinkers with difference. The world, in their eyes, has been so profoundly consumed by the same and universalizing logic of capital that they consider all particularities as only surface effects of capital. Many anti-colonial thinkers, on the other hand, who were both universalists and humanists at the same time, began by taking difference seriously: this place, my skin colour, my identity, my people, and so on. Even Frantz Fanon, the most universalist of them, began with the fact of his blackness. He questioned it but still it was his blackness, and not a universal theory of placeless capital, that remained his point of departure. None of them—the anti-colonial thinkers we have considered here—froze their ideas of difference into any form of essentialism. Difference, for them, was part of the human condition. Someone like Senghor wanted to celebrate it—something colonial domination seldom allowed. To be able to celebrate difference without either closing himself off to others or losing himself in some universal sameness was, for Senghor, a condition of freedom. Difference does not tear me off from others; difference is what connects me to them. It is because they exist that I know I am different. Such would have been his position. It did not mean, as I said in the very beginning, the absence of conflict. After all, what in life can be outside of the field of power? But difference, thus conceived, is necessarily open to the in-between, the hybrid, and the interstitial. Postcolonial criticism preserved and developed this impulse that lay deep in the history of what I have called the dialogical side of anti-colonial thinking. Dening anticipated much of this, because in the histories he wrote and thought, the past and its people were caught up in the politics of difference. His Gooch, his Marquesans could not be thought without thinking the in-between that mediates all experience of difference. For Dening, difference and the in-between— his beaches—were a part of his understanding of human existence. He would often say: all history is cross-cultural history.[51] Indeed it is only when we read Dening and people such as Senghor and Fanon together that we realize the existential dimension of postcolonial thinking. It is Dening's success in giving us a sense of history in which humans have no choice but to chance their all for the joy of experiencing the thrills and dangers of difference that we begin to see what the struggles of anti-colonial thinkers such as Senghor or Fanon or Césaire or Gandhi were all about: to make our enjoyment of difference not a condition of enslavement of one by the other but a state of freedom.

[51] See Greg Dening, *Performances* (Chicago: University of Chicago Press, 1996).

4

FROM CIVILIZATION TO GLOBALIZATION
The 'West' as a Shifting Signifier in Indian Modernity*

I feel honoured to have been invited to deliver a couple of lectures in this series that allows scholars who base their thoughts on the historical experience of India to exchange notes with those who think out of the experience of this great nation. I am also grateful to the authorities that organized this series for their hospitality and the invitation that made my visit possible.

I will tell you a little bit about my background before getting into my lecture, in hopes to illustrate the way in which China influenced my intellectual development in India and elsewhere. I was raised during a time in the history of the youth of India when they were deeply influenced by Maoist political thought. Subaltern Studies, the historical series I am associated with, was started by a group of Indian historians drawn to Mao's teachings, and for whom Mao was a figure of inspiration. In addition, there was a global romance about peasant revolutions—not just because of China but also because of the Vietnam War.

* This essay is an edited version of a lecture delivered as part of the West Heavens Project at the Shanghai Art Museum in December 2010 and published in *Inter-Asia Cultural Studies* 13, no. 1 (2012): 138–52. I remain grateful to the organizers of the project who invited me to present this lecture and to the Shanghai audience whose many questions and comments I found most instructive.

A few years later, I went to Australia for my PhD. I still remember how I felt when I first met Chinese students in Australia. I remember hoping they would all share my enthusiasm for the Cultural Revolution, but they were all against it! I remember arguing angrily with a Chinese woman. As I said to her 'but Mao had such beautiful ideas', she countered me by saying 'but what's the use of ideas that don't work?' I wrote home to my friends saying that these students must have been counter-revolutionaries, the 'wrong' type of Chinese from my point of view! I waited long for the right type of Chinese students, but they never came. I finally had to reconcile myself to the possibility that I would never meet someone who might have a word or two to say in favour of the Cultural Revolution. I did hear some good things much later but they were very qualified and measured statements. It was clear that the Great Proletarian Cultural Revolution was not what we had made it out to be.

The first batch of Chinese students coming out of China, it seemed to me, were as romantic about the West as we were about China. Our romanticism of China came from a long tradition of Western romanticism. I remember all the Western intellectuals—historians, economists, and journalists—who went to China during the Cultural Revolution and wrote books about how beautiful it was. If you read their descriptions, you would think the revolution was a heaven on earth. It took me a long time to accept the change in China and it took me even longer to realize the wrong things done in the name of the Cultural Revolution and about the sufferings they imposed on many. There were many things we did not know about Chinese socialism. We did not know about the famine that followed the Great Leap Forward, for instance. I still remember defending backyard furnaces. So coming to China for me was a matter of experiencing very mixed and profound feelings.

What I want to speak about here is a question that I have raised a few times before in conversations with Indian and Chinese friends. 'I understand and even support your desires to becoming superpowers', I say to them.

But when you come truly to dominate the world effectively, what terms of criticism will you provide to your victims so they can criticize your domination? In other words, what resources will you produce from within your tradition that others will use to criticize you?

In posing this question, I begin from the premise that no power-ful country can ever be completely benign. If a country or a nation becomes powerful in a worldly sense, they will end up oppressing some group or other either internally or externally. So if a powerful nation is to be good for itself, it has to take responsibility for its power and create terms that its victims can use to criticize it.

This is the proposition I want to illustrate by looking at how the meaning of Europe or more generally the West has changed in India from the colonial period—I will be mainly concerned with the period c. 1890s to now, the last few decades, that is, when India has seen the rise of a new middle class, a surge towards urbanization, a globalized media, a competitive consumerist culture, a public life rocked constantly by allegations of large-scale corruption, and a capitalism innovative and dynamic in certain areas such as IT while absolutely 'red in tooth and claw' when it comes to resources and real estate. I do not ask about the meaning of the West out of idle curiosity, however. Behind it lies my larger question.

There is no doubt that Europe and Europeans once dominated this planet. By the end of the nineteenth century, 80 per cent of the surface of the earth was under the rule of one European power or another. Since 1945, however, we have seen a retreat of the colonial great pow-ers of Europe and the rise of superpowers such as the United States and once the Soviet Union as well. China and India today aspire to similar superpower status. China has already achieved a lot more of it than India. A superpower that dominates us surely dominates us economi-cally, militarily, and technologically. It also undoubtedly influences our imagination—the twentieth century, which became the American cen-tury, cannot be imagined, for example, without the global dominance of Hollywood or certain American institutional imaginaries (such as institutes of technology in various countries modelled on MIT). Yet a distinction remains to be made between European colonial domination of others and the sheer economic, military, and cultural weight of a superpower. The distinction is this: when European powers became imperial–colonial 'lords of the humankind' from the period of the Renaissance to that of the Enlightenment and into the nineteenth cen-tury, they also gave their victims the terms and categories of thought with which to critique and challenge European domination. Two such great 'weapons of criticism' forged in the European workshop of the nineteenth century—but with their intellectual genealogies stretching further back into history—were Marxism and Liberalism, both wielded with great effect by many decolonizing nations and thinkers who criticized European domination. That is why I raised the question that if tomorrow China or India were to become a superpower, would we simply dominate in the ways the Americans have dominated? Or would we dominate in such a way that our very domination will create visions of humanity that the rest of humanity would be able to use against us? So I think if a real superpower or a dominating power wants to be good in spite of knowing that no power is benign, it has to create a certain kind of contradiction or criticism within itself. It needs to develop a culture of self-criticism at the same time as it develops into a powerful player in the affairs of the world.

Will we move beyond the horizons of European thought as China and India become dominant, powerful countries in this century? Will India and China produce new grounds for thinking on which humanity will meet as one? This is an important question for our times. Certain important problems we look at today are global in scope: climate change is a global problem, food security is a global problem, terrorism is a global problem, and water shortage, energy crisis, and so on are global problems. I recently read an Indian report that said for the first time in Indian history India has had to order an entire tanker of water from Alaska. The Chinese building of dams in the Himalayas worries Indians because the two countries do not have a water treaty. Yet, given the global or planetary nature of so many of our contemporary crises, the model of thinking that said that 'my development will have to come at your cost' will clearly not work in the long run. As we develop separately as different nations, we also have to develop some sense of commonality.

The last time I was in China—in September 2010—I was quite struck by discussions in English language Chinese newspapers on the need to move from the 'Made in China' phase to the 'Created in China' one. I assume that these newspaper writers had material things in mind when they spoke of things being 'created in China'—something like cars and gadgets of Chinese design. But European domination of the world went much further than designing material objects by creating concepts that framed some of the normative ideas for all of us. Can India and China aspire to the same role?

It is to ask this question that I want to share with you an Indian chapter in the history of the much-discussed—and today much-tainted—word 'civilization'. Around that word of European origin were created a series of meanings that, by attaching many possibilities to the word, allowed for the common meeting ground between European colonial masters and those whom they dominated. The question is this: how does a powerful country, which cannot avoid dominating others because it is powerful, create a culture of understanding itself as internally plural and thus help the dominated also to create a plurality of their own selves? It is the politics of creating pluralities within ourselves that, I submit, creates a common ground, a ground for dialogue in a world that is marked by inequalities of all kinds.

I am going to use the concept of civilization as a historical example of what I have in mind. 'Civilization' is a word that belonged originally to European vocabularies but around which a plurality of 'Europes' and of 'Indias' were created, creating thereby a common ground that I will call 'civility'. What I do here is to defend the idea of civility. Gandhi was a master at civility, even with people he fought against. Once, for example, in his South African years, when a proposed strike of Indian labourers in 1914 appeared to coincide with a strike of railway engine drivers, he wrote a letter to South African Minister (later General) Jan Christiaan Smuts voluntarily postponing the strike by Indians saying he did not want to attack the government when it was already weakened by another major strike, but would wait for that other strike to be over and then commence his. When Gandhi was later put in prison by Smuts, he actually made a pair of sandals as part of his prison labour and presented them to Smuts. Smuts, in turn, returned them as gifts to Gandhi on the latter's 70th birthday, remarking that it was his bad luck to be in a situation once where he was obliged to imprison this man. Or take another example of civility. Gandhi made some comments in 1934 in a newspaper in which he explained a terrible earthquake in Bihar as divine chastisement for the sin of untouchability. Rabindranath Tagore disagreed very strongly but before publishing his disagreements he actually wrote to Gandhi asking if had really made those comments, and mentioning that he proposed to oppose Gandhi publicly if Gandhi would verify that the comments were indeed his. Gandhi wrote back saying yes, those comments were his own, and that Tagore should feel welcome to oppose them, which Tagore did. This was civility in opposition.

Let me begin with the word 'civilization'. This word was critical to the story of European imperialism. European domination of the world was often justified by what the Europeans saw as their civilizing mission. Others were barbaric and savage so they needed their help in civilizing, except they always thought of the Indians and Chinese as bearers of ancient civilizations who had fallen on bad times—they were civilizations in decline. It was very clear, however, that the more uncivilized the Europeans thought some people were, the more freedoms Europeans allowed themselves to marginalize them.

Many prominent scholars, including, famously, the historian Lucien Febvre and the linguist Émile Benveniste, have written histories of this word that first came into use in French in the 1760s and then into English in the following decade. John Stuart Mill wrote a famous essay on the topic in 1836. Brett Bowden's recent book, *The Empire of Civilization: The Evolution of an Imperial Idea*, updates this history, bringing it up to our contemporary times.[1] I do not wish to cover all that familiar ground. Nor will I do an anti-Orientalist or anti-Samuel Huntington critique of this term—simply because I take such critiques for granted. I want to begin by demonstrating to you how, from about the 1880s to the 1950s, there arose a historical situation that enabled leading Indian nationalists to develop a close connection between the idea of civilization and the related idea of civility and turn them into instruments of a critical dialogue with Europe as part of their struggle for freedom from European domination. The ideas of civility and civilization, as is well known, arose at different times in European history; the word 'civility' being older than the word 'civilization'. In bringing the two words together, Indian nationalists were unwittingly restoring a connection that had become breached through usage. For while the word 'civilization' in its late nineteenth-century incarnation could refer to achievements in the sphere of material culture alone, at its inception the word also connoted a certain 'civil' state of being, for its source lay, at least in its usage in eighteenth-century France, in religion's call 'to confraternity, to soften our hearts'.[2] The intimacy between civility and religion was, again, a fraught one—several commentators have pointed

---

[1] Brett Bowden, *The Empire of Civilization: The Evolution of an Imperial Idea* (Chicago: University of Chicago Press, 2009).

[2] Bowden, *The Empire of Civilization*, p. 27.

to the tradition of the word 'civil' often referring to that which was not religious (as in the expression 'civil marriage').[3] The connection at origin between 'civility' and 'civilization' was also broken by later imperialist practices of domination, for members of imperial nations could be both 'civilized' on their own terms and be 'rude' and 'barbaric' towards others at the same time. To turn the question of being civilized by the European into a question of human civility itself was a major strategic achievement of Indian nationalist thinkers.

'Civilization' was a key word in European vocabulary from the beginning of the nineteenth century. The hierarchical scale of human civilization that the thinkers of the Scottish Enlightenment developed formed a very important element in British thinking about India. But Indian nationalists made it their own in producing critiques of the West. As Rabindranath Tagore remarked in 1941, the last year of his life, the word 'civilization' that had been translated into Bengali (and Hindi) as *sabhyata* actually had no equivalent in 'our languages'.[4] Yet it came to be of much use to Indian nationalist critics of the West.

The Indian voices I want to consider here belong to four iconic Indians: Swami Vivekananda, originally known as Narendranath Datta, the first Indian religious activist to bring a 'modern' version of Hinduism to the West; Rabindranath Tagore, India's pre-eminent poet who was awarded the Nobel Prize in literature in 1913; Mahatma Gandhi, who I suppose needs no introduction; and Jawaharlal Nehru, the first prime minister of independent India.

Between them, these intellectuals also cover the period of the anti-colonial movement in India and the years of transition to a post-colonial state. They are all personalities who had some impact on the West and in the world generally. There was, however, a rhythm to the timing and the nature of their impact: their impact was heightened whenever Western intellectuals entertained doubts about validity and the mission

[3] See the discussion in Clifford Orwin, 'Citizenship and Civility as Components of Liberal Democracy', in *Civility and Citizenship*, ed. Edward C. Banfield (St Paul, MN: Professors of the World Peace Academy, 1992), pp. 75–94.

[4] Rabindranath Tagore, 'The Crisis in Civilization' ['Sabhyatar Shankat'], in *The Collected Works of Rabindranath [Rabindrarachanabali]*, vol. 13 (Calcutta: Government of West Bengal, 1961, centenary edition), p. 407. There is an English version of the essay in *The English Writings of Rabindranath Tagore*, vol. 3, ed. Sisir Kumar Das (Delhi: Sahitya Akademi, 1999), pp. 724–6.

of their own civilization. Absent this doubt, the impact of Indian critiques of the West is immediately reduced. This see-saw feature of the historical career of the word 'civilization' as it moved back and forth between the West and the East is an index of the historical role it played in creating room for dialogue—a middle ground—between the colonizer and the colonized.

My first case in point is Swami Vivekananda, who won recognition in the West at a time when very few male intellectuals in Britain or the United States entertained any doubts about the global mission of the West. For, by the time Africa was being opened up for colonial rule and exploitation towards the end of the nineteenth century, decades of stable European economic growth and material prosperity had made the idea of progress seem palpably true. In fact, so deeply ingrained was this idea and so confident were the Europeans of ways of measuring it, that the British in India regularly published annual and decennial statistical reports in the second half of the nineteenth century called 'Reports on Moral and Material Progress of India'. Here, again, Brett Bowden has an excellent discussion of how the idea of civilization morphed into the idea of progress.[5]

Vivekananda made his name by speaking successfully at the first World Parliament of Religions held in Chicago in 1893. (The recent clamour over 9/11 has made many Indians forget that 11 September also marks the anniversary of this historic lecture.) Vivekananda reportedly abandoned the stiff formality of the gathering to address his audience as 'Sisters and Brothers of America' and was an instant success. His representation of Hinduism in America and in Britain in the 1890s won him immediately a large number of followers in these counties.

Now, the letters that he wrote in this period from America and Europe to his disciple back in Madras (Chennai), Alasinga Perumal, show clearly that Vivekananda understood how very 'political' the idea of 'civilization' was and how very closely it was connected to the colonial enterprise. A letter dated 6 May 1895 and addressed to Perumal describes his 'success' in the United States: 'India is now in the air, and the orthodox [Christian clergy] … are struggling hard to put out the fire.' He then goes on to say:

5 Bowden, *The Empire of Civilization*, Chapter 3.

If you could send and maintain for a few years a dozen well-educated strong men to preach in Europe and America, you would do immense service to India, both morally and politically. Many of the Western people think of you as a nation of half-naked savages, and therefore only fit to be whipped into civilization. If you three hundred millions become cowed by the missionaries…, what can one man do in a distant land?[6]

Yet, for all the charm of the 'success' that the Swami wrote home about, the fact remains that an overwhelming majority of the people in the West who actually accepted and felt drawn towards the teachings of Vivekananda were women and not men. Much recent research supports this conclusion and, in fact, there is quite telling evidence even in what he wrote at the time. Here is a letter, for instance, written from Massachusetts to Perumal on 20 August 1893: 'From this village I am going to Boston tomorrow. I am going to speak at a big Ladies' Club here…. I must first go and buy some clothing in Boston. If I am to live longer here, my quaint dress will not do. People gather by hundreds in the streets to see me.'[7] Apparently one reason why a few days after his first arrival in Chicago he left the city for Boston was that 'the man in the street stared and poked at him as at some object of curious and dubious nature'—there were also considerations of costs. But Boston itself was not much different.

I landed [in Boston] … a stranger in a strange land. My coat was like this red one and I wore my turban. I was proceeding up a street in a busy part of town when I became aware that I was followed by a great number of men and boys. I hastened my pace and they did too. Then something struck my shoulder and I began to run, dashing around a corner and up a dark passage, just before the mob in full pursuit swept past—and I was safe![8]

'So', he continued in the previously cited letter, 'what I want is to dress myself in a long black coat, and keep a red robe and turban to wear when I lecture. That is what the ladies advise me to do, and they are the rulers here, and I must have their sympathy'.[9]

[6] Vivekananda, 'Letter to Alasinga Perumal, 6 May 1895', in *The Complete Works of Swami Vivekananda*, vol. 5 (Calcutta: Advaita Ashram, 1995, Mayavati Memorial edition), pp. 79–80.

[7] Vivekananda, 'Letter to Alasinga Perumal, 20 August 1893', in *The Complete Works of Swami Vivekananda*, vol. 5, pp. 18–20.

[8] Marie Louise Burke, *Swami Vivekananda in the West: New Discoveries—His Prophetic Mission*, vol. 1 (Calcutta: Advaita Ashram, 1998 [1958]), pp. 19, 20.

[9] Vivekananda, 'Letter to Alasinga Perumal, 20 August 1893', pp. 18–19.

Or take another letter dated 2 November 1893 in which Vivekananda reproduces a newspaper report of one of his lectures: 'Ladies, ladies, ladies packing every place—filling every corner, they patiently waited and waited while the papers that separated them from Vivekananda were read.'[10] In fact, a contemporary observer, Mrs S. K. Blodgett, who was present at the Parliament of Religions when Vivekananda opened his maiden speech by addressing the assembled gathering as 'Sisters and Brothers of America', had this to say of women's immediate reaction to the Hindu monk:

> When that young man got up and said, 'Sisters and Brothers of America', seven [?] thousand people rose to their feet as a tribute to something they knew not what. When it was over I saw scores of women walking over to the benches to get near him, and I said to myself, 'Well, my lad, if you can resist that onslaught you are indeed a GOD!'[11]

This is an interesting story, I suggest, of the West being rendered plural by the way Vivekananda addressed the West. His discourse appealed more to women than men, and this won him the platform he sought. There is a buried history here of American feminism or at least of women's activism that I can only parenthetically acknowledge and but cannot bring out in any detail. But incidental information available in Vivekananda's biographies does tease our imagination. One of Vivekananda's early hostesses and patrons in Boston, Ms Kate Sanborn, was herself a lecturer and author who wrote about country life and composed small poems for friends that clearly spoke of her thoughts about men: 'Though you're bright / And though you're pretty / They will not love you / If you're witty.'[12] Another of the Swami's hostesses, Kate Tannat Woods, was also a lecturer and author who wrote 'many books' including *Hester Hepworth*, 'a story of the witchcraft delusion'.[13] But these were clearly individuals and families interested in looking beyond the West, sometimes influenced by American transcendentalism. In the Woods family, for instance, it was said over a few generations

[10] Vivekananda, 'Letter, 2 November 1893', in *The Complete Works of Swami Vivekananda*, vol. 5, p. 20.

[11] Burke, *Swami Vivekananda in the West*, p. 81.

[12] Burke, *Swami Vivekananda in the West*, p. 23.

[13] Burke, *Swami Vivekananda in the West*, pp. 42–3.

that Vivekananda and Mahatma Gandhi 'were more Christlike than any the world has known'.[14]

If it were the 'ladies' of the West—and men interested in 'counter-culture'—who received Vivekananda's critique of the West enthusiastically, the situation was not all that different for Mahatma Gandhi when he first came to London in the 1880s—a few years before Vivekananda went to Chicago—as a student. His inspiration came, as his great-granddaughter Leela Gandhi has shown in her imaginative book *Affective Communities*, from non-mainstream personalities such as the homosexual and anti-imperial writer Edward Carpenter or the vegetarian, animal-welfarist, and anti-imperial Henry Salt.[15]

At the end of the nineteenth century, when most of the major leaders and thinkers of the West were brimming with confidence about the righteousness of European empires and their civilizing missions, Indian interlocutors of the West could only speak to those parts of the West that were themselves marginalized: spiritualists, women, homosexuals, vegetarians, and so on. Imperial success, as Ashis Nandy put it in his provocative book, *The Intimate Enemy*, had made the dominant 'European personality' hyper-masculine (Nandy's term), sidelining all that could be considered—from the psychological point of view that Nandy assumes—feminine or childlike in the history of the West. Readers of Nandy will remember how brilliantly he uses the biography and writings of Rudyard Kipling to illustrate this point.[16]

It was only after the end of the First World War that claims of civilizational superiority of the West came to be questioned by Western intellectuals themselves. Some of the mood of the period is captured in the following lines that the English political scientist Harold Laski wrote in June 1923 to his friend Felix Frankfurter, a Harvard professor and later a judge at the Supreme Court of the United States:

> The truth is, dear Felix, that we ought not to stay in India. Literally and simply, we are not morally fit to do the job. On all of which please read E. M.

[14] Burke, *Swami Vivekananda in the West*, p. 43. For the transcendentalist connection, see Burke, *Swami Vivekananda in the West*, p. 26.

[15] Leela Gandhi, *Affective Communities: Anti-Colonial Thought, Fin-de-Siècle Radicalism, and the Politics of Friendship* (Durham, NC: Duke University Press, 2006), Chapters 3–4.

[16] Ashis Nandy, *The Intimate Enemy: Loss and Recovery of Self under Colonialism* (Delhi: Oxford University Press, 1983), Chapter 1.

Forster, *A Passage to India*.... I add my grave doubts whether the Indians can govern themselves. But it is better for them to make efforts than to have this running sore at the heart of things. If they fail, let it be their failure. Our success (if it were not too late) would only deepen their sense of inferiority.[17]

What thus came under a dark cloud of doubt in this period was the very idea that had become triumphant by the end of the nineteenth century: that the West was civilizationally superior to the rest of the world or that its civilizational superiority gave it the right to rule others. It was in this period that intellectuals in the West were more prepared to listen to criticisms of their civilization coming from other places, and it was no accident that it was in this era that both Mahatma Gandhi and Rabindranath Tagore, perhaps the two finest products of the Indo-British cultural encounter, emerged as major critical voices from outside the West. Both Tagore and Gandhi were universalist in their orientation. Profoundly committed to the welfare of Indians, they were not nationalist in any narrow sense. They also had their own significant differences, a pointer to the fact that even among themselves, the best of the Indian leaders, while agreeing on the importance of being civilized, could only disagree on what might be the most proper meaning of the word. 'Civilization' was a critical word in the Gandhi's vocabulary too, except that it meant usually the industrial way of life to which he was opposed. The one famous tract that Gandhi wrote in 1909 on the subject of self-rule in India, *Hind Swaraj*, contained a whole chapter on the subject where, following Edward Carpenter, he called civilization 'a disease'.[18] Gandhi's views are relatively well known, so I will not expand on them. Both Gandhi and Tagore rejected the idea that material culture or artefacts alone could stand for civilization. They also rejected as insulting the idea that it was Europe's task to civilize others. Yet they carried on through their lives a complex conversation with the West precisely on the question of what it meant to be civilized. They thus converted the question of civilization into a question of civility. But their answers were sometimes very different.

[17] Kingsley Martin, *Harold Laski (1893–1950): A Biographical Memoir* (New York: Viking, 1953), p. 58.

[18] M. K. Gandhi, *Hind Swaraj and Other Writings*, ed. Anthony J. Parel (Cambridge: Cambridge University Press, 2007 [1997]), p. 34.

In a collection of essays that he wrote mostly in the last decade of his life (he died in 1941), Tagore summed up his views on the role of Europe in Indian history. He was not unaware of the blemishes that Europe carried in her history by having oppressed other peoples and having taken over their lives and lands. In the title essay of the book *Kalantar* (Change of Times), Tagore wrote thus about the negative side of the idea of 'civilization' that Europe preached to the colonized.

> Gradually, we saw that outside of the nations Europeans considered their own, the torch of European civilization was [used] not for the purpose of illumination but for starting fires. That is why one day China's heart was bombarded with cannon balls and balls of opium. Schuster's *Strangling of Persia* ... [shows] how 'civilized' Europe once strangled with both hands young Persians determined to give their lives to liberating Persia from long-term inertia.... On another side, everybody knows how in the Congo region of Africa European rule transformed into indescribable horror.... The Great War has suddenly lifted a curtain on Western history.... We watched Japan, the leading student in Europe's classroom, in Korea, in China, laughing off criticisms with examples from European history.... The Europe that once called ... Turkey inhuman ... now hosts the indiscriminate terror of fascism in her open courtyard.[19]

Indeed in his last essay 'Crisis in Civilization', penned in 1941, Tagore—faced with the barbarism of the Second World War—struck a despondent note on the question of European civilization: 'I had at one time believed that the springs of civilization would issue out of the heart of Europe. But today when I am about to the quit the world that faith has gone bankrupt altogether.' Yet he refused to give up his 'faith in Man'.[20] Or, consider his judgement about the place of Europe in Indian history:

> The advent of the English in Indian history was a strange affair. As human beings, they remained much more distant from us than even the [foreign] Muslims. But no foreign nation can match the depth and pervasiveness of the intimacy that the English, as ambassadors of the spirit of Europe, have forged with us.[21]

---

[19] Rabindranath Tagore, 'Change of Times' ['Kalantar'], in *The Collected Works of Rabindranath: Change of Times* [*Rabindrarachanabali: Kalantar*] (Calcutta: Government of West Bengal, 1968), pp. 214–15.

[20] Rabindranath Tagore, 'Crisis in Civilization', in *The English Writings of Rabindranath Tagore*, vol. 3, pp. 724–6.

[21] Tagore, 'Change of Times', pp. 210–11.

What made this possible? Tagore's answer was fourfold. First was modern science or reason that Europe brought to India: 'Everyday she conquers the world of knowledge, because her pursuit of reason is pure, free as it is from feelings of personal attachments.'[22] The second important European idea to have an impact on India was the idea of equality before the law:

> One message contained in the new [British] rule was that crime was judged independently of the persons involved.... Whether a Brahman killed a Shudra or Shudra a Brahman, the offence of murder belonged to the same class and the punishment was the same.[23]

Third was the idea that no human being could be a property of another: the effort, as Tagore put it, against 'converting humans into commodities'.[24] And, finally, there was the message of self-determination or self-government that Tagore saw as another fundamental message of Europe:

> That, today, in spite of all our weaknesses we can attempt to change the situation of our nation and the state is due to our taking a stand on the ground of [a European] theory.... It is on the strength of this theory that we fight clamorously with such a powerful government over demands we would never been able to dream of raising with the Mughal emperor.[25]

And what was this theory? It was the theory of sovereignty, both of the individual and the nation. 'This is the theory expressed in the poet's line', wrote Tagore; the poet in question was no other than the Scottish national poet Robert Burns and the line was one from a famous song he wrote in 1795: 'A man is a man for all that.'[26]

In other words, for Tagore as for Gandhi, criticisms of European civilization were not a way of ignoring the fact that any civilization was plural and multiple when looked at from the inside. It was a civilization's capacity to furnish itself with tools for self-criticism and, therefore, for self-improvement that impressed Tagore in the end. Of the Spanish–English relations, for example, he would say: 'We have ...

---

[22] Tagore, 'Change of Times', pp. 210–11.
[23] Tagore, 'Change of Times', pp. 210–11.
[24] Tagore, 'Change of Times', pp. 210–12.
[25] Tagore, 'Change of Times', p. 212.
[26] Tagore, 'Change of Times', p. 212.

witnessed from this distance how actively the British statesmen acqui-
esced in the destruction of the Spanish Republic. On the other hand,
we also noted with admiration how a band of valiant Englishmen laid
down their lives for Spain.'[27] The general principle involved here was
spelt out as a part of a lecture he gave in 1923 and then reproduced
verbatim in a letter written to an Oxford-based academic in 1934: 'We
have seen Europe cruelly unscrupulous in its politics and commerce,
widely spreading slavery over the face of the earth in various names and
forms. And yet, in this very same Europe, protest is always alive against
its own inequities.'[28]

To be civilized, then, was to have a capacity for self-reflexivity, to
be able to create one's own critique. That was the kernel of civility.
Conversation with Europe about civilization was valuable because
Europeans could be self-reflexive.

✿ ✿ ✿

With the coming of independence in 1947, however, the line of criticism that Tagore and Gandhi had developed lost steam. There are many
reasons for it. Let me mention two critical ones, one external and the
other internal to India. The 1950s and 1960s were in some ways a rerun
of the years from 1870 to 1900. With the defeat of Nazism, Fascism, and
Japanese militarism (all products, predominantly, of the interwar period),
and the unprecedented material prosperity of the post-war West, the
idea of progress returned in a new guise, now known under the various
names of modernization, economic growth, and political development.
Developing countries such as India participated in that optimism. There
was, of course, the Cold War and a sense of competition, symbolized by
the space race, between the ideas of socialism and capitalism. There was
the non-aligned movement headed by India for a while but that was a
political choice. What seemed invincible was the industrial way of life
whose praise was sung by many an American theorist, ranging from Walt
Whitman Rostow (the theorist of economic take-off), James Burnham

[27] Tagore, 'Crisis in Civilization', pp. 724–5.

[28] The lines occur in a 1923 lecture entitled 'The Way to Unity' and are
repeated in a 1934 letter written to Professor Gilbert Murray, published
together under the title 'East and West' in *The English Writings of Rabindranath
Tagore*, vol. 3, pp. 349, 462.

(the theorist of managerial revolution), and through to Daniell Bell (the man who spoke of post-industrial society). The industrial way of life as such now seemed truly beyond question. The global, Indian voice of this period was that of the first prime minister, Jawaharlal Nehru. Nehru's vision and spirit have recently received an astute interpretation at the hands of Sunil Khilnani who wrote: 'Nehru wished to modernize India, to insert it into what he understood as the movement of universal history.'[29] With this transition to the era and the mantra of modernization, the civilizational critique lost its appeal to Indian leaders. It was as though Nehru's India, as Khilnani puts it, 'had to move forward by one decisive act that broke both with its ancient and its more recent history. The rationalist, modernist strain in Nehru's thinking ... obliterated the attachment to the heritage of an Indianness rooted in the past'.[30]

The other factor that destroyed civilizational thinking was developments from the 1930s that profoundly rejected, for good or bad, the assumption of national unity that underlay the very idea of there being an Indian civilization. Muslims criticized the apparent Hinduness of the idea; the lower castes and the ex-untouchables, as they came into political power and consciousness, increasingly saw the claim to civilization as based on texts produced by the Brahmins and the upper castes. This latter critique, going to back to Phule, Ambedkar, and others, has become an integral part of today's culture of democracy in India.

Perhaps the death of the Gandhi's civilizational critique of modernity and the subsequent transition to the values and vision of modernization is best captured in an exchange of letters that took place between Gandhi and Nehru in 1945, a little more than a year before independence. Gandhi wrote to Nehru:

> I still stand by the system of government envisaged in *Hind Swaraj*.... I am convinced that if India is to attain true freedom and through India the world also, then sooner or later ... people will have to live in villages, not in towns.... Crores of people[31] will never be able to live in peace with each

[29] Sunil Khilnani, *The Idea of India* (New York: Farrar, Strauss, Giroux, 1998), p. 8.
[30] Khilnani, *Idea of India*, p. 132.
[31] 1 crore =10 million.

other in towns and palaces.... You must not imagine that I am envisaging our
village life as it is today.... My ideal village will contain intelligent human
beings. There will be neither plague, nor cholera, nor small pox; no one will
be idle, no one will wallow in luxury.[32]

To which Nehru replied: 'A village, normally speaking, is backward
intellectually and culturally and no progress can be made from a backward environment.... We have to ... encourage the village to approximate more to the culture of the town.'[33]

Yet there was one legacy of the civilizational critique of imperialism that nobody, not even Nehru, could reject or even wanted to
discard, and that is India's adoption, on independence, of the principle
of universal adult franchise—in short, a foundational aspect of Indian
democracy. Indian institutions and social practices are undemocratic in
many respects, but India is surely unique among developing countries
and among her neighbours for having sustained a tradition of, on the
whole, free and fair elections for 60 years. Khilnani, it seems to me, is
only half right in saying:

Contrary to India's nationalist myths, enamoured of immemorial 'village
republics', pre-colonial history little prepared it for modern democracy. Nor
was democracy a gift of the departing British. Democracy was established
after a profound historical rupture ... [that] incited them to imagine new
possibilities.[34]

Khilnani is right in emphasizing that 'democracy'—giving non-
literate peasants the rights of citizenship—represented a rupture in
Indian history but he underestimates the role that the 'nationalist
myths', myths celebrating Indian civilization and an allegedly deep
republican tradition, played in giving Indian leaders the courage that
enabled them to take the historically unprecedented step of making
peasants, overnight, into citizens. Thus, he overlooks the fact that what
gave Indian leaders the courage to defy the dictum of a John Stuart Mill
that 'there could not be any universal franchise without any universal
adult education' was the assumption that our ancient civilization had

[32] M. K. Gandhi, 'Letter to Nehru, 5 October 1945', in *Hind Swaraj and Other Writings*, pp. 150–1.
[33] Jawaharlal Nehru, 'Letter to Gandhi, 9 October 1945', in *Hind Swaraj and Other Writings*, pp. 152–3.
[34] Khilnani, *Idea of India*, p. 17.

done the job of literacy and prepared the peasant for shouldering the burden of citizenship. If I may quote from my book *Provincializing Europe*, where I have touched upon this issue:

> In defending the new [Indian] constitution and the idea of 'popular sovereignty' before the nation's Constituent Assembly on the eve of formal independence, Sarvepalli Radhakrishnan, later to be the first Vice-President of India, argued against the [Western] idea that Indians as a people were not yet ready to rule themselves. As far as he was concerned, Indians, literate or illiterate, were always suited for self-rule. He said: 'We cannot say that the republican tradition is foreign to the genius of this country. We had it from the beginning of our history'.[35]

Radhakrishnan's statement is an indication of how much the introduction of democracy in a country such as India owed to the labour of those—such as Gandhi or Tagore—who adopted the European idea of 'civilization' and worked it to anti-colonial and democratic ends. It is no wonder that Gandhi kept calling for universal adult franchise from as early as 1921. What Khilnani does not appreciate enough, it seems to me, is how nationalist myths about the pasts of India helped our nationalist leaders to develop a faith in the masses. Without that faith, right or wrong, there would not have been any experiment in mass democracy in India. Indian democracy originated thus in a gesture of civility on the part of the elite towards the masses.

※ ※ ※

Today, with a consumerist revolution occurring in India, the West having lost all civilizational status with the demise of formal empires, and the rise to political power of low-caste parties and populations in India, the civilizational/spiritual understanding of national life lies much diminished in significance, if not reduced to a nullity. My main purpose in discussing it was to show how in the age of imperial— as distinct from superpower—domination, the very word 'civilization', much debated on all sides as to its true content, provided a middle ground on which both the colonizer and the colonized could meet in a spirit of conversation across the differential of power and hierarchy.

[35] Dipesh Chakrabarty, *Provincializing Europe: Postcolonial Thought and Historical Difference* (Princeton, NJ: Princeton University Press, 2000 [2007]), p. 10.

The West does not any longer connote any civilizational superiority. Nor does it act as any kind of middle ground any more in the politics of culture. But the West still stands for a materially powerful culture, though now shorn of all the messages of humanism or liberalism that a Tagore or even a Nehru read into it. And politics of culture in India today cannot be separated from the presence of media and consumerism in Indian public life. So let me illustrate, in drawing to a close, what happens to a conflict over the West as a sign when the sign itself cannot any longer mediate the conflict.

In February every year now, young Indians celebrate Valentine's Day. This has become quite a cultural craze in urban India. On 24 January 2009, a bunch of men belonging to a self-styled Hindu outfit called the Ram Sene (Warriors of Rama) physically assaulted young women visiting a pub in the town of Mangalore in Karnataka. The state government, run by the Hindu party Bharatiya Janata Party (BJP), were initially soft on the perpetrators of this violence, especially their leader Pramod Muthalik, a person with a long past in Hindu-style politics. Muthalik apologized for hitting women but not for the attack on pubs and other things he considers inimical to Indian culture. His next programme, he announced, was to resist the celebration of Valentine's Day for it was 'un-Indian'. He said his group would forcibly abduct and marry off any young couple found being romantic in public. In a television interview with CNN-IBN, he explained: 'Why should one declare one's love only on one particular day of the year? In India, we love our partners everyday!' There has been violence by other groups before against the observance of Valentine's Day. Feminists this time formed an alliance called the 'Consortium of Pubgoing, Loose and Forward Women' who on 5 February 2009 started a campaign of collecting and sending Muthalik and his men pink *chaddis* ('chaddi' is the Punjabi–Hindi word for 'underwear') from all over the country. More than 12,000 chaddis were collected. The campaign has been very powerful in the English language media. The *Times of India* ran an animation. Unfortunately, I cannot reproduce the animation here for technical and copyright reasons, but I will discuss its contents briefly to help underscore my point. The animation showed a talking head of Muthalik being forced into silence by one pink chaddi after another flung on his face until he is completely gagged and cannot move his lips.

It is an interesting debate for me to watch, as someone living outside of India, to notice how different the West has become in its connotation. Around Valentine's Day, there were reports of the amount of money people had spent on conspicuous consumption. All the big hotels were booked up, people booked dinners involving payments that were sometimes ten times a full professor's monthly salary. So there were three things coming together: consumerism, the importance of the media, and the question of 'Westernized' women. But what was the West? What did it signify?

The West is no longer a question of civilization but of a certain kind of aggressive pursuit of freedom in consumption and lifestyle, focused on the freedom of the individual to express him or herself and not be oriented to a community except in seeking protection in public life from violence and oppression that could be directed towards such expression-seeking individuals. On the other side stands a very violent, oppressive, and patriarchal construction of 'tradition', mortally opposed to this figure of the individual that it construes the 'Western' as 'foreign' and a threat to 'tradition' and which therefore subjects the allegedly Westernized women to patriarchal and undemocratic violence.

Indian feminists obviously deployed a lot of bantering, in-your-face kind of humour in this animation campaign. Some of the humour could even be considered queer. Nor do I question the powerful mobilization they achieved in this campaign against a bunch of goons. But at the same time, I cannot but notice the complete absence of a middle ground in this conflict. On the one side are Muthalik and his men, threatening a Western-style expression of love and sexuality with violence, embodying intolerance and thuggery. On the other side is this animation that also ends with a symbolic gagging of Muthalik as though those fighting for their right to choice of lifestyle and freedom also would rather silence opposition than engage in any conversation with it. The West here is a figure split completely between the idea of immoral sexual promiscuity on the one hand and the right to sexual expression, consumption, choice, and lifestyle on the other. Straddling these divisions is the emerging rich–poor divide.

* * *

One may ask: Why should we care about civility? Is not intolerance the only fitting answer to the intolerance of a Muthalik? Besides, many

Indian friends, who have seen Dalit leaders of recent times deliberately use, to great effect, uncivil language towards the upper caste, ask: Is not civility an elitist project? Does it not hide claims to privilege? Well, you only have to visit India to know that the classes that suffer the basest forms of incivility are the subaltern classes, not the wealthy or powerful elites. Besides, I agree with the old argument of Edward Shils's: institutions of civil society decay if there is no civility in public life, no culture of respect for the lives of others.[36]

But that is an argument internal to India. Maybe it applies to China too, but I do not know. The important issue that I wanted to extract from my short history of the work that the word 'civilization' performed for Indian nationalists of a bygone era is this: Indian nationalism as practised by the likes of Vivekananda, Gandhi, Tagore, or Nehru in the context of British rule was based on certain debatable but key terms supplied by Europe but shared on both sides. Civilization was one such key word. Its meaning was unstable; it differed in different hands. Gandhi and Tagore even famously clashed a few times over its meanings. Yet it was this sharing of some critical terms that created a room for dialogical manoeuvres even within the vice grip of power. And that was because in sharing with the colonized the two overarching themes of modernity—human control over the forces of nature and human freedom from oppression by other humans—Europe exhibited enough contradictions within herself to provide the colonized with terms with which to criticize her doings. In the concrete, these produced the kinds of friendships, alliances, hybridities, and ambivalences that Ashis Nandy, Leela Gandhi, Homi Bhabha, and others have written about.

This returns me to the question with which I began. As I welcome the prospect of China and India taking their place among the dominant nations of the world, I wonder if they would help create new visions of humanity and help humans achieve justice and fairness in a world racked by problems of planetary proportions: climate change, food security, global refugees and asylum seekers, failed states, and terrors of various kinds. Or would we continue to think of the world through ideas that became global during the era of European ascendancy, and that still constitute our vision of civility, even as Indian and Chinese

---

[36] Edward Shils, 'Civility and Civil Society', in *Civility and Citizenship*, pp. 1–15.

national elites pursue the American model of domination through economic, military, and technological means and the actual prospect of achieving civility between the powerful and the powerless recedes into a horizon that seems increasingly distant? For me, it still remains an open question, for I hope that one day the aspiration to move from 'Made in China' to 'Created in China' will relate not only to things material (such as the designs of cars) but to visions of humanity as well. But for this to happen, critiques of China, India, the United States, and the West generally will have to issue from some shared ground of thinking. I take the conversations represented by these series of lectures to be working towards creating this possibility.

5

FRIENDSHIPS IN THE SHADOW OF EMPIRE
Tagore's Reception in Chicago, c. 1913–32*

'Only those are to be judged friendships in which the characters with age have been strengthened and matured.'

—Montaigne, 'Of Friendship'[1]

'This is *The Scoop*. Reserve space in the next number for Rabindranath Tagore', wrote the American poet Ezra Pound from London to Harriet

* Lightly edited from 'Friendships in the Shadow of Empire: Tagore's Reception in Chicago, circa 1913–1932', *Modern Asian Studies* 48, no. 5 (September 2014): 1161–87. My foremost thanks go to Mukta Dutta Tomar, India's consul general in Chicago in 2011, who prodded me to write this paper. Thanks are due to audiences at the University of Technology, Sydney, the Australian National University, Canberra, the Art Institute of Chicago, and Visva-Bharati University for their responses to an earlier version of this paper. I am grateful to Devleena Ghosh, Debjani Ganguly, Assa Doron, Heather Goodall, Biswajit Roy, Uday Narayan Singh, Don and Barbara Willard, Bill Brown, James Chandler, Rochona Majumdar, and to referees of *Modern Asian Studies* for their comments; to Tapati Mukherjee, director, Rabindra Sadan, for access to the papers of Rabindranath Tagore; to the staff of the Regenstein Library, the University of Chicago, for their courteous assistance; and to Arnab Dey, Gerry Siarny, Ranu Roychoudhuri, Lorena Mitchell, and Esther Mansdorf for their help at different times with my researches and computer issues.

[1] Michel de Montaigne, 'Of Friendship', in *Montaigne: Selected Essays*, trans. Charles Corron and W. Hazlitt and ed. Blanchard Bates (New York: The Modern Library, 1949).

Monroe, the editor of the newly founded Chicago magazine *Poetry* in October 1912.[2] Unheard of until then in the fledgling literary circles of Chicago, Tagore, whose *Gitanjali* had just caused a stir in London, was published in *Poetry* in December 1912 with an introductory note from Ezra Pound and, through a serendipitous turn of events, soon found himself in the city of Chicago in January 1913 as a guest of the magazine that was the first to publish him in America.

This chapter is in part a contribution to the growing biographical literature on Tagore. His visit to the University of Chicago is mentioned in his multi-volume biographies available in Bengali and in the literature on Chicago's modernism in the early part of the twentieth century but not in any detail.[3] The University of Chicago hosted a lecture by Tagore on 23 January 1913 when he spoke on the topic of ideals of the ancient civilization of India, a lecture he repeated later at Harvard and then included in a revised form in his book *Sadhana*.[4] But there remains no institutional memory of the visit. In 1961, when Humayun Kabir, then the Minister for Scientific Research and Cultural Affairs in the Indian government, approached the University of Chicago philosopher Richard P. McKeon for advice regarding a 'proposed Tagore Commemorative Volume', the professor had no recollection of the poet's visit to his own university.[5] The first part of this chapter provides a sketch of certain institutional and cultural developments in the city that laid the ground for Tagore's reception in Chicago in 1913. In particular, I tell the story

[2] Harriet Monroe, *A Poet's Life: Seventy Years in a Changing World* (New York: McMillan, 1938), p. 262.

[3] Krishna Dutta and Andrew Robinson, *Rabindranath Tagore: The Myriad-Minded Man* (New York: St Martin's Press, 1996); Rathindranath Tagore, *On the Edges of Time* (Bombay: Orient Longman, 1958); Sujit Mukherji, *Passage to America: The Reception of Rabindranath Tagore in the United States* (Calcutta: Bookland, 1964); Ellen Williams, *Harriet Monroe and the Poetry Renaissance: The First Ten Years of Poetry, 1912–1922* (Chicago: University of Illinois Press, 1977). A quite informative essay is Stephen N. Hay, 'Tagore in America', *American Quarterly* 14 (1962): 439–63. Leisl Olson's forthcoming book, *Modernism Made in Chicago*, also has some discussion of this visit.

[4] Prabhatkumar Mukhopadhyay, *Rabindrajibani o rabindrasahityaprabeshok*, vol. 2 (Calcutta: Visva-Bharati, 1977, 4th edn), p. 412.

[5] McKeon to Humayun Kabir, 29 June 1960, Richard Peter McKeon Papers, Box 44, Folder 10, Regenstein Library (hereafter RL), Special Collection (hereafter Sp. Colln), University of Chicago.

of how he came to give this lecture at the University of Chicago, based
on some unpublished and hitherto unknown material preserved in the
Special Collections of the Regenstein Library of the university.

My larger interest, however, is in discussing how Tagore was understood and imagined by sections of the Chicago literati who hosted his
visit and by the authorities of the university who invited him to deliver
the lecture. To this end, the second part of the chapter provides an
interpretive reading of the bond of friendship that Tagore developed
with Harriet Moody, a prominent Chicago entrepreneur and literary
personality who hosted Tagore and his family in 1913, and made her
apartments in London and New York available to the poet for accommodation on other occasions. Not romantic or even intimate in any
obvious sense, it was nonetheless a strong and enduring friendship
between two people of very different backgrounds and personalities.
The historian Stephen Hay once likened this friendship to 'a golden
thread [running] through all his [Tagore's] visits to America'.[6] I offer
a reading of Tagore's letters to Moody—preserved in the Regenstein
Library of the University of Chicago—in light of Moody's views of this
friendship that I have derived from other sources including some of
her letters preserved in the Tagore archives (Rabindra Sadan) at Visva
Bharati University in West Bengal, India.

What connects the two parts of the chapter is the question of how
the British Empire cast its shadow on the reception of Tagore's personality and work outside of the subcontinent. Whether or not Tagore was
a loyal subject of the empire was, as we will see in the case of his visit
to the university, a matter of crucial concern to the authorities. But it
is also clear, both from the history of Tagore's visit to the University of
Chicago and from his reception by personalities associated with the
magazine *Poetry*, that an idealistic view of something called 'Indian
civilization'—of which Tagore was seen as both an embodiment and
purveyor and which was seen as possessing some answers to the major
problems that appeared to ail the West—weighed quite substantially
with those who promoted his cause in the United States. The pleasure
of conversation with a person who was seen as bearing a civilizational
message often helped his friends and others to override the tensions
that could have arisen from the differences of gender, class, race, or

6 Hay, 'Tagore in America', p. 443; Mukherji, *Passage to America*, p. 70.

even from the sheer ignorance, on both sides, of actual cultural and historical differences. I use Tagore and Moody's relationship to illustrate this point that figures in the first part of the chapter as well. The tendency to look at the world through a framework of contending civilizations that was once prevalent and that is now rightly critiqued, I argue, enabled certain human exchanges that would be much more difficult to transact today when the idea of 'civilization' lies in ruins. I treat Harriet Moody's unequal relationship to Tagore as a parable of friendship that was made possible by the civilizational discourse that marked the cultural politics of the empire in the period between the two World Wars.[7]

A Poet and a City

In a note that she prepared as a tribute to Tagore on his 70th birthday, Harriet Monroe acknowledged that 'the founder and editor [of *Poetry*] had never heard of Tagore' until Ezra Pound, the magazine's foreign correspondent resident in Britain, had seen Tagore's poems discussed in the London *Times*. Pound met with the poet who was then visiting England, and 'induced him to permit the sending of some of the *Gitanjali* poems to the new poets' magazine in Chicago'.[8] Tagore would not have had any reason to know of this new magazine either. *Poetry: A Magazine of Verse* was founded in 1912. It was made possible by a growing sense of cosmopolitanism among some of the leading citizens of Chicago when a number of businessmen who had made money in the preceding few decades began to take an interest in building some of the cultural institutions of the city.[9] Harriet Monroe (1860–1936), the editor of the magazine, was the daughter of a lawyer and worked as an art critic for the *Chicago Tribune*. In 1911, in a gesture that one could read as a sign of the times, she called upon

---

[7] For more on this, see my essay 'From Civilization to Globalization: The "West" as a Signifier in Indian Modernity', *Inter-Asian Cultural Studies* (Taiwan) 13 (2012), an edited version of which is reproduced in this volume (chapter 4).

[8] Harriet Monroe's typed note, 'Tagore in Chicago', *Poetry: A Magazine of Verse* Records [hereafter *Poetry* Records], Box 41, Folder 3, eventually published in *The Golden Book of Tagore* issued to mark the poet's 70th birthday, p. 1, RL, Sp. Colln, University of Chicago. See also Monroe, *A Poet's Life*, pp. 261–2.

[9] See Williams, *Harriet Monroe*, 'Introduction'.

and persuaded a 100 Chicagoans to pledge $50 a year for 5 years to support a magazine of poetry that would have for its motto a line from Walt Whitman: 'To have great poets there must be great audiences too.'[10] Once the Tagore poems were published, the *Chicago Tribune* devoted an editorial to discussing the magazine's international aspirations in the course of which it mentioned Tagore. Soon after, writes Monroe in her aforementioned note:

> We were amazed to receive a letter signed by a young Tagore in the University of Illinois (Urbana-Champaign) saying 'My father is visiting me here and would like a few copies of the magazine containing his poems'. This was news indeed—the distinguished Oriental poet, whom I had supposed to be at home if not still in London, was for a time our neighbour in my own state! I wrote to him at once, inviting him to Chicago, and Mrs William Vaughn Moody, widow of the poet, seconded the invitation with an offer of her generous hospitality.

The actual letter from Rathindranath, Tagore's son, shows how little in fact the Tagores on their part knew about the magazine in which the poems had been published. The letter referred to the magazine as *Poetry Review* and addressed Ms Monroe as 'Dear Sir'.[11]

The person who was instrumental to the University of Chicago inviting Tagore to give a lecture was Edwin Herbert Lewis (1866–1934). The two major Bengali biographers of Tagore, Prabhatkumar Mukhopadhyay and Prasanta Pal, both mention him but get his details wrong.[12] Edwin Lewis was a professor of English who held two PhDs—one in Latin from Syracuse University, which he acquired

---

[10] Williams, *Harriet Monroe*, pp. 17, 21.

[11] Monroe, 'Tagore in Chicago', pp. 1–2. The actual letter from Rathindranath Tagore read thus: 'Dear Sir, Mr. Rabindranath Tagore, who has recently arrived here, would appreciate very much if you kindly send him two copies of the December issue of the *Poetry Review* in which some of his poems were published. Thanking you in anticipation, I remain, Yours truly, R. N. Tagore. Jr.' The letter was dated 9 December 1912. The address given was 508 W. High Street, Urbana, Illinois (*Poetry* Records, Box 41, Folder 3, RL, Sp. Colln, University of Chicago). The incident is also described in Monroe, *A Poet's Life*, p. 320.

[12] Mukhopadhyay, *Rabindrajibani*, p. 412, describes him as a professor at the University of Chicago but Lewis had ceased to be a professor at the university towards the end of the 1890s. Prasantakumar Pal, *Rabijibani, 1908–1914*, vol. 6 (Calcutta: Ananda Publishers, 1993), p. 351, calls him the 'director' (*adhikarta*) of the Lewis Institute. Lewis was a professor at the institute but

in 1892, and one from the English department of the University of Chicago obtained in 1894. He was the first doctorate produced by the latter department. He taught at the university between 1892 and 1899. While teaching at Chicago, he also began to teach at the newly set up Lewis Institute (1895), a polytechnic school that was founded with help of money bequeathed by a real estate investor, Allen C. Lewis, who took great interest in vocational and practical education. The institute was set up with the aim of providing education in the mechanical and liberal arts and training in domestic economy, and is said to be the first junior college in the country. From 1899, Lewis became a full-time professor at this institute where he also held administrative responsibilities and worked until his retirement in 1934. He died in Palo Alto in 1938.[13]

The establishment of the Lewis Institute was also a sign of certain cultural stirrings and demographic developments in the city of Chicago. The city's population grew from around 300,000 in 1870 to more than a million by 1890.[14] Several developments in the last decade of the nineteenth century point to the city's young but confident and growing cultural profile: in 1882, the Chicago Academy of Fine Arts (1879) renamed itself the Art Institute of Chicago; the University of Chicago was set up in 1892; and the World's Columbian Exposition was held in 1893, coinciding with the visit of Swami Vivekananda to the city.[15]

In 1890, Frank Wakely Gunsaulus, a pastor at the Plymouth Congregational Church, near where the Illinois Institute of Technology (IIT) stands today, gave a sermon that became famous in Chicago as the 'Million Dollar Sermon'. In that sermon, Gunsaulus said that if someone were to give him the gift of a million dollars he could 'build a school where students of all backgrounds could prepare for

---

never its director though he held several administrative positions. See biographical notes in Edwin Herbert Lewis Papers, RL, Sp. Colln, University of Chicago.

[13] See biographical notes in Edwin Herbert Lewis Papers, RL, Sp. Colln, University of Chicago.

[14] Dennis McClendon, 'Chicago Growth, 1850–1890: Maps by Dennis McClendon' (no year given), available at http://tigger.uic.edu/depts/ahaa/imagebase/chimaps/mcclendon.html (last accessed on 30 March 2012).

[15] See, for example, the discussion in Daniel J. Cahill, *Harriet Monroe* (New York: Twayne Publishers, 1973), Chapters 1 and 2.

meaningful roles in a changing industrial society'.[16] Inspired in part
by this sermon, Philip Danforth Armour, one of the city's businessmen, left money in his will to start an educational institution for the
non-elite—the Armour Institute of Technology. This institute and the
Lewis Institute later merged in 1940 to form the Illinois Institute of
Technology. Gunsaulus served as the director of the Armour Institute
from its founding in 1892/3 to his death in 1921. Gunsaulus was also
one of those who pledged support to the *Poetry* magazine from its very
inception in 1912.[17]

The letter that Harriet Monroe received from Tagore's son,
Rathindranath, was dated 9 December 1912. By the 14th of that
month, enough letters had been exchanged for Tagore to write to
Monroe saying that he might come to Chicago for 'two or three weeks'
during the Christmas vacation, though he mentioned in a later letter
(25 December) how greatly reluctant he felt about 'visiting big towns,
where I am likely to be drawn into all kinds of engagements, which
bewilder me. To tell you candidly, this is the reason why I am hesitating
to go to Chicago or to Boston.'[18] This was actually no false modesty.
Tagore wrote very similar letters to friends back home at this time.
On 30 December, for instance, he wrote to his nephew Satyaprasad
Gangopadhyay that he was 'hiding away in a corner of Illinois' after
reaching America. 'Have avoided the nuisance of big cities', he wrote,
and added: 'I have received an invitation from Chicago but feel no
desire to go there.... Rathi [Rathindranath, his son] and *bouma* [lit.
'bride-mother', Rathindranath's wife] are visiting Chicago during the
Christmas holidays.'[19] Rathindranath and his wife, Pratima Devi, did
meet with Monroe and Edwin Lewis while in Chicago. Monroe wrote

[16] Illinois Institute of Technology, 'The Sermon and the Institute', 2013,
available at http://www.iit.edu/about/history/ (last accessed on 28 March
2012).

[17] Williams, *Harriet Monroe*, pp. 16–17.

[18] Tagore to Harriet Monroe, letters dated 14 December 1912 and 25
December 1912, *Poetry* Records, Box 41, Folder 3, RL, Sp. Colln, University
of Chicago. In his letter of 4 January 1913, Tagore actually said: 'Please do not
think for a moment that I shall leave this country without visiting Chicago and
thanking you for the kind feelings you have towards me.'

[19] Tagore's letter to Satya dated 30 December 1912, in 'Letters',
Rabindrabiksha, ed. Anathnath Das, no. 29, 7 August 1996 (Santiniketan:
Visva-Bharati, 1996), p. 28.

to Tagore on 3 January 1913: 'It grieves me that you are in such dread of big cities as to hesitate to come to Chicago' and promised to make the visit 'as quiet ... as you desire'.[20]

Tagore at the University of Chicago

Monroe and her friends felt that Tagore needed to be invited by a prestigious institution of the city. Edwin Lewis wrote to the then president of the University of Chicago, Harry Pratt Judson (1849–1927, president 1907–23), on 17 December 1912 requesting him to invite Tagore to deliver a series of lectures—the original number Lewis had in mind was five—at the university. Judson, however, had not heard about Tagore. It is interesting to see Lewis describe Tagore to Judson as someone who was more 'level-headed' than, say, Vivekananda and as a loyal votary of the empire. 'May it not be possible', asked Professor Lewis of the president, 'to arrange that Mr. Tagore, the most eminent man of letters in all India, should give *five* lectures at the University in January or February, on "Religious Ideals"? I feel certain that his treatment of the subject would be eminently sane, and that he is a fine speaker.' He then went on to describe Tagore's father as the founder of the Brahmo Samaj, a reformist Hindu sect that, said Lewis, 'has always been free from nonsense' and added, in an implicit but obviously slighting reference to Vivekananda's visit to the city: 'Chicago has not heard a thoroughly scholarly and level-headed Hindoo since 1893, when Moozumdar [a Brahmo preacher] was here.'[21]

Lewis was trying to assure Judson that Tagore was no rabble-rousing nationalist and that his loyalty to the British Empire was unquestionable. The president's office appears *not* to have responded to this request with any sense of urgency, for Lewis did not hear back from them for about a month. Indeed it is uncertain if Lewis was not merely trying to keep Tagore's interest in the prospect of a visit to the city alive when he wrote thus to the poet on 23 December: 'I called up President Judson. He expressed the liveliest desire to hear your lecture, but said he could

[20] Harriet Monroe to Tagore, 3 January 1913, cited in Pal, *Rabijibani*, vol. 6, p. 352.
[21] E. H. Lewis to President Harry Pratt Judson, 17 December 1912, Administration Records of the Presidency of Harry Pratt Judson, Box 80, Folder 8, RL, Sp. Colln, University of Chicago.

not tell until next week—after the holiday recess—whether it would be possible to arrange dates in January.'[22] The president's secretary, D. A. Robertson, actually wrote to Lewis on 13 January. The president would not arrange for 'five' lectures by Tagore; there would be only one lecture, and preferably on 'his own poetry and modern Bengali literature' rather than on 'the religions of India' as Lewis had suggested.[23] Lewis wrote back somewhat plaintively to the president's secretary on 15 January. He was no longer sure that the president's office would lend a sympathetic ear to his request:

> I earnestly beg the President to write directly to Mr Tagore … and invite him. It was I who wrote to him first. I felt it a disgrace that a man who commands an audience of 20,000 people any time he chooses to speak in Calcutta should be within so short a distance of Chicago and not be invited by the most distinguished intellectual interests of our Babylon to appear here.

Lewis was even uncertain that the university would pay Tagore a decent honorarium: 'As to an honorarium, I don't suppose he will accept one. But … I would rather pay $50 myself than see him offered less.' He played up again the allegedly conservative and pro-imperial nature of Tagore's political positions: 'He is a good spirited man, & England has him to thank that Bengali disaffection did not burst into flame four years ago [around the issue of the first partition of Bengal by Lord Curzon].'[24]

[22] E. H. Lewis to Tagore, 23 December 1912, cited in Pal, *Rabijibani*, vol. 6, p. 352.

[23] 'Secretary to the President' to Lewis, 13 January 1913, Administration Records of the Presidency of Harry Pratt Judson, Box 80, Folder 8, University of Chicago, RL, Sp. Colln. David Allan Robertson (1880–1961) was an alumnus of the University of Chicago. He was a junior faculty member in the Department of English from 1904 to 1923, and also had the title of dean from 1919 to 1923. He then served as an assistant director of the American Council of Education from 1924 to 1929. Personal communication from Professor John Boyer, dean of the college, University of Chicago, dated 26 December 2012.

[24] Lewis to Mr Robertson, 15 January 1913, Administration Records of the Presidency of Harry Pratt Judson, Box 80, Folder 8, RL, Sp. Colln, University of Chicago. In her autobiography, Harriet Monroe remembers Tagore from his 1913 visit as 'bitter about the British subjection of his country' that he likened to 'a great steel hammer, crushing persistently the spirit of the people' (Monroe, *A Poet's Life*, p. 321).

Tagore, unaware of the work that Lewis had been doing behind the scene, chose to speak on the ideals of civilization in ancient India, and the university, finding the topic closer to religion than to poetry, decided to offer him accommodation at the Quadrangle Club where, as the president's secretary pointed out in an internal memo, 'University preachers are put up'. And it was again a supposedly conservative, pro-imperial Tagore who proved attractive to the authorities of the university. 'To Tagore', wrote the president's secretary in the same memo, inflating by some considerable degrees the sales pitch of Edwin Lewis, 'the British Government owes more than to say any man the present control over the Bengal situation. That hot-bed of Indian disturbances seems to be utterly under Tagore's control and when he speaks in Bengal or Calcutta, he often gets an audience of 22,000 people.'[25]

Misrepresentations of Tagore were not peculiar to his friends at Chicago but they say something about the way the Orient was seen by many intellectuals in the West in the years immediately before and during the Great War. Consider how Harriet Monroe recalled Tagore's 1913 visit in her short reminiscence, 'Tagore in Chicago': 'I remember how excited we were when they [the Tagores] arrived. Devotional poetry is rarely of value considered as poetry, but these were beautiful devotional poems, and the religious feeling they expressed was a tribute to the universal God of all races and creeds.' And again:

We used to spend evenings around Mrs. Moody's fire, listening to the chanting of poems in Bengali, or the recitation of their English equivalents, and feeling as if we were seated at the feet of some ancient wise man of the East, generous in his revelations of beauty. He talked also about his native country and the meaning of that huge word 'India', and about his hope for more friendly consideration from the governing powers of the world.[26]

Lewis's and Ezra Pound's initial assessments of Tagore's poetry also contained elements that spoke as much of a lack of comprehension on their part as of their own imaginations of Bengal or more generally

[25] Memorandum to Mr James A. Field from 'DAR', dated 14 January 1913, Edwin Herbert Lewis Papers, Box 8, Folder 7, RL, Sp. Colln, University of Chicago.

[26] *Poetry* Records, Box 41, Folder 3: Typescript titled 'Tagore in Chicago', pp. 1–2, RL, Sp. Colln, University of Chicago.

the East. In the short introduction Pound wrote for Tagore's poems published in *Poetry*, he declared these poems to be 'an event in the history of English poetry and of world poetry.... I do not use these terms with the looseness of contemporary journalism'. And, then, without knowing a word of Bengali, he proceeded to speak thus in very high praise of the language and its poetry:

> These poems are cast, in the original, in meters perhaps the most finished and subtle of any known to us. If you refine the art of the troubadours, combine that with that of Pleiades, add to that the sound-unit principle of the most advanced artist in *vers libre*, you would get something like the system of Bengali verse. The sound of it when spoken is rather like good Greek, for Bengali is the daughter of Sanscrit which is a kind of uncle or elder brother of the Homeric idiom.... The Greeks gave us humanism. The Bengali brings us the pledge of calm which we need overmuch in an age of steel and mechanics.[27]

After such lavish and irresponsible dispensation of praise, it was not surprising that Pound should write complainingly to Harriet Monroe the very next year that 'Tagore's philosophy hasn't much in it for a man who felt the pangs [of] and has been pestered with western civilization'.[28]

The search for an alternative civilization that would speak to those 'pestered' with the Western one and provide them with 'the calm [they] need[ed] overmuch in an age of steel and mechanics' can be seen to be also at work in the admiration that Edwin Lewis felt for Tagore as he introduced the poet to readers in Chicago. On 15 January 1917, Lewis presented a paper to the Chicago Literary Club entitled 'The Work of Tagore'.[29] Later, he drew on parts of this essay to write another piece of which only a fragment has survived. This fragment continues a completely unrealistic and enchanted view of Tagore that asserts: 'Dr. Tagore's own personality is what it is, very simple and full of faith in God, because he was born into one of the finest homes on earth, where no quarreling was ever heard, where he was never plunged

---

[27] Ezra Pound, 'Tagore's Poems', *Poetry: A Magazine of Verse* 1 (1912): 92.

[28] Pound to Monroe, 22 April 1913, cited in Williams, *Harriet Monroe*, p. 64.

[29] Edwin Herbert Lewis, *The Work of Tagore* (Chicago: Chicago Literary Society, 1917), Edwin Herbert Lewis Papers, Box 8, Folder 7, RL, Sp. Colln, University of Chicago. This essay was read before the Chicago Literary Club on 15 January 1917 and 275 copies were printed for the members. See note published at the end of the chapter.

into mental struggles on the question of authority.'[30] Such misunderstandings were common in the history of Tagore's reception in the West, and they were sometimes even productive. Lewis, for instance, got involved in the activities of a Hindusthan Association of America, which was set up with its headquarters in Urbana (Illinois) subsequent to Tagore's first visit. Lewis contributed regularly to its magazine, *The Hindusthanee Student*. His contributions show how deeply images of India, and that of Tagore, were caught up in debates to do with the mechanical–industrial civilization of the United States.[31] This discussion was, of course, part of much larger Western discourse in the 1910s and the 1920s as to what the West could learn from the 'ancient ideals' of India.[32]

Introducing Harriet Moody

The person Tagore felt closest to during his time in Chicago and with whom he forged a particular kind of friendship that lasted until she died was Mrs Harriet Vaughn Moody (1857–1932). It was to her, after all, that he dedicated his book *Chitra*, an English rendering of his Bengali play in free verse, *Chitrangada*. 'I am sure', he wrote in a letter dated 14 February 1914 to Mrs Moody, 'you have got my *Chitra* by this time and have forgiven me for the liberty I have taken in dedicating it to you without waiting for your permission'.[33] In a follow-up letter of 10 March 1914, the claim on friendship is stronger. 'My dear Friend', it runs,

[30] Untitled and unfinished essay in Edwin Herbert Lewis Papers, Box 8, Folder 7, RL, Sp. Colln, University of Chicago.

[31] The issues of *The Hindusthanee Student* are available at http://www.saa-digitalarchive.org/item/20110930-387 (last accessed on 1 April 2012).

[32] When the well-known historian of Asian art A. K. Coomaraswamy and his wife came to stay with Mrs Moody around 1916—on Tagore's introduction—Coomaraswamy was apparently in the habit of pronouncing that 'India … is now finished, and that the only soil upon which ancient Indian artistic ideals can flourish and develop is the soil of the west'. Harriet Moody's letter to Alice Corbin Henderson, cited in Olivia Howard Dunbar's *A House in Chicago* (Chicago: University of Chicago Press, 1947), p. 130. Dunbar, unfortunately, did not care much about carefully dating the letters she quoted from.

[33] Tagore to Moody, 14 February 1914, Papers of Harriet Brainard Moody (hereafter PHBM), Box 2, Folder 22, RL, Sp. Colln, University of Chicago.

In memory of the delightful evenings we had, reading *Chitra* by your fire-side, I dedicated that little lyrical drama of mine to you, hoping that the dedication will remind you of how deeply I value your friendship. I purposefully omitted to ask you [for] permission. It was to add to the list of the already numerous transgressions you had allowed your poet in the generous exercise of your forbearance.[34]

Claims of friendship come through strongly in a letter Tagore wrote from Calcutta on 18 February 1915 outlining his intention to visit Japan in September that year. It refers rather playfully to the demands of Harriet Moody's businesses while pleading with her to join his party on the trip:

Did we not plan this meeting at your fireside? ... Don't you plead business. Business should never be one-sided, it must not fix your mind to its profits only, there must come times when you should recklessly rush to losses and be glad. The element of loss is the element of poetry in business. Business would be deadly to the spirit of man if it were wholly successful. There should be at least one poet among your ... advisers to represent this side—the freedom from the tyranny of the desire for success.[35]

Tagore and Harriet Moody met again for a few days when Tagore visited the United States in 1916 and then in 1920–1 when he visited the country for about four months and spent a few days in Chicago as her guest. They also met briefly, later and in passing, in Rome and London in the 1920s.[36] Their letters were not always a two-sided affair. There are some letters from Mrs Moody to Tagore that are now preserved at the Tagore archives in the university he set up.[37] But from the internal evidence of the letters written by Tagore that are now preserved at the University of Chicago, it can be easily seen that very few, maybe one or two, of them were written in response to letters from Mrs

[34] Tagore to Mrs Moody, 10 March 1914, PHBM, Box 2, Folder 22, RL, Sp. Colln, University of Chicago.

[35] Tagore to Harriet Moody, Calcutta, 18 February 1915, PHBM, Box 2, Folder 22, RL, Sp. Colln, University of Chicago.

[36] See Prabhatkumar Mukhopadhyay, *Rabindrajibani o rabindrasahityaprabeshok*, vol. 3 (Calcutta: Visva-Bharati, 1953[1992]), pp. 66–75; Prasantakumar Pal, *Rabijibani*, vol. 8 (Calcutta: Ananda Publishers, 2001), pp. 61–6.

[37] These letters may be found in Papers of Rabindranath Tagore (hereafter Tagore Papers), File No. 246, Visva-Bharati University, Santiniketan, India.

Moody. That fact itself suggests a certain kind of lopsidedness—if not a one-sidedness—to this friendship, a theme I shall revert to in the concluding section of this chapter.

Several of Tagore's letters to Harriet Moody have a touch of the sentimental about them. 'I must tell you how truly your friendship has become a part of our life', he told her in a letter written from a ship in April 1913.[38] 'I thought I would startle you one fine morning in June by presenting myself at your door and quite naturally taking my seat at your breakfast table', he wrote in a letter dated 13 May 1918, after he had just cancelled a trip to America on account of false rumours being spread in the United States about his politics, this time painting him as a revolutionary who worked against the British empire.[39] On 23 December 1920, Tagore sent Mrs Moody a poem as 'a gift of one who has carried home across the sea the memory of your friendship as one of the best boons that your country has given him'.[40] The last time Tagore visited the country in 1930, he did not travel to Chicago.[41] But his letters are full of tender sentiments. 'Dear friend', he wrote on 12 October 1930 soon after landing in New York and in words that recall some lines of a famous song of his ('Ogo Bideshini' [Oh, My Foreign Lady]): 'After a long wandering I have come at last at your gate. But your dear face is not yet seen.'[42] A few days later he wrote again: 'I shall never forgive my fate if I ever go away without seeing you.'[43] This was in 1930. Mrs Moody's businesses had been badly hurt by the Great Depression and she must have pleaded inability to visit Tagore, for he writes on 5th December: 'I understand your difficulties and it will cause me pain if I know that you have strained your resources too much in order to come to see me. In any case, I am sure of your affection and

[38] Tagore to Harriet Moody, 16 April 1913, PHBM, Box 2, Folder 22, RL, Sp. Colln, University of Chicago.

[39] Tagore to Harriet Moody, Calcutta, 13 May 1918, PHBM, Box 2, Folder 22, RL, Sp. Colln, University of Chicago.

[40] Tagore to Harriet Moody, Mama Farms, Napanoch, 23 December 1920, PHBM, Box 2, Folder 22, RL, Sp. Colln, University of Chicago.

[41] Mukhopadhyay, *Rabindrajibani*, vol. 3, pp. 425–9.

[42] Tagore to Harriet Moody, 12 October 1930, PHBM, Box 2, Folder 22, RL, Sp. Colln, University of Chicago.

[43] Tagore to Harriet Moody, 16 October 1930, PHBM, Box 2, Folder 22, RL, Sp. Colln, University of Chicago.

I am deeply satisfied.'[44] The last letter from Tagore preserved in the Moody papers is dated 15 December 1930, written a day before he was to leave New York for England. It simply said: 'Dear friend, Good Bye. With love and kind wishes, Rabindranath Tagore.'[45] Mrs Moody died in 1932.[46]

Harriet Converse Tilden (Brainard) Moody was born in 1857 in Ohio to a family that saw money after moving to Chicago in the late 1860s. Harriet Moody obtained her parents' 'reluctant consent' to study at Cornell University and came under the influence of her mentor and professor Hiram Corson, who taught English literature but was a devoted student of Madame Helena Blavatsky, the Theosophist leader. It is possible that Corson passed on to Ms Moody a certain view of the Orient.[47] Sometime in the early 1880s Harriet Converse Tilden married Edwin Brainard, 'a wealthy Chicago lawyer' and a son of Dr Daniel Brainard, a native of New York trained in Philadelphia who founded Rush Medical College (now incorporated into Rush University) in Chicago in 1837, the same year in which the city received its charter. The marriage was said to have taken place 'over the violent objections of her father'. The marriage was short-lived and a year after the couple divorced in 1885, Harriet Tilden's once-wealthy cattle-shipper father died leaving her and her mother without enough money to afford the luxury they were used to. Financial circumstances forced Harriet Tilden Brainard to become a school teacher, but the income was not sufficient. Harriet, we are told, was on the lookout for other opportunities. Here, again, the growing sophistication of the city's middle class' taste in consumption came to her aid. A friend suggested that Harry Gordon

[44] Tagore to Harriet Moody, 5 December 1930, PHBM, Box 2, Folder 22, RL, Sp. Colln, University of Chicago.

[45] Tagore to Harriet Moody, 15 December 1930, PHBM, Box 2, Folder 22, RL, Sp. Colln, University of Chicago. The letter cited in note 34 gives Tagore's date of departure from New York.

[46] See the letter from Edith Kellog, Harriet Moody's secretary, to Tagore: 'The last two or three years of her life seem to me to have been very tragic; but she was working hard all the time, trying to recover her fallen fortunes' (Edith Kellog to Rabindranath Tagore, 12 November 1932, Tagore Papers, File No. 246, Visva-Bharati University).

[47] Dr Eugene Corson, the son of Professor Corson, dedicated his book on Madame Blavatsky to Harriet Moody as 'she had suggested [it] to me'. Dunbar's *A House in Chicago*, p. 22n5.

Selfridge (1864–1947)—then an employee in the Chicago departmental store Marshall Fields but later the founder of the famous British Selfridges—was looking for 'new gourmet food items' for the chain. Harriet sent off to him 'some items she had prepared in her mother's kitchen'. So successful were her culinary creations that in 1890 she started her own company, Home Delicacies Association, which flourished between 1890 and 1929. It later expanded into London, thanks to the Selfridge connection.[48] Over time, she would cater to the railways and 'fashionable private clients'. In 1920, she opened a restaurant, Le Petit Gourmet, in Chicago's Italian Court. Throughout the 1920s she organized poetry nights where 'Carl Sandberg, Robert Frost, Edna St. Vincent Millay', and many others would read their work. An unsigned note in Harriet Moody's papers describes the restaurant as a 'veritable institution of Chicago as well known as the lions at the entrance of the Art Institute'.[49] Mrs Moody's businesses suffered in the financial crisis of 1929 when she had to sell out. The Italian Court at 615 North Michigan Boulevard, constructed in the 1920s, was razed in the 1960s to make room for office buildings.[50]

In 1894, Harriet Brainard bought the property at 2970 Groveland (now Ellis) Avenue where the Tagores—Rabindranath, his son Rathindranath, and his daughter-in-law Pratima Devi—would eventually come to stay in January 1913. Harriet's friend and boarder, Martha Foote Crow, who taught English literature at the University of Chicago and who stayed there in the 1890s, introduced her to the young poet and dramatist William Vaughn Moody, then an assistant professor of English

[48] In an untitled manuscript article on the history of the Home Delicacies Association, Harriet Moody notes that the first demand was for 'home made ginger bread' for Marshall Field's 'new tea room' (PHBM, Box 3, Folder 2, RL, Sp. Colln, University of Chicago).

[49] PHBM, Box 3, Folder 3, RL, Sp. Colln, University of Chicago.

[50] I have used Olivia Howard Dunbar's *A House in Chicago* and the following web-based sources to put together some of the basic facts of Harriet Moody's life: 'Anatomy of a Restaurateur: Harriet Moody', 2011, available at http://restaurantingthroughhistory.com/2011/06/16/anatomy-of-a-restaura[n]teur-harriet-moody/ (last accessed on 26 March 2012); 'Guide to the Harriet Brainard Moody Papers, 1899–1932', available at http://www.lib.uchicago.edu/e/scrc/findingaids/view.php?eadid=ICU.SPCL.MOODYHB (last accessed on 26 March 2012); and 'History of the Rush Medical College', available at http://www.rushu.rush.edu (last accessed on 26 March 2012).

and rhetoric in the same institution. They shared a deep friendship but did not marry until Mrs Tilden, Harriet's mother, who was opposed to their union, died in 1908. This was also the year William Vaughn Moody was awarded an Honorary DLitt by Yale. Harriet and William got married in 1909, a year before William Moody died, sadly, of brain cancer at the age of 41.[51] Harriet Moody went travelling for some time and then threw herself into her businesses and acted as a generous host to many writers and poets who visited the city. Approached by Harriet Monroe, she agreed—though she had initially begged off—to host the Tagores, barely two and a half years after she had become a widow.[52]

This was not an easy decision to make. Harriet Moody has left us her own description of the moment. Widowed, she 'had been away from home for almost two years, seriously occupied, and ... had just come home to rest' when she received a message from Harriet Monroe that Monroe 'had invited a most distinguished poet (Tagore) to give an address here' and desperately needed her to host him. 'But I was adamant', she writes. 'I had freed myself ... from all sense of duty or obligation, and I declined to undertake this responsibility'. Next morning, however, her thoughts changed. 'It came to me that my home, which had been the home of a poet, could not close its doors to a brother poet.' She agreed to host Tagore and his family and 'got and read his book of verse, most carefully'.[53] Harriet Moody describes in her own words her first impressions of Tagore: 'A light powdery snow began to fall just as I was watching for him, and as he arrived, it fell on his picturesque black velvet cap and on his flowing white beard, giving a romantic aspect to his appearance.' While others 'settled themselves in the unobtrusive places in the living room, ... the poet came and

---

[51] 'Guide to the Harriet Brainard Moody Papers, 1899–1932', available at http://www.lib.uchicago.edu/e/scrc/findingaids/view.php?eadid=ICU.SPCL. MOODYHB (last accessed on 26 March 2012).

[52] Dunbar, *A House in Chicago*, p. 93.

[53] William Vaughn Moody, *Letters to Harriet*, ed. Percy Mackaye (Boston and New York: Houghton Mifflin Company, 1935), p. 407. The situation is also described in Monroe's *A Poet's Life*, p. 320: 'Alice [Corbin] and I found ourselves in a predicament. *Poetry* had no fund for entertainment, and neither of its editors could make room, in her contracted family quarters, for this foreigner from afar and his son and daughter-in-law.... So once again Mrs. Moody, friend of poets, came to the rescue.'

set beside me, before going to his own room'.[54] They talked, and thus began a friendship that was to last for the rest of her life.

A Parable of Friendship

Friendship has been an arresting and difficult question in the philosophical literature on the subject: it is perhaps a universal question for humans that also becomes historically inflected in different times at different places. Tagore's 'friendship' with his admirers in Chicago no doubt had a historical and contextual side to it. Nationalism, empire, historically formed patterns of patriarchy and gender-relations, colonial rule, and assumptions of white supremacy and other related issues of the time undoubtedly left their imprint on what Tagore and his correspondents wrote by way of expressing their feelings. One cryptic way in which issues of imperial rule, for example, are referred to in the correspondence and papers that I have read is through passing references to that great and controversial figure of the British Empire in the nineteenth century: Joseph Rudyard Kipling (1865–1936). Edwin Lewis's short 1917 essay 'The Work of Tagore' ends by indirectly alluding to Kipling's 'Ballad of East and West' in the context of the Great War: 'In the trenches and the dugouts the sons of gentlemen are not singing McAndrew's hymns to the steam engine, or anything to the effect that East and West shall never meet' (implying that the soldiers were now asking for copies of *Gitanjali*).[55] Tagore himself made an uncharacteristically slighting reference to Kipling in a letter to Harriet Monroe written on 19 December 1919 [1914?], while discussing his prize. He described the nuisance of public adulation but stated that he was yet 'rejoicing in the fact that the East and the West will ever touch each other like twin gems in the circlet of humanity' and observed 'how they had met long before Kipling was born and will meet long after his name is forgotten'.[56]

[54] Moody, *Letters*, p. 407. Monroe thus describes her impressions of Tagore's appearance: 'Tagore was a patriarchal figure in his gray Bengali robe, with a long gray beard fringing his chin. His features were regular and Aryan, his skin scarcely darker than a Spaniard's' (Monroe, *A Poet's Life*, pp. 320–1).

[55] E. H. Lewis, *The Work of Tagore*, p. 16.

[56] Tagore to Harriet Monroe, 31 December 1913, *Poetry* Records, Box 41, Folder 3, RL, Sp. Colln, University of Chicago.

Indeed it is ironical today to go back to Kipling's poem 'The Ballad of East and West' so many years after Tagore thought of his prize as a refutation of what was seen as Kipling's dictum. It is ironical because this poem that has been misunderstood for a long time as an arrogant imperialist statement about the immiscibility of the East and the West was actually about the feelings of mutual respect that a British soldier and his Indian counterpart could experience while suddenly finding themselves facing each other in the course of an armed chase across the border on the North-Western Frontier. Here is the first stanza of the poem that has unfortunately always stood for the (mostly unread) whole:

> Oh East is East, and West is West
> And never the twain shall meet
> Till Earth and Sky stand presently
> At God's great Judgment Seat.

And here is the stanza that follows:

> But there is neither East nor West
> Border, nor Breed, nor Birth
> When two strong men stand face to face
> Tho' they come from the ends of the earth.[57]

The Kipling poem is incidental—though not irrelevant—to our story. Friendships are, as Mary Lago said of Tagore's friendship with Rothenstein—'imperfect encounters'.[58] Besides, letters could be misleading guides to feelings. There is much that goes unsaid in human affairs and much that remains inexpressible. In concluding this chapter, then, I want to turn to Tagore's friendship with Mrs Moody to ask how, if at all, the discourse of civilization I have alluded to before made possible this 'friendship' that, on today's reading, seems to have been very unequal in more than one respect. One area of obvious inequality is in the very sources I use here to reconstruct this friendship. There are

[57] Rudyard Kipling, *Ballads and Barrack-Room Ballads* (New York: Macmillan, 1897), pp. 3–11. See also the comments in Robert W. Smid, *Methodologies in Comparative Philosophy: The Pragmatist and Process Traditions* (Albany, New York: State University of New York Press, 2009), p. 1.

[58] Mary M. Lago, *Imperfect Encounter: Letters of William Rothenstein and Rabindranath Tagore, 1911–1941* (Cambridge, MA: Harvard University Press, 1972).

some letters from Mrs Moody available in the Tagore archives. But her voice is also available in the biography that a younger woman, Olivia Dunbar, wrote of her in 1947 in which there are some direct quotations from her. It also helps that Dunbar often expresses an understandable impatience with many of Tagore's sentiments, an impatience that Mrs Moody clearly did not share. This makes it easy to distinguish the biographer's voice from that of the subject of the biography.

Many cultural and historical differences separated Rabindranath Tagore and Harriet Moody from each other. Their perceptions of each other—at least in the way they represented them in writing—were coloured by these differences. This is what Tagore wrote to a friend back home from Chicago about Mrs Moody. Early impressions, but the grid of sentiments is recognizably gendered in a culture-specific way and, in fact, assimilates Harriet Moody to the character of the mother created by Tagore himself in his famous novel *Gora* (1909; 1910):

> I really like Mrs. Moody a lot.... There is a natural generosity in her hospitality. Her heart pours out motherly feelings in abundance and they flow in diverse streams. It is not just us [Tagore's family], these feelings comfort whoever comes into contact with her. Not for a single day since arriving here have I felt like I was staying with someone who is not one of my own.... There is another quality of women here that ... leaves me enchanted. I have noticed that their wifely devotion is not constricted in any sense.... She [Mrs Moody] cares for her husband's work, his writings and for all his [other] pursuits in life as she would for a child. I feel so happy to see that no aspect of his work is alien to her heart.... She is highly educated ... and may even be called wealthy. This combination of [worldly] efficiency with a capacity to feel for others is what I consider the ideal of womanhood. And when you add to that education and a sense of literature, you add gemstones to gold.... [I]t is this highest expression of womanhood that pleases me the most. This is what I have sought to express in [the character of] Anandamoyee in [my novel] *Gora*.[59]

How did Harriet Moody feel about Tagore's claims on her friendship? Some of the comments made by her biographer Olivia Dunbar give us a glimpse of the relationship as it may or could have seemed from Harriet Moody's side or at least from the perspective of her biographer. 'The younger Tagores', writes Olivia Dunbar combining a biographer's

[59] Tagore's undated (1913) letter cited in Prasantakumar Pal, *Rabijibani*, vol. 2 (Calcutta: Bhurjapatra, 1985), p. 362.

distance from and empathy for her subject's feelings, 'in filial deference
to Rabindranath, scarcely spoke at all in his presence.... [And] Harriet
was an eager seeker of wisdom; Tagore, the seer, was accustomed to
dispense it. Figuratively kneeling at the feet of the Oriental, the middle
westerner did not find herself repulsed.'[60]

Clearly, this was not a friendship between two people who were
equal or similar in any obvious way. Nor was Tagore an easy person to
be around. Here is Dunbar again: 'During the weeks that followed, for
this visit was no overnight affair, East and West accomplished a happy
fusion. It is possible, of course, that the adjusting was largely on the part
of the Occidentals, for Mr. Tagore may have been a little exigent in an
unintentional and charming way.' A note from Harriet Moody written
to a friend at this time indirectly supports Dunbar's observations:

> I am more than sorry to have missed seeing you when you were in Chicago.
> I am sure it would be difficult for you to imagine just the kind of restraint
> that fell over my household because of the presence in it of Mr Tagore. Not
> that he would wish to restrain us in any way; but his preoccupations of mind
> are such as to leave him quite oblivious of the current [of] life about him
> and the result is that we have to adjust ourselves when he is here, to possible
> changes in his plans.

Dunbar comments: 'Evenings in 1970 were now devoted to listening to
Mr Tagore, either to his talk, *which did not mean conversation*, or to his
reading of his own poetry.'[61]

In parenthesis, we may also note Tagore's usual dependence on
people around him for the management of everyday chores. It would
be wrong to suggest that such dependence was something he forced on
others. As in Mrs Moody's case, the behaviour was often a mark of the
unusually deep reverence that people felt in his presence. R. F. Rattray,
who looked after Tagore during his trip to Boston in 1913, wrote:
'[I]t was rather trying that he [Tagore] was so helpless in practical
matters, leaving them to others. But others felt it to be a privilege to
serve him.'[62] However, it is difficult for us not to miss the complete
absence of any self-irony in a letter that Tagore wrote home soon after

---

[60] Dunbar, *A House in Chicago*, pp. 94–5.

[61] Dunbar, *A House in Chicago*, p. 94 (emphasis added).

[62] R. F. Rattray, *Poets in the Flesh: Tagore, Yeats, Dunsany, Stephens, Drinkwater*
(Cambridge, MA.: The Golden Head Press Ltd, 1961), p. 4.

reaching Urbana. '*Bhai* [Brother] Satya', he wrote to his nephew on 8 November 1912,

> we have arrived in America. We have rented a house in Illinois and our domestic life is in full swing. It is almost impossible to get servants or maid-servants here ... the housewives here do all household work themselves, and even the head of the family has to pitch in. Yesterday afternoon we saw a local professor washing his own clothes. One advantage is that this [labour] carries no indignity—for everyone except the very rich is in the same situation. We are not very rich either, so we have had to adopt the same means.

'We'? The very next sentence in the letter clarifies, almost unselfconsciously, who the 'we' of Tagore's sentence was: '*Bouma* [daughter-in-law; Tagore translated the expression as 'bride-mother'] is doing all the work of cooking, feeding [us], and cleaning the house.'[63]

Not only was Tagore's friendship with Mrs Moody unequal, the exchanges themselves were sometimes strange, at least from the point of view of Moody's biographer. It is not at all clear from the correspondence that Tagore understood or appreciated Harriet Moody's business acumen or the challenges she faced in that domain. If Harriet Moody had anything of her biographer's taste in feelings and self-expression, a certain clash of sentiments in this genuine friendship would have been unavoidable. Some of Tagore's letters to Mrs Moody concerned, for example, his own feelings of harassment at the public adulation he was subjected to in India on receiving the Nobel Prize. 'I am passing through an ordeal', he writes in a letter dated 23 December 1913. 'My time is uselessly wasted in trivial formalities. I am also assailed by the curiosity of the multitude. This burden of wasted days which brings me neither work nor rest is an enormous strain for me.'[64] 'A few months later', Dunbar continues in a disapproving tone, 'Harriet found herself appealed to in so urgent a strain that it must have chagrined her to acknowledge that in this case no solacing action was really within her power'. The comment was caused by a letter that Tagore wrote on 22 January 1914:

---

[63] Tagore's letter to Satyaprasad Gangopadhyay, 8 November 1912, in *Rabindrabiksha*, vol. 29, 7 August 1996, p. 26.

[64] Cited in Dunbar, *A House in Chicago*, p. 104.

I am still suffering from Nobel Prize notoriety and I do not know what
nursing home I can go to ... [to] get rid of this my latest and my greatest
trouble. To deprive of me of my seclusion is like shelling an oyster—the
rude touch of curiosity is all over me. I am pining for some shade of
obscurity.... Why do I not have a word of sympathy from you in my time
of distress?[65]

Readers of Tagore will know that he wrote in very similar terms to
other correspondents as well, both within Bengal and outside. There are
many letters in Bengali that he wrote in this vein but let me quote from
an English one to the British painter, Sir William Rothenstein, written
on 18 November 1913 where Tagore described his plight caused by
public adulation in Bengal that had reached manic proportions: 'It is a
very great trial for me. The perfect whirlwind of public excitement it
has given rise to is frightful. It is almost as bad as tying a tin at a dog's
tail making it impossible for him to move without creating a noise and
collecting crowds all along.'[66] In Bengali, the sentiment sounds particularly playful and self-mocking; but they also speak of an inner sense of
loneliness that perhaps made Tagore look for solace in the friendship
of someone like Harriet Moody. Moody's biographer, Dunbar, however,
could not think her way to imagining what an appropriate response
could have been on Harriet's part. Tagore's letter represented a cultural
impasse for her. She comments, somewhat acidly but not unreasonably
from her own point of view: 'Few of the notable persons to whom this
prize has been awarded, particularly when awarded *in absentia*, can
have found the experience so upsetting.'[67]

But consider Harriet Moody's own feelings—as expressed in the few
letters quoted in her biography. Her admiration for Tagore, whom she

[65] Tagore to Harriet Moody, 22 January 1914, PHBM, Box 2, Folder 22, RL,
Sp. Colln, University of Chicago; Dunbar, *A House in Chicago*, p. 105.

[66] Tagore's letter to Rothenstein, cited in Mukhopadhyay, *Rabindrajibani*,
vol. 2, pp. 446–7n2. Tagore used this simile in some of his Bengali writings
and speeches too. It was difficult for him to handle this sudden adulation by
many who had lampooned and made fun of his writings in the past. Mohitlal
Majumdar, the Bengali poet and critic, was reported to have said that in a public
speech Tagore likened many of these 'admirers' to 'village boys who tie a tin to
the tail of a dog and chase it through the streets with shouts' (Pal, *Rabijibani*,
vol. 6, p. 451, citing Nirad C. Chaudhuri, 'Tagore and the Nobel Prize', *The
Illustrated Weekly of India*, 11 March 1973).

[67] Dunbar, *A House in Chicago*, p. 105.

often capitalized as 'the Poet', remained deep and genuine throughout her life. She once wrote to a friend around the second visit of Tagore (c. 1916): 'Nothing I can say of Mr. Tagore is altogether adequate. He is himself inexpressible and in many ways more uplifting in his influence than ever, though perhaps a trifle less simple in his outer bearing [after the award of the Nobel Prize].'[68] Yet she was also deeply disappointed that Tagore, once the reception to him cooled in United States towards the end of the 1910s (caused in part by word about his alleged opposition to British rule in India) and his efforts to raise money for his university proved abortive, turned away from the country, seeing it as coldly capitalist and lacking a soul. As Tagore wrote to his friend Charles Freer Andrews on 17 December 1920: 'I should not let my dignity be soiled by the sordid touch of her [American] dollars;—mere lack of means should not be allowed to mock the majesty of soul, seeking its crown in the foolscap of the bank cheque.'[69] Mrs Moody was pained by this attitude. She wrote to her friends Frank and Mary Swinnerton in August 1925:

> I don't know whether you feel as I do, but to me it always seems that Robi Babu's absolute severance from his exterior environment unfits him for getting the real quality of American life or from knowing the deeper truth about his friends and our outstanding leaders, although his own magnificent initiative is of course valuable. But I feel that it is somewhat defeating to have it so coupled with misapprehension about others. Nothing but his settled conviction that America is hostile, mediocre and commercial has prevented his coming back this time.

Olivia Dunbar comments: 'These may have been the first or perhaps the only almost-critical words that ever came from this most constant of the philosopher's disciples. But her devotion to him was by no means lessened.'[70]

---

[68] Dunbar, *A House in Chicago*, p. 133. On Mrs Moody's habit of 'capitalizing' 'the Poet', see p. 131.

[69] Tagore's letter quoted in Pal, *Rabijibani*, vol. 8, p. 49. His feelings of ambivalence about raising money in America by going on lecture-tours began with the very first of such tours in 1916 when he wrote to Harriet Monroe complaining about his lack of leisure: 'I shall try to look cheerful and go on dancing to the tune of your American dollar' (Tagore to Monroe, 6 October 1916, *Poetry*, Box 41, Folder 3, RL, Sp. Colln, University of Chicago).

[70] Dunbar, *A House in Chicago*, p. 227.

As one can see, Mrs Moody was charging her favourite poet-philos-
opher with nothing less than the accusation that he did not understand
America, her country. Tagore, on his part, could also complain—having
been rebuffed by American financiers—that they did not understand
his mission in India. Yet what allowed this friendship to be continued
on both sides across the 1920s when Tagore and Mrs Moody could not
or did not meet? What did they each get out of this very 'imperfect
encounter'? What light does this story shed on what one may call, after
Derrida, the politics of friendship in the age of Empire?[71]

A slight detour into Derrida's discussion of Aristotle on friendship
may actually help us to see eventually how what I have called 'the civilizational framework' of the interwar period may have helped sustain
the relationship between Tagore and Moody, a relationship that today
would have been plagued by understandable contemporary anxieties
about inequalities of gender, race, and culture. The point is one needs
confidence to decide to invest in a friendship in the face of certain
obvious elements of inequality, hierarchy, or difference. From where
did Mrs Moody, for instance, draw the confidence she needed to sustain
her role as a 'refuge' for Tagore?

We can take our cue from a point Derrida makes in the course of reading Aristotle's *Nicomachean Ethics* and *Eudemian Ethics* via Montaigne's
essay 'Of Friendship' without thereby having to commit ourselves—as
Derrida also does not—either to Aristotle's sense of social hierarchy
or his politics of gender.[72] Opening with the apostrophe attributed to
Aristotle, 'O my friends, there is no friend', Derrida meditates on the
seeming contradiction of this statement: 'If there is "no friend", then
how could I call you my friends, my friends?'[73] As he moves carefully
through Aristotle's texts, Derrida reads the contradiction as indicative

<hr>

[71] Jacques Derrida, *Politics of Friendship*, trans. George Collins (London: Verso,
1997). On some of these questions, also see Leela Gandhi, *Affective Communities: Anticolonial Thought, Fin-de-Siècle Radicalism, and the Politics of Friendship*
(Durham: Duke University Press, 2006).

[72] *Nicomachean Ethics* and *Eudemian Ethics* in *The Complete Works of Aristotle*, ed. Jonathan Barnes, vol. 2 (Princeton, NJ: Princeton University Press,
1984), pp. 1729–1867 and 1922–1981 respectively; Montaigne, 'Of Friendship',
pp. 59–73.

[73] Derrida, *Politics*, p. 1. On the attribution (by Diogenes Laertius) of the
statement to Aristotle, see pp. 207–11.

of the 'two times' (*deux temps*) or the *contretemps* that make up the structure of friendship, thus playing both on the meaning of this word (small disagreement, unexpected setback) and its formation (*contre* = other, *temps* = time). He then expounds as follows—reading Aristotle faithfully but creatively—on the relation of friendship with the question of time. True friends are rare and finding them involves selection and judgement and thus time. But once made and stabilized, friendship belongs to another order of time where the passage of days on the calendar cannot corrode it. The highest order of friendship thus involves a decision—a judgement—*to love*, even before one knows that one will be loved in return. Derrida then develops Aristotle's propositions into the statement: '*It is more worthwhile to love* than *to be loved*.'[74] The highest order of friendship—one that is not based on utility or pleasure, as Aristotle would put it in his schema—places a greater premium on the act of loving—'to love'—than on being the object of human love. Those who 'prefer to be loved', says Derrida, following Aristotle's lead again, 'seek honours, distinction, signs of recognition'.[75] 'To love' thus represents a position devoid of the utility, pleasure, or narcissism that marks the position of the beloved. It is also necessarily the more *human* position in friendship as the object of one's affection need not be a living human being; it could be a deceased person or even inanimate, as Derrida points out, extending Aristotle.[76]

If Tagore saw in Harriet Moody a 'mother', that is, a source of comfort, a refuge—which is what his letters cited above would suggest—then he put himself in the place of being loved and not in the experience of what Aristotle would have called 'primary friendship', where loving was the more important activity than that of being loved.[77]

---

[74] Derrida, *Politics*, pp. 7, 8. Cf. Aristotle, *Eudemian Ethics*, book VII, p. 1960: 'Its [primary friendship's] function is an activity, and this is not external, but in the one who feels love.' See also p. 1961. *Nicomachean Ethics*, book VIII, p. 1828.

[75] Derrida, *Politics*, p. 10. Cf. Aristotle, *Nicomachean Ethics*, book VIII, p. 1832: 'Most people seem, owing to ambition, to wish to be loved rather than to love.'

[76] Derrida, *Politics*, pp. 10–11. Cf. Aristotle, *Nicomachean Ethics*, book VIII, p. 1829: 'Love may be felt just as much towards lifeless things.' See also *Eudemian Ethics*, book VII, p. 1960.

[77] 'Love is like activity, being loved like passivity' (Aristotle, *Nicomachean Ethics*, book IX, p. 1846).

For Aristotle, mothers were a figure of primary friendship even in the apparent inequality of the mother–child relationship, for the 'desirable' side of friendship, Aristotle wrote, 'lie[s] in loving rather than in being loved, as is indicated by the delight mothers take in loving'.[78] I am not suggesting Harriet Monroe's feelings were actually those of a mother, whatever Tagore may have made of them. The figure of the mother stands here for a certain measure of generosity that stems from the confidence of one's judgement and decision to be a friend. Moody's own words suggest that she was aware of the social and historical differences, or even of the inequalities, that inhered in this relationship. There was little between them of what we today would regard as 'conversation' between equals. The verbal transactions appear to have been mostly one-sided—'he was the one who talked straight on, without waiting for a reply'. Yet she did not take long to sense a communion with Tagore—'it seemed as if he were speaking from the depths of my own being'—and thus made the decision to care for him, to offer him her friendship, 'for there was never a moment when he was strange to me'. With hindsight and through the work of memory, Harriet Moody telescoped the process by which she decided to be a friend of Tagore's into the very first moment of their meeting. 'I had just come from an ocean journey', she wrote narrating the impact of Tagore's arrival in her house on that fateful day of 19 January 1913:

> The poet's voice was like the lapping of waves, quiet, rich, sustained. I was soothed and heartened as I listened to him. He was one who talked straight on, without waiting for a reply. This did not seem in the least wearisome. Like all significant conversations, it seemed as if he were talking from the depths of my own being. It was as if we were conferring, after a long separation, about the fundamental doctrines of a common early home, under the teaching and influence of the same father and mother. There was never a moment when he was strange to me, although he commanded my quiet reverence.[79]

The strength of generosity is written all over that concluding phrase: 'He commanded my quiet reverence.' 'He commanded' and her reverence was 'quiet'—there is no illusion here about inequality and hierarchy signalled by speech. Yet 'there was never a moment when

---

[78] Aristotle, *Nicomachean Ethics*, book VIII, p. 1832.

[79] Moody, *Letters*, pp. 407–8.

he was strange', which also means the reverence offered was sure of itself. It was not conflicted in any way. There was no conversation as commonly understood and yet, says Moody, there was a 'significant conversation'. There is a word that Tagore once used to express the strength he sensed in Mrs Moody. The word was 'forbearance', an originally legal sixteenth-century word referring to a process of delaying—that is, not foreclosing—on debts that might be owed to oneself.[80] I refer again to the letter he wrote to Harriet Moody when telling her that he had dedicated his play *Chitra* to her: 'The already numerous transgressions you had allowed your poet in the generous exercise of your *forbearance*.'[81] What thus took Tagore's relationship with Harriet Moody forward and gave it the quality of friendship was his recognition of her strength—though he expressed it in the culturally specific idiom of motherhood and through the metaphor of forbearance—and Harriet Moody's capacity and willingness to take joy in the activity of loving rather than in the passivity of being loved.

But my point is not biographical, or at least not merely biographical. How does one understand Harriet Moody's statement that 'there was never a moment' when Tagore was 'strange' to her, although 'he commanded [her] quiet reverence'—in the face of all the evidence of strangeness and inequality that both Dunbar and Moody herself furnish? Leaving aside what may have been purely matters of personality with both Tagore and Moody, the bit about Mrs Moody's 'quiet reverence' takes us back to the scene in her living room as described by Harriet Monroe (see above): 'We used to spend evenings around Mrs. Moody's fire, listening to the chanting of poems in Bengali, or the recitation of their English equivalents, and feeling as if we were seated at the feet of some ancient wise man of the East, generous in his revelations of beauty.'[82] Tagore thus seems to have come across as 'some ancient wise man of the East' bearing in his person a civilizational message to weary souls of the West. On this point, the few letters from Mrs Moody that survive in the Tagore archives are telling. On 31 January

---

[80] See 'Online Etymological Dictionary', available at <http://www.etymon-line.com/index.php?search> (last accessed on 8 February 2014).

[81] Tagore to Mrs Moody, 10 March 1914, PHBM, RL, Sp. Colln, University of Chicago.

[82] *Poetry* Records, Box 41, Folder 3: Typescript titled 'Tagore in Chicago', pp. 1–2, RL, Sp. Colln, University of Chicago.

1913, soon after the first visit by the Tagores, Harriet Moody wrote to Rabindranath to say with 'reverent affection': 'I cannot tell you what you have done for me.'[83] Addressing him as 'Dear Friend and Beloved Master', she wrote on 9 May of the same year describing—indeed the Christian associations are hard to miss—how a letter from the poet had not only called her to an 'uplifted mood', it also showed her that 'you have walked upon the waves and they have not flowed over you'.[84] A letter dated 21 November 1913, congratulating Tagore on his being awarded the Nobel Prize, explains the quasi-religious aspect of her friendship: 'For myself, it is a mystic joy that you have dwelt within my walls, and have given me this great privilege of calling you my friend.'[85]

Thus, Tagore saw himself as a bearer of a civilization he called 'Indian'; his friends in Chicago thought of it as something 'Eastern'. Mrs Moody's relationship to this civilization as she saw it embodied in the poet was quasi-religious or, in her words, 'mystic'. She was aware of the differences, inequalities, and the asymmetries of this friendship: he was not a good listener, he did most of the talking, one's plans had to readjusted to suit his presence. Yet she gave freely and confidently her affection and forbearance. A certain way of understanding the world through a framework of 'civilizations' once worked simultaneously as a justification as well as a powerful critique of the empire. But this particular story of friendship shows how it also made it possible for unexpected friendships to flourish across many obvious inequalities and hierarchical differences.

[83] Moody to Tagore, 31 January 1913, Tagore Papers, File No. 246, Visva-Bharati University.
[84] Moody to Tagore, 9 May 1913, Tagore Papers, File No. 246, Visva-Bharati University.
[85] Moody to Tagore, 21 November 1913, Tagore Papers, File No. 246, Visva-Bharati University.

6

ROMANTIC ARCHIVES
Literature and the Politics of Identity in Bengal*

A letter from a friend in Calcutta recently put to me this question: Will the investment in Bengali literature that marked Bengal's colonial modernity survive the impact of globalization?

> Bengalis have lost their appetite for [Bengali] literature, [said my friend]. The reading habits of the Bengali public have changed so much that were someone to write a *Pather Panchali* [a famous novel published in 1927] today, they would not be able to attract the attention of readers unless a well-known filmmaker created a hyped-up film version of it.... I am sure you will agree that literary work needs a certain environment for its growth. This environment that you have seen in Calcutta in the past is now disappearing. And nobody seems to care.[1]

The letter voiced a sentiment that is not uncommon among my literary-minded friends in the city. It seems plausible that Bengali

* Edited from *Critical Inquiry* 30, no. 3 (Spring 2004): 654–82. Versions of this paper were presented as the Mary Keating Das lecture (2003) at Columbia University, at a meeting of the South Asian Studies Group in Melbourne, and at the Centre for Studies in Social Sciences, Calcutta. I am grateful for audiences at these meetings and to James Chandler, Gautam Bhadra, Rochona Majumdar, Muzaffar Alam, Bill Brown, Tom Mitchell, Gauri Viswanathan, Kunal Chakrabarti, Sheldon Pollock, Clinton Seely, Carlo Ginzburg, and Biswajit Roy for comments on an earlier draft. Special thanks to Anupam Mukhopadhyay in Calcutta and Rafeeq Hasan in Chicago for assistance with research.
[1] Raghab Bandyopadhayay, letter to author, 26 June 2002.

language and literature do not possess the cultural capital they once did in the state of West Bengal. The magazine *Desh*, a periodical that for long has attempted to capture the cultural essence of the literary-minded sections of the Bengali middle classes—the so-called bhadralok—suddenly changed a few years ago from being a weekly to a biweekly publication. Why? I asked another Bengali friend who seemed informed on these matters. I was told that the readership for the magazine was a declining and ageing readership. Younger people did not read the magazine, not in the same numbers anyway.

For a long time, the comportment of being a modern Bengali person has had much to do with certain kinds of personal investment in Bengali language and literature. Sometime in the nineteenth century, in the mist of times that for the bhadralok have been partly historical and partly fabulous, things happened in British Bengal that made books and literature central to modern Bengali identity.[2] Two factors helped to reinstitute the nineteenth century and its consequences into the cultural ambience of late twentieth-century Calcutta. One is the fact that the emancipatory optimism of the Left—elaborated in the revolutionary poetry and songs of the 1940s that retained their popularity into the sixties—drew heavily on the heritage of the nineteenth century until the Maoist Naxalite movement (c. 1967–71) began to question that inheritance. The other was the Tagore centenary year of 1961. The poet and along with him the nineteenth and early twentieth centuries were reinvented for my generation of educated Bengalis in myriad ways by the All India Radio, the Gramophone Company, the government of West Bengal, and a host of other major institutions in the city.

It is difficult to avoid the impression today that educated, well-to-do families are divesting from Bengali language and literature when it comes to their children's education. The new and global media help unfold new possibilities for cultural production. The more celebrated new Bengali writers often write in 'global English'. At any rate, a sense of distance from the nineteenth century and all that it stood for is now in the air among the young. Even the book, which perhaps became the most favoured material–cultural object of educated Bengalis over the

---

[2] See Dipesh Chakrabarty, *Provincializing Europe: Postcolonial Thought and Historical Difference* (Princeton, NJ: Princeton University Press, 2000), in particular Chapters 5–7.

last two centuries, is portrayed as a thing of the past in the words of a song of a contemporary Calcutta band:

Ananda Sen
Used to read books.
The time was 1972.
Browning, Tennyson, Arthur Miller
Romance, travel, and crime-thriller
But devaluation made the rupee bekar [useless]
Sen only reads the newspaper[3]

There is something interesting—in the context of our present discussion—about this song, released in 2001. It ostensibly describes a cultural memory of a loss, the loss of the book, attributed in the song to the economic conditions of the country. The memory in the song goes back about three decades to 1972. Yet, in an unintended fashion, the song also describes the death of the Bengali nineteenth century as well. For this century, it would appear, had quietly left its mark on the reading habits of the fictitious Mr Ananda Sen. Browning and Tennyson were, after all, two of the most popular poets among Bengali readers of English literature in the second half of the nineteenth century.

The long Bengali nineteenth century is perhaps finally dying. It may, therefore, make sense to treat its death as a proper object of historical study. In the context of the remarks made by my friend whose sentiments made me think of the subject of this essay, I want to ask: what was the nature of the bhadralok investment in literature and language that once made these into the means of feeling one's Bengaliness? Here it is useful to pay some attention to the works of Dinesh Chandra Sen, the pioneering historian and a lifelong devotee of Bengali literature.[4] Once hailed as the foremost historian of Bengali literature, he was lampooned by a younger generation of intellectuals in the 1930s who faulted his sense of both politics and history. It is the story of the early reception and the later rejection of Sen's work

[3] Chandrabindu, 'Ananda Sen', *Gadha*, audio cassette, 2001.
[4] Bengalis did not have second names until the coming of the British. During colonial rule, Bengali men began to split names made up of compound words in order to produce middle names. Thus, Dineshchandra became Dinesh Chandra. I will simply follow this custom in spelling the name of Sen even in passages translated from Bengali. My focus on Sen also necessarily limits the aspects of Bengali literature I deal with here.

that I want to use here as a way to think about the questions raised by my friend.

A few biographical details are in order. Born in a village in the district of Dhaka in 1866, Dinesh Chandra Sen (or Dinesh Sen for short) graduated from the University of Calcutta with honours in English literature in 1889 and was appointed the headmaster of Comilla Victoria School in 1891 in Comilla, Bangladesh. While working there, he started scouring parts of the countryside in eastern Bengal in search of old Bengali manuscripts. The research and publications resulting from his efforts led to his connections with Ashutosh Mukherjee, the famed educator of Bengal and twice the vice chancellor of the University of Calcutta (1906–14 and 1921–3). In 1909, Mukherjee appointed Sen to a readership and subsequently to a research fellowship in Bengali at the university.[5] Sen was eventually chosen to head up the postgraduate department of Bengali at the University of Calcutta when that department—perhaps the first such department devoted to postgraduate teaching of a modern Indian language—was founded in 1919. Sen served in this position until 1932. He died in Calcutta in 1939. Sen produced two very large books on the history of Bengali literature: *Bangabhasha o shahitya* (Bengali Language and Literature) in Bengali, first published in 1896, and *History of Bengali Language and Literature* (in English), based on a series of lectures delivered at the University of Calcutta and published in 1911.[6] He also produced many other books including an autobiography. All his life, Sen remained a devoted, tireless researcher of Bengali language and literature.[7]

[5] See Supriya Sen, *Dineshchandra* (Calcutta: Jijnasa, 1985), p. 39.

[6] For a factual revision of Dinesh Sen's research findings, see 'Appendix to the Eighth Edition', prepared by Dr Prabodh Chandra Bagchi MA DLitt (Paris)', in Dinesh Chandra Sen, *Bangabhasha o shahitya*, ed. Asitkumar Bandyopadhyay, 2 vols (Calcutta: West Bengal State Book Board, 1991), vol. 2, pp. 868–89.

[7] Biographical details on Dinesh Sen are culled here from his autobiography, *Gharer katha o jugashahitya* (Calcutta: Jijnasa, 1969 [1922]); S. Sen, *Dineshchandra*; biographical note entitled 'The Author's Biography' published in D. C. Sen, *Bangabhasha o shahitya*, vol. 1, pp. 43–5; and 'The Author's Life', in Dinesh Chandra Sen, *Banglar puronari* (Calcutta: Jijnasa, 1939), pp. 1–32. A later reprint of this book (1983) says in a publisher's note that this short biography given in the first edition contains some factual errors. But the facts stated here seem to stand corroborated by other sources.

Sen, today, is truly a man of the past. His almost exclusive identification of Bengali literature with the Hindu heritage, his idealization of many patriarchal and Brahminical precepts, and his search for a pure Bengali essence bereft of all foreign influence will today arouse the legitimate ire of contemporary critics. It is not my purpose to discuss Sen as a person. But, for the sake of the record, it should be noted that, like many other intellectuals of his time, Sen was a complex and contradictory human being. This ardently and (by his own admission) provincial Bengali man loved many English poets and kept a day's fast to express his grief on hearing about the death of Tennyson.[8] For all his commitment to his own Hindu-Bengali identity, he remained one of the foremost patrons of the Muslim–Bengali poet Jasimuddin.[9] The inclusion of a poem by Jasimuddin in the selection of texts for the matriculation examination in Bengali in 1929, when Hindu–Muslim relations were heading for a new low in Bengal, was directly owing to Sen's intervention at the appropriate levels.[10] And his patriarchal sense of the extended family

[8] See S. Sen, *Dineshchandra*, p. 19.

[9] Sen's relationship to Jasimuddin is the subject of the latter's reminiscence in *Smaraner sharani bahi* (Calcutta: Antara, 1976). Jasimuddin writes:

Here was a man who took me from one station in life to another. My student life perhaps would have ended with the I.A. [Intermediate of Arts] degree if I had not met him. Perhaps I would have spent my life as an ill-paid teacher in some village school. I think of this not just only once. I think this every day and every night and repeatedly offer my *pronam* [obeisance] to this great man. (Jasimuddin, *Smaraner sharani bahi*, p. 71)

[10] Wahidul Alam writes:

I was surprised when in 1929 I read Jasimuddin's poem 'Kabar' in Calcutta University's selection of Bengali texts for the Matriculation examination. A poem by a Muslim writer in the Matriculation selections! And that too under the auspices of the University of Calcutta? ... A teacher of mine told me a story about this. There was forceful opposition in [the University's] Syndicate to the inclusion of a student. But Dr. Dinesh Sen was the number one advocate for Jasimuddin.... Apparently, he countered the opposition by saying, 'All right, please be patient and just listen to me recite the poem'. He had a passionate voice and could recite poetry well. He read the poem with such wonderful effect that the eyes of many members of the Syndicate were glistening with tears.

did not stop him from encouraging his daughters-in-law to pursue higher studies.[11]

Romanticism and the Project for a National Literature

What once made the word Bengali more than a mere ethnic tag and gave it a seductive ring for many was the phenomenon of a romantic, anti-colonial nationalism in Bengal that flourished in the period c. 1890–1910.[12] Its high point was the so-called Swadeshi (*swadesh*: 'one's native land') Movement (1905–8) organized to protest, and eventually reverse, the first partition of the province of Bengal executed by the British—ostensibly for administrative reasons—in 1905.[13] At the centre of this romanticism was a perceived connection between identity and aesthetic activity in the realms of art, music, literature, and language. Perhaps the best intellectual expression of this outlook—coloured, as the following quote will show, by a heavy tint of early nineteenth-century German talk of the spirit—comes from the pen of Aurobindo Ghosh, a revolutionary leader of the Swadeshi Movement, who wrote this in 1909:

> The needs of our political and religious life are now vital and real forces and it is these needs which will reconstruct our society, recreate and remould our industrial and commercial life and found a new and victorious art, literature, science, and philosophy which will not be European but Indian. The impulse

---

Wahidul Alam, 'Kabi Jasimuddin', *Alakta* 5, no. 2 [1983], quoted in Titash Chaudhuri, *Jasimuddin: Kabita, gadya o smriti* (Dhaka: Bangla Academy, 1993), p. 172.

[11] See S. Sen, *Dineshchandra*, pp. 86–7.

[12] *Romantic*, being a word of global provenance, is hard to define with respect to any particular national experience of romanticism. However, most Bengali romantics discussed here have shared with the Schlegel brothers the idea that 'the truly Romantic' was constituted by 'a certain radiance, or fluorescence, of the literary work which makes it transcend the necessarily limited scope of human language and open a vista into the infinite'. Friedrich Schlegel's fragment that 'we should make poetry ... sociable and society poetical' would also have met with their enthusiastic approval (Ernst Behler, *German Romantic Literary Theory* [Cambridge: Cambridge University Press, 1993], pp. 78, 157).

[13] Sumit Sarkar's *The Swadeshi Movement in Bengal, 1903–1908* (Delhi: People's Publishing House, 1973) is a rich account of the history of this movement.

is already working in Bengali art and literature. The need of self-expression for the national spirit in politics suddenly brought back Bengali literature to its essential and eternal self and it was in our recent national songs that this self-realisation came. The lyric and the lyrical spirit, the spirit of simple, direct and poignant expression, of deep, passionate, straightforward emotion, of a frank and exalted enthusiasm, the dominant note of love and bhakti (sentimental devotionalism), of a mingled sweetness and strength, the potent intellect dominated by the self-illuminated heart, a mystical exaltation of feeling and spiritual insight expressing itself with plain concreteness and practicality—this is the soul of Bengal. All our literature, in order to be wholly alive, must start from this base and, whatever variations it may indulge in, never lose touch with it.[14]

It was sometime between 1872—when Ramgati Nyayaratna, a scholar of Sanskrit, published one the first histories of Bengali literature—and 1896 when Dinesh Sen came out with *Bangabhasha o shahitya*—that this literary–ethical project of being Bengali itself came into being. A quick comparison between Nyayaratna's history of Bengali literature and that of Dinesh Sen is telling in this respect. Nyayaratna's book *Bangalabhasha o bangalasahityavishayok prastav* (A Motion Concerning Bengali Literature and the Bengali Language) (1872) used the word 'Bengali' simply to refer to an ethnic group. As Nyayaratna himself said in his preface to the first edition, the entire first chapter of the book was dedicated to solving problems with the dating of Bengali language and the script.[15] The rest of the book did not in any way address the question of being Bengali. Sen's work, on the other hand, was all about the meaning of this question. Commenting on the difference between the two scholars, Dr Asit Kumar Bandyopadhyay, who edited a recent reprint of Nyayaratna's book, writes:

The goldmine of medieval Bengali literature was discovered by Dinesh Chandra Sen.... His point of view was particularly different from that of Nyayaratna.... Ramgati's mind had been moulded by the heritage of

[14] Aurobindo Ghosh, 'The Awakening Soul of India' (1909), in *On Nationalism*, ed. Sri Aurobindo (Pondicherry: Sri Aurobindo Ashram, 1996, 2nd ed.), p. 404.

[15] See Ramgati Nyayaratna, *Bangalabhasha o bangalasahityavishayok prastav*, ed. Asit Kumar Bandyopadhyay (Calcutta: Supreme Book Distributors, 1991 [1872]), p. xv. This edition works off a later edition edited and published by Nyayaratna's son Girindranath Bandyopadhyay.

Sanskrit language and literature.... For Dinesh Chandra was well acquainted with English literature of the Victorian period and had also read with attention histories of English, French, and German literatures.... Educated Bengalis, who were searching for the roots of the distinctiveness and for pride in the Bengali way of life ... welcomed him as the true historian of Bengali literature.[16]

Indeed the impact of the publication of *Bangabhasha o shahitya* is captured in what Rabindranath Tagore wrote in praise of the book when it went into the second edition: 'Dineshbabu ['babu' is an honorific term in Bengali] surprised us all when the first edition of this book came out. We never knew that there was such an enormous affair called ancient Bengali literature. We got busy familiarizing ourselves with the stranger.'[17]

A project for a national literature looked on literature as an expression of the national spirit. This national spirit was expected to act as an antidote to all the mundane interests that otherwise divided the Bengali people—the Hindus from the Muslims, the lower castes from the upper castes, and the elite from the masses. Literature, in that sense, was seen as innately political. The Bengali intellectual's faith in the work of the spirit was articulated in what Aurobindo said in 1909 about the Italian patriot Mazzini—a veritable icon of romantic nationalism in India: 'Mazzini lifted the country from [a] ... low and ineffective level and gave it the only force which can justify the hope of revival, the force of the spirit within, the strength to disregard immediate interests and surrounding circumstances.... The spiritual force within not only creates the future but creates the material for the future.'[18] A similar appreciation of the national spirit animated all that was said about lit-

[16] Nyayaratna, *Bangalabhasha* , pp. vi–vii.

[17] Rabindranath Thakur [Tagore], 'Bangabhasha o shahitya' (1902), in *Rabindrarachabali: janmashatabarshik shongskoron*, 13 vols (Calcutta: Government of West Bengal, 1961), vol. 13, p. 806.

[18] Aurobindo Ghosh, 'The Power That Uplifts' (1909), in *On Nationalism*, p. 456. Indian romantic-political readings of Mazzini and the Italian Risorgimento would make a fascinating area of research. Gita Srivastava's *Mazzini and His Impact on the Indian Nationalist Movement* (Allahabad: Chugh Publications, 1982) makes an indifferent beginning. See also N. Gangulee, introduction to Giuseppe Mazzini, *Giuseppe Mazzini: Selected Writings* (London: Lindsay Drummond, 1944?), p. 38: 'It was in [a] ... study-group in Calcutta that I first came to read Mazzini's writings.'

erature in the 1890s and 1900s. Dinesh Sen treated the 'folk' literature of Bengal as 'expressions of all the poetry of the race'. They were 'read and admired by millions—the illiterate masses forming by far the most devoted of their admirers'.[19] In a lecture on 'national literature' given at an annual meeting of the newly founded Bangiya Sahitya Parishad (Bengali Literary Academy, 1893), Tagore put an ingenious gloss on the Sanskrit/Bengali word for literature, *sahitya*. 'The word "sahitya"', he said,

> is derived from the word 'sahit' [being with]. Considered in its constitutional sense, then, the word suggests the idea of being together. This togetherness does not simply relate to thoughts, languages, or books. No deep intimacies between human beings, between the past and the present, or between the distant and the near can be forged by means other than those of literature. The people of a country lacking literature have no ties binding one another. They remain divided.[20]

Sen's *History of Bengali Language and Literature* actually offered some anecdotal evidence of this alleged spiritual bond between the educated elite and the non-literate masses enabled by the shared pleasures of 'folk' literature:

> In 1894, I was residing in Tippera. It was early in June; the clouds had gathered on the horizon, and round the [S]ataratan Matha [monastery] of Comilla, they had made the darkness of night a shade more black. An illiterate Vaishnava [literally, of the god Vishnu] devotee, an old man of seventy, was singing the following song of Chandi Das [a medieval Bengali poet], playing on a lute made of a long gourd.
>
> 'Dark is the night and thick are the clouds,
>
> How could you, my beloved, come by the path in such a night? ...'
>
> I suddenly heard his voice become choked with tears, and he could not proceed any more. On his coming to himself, ... I asked him the cause of his tears. He said, it was the song.... He did not consider the song as an ordinary love-song. Here is his interpretation,—'I am full of sins.... In deep distress I beckoned Him to come to me.... I found Him waiting at the gate of my house. It cannot be any pleasure to Him to come to a great sinner like me,—

---

[19] Dinesh Chandra Sen, *History of Bengali Language and Literature* (Calcutta: University of Calcutta, 1911), p. 167.

[20] Tagore, 'Bangla jatiya sahitya (1895–96)', *Rabindrarachanabali* 13: 793.

the path is so foul, but by my supreme good fortune the merciful God took it.... The thought of His mercy choked my voice....'

Tears were dropping from the eyes of the old man ... as with his right hand he was still playing on the lute.[21]

Sen considered this an 'instance of [the] spiritualization of ideas even by rural and illiterate people in Bengal'.[22] Sen's anecdote allows us an insight into the romantic–nationalist construction of the past. In what he wrote on folk and national literature in the period 1880–1910, Rabindranath Tagore theorized just such a past. He expressed the hope that Bengali literature would act as 'the live umbilical cord' helping to bind together the past, the present, and the future of the Bengali people 'in all their intensity and greatness'.[23] Such collapsing of different times would defy the logic of the historian. Tagore remarked once with respect to the literature of the rural 'folk':

One or two hundred years do not make much difference to the age of these poems. Looked at from this point of view, rhymes put together by a village poet, say, fifty years ago may be seen as contemporaneous with the compositions of Mukundaram [sixteenth–seventeenth centuries]. For the waves of time cannot assault with any force the place where the soul of the village survives.[24]

Or, as he put it elsewhere: 'Fragments of many ancient histories and memories lie dispersed in these [rural nursery] rhymes. No archaeologist can put them together in order to make them into a whole. But our imagination [*kalpana*] can attempt to create out of these ruins a distant-and-yet-close relationship with that forgotten and ancient world.'[25]

If literature was indeed so inherently political, one can then look on Sen's passionate wanderings in the Bengal countryside around

[21] D. C. Sen, *History of Bengali Language and Literature*, pp. 127–30.

[22] D. C. Sen, *History of Bengali Language and Literature*, p. 127.

[23] Rabindranath Tagore, 'Jatiya shahitya' (1895–6), quoted in Gautam Bhadra and Deepa Dey, 'Chintar Chalchitra: Bangiya Shahitya Parishat (1300–30)', *Sahitya Patrika* 38 (1994–5): 47.

[24] Quoted in Bhadra and Sen, 'Chintar Chalchitra', p. 57. Also see Rabindranath Tagore, 'Gramyo sahitya', *Rabindrarachabali* 6: 642.

[25] Quoted in Bhadra and Sen, 'Chintar Chalchitra', p. 57. Also, see Rabindranath Tagore, 'Chhele bhulano chhora', in *Rabindrarachabali* 6: 585.

Chittagong and Tripura in his twenties—looking for old manuscripts—as a variety of romantic–political activism. His narrative highlights the spirit of sacrifice that Aurobindo spoke of in his praise for Mazzini. On occasions, Sen seems to have received support from interested officials who sent their liveried assistants along to help him. But often the search was lonely, all his own, at his own expense, and at great risk to his health and safety. In Sen's own words:

> The sight of liveried government orderlies or peons would frighten villagers. [The presence of] such personnel in fact hindered the collection of manuscripts, so I would [often] go alone. Sometimes I would be travelling in the hills until nightfall. At times I would simply have to summon up ... courage and trek through rain and storm or through terrifying jungles at night.... Only a person as wretched as I would go around collecting manuscripts in this manner, abandoning all hopes for living. How often I would hurt from all the travelling I did and would cry [from pain] if I touched the wounded part of my body.[26]

Colonial Romantics and Their Anxieties

Sen's work makes visible two major—and related—anxieties that drove the romantic-political project of a national literature. The first, as we have seen, was the concern to find a spiritual ground on which to erect national unity.[27] This quest for unity made it necessary to use literary material to create a family romance of the nation. That romance, in turn, was deeply marked by some other male anxieties concerning home, gender, and sexuality. This, as such, is not surprising. Feminist historians have often documented such anxieties for nationalisms generally, both in India

---

[26] D. C. Sen, *Gharer katha o jugashahitya*, pp. 124–5.

[27] This indeed was one of the reasons Tagore welcomed *Bangabhasha o shahitya*. Sen's book had 'brought to life' the true history of Hindu–Muslim relationship by showing that 'a close relationship existed between Hindus and Muslims, that there was a path of friendship between them in spite of many troubles and disturbances'. This, Tagore added, was 'truly historical, something that should always be made known. For this is the story of the land, it is not a fact concerning some specific people' (Tagore, 'Bangabhasha o sahitya', *Rabindrarachabali* 13: 807).

and elsewhere.[28] What is interesting about this particular story, however, is what Sen's writings tell us about the reception of European romanticism in the Bengal of the late nineteenth and early twentieth centuries.

As historians of modern Bengali literature well know, poets such as Byron, Shelley, Keats, and Wordsworth—as well as Milton (introducing a note of classicism) and Shakespeare—were enduring icons in the worlds of nineteenth-century Bengali poets.[29] I do not have the space here to discuss the topic in any detail. We know Michael Madhusudan Datta, Rangalal Bandyopadhyay, Hemchandra Bandyopadhyay, and Biharilal Chakrabarty—important names in nineteenth-century history—were influenced and inspired by these poets.[30] This history awaits detailed research, but anecdotal evidence suggests that well into the early part of the twentieth century, Bengali poets remained enthusiasts of English romantic and classicist poetry. The following description of a literary exchange between the romantic-nationalist poet Dwijendralal Roy (1863–1913) and his friend Lokendranath Palit, a well-known and colourful personality of the day, could be considered typical:

[28] See, for example, Lynn Hunt, *The Family Romance of the French Revolution* (Berkeley: University of California Press, 1992); Carla Hesse, *The 'Other' Enlightenment: How French Women Became Modern* (Princeton, NJ: Princeton University Press, 2001); Tanika Sarkar, *Hindu Wife, Hindu Nation: Community, Religion, and Cultural Nationalism* (New Delhi: Permanent Black, 2001); and Rochona Majumdar, 'Marriage, Modernity, and Sources of the Self: Bengali Women c.1870–1956', PhD diss., University of Chicago, 2003, esp. Chapter 2, 'Debates on Dowry in Colonial Bengal'.

[29] See Priyaranjan Sen, *Western Influence in Bengali Literature* (Calcutta: Academic Publishers, 1966 [1932]); Harendra Mohan Das Gupta, *Studies in Western Influence on Nineteenth-Century Bengali Poetry, 1857–1887* (Calcutta: Semushi, 1969 [1935]); Ujjvalkumar Majumdar, *Bangla sahitye pashchatya probhab* (Calcutta: Dey's, 2000); and Michael Madhusudan Datta, *The Slaying of Meghnada: A Ramayana Revisioned in Colonial Calcutta*, trans. Clinton B. Seely (New York: Oxford University Press, 2004).

[30] That the young Michael often modelled not only his writings but even his personal letters in the 1840s on those of Byron has been noted by a couple of recent commentators. See Ghulam Murshid, *Ashar chhalane bhuli: Michael-jibani* (Calcutta: Ananada, 1997 [1995]), pp. 55–6. Murshid credits William Radice of the University of London with having been the first to notice similarities between Byron's letters published in Thomas Moore's life of the poet and those written by the young Michael, see p. 9. The other poets mentioned here often simply inserted lines translated from English romantic poets into what they wrote in Bengali.

Loken has an amazing and unending capacity to understand poetry! He understands Byron without any effort. Shelley he is even more at ease with. The other day I had a big argument with him about Byron and Shelley. I started reading out from *Manfred*. Listening to it, he suddenly jumped out of his chair with sheer enthusiasm and said, '*Oh, maddening!* [in English in original] No more, no more, please don't read any more. Let me think.' Saying this, he remained self-absorbed in a serious mood for about a quarter [of an hour]. What a connoisseur he is! You cannot compare him with the likes of us. A Bengali man gets all excited if he can rhyme three lines using words like '*mondo* [gentle], *mondo, shugondho* [fragrance]' and thinks to himself: 'What a poet I have become!' ... Good writing requires ... truly good education.... Shelley, Byron, Keats, Shakespeare, our Vaishnava poets, Vyas [the mythical writer of the *Mahabharata*], Valmiki [the mythical writer of the *Ramayana*], Kalidas, Hugo—unless you read these great poets with sincere devotion you cannot any longer become a great poet by dint of any magical 'abracadabra', not today.[31]

Dinesh Sen came from the same cultural stock as Dwijendralal Roy. His enthusiasm for Scott, Milton, Tennyson, and for the Lake poets is well known; he could even recite some of their poetry from memory.[32] I have not had the opportunity to investigate in more detail Sen's reading practices. But references to the heroines of Byron, Shakespeare, and others in some critical passages in his *History of Bengali Language and Literature* allow us to see how an intimate, yet troubled, relationship to European romanticism determined the nature of Sen's pursuit of the folk. Consider, for instance, the following passage from Sen's *History of Bengali Language and Literature* in which he is seeking to argue with his own English-educated Bengali readers as to why they should not seek their ideals of romantic love in European poetry. They should instead look in the direction of Behula, Khullana, and Ranjavati—all heroines from the so-called middle period who were to become household names thanks, in large part, to Sen's own writings:

The enlightened section of our community who are fond of displaying their erudition in English literature, who are never weary of admiring a Cordelia, a Haidee or even a Donna Julia and who quote from the English translation of Virgil to shew their appreciation of Dido's love, would not care to read

[31] Quoted in Debkumar Raychaudhuri, *Dwijendralal: Jibon* (Calcutta: Basudhara Prakashani, 1965), pp. 404–5.
[32] See 'The Author's Life', in D. C. Sen, *Banglar puronari*, p. 14.

the story of Behula—the bride of Laksmindra, whose unflinching resolution and sufferings for love rise higher than many a martyrdom; or of Khullana, the loving damsel of Ujani, whose beauty, tender age, sufferings and fidelity all combine to make her one of the finest creations of poetic fancy; or of Ranjavati—the wife of King Kadna Sen of Maynagar whose resignation was as great as her austerities that stripped even death at the stake of its natural horrors.[33]

Cordelia, Haidee, Donna Julia: all names of heroines with strong imprints of individuality on their personalities. They were characters who made their own choices in matters of love, individuals—as a recent commentator on Byron has put it—'in possession of the means of erotic self-assertion'.[34] Besides, Donna Julia and Haidee were even portrayed as proactive seducers of Don Juan in Byron's long poem of the same name, as part of the politics of what, to quote a contemporary critic, 'Coleridge might have called Byron's "sexual Jacobinism"'.[35] For Byron, surely, sexual liberty was part of liberty as such and formed a core of his critique of emerging bourgeois domesticity in his own country.[36] It is important to note that Sen does not deny the appeal to Bengali men of sexually and politically 'liberated' women. He indirectly documents that for the 'modern', romantic, English-educated Bengali man, European literature portrayed women who were exciting and attractive. Why, then, should Bengali men turn to their 'own' folk literature that they, said Sen, were 'naturally best fitted to appreciate'?

Sen's argument, as it unfolds, expresses a fear of that which also seemed attractive. It was an argument that appears to have arisen from a sense of erotic, if not sexual, despair. Bengali men's 'appreciation of

---

[33] D. C. Sen, *History of Bengali Language and Literature*, pp. 397–8.

[34] Charles Donelan, *Romanticism and Male Fantasy in Byron's 'Don Juan': A Marketable Vice* (Basingstoke, Hampshire: MacMillan Press, 2000), p. 48. See also the discussion in Chapters 3 and 6.

[35] The expression 'sexual Jacobinism'—and the idea that this is how Coleridge might have described Byron's politics—comes from Malcolm Kelsall, 'Byron and the Romantic Heroine', in *Byron: Augustan and Romantic*, ed. Andrew Rutherford (New York: St Martin's Press, 1990), p. 57. Moyra Haslett, *Byron's 'Don Juan' and the Don Juan Legend* (Oxford: Clarendon Press, 1997), p. 185, employs a very similar expression. The comments are inspired by, among other things, Samuel Taylor Coleridge, *Biographia Literaria*, ed. Nigel Leask (London: J. M. Dent, 1997), Chapter 23.

[36] See, in particular, Haslett, *Byron's 'Don Juan'*, chapters 1–3, 5.

the romantic motives of European literature', said Sen, was 'fraught
with disastrous results to our society'. Why? Sen's answer did not in
the least glorify actually existing Bengali families. These families, he
wrote, left 'no room for the betrothed pair to have the slightest share
in the mutual choice'.[37] Sen's romantic critique of Bengali domestic
arrangements takes an even more searing form in a few other sentences
in his *History*. 'In this country', he said,

> a blind Providence joins the hands of a mute pair who promise fidelity,
> often without knowing each other. When the situation grows monotonous,
> losing colour and poetry, both men and women are treated to lectures on
> the purity of the nuptial vow, and to promises of rewards in the next world.
> They fully believe in the sanctity of marriage, and are ready to sacrifice
> sentiment to stern duty. But human passion cannot be altogether repressed,
> and where it over-rides the ordinances of the Shastras [scriptures], it rushes
> forward with extraordinary strength, all the greater for the attempt at
> forcible suppression.[38]

This was *not* the language of a conservative believer in tradition.

We now begin to see Sen's predicament, and clearly it was not his
alone. Byron was exciting, but Sen was scared of the consequences of his
sexual politics. European romanticism had given rise—among Bengali
men—to a critique of the Bengali home and its conjugal arrangements.
Part of this critique was indeed a desire for 'liberated' women, which
Sen had taken to heart. However, like many of his contemporaries, Sen
feared that the emphasis on the autonomy of the individual in domestic and conjugal life could only make men profoundly unhappy in a
land where the bonds of the extended family with its own long history
seemed indissoluble. This is one of the few places in the book where
Sen admits both his despair as a romantic individual and the practical
utility—from a pragmatic point of view—of the ideal of self-sacrifice that
he found elaborated in Bengali literature. That is why his idealization of
the Bengali family—his family romance that underpinned the 'national
literature' project—ultimately rests on an impulse that is far from
romantic. For he says, quite plainly: 'Indeed, in a place where a joint and
undivided family system required a man to live and eat together with
all his near kinsmen, it would be impossible to live in harmony without

---

[37] D. C. Sen, *History of Bengali Language and Literature*, p. 398.
[38] D. C. Sen, *History of Bengali Language and Literature*, p. 117.

elevating the domestic duties into the highest virtues.'[39] This was not a spiritual defence of the arrangements that *actually existed* within Bengali homes. It was more a desperate search for a romanticized 'tradition' that would make room for the new individual, both male and female, while allowing the pursuit of happiness in a land in which the past did nothing to validate the European humanist ideal of the individual. For Sen and his cohorts, the only solution seemed to be a romanticized notion of the extended family itself. It would be harmonious enough to accommodate within its regime the companionate form of marriage, and yet it would tame any potential for mixing sexual liberty with political liberty. Such a family would act as a metaphor for the nation. Without families of this kind, as Sen put it, 'it would be impossible to live in harmony'. His talk of 'elevating the domestic duties into the highest virtues' was actually making a virtue out of perceived necessity.[40]

In Bengali literature, Sen reasoned, the 'virtue' of domestic duty had been preached for generations. This literature—and not the existing arrangements in the family—seemed to offer spiritual solutions to what ailed the spirit of the English-educated, romantic Bengali man. Sen writes: 'No other nation has ever given so high a value to domestic duties, identifying them so closely with the spiritual.'[41] It was literature—its folk, medieval, and Vaishnava traditions, and the translated Puranas in particular—that had supplied 'inexhaustible examples' of 'obedience to parents, loyalty to the husband, devotion to brothers and sacrifices to be undergone for guests, servants and relations'.[42] In fairness to Sen, it must be said that he did not preach patriarchal values—the examples of Sita, Savitri, Damayanti, Shakuntala, and Behula—only to women. He preached to all, both men and women, the ideas of a harmonious system of hierarchy and of voluntary and willing submission to authority facilitated by the feeling of devotion (*bhakti*) to duty. 'Rama who left the throne ..., and Visma, who took the vow of celibacy, ... Hanumana [who] typif[ied] devotion to a master, and Ekalavya to the religious preceptor' were the ideal characters he held up to his male readers.[43]

[39] D. C. Sen, *History of Bengali Language and Literature*, p. 879.
[40] D. C. Sen, *History of Bengali Language and Literature*, p. 879.
[41] D. C. Sen, *History of Bengali Language and Literature*, p. 879.
[42] D. C. Sen, *History of Bengali Language and Literature*, p. 878.
[43] D. C. Sen, *History of Bengali Language and Literature*, p. 879.

With hindsight, we know that the fear that Sen and his contemporaries had of 'unbridled' individualism in conjugal life destroying the social fabric of the extended family overstated reality. But that is the wisdom of hindsight. What we have to notice is that the desire for harmony in the extended family and in national life in general may itself have been a modern ideal that developed only after the coming of the British rule. Pre-British Bengali literature surely does not fight shy of conflict between family members, nor does it preach any general message of harmony. The ideas that allowed many to see the caste system, the patriarchal extended family, the village, and other collectivities as potentially harmonious entities owed themselves, I suspect, to European education. To press into the service of domestic harmony the 'virtue' of self-sacrifice and loyalty to one's social superiors was a modern development. While it battled what it saw as Western individualism, it was itself most likely a product of the romanticism and classicism that came with the West.

From the Ruins of 'National Literature'

The romantic project of a 'Bengali national literature' came apart in the 1920s and 1930s as demand for a separate Muslim homeland gained momentum in the subcontinent as a whole. The politics of Bengal now were drawn into the politics of the rest of India. Besides, women, the working classes, and the lower castes all increasingly asserted themselves in political and public life using the language of rights. Literature alone could not produce the 'national spirit' anymore. That the formation of a Bangiya Sahitya Parishad (Bengal Literary Academy) in 1893 did not address the needs of Bengali Muslims became clear from early in the second decade of the twentieth century. A near-absolute breach between Hindu and Muslim intellectuals took a long time to develop. But as early as 1911, Muslim intellectuals in Calcutta set up a separate Muslim literary association (Muslim Sahitya Samiti) as they found the Bangiya Sahitya Parishad too Hindu for their taste. The renowned linguist Muhammad Shahidullah, who was one of the organizers of the new association, thus remembered the circumstances leading to its formation. His prose clearly speaks of Muslim and Hindu Bengalis as 'us' and 'them':

> I passed the B.A. examination in 1910. I came in contact with several enthusiastic young men at that time. Among them were Mohammed

Mozammel Huq, Mohammad Yakoob Ali Chaudhuri, Maulvi Ahmad Ali, Muoinuddin Hussain, and others.... Some of us were members of the Bangiya Sahitya Parishad. There was no discrimination made there between Hindus and Muslims. Yet our literature was so poor that taking part in their meetings made us feel like the way the poor feel inside the houses of their wealthy relatives. We felt wanting in spirit. We thought we should have our own literary association without cutting off relations with the Bangiya Sahitya Parishad. With this purpose in mind, a meeting was convened on 4th September 1911 at No. 9, Anthony Bagan Lane, Calcutta, at the house of Maulvi Abdul Rahman Khan.... I was unanimously elected the secretary.[44]

The formation of the University of Dhaka in 1921 gave a further boost to Muslim literary activities and aspirations. Besides, constitutional reforms initiated between 1919 and 1935 by the colonial government introduced limited but critical forms of electoral politics that only deepened and intensified the competitive currents between Hindus and Muslims and between the upper castes and the so-called depressed classes.[45] During this period the Indian National Congress became a 'mass' political organization under the leadership of Gandhi, and the Muslim League found 'mass' political methods for pressing home the demand for Pakistan. Politics itself was no longer—except in the idealist proclamations of Gandhi and Gandhians—about transcending interest. It became more a calculus of creating 'general' interests around class, caste, religious, or 'secular-Indian' communities. Attributed more to interest than to spirit or virtue, politics would increasingly come to be seen as arising not from the 'spirit' but from the dynamic of the social structure. This was a dynamic that emergent new disciplines of the social sciences were far more suited to study and address than art or literature. One could politicize literature, distinguish political from so-called non-political literature, or read literature politically in the interest of social justice. But that was different from literature itself being by definition a fount of the political. The rational procedures of

____

[44] Muhammad Shahidullah, 'Bangiya muslim sahitya patrika', in *Shahidullah rachanabali*, ed. Anisuzzaman, 4 vols (Dhaka: Bangla Academy, 1994), vol. 1, p. 471. For more details on this event and on later developments, see Khondkar Siraj ul-Huq, *Muslim sahitya samaj: Samajchinta o sahityakarma* (Dhaka: Bangla Academy, 1984), pp. 93–177.

[45] See Pradip Kumar Datta, *Carving Blocs: Communal Ideology in Early Twentieth-Century Bengal* (New Delhi: Oxford University Press, 1999).

the social sciences now seemed much better suited to address national-political needs.

It is not surprising that Dinesh Sen's works should lose their charm for many younger Bengali intellectuals in this period. To them, Sen seemed like an intellectual dinosaur, representing increasingly obsolete methods and assumptions of research in reconstructing the past of the Bengali people. More than that, he seemed out of step with the moves the main nationalist party, the Indian National Congress, had taken. Sen's politics of projecting a 'national Bengali identity' now sounded to some as a special plea for a Bengal that excluded from its territory other Indians who did not speak Bangla. His position would thus be seen by some as opposed to the ideals of a pan-Indian nationalism with which the Congress increasingly confronted the Muslim demand for a separate homeland. The linguist Sunitikumar Chattopadhyay strongly criticized the idea of 'Greater Bengal', an expression that Sen used as the title of his last book. 'We cannot afford to forget', said Chattopadhyay, 'that the land of Bengal is part of India; that Bengalis are part of a cluster of Indian nationalities and have no other identity separate from India'. 'Bengali culture', he said, himself forgetting the Bengali Muslim, 'is part of Indian culture—there is no Bengali culture opposed to the latter'.[46]

Perhaps the most severe criticisms of Sen came in the columns of a Calcutta-based journal started in 1924, *Shanibarer chithi* (Saturday's Mail), devoted to humorous, witty, but often hurtful, criticisms of writers and literary fashions.[47] The poet Jasimuddin in his reminiscences of Sen in this period captures with sympathy and compassion the extent of Sen's marginalization and his harassment at the hands of young and

[46] Sunitikumar Chattopadhyay, 'Brihattara banga', in his *Bharat-sanskriti* (Calcutta: Mitra and Ghosh, 1939), pp. 155–75. This essay was dropped from the second edition of the book. Thanks to Gautam Bhadra for bringing this essay to my attention. The same criticism was made (probably by the same author) in an unsigned essay entitled 'Itihash noy' (Not History) that ridiculed Sen's *Brihat banga*. See Anon., 'Itihash noy', *Shanibarer chithi* (August–September 1936): 1301–15. Bengali Muslim nationalism that repudiated both Hindu Bengali nationalism *and* any idea of a larger 'Indian nationalism' eventually gave the lie to Chattopadhyay's contention as well.

[47] An informative account of the history of this journal is provided in Shonamoni Chakraborty, '*Shanibarer chithi' o adhunik bangla sahitya* (Calcutta: Aruna Prakashani, 1992).

irreverent researchers.[48] Around 1928–9 and 1936–7, the journal published several articles virulently criticizing Sen, including a long essay published in instalments and sarcastically entitled—in mock-Persian—*Dineshnama*, or the 'The Tale of Dinesh'. These essays and reviews sometimes acknowledged the pioneering role that Sen had played as a historian of Bengal. But they made fun of his many factual errors, faulty argumentation, his tendency to go on publishing new editions of *Bangabhasha o shahitya* without familiarizing himself with recent research, and, above all, the obsolete sentimentalism of his method. The accusations amounted to the charge—and the *Chithi* said it literally in some of its issues—that what Sen had written was not objective and scientific history; it was more like imaginative literature. Sen's book *Brihat banga* (Greater Bengal), they asserted (not altogether unreasonably), was not history but 'a novel'.[49]

The language of criticism in *Shanibarer chithi* was often harsh and sometimes vicious.[50] But the charges stuck and were repeated by others. Nalinikanta Bhattashali, a respected historian of Bengali literature,

---

[48] Jasimuddin mentions Sunitikumar Chattopadhyay among the leaders of the group opposed to Sen. See Jasimuddin, *Smaraner sharani bahi*, pp. 61, 68. For a recent critical appreciation of *Brihat banga*, see Gautam Bhadra, 'Itihashe smritite itihash', *Visva-Bharati patrika* (July–September 1994): 134–43.

[49] See the following entries: 'Dineshnama' (The Tale of Dinesh) and 'Bangabhasha o sahitya', *Shanibarer chithi* (March–April 1929): 142–80, 214–26, and 'Dineshnama' and letter by Bhimrul Sharma, *Shanibarer chithi* (April–May 1929): 312–36, and (May–June 1929): 440–4. These essays described Sen as a 'flatterer' of powerful people at the university while also being a 'tyrant' to his subordinates. His 'histories' were termed fables and his autobiography mocked. The letter from Sharma described Sen as 'moon-struck' and pointed to several factual errors in his books. Among the other issues of *Shanibarer chithi* that targeted Dinesh Sen were (October–November 1928): 826; (December 1928–January 1929): 994–1004; (February–March 1929): 998–1004; (April–May 1936): 1002, 1022–3, 1143–4; (June–July 1936): 1128–31; (August–September 1936): 1301–15, 1338–42; (September–October 1936): 1612–13; and (November–December 1936): 192–3. *Shanibarer chithi* used to be dated according to the Bengali calendar. I have converted the months and years into those of the English calendar.

[50] The essay on *Brihat banga*, for instance, indicated the 'thickness' of Sen's head by suggesting that it be used as a nutcracker. Some of the articles referred to in note 49 accused him of stealing other people's research and of committing academic fraud.

acknowledged the value of Dinesh Sen's pioneering work in his introduction to a 1936 edition of the Bengali *Ramayana*. But that was about
the only praise that Bhattashali could offer Sen. 'The gap', he added,

> between histories of literature written at the time of the first publication of
> *Bangabhasha o sahitya* and those written now is as large as the gap between
> the year 1837 in the reign of Victoria and 1901.... *Bangabhasha o sahitya* is
> now in its sixth edition. It is true that Dineshbabu has attempted to mend
> [the book] clumsily—and within the limits of his knowledge and intelli-
> gence—by adding some recent findings here and there. But the structure of
> the book has not changed and it has, as a whole, acquired an appearance as
> terrible as that of the patchwork quilt of a *fakir*.

Bhattashali's colourful prose did not stop there:

> Dineshbabu blithely ignores the majority of researchers and their research
> of the last thirty years. He does not discuss if he has read them, discussed
> them, or why he considers them unacceptable. Without including any of
> these [discussions] in the book, Dineshbabu simply tows along this worn-
> out, sluggard boat of his—filled with goods whose time has expired—from
> the station [in English in original] of one edition to another! Such a strange
> phenomenon can happen only in a lifeless country like ours.[51]

A Question of Method

Let us put aside for the moment the harshness of the criticism that
Sen faced.[52] Bengali intellectuals are, after all, no strangers to vicious
criticism. Let me at the same time ignore the lack of wisdom in Sen's
indefensible refusal to update research and methods and in his tendency towards sentimentalism. Nor do I want to pursue here the point

[51] Nalinikanta Bhattashali, introduction to *Mahakabi krittibasrachita rama-
yan*, ed. Bhattashali (Dhaka: P.C. Lahiri, 1936), pp. i–viii. I owe this reference
to Gautam Bhadra.

[52] For the sake of record, I should mention that Sajanikanta Das, the founding editor of *Shanibarer chithi*, later repented his action in print. His posthumously published book, *Bangla gadyashitye itihash* (History of Bengali Prose)
(Calcutta: Mitralaya [?], 1975 [1963]), says in its dedication: 'Once, driven by
the frivolity of youth, I wrote 'Dineshnama' in *Shanibarer chithi*. Not only did
the generous-hearted Dinesh Chandra forgive me in his old age, he even blessed
me from his heart. Sadly, I could not make amends when he was alive. I do so
now.' Thanks to Gautam Bhadra for this reference.

that Muslim nationalists never fully identified with the Hindu romantic project. I want to focus instead on a question about method that the criticism of Sen, in effect, raised. It seems to me that what was at issue in this story was an important question about what constituted the archives for collective pasts and how such archives could be accessed. For those who, like Sen and others of his generation, had seen literature as quintessentially political, the past was constituted, ultimately, not merely by historical evidence but also by emotional and experiential recollections of the past. The past in that sense could fuse with the present. It was inhabitable in spirit. Sentiments and emotions were thus a part of the method of both constituting and accessing a collective past.[53] For the generation that painstakingly built up the principles of 'scientific' history and dispassionate analysis, however, the archives lay in pieces of objective evidence coming down from the past. One's subjective feelings were merely personal. I am not suggesting that this change happened in a day. Nor do I mean to say that 'objective' history writing did not have its own share of romances. I am simply drawing a contrast between two different modes of constituting and accessing the past in order to highlight a point in my argument.

That sentiments were a part of the romantic method Sen employed in constituting the past can be demonstrated easily with reference to the problem known as the Chandidas puzzle in the history of Bengali literature. For a long time, the name Chandidas was known among students and other readers of 'medieval' Bengali literature. It was known from the biographies of the popular fifteenth- and sixteenth-century Bengali religious saint Chaitanya that he loved listening to song-poems composed by a Chandidas. The discovery of new texts in the second decade of the twentieth century, however, and a growing appreciation

[53] Scholars who have continued in Sen's footsteps have never felt embarrassed about treating literature sentimentally. See, for instance, Shankariprasad Bosu, *Chjandidas o bidyapati* (Calcutta: Dey's, 1999 [1960/1]), p. 28:

> It was in his heart, and not his head, that our teacher Dinesh Chandra received the inspiration for writing a history of literature. So the history he wrote was marked by a certain indispensable element of sentimentalism. What looks like uncontrolled sentimentalism from one point of view, sounds like a song [celebrating] the surrender of the self when approached from another. In entering the world of Chandidas's life, I will respectfully follow my predecessor Dinesh Chandra.

of historical methods of research produced a problem for historians of Bengali literature. It began to look likely that there had been many different poets who signed off their compositions with the same name of Chandidas (with different prefixes). Their proper identification, therefore, called for historical circumspection and careful collection and reading of evidence. Manindramohan Bose, a lecturer at the University of Calcutta, posed the problem in a series of essays published in the journal of the Bangiya Sahitya Parishad around 1925 or 1926, pointing out ways in which some aspects of this puzzle could be solved by attending to particular aspects of the evidence.[54]

Sen refused to see the problem in historical terms. It was not that he was intellectually incapable of appreciating the methodological issues under discussion. In endorsing the first volume of Bose's edition of the poems of Deena Chandidas (one of the Chandidases), Sen referred approvingly to 'the famous historian at the University of London, Professor L.D. Barnett' who allegedly advised 'students to exercise scepticism in historical discussions' so that they did not accept any existing conclusions without proper examination. Scepticism, and not sentimentalism, said Sen, was central to 'scientific research'. 'Writing guided by emotions and enthusiasm', Sen wrote almost echoing his critics, 'may be poetic and attractive to the heart but it does not amount to scientific research'. He commended Bose for following the path pointed out by Barnett.[55]

Yet consider his own response in *Bangabhasha o shahitya* to the charge that the identity of any particular Chandidas needed to be established through careful research and that, by treating the different Chandidases as though they were one person, he had in fact distorted history. Sen retreated into a passage he had written in the very first edition of the book and dug his heels further into, as it were, the treacherous grounds of sentimentalism. In the very first edition (1896), he had said, with reference to Chandidas: 'The reader will

---

[54] See Manindramohan Bose, 'Introduction', *Deena chandidaser padabali*, 2 vols (Calcutta: University of Calcutta, 1938), vol. 2, p. 9. See also the chapter called 'Chandidas shamashya' in Muhammad Shahidullah, *Bangla sahityer katha: Madhyajug*, 3 vols (Dhaka: Rennaisance Printers, 1967–8), vol. 2, pp. 40–68.

[55] Quoted in Bose, 'Opinions on the First Volume', *Deena chandidaser padabali* 2: 1–2.

forgive me. The historian is meant to hide his own opinion in describing a subject. I am unable to follow that rule.... I would not have discussed ancient Bengali literature if it had not been for the enchanting power of Chandidas's poems. Hence ... the many digressions.'[56] In the second edition (1901) he made a few changes to this paragraph. After the sentence, 'The reader will forgive me', he added: 'Chandidas's poems have been the source of many a tear of joy and sorrow since my childhood. I cannot tell if the intense emotions of my heart will make it impossible for me to present a proper discussion of his poems.'[57] The rest of the paragraph more or less remained the same. But faced in the 1920s with growing discussions of the need to deploy historical and linguistic methods of reasoning, particularly in relation to Chandidas, Sen made his defiance of history ever more obstinate and wilful. This particular paragraph was now expanded to incorporate the following:

> For many years now I have recited the name of Chandidas as if it were the Gayatrimantra [a mantra Brahmins are expected to recite every day]. No one, not even my wife and sons, are as close to me as this great poet. Nobody in the world has given me more pleasure than he. From this acquaintance cultivated over half a century, I can now tell if a poem bears his [characteristic] 'tune'.

And then came the final anti-historicist declaration: 'I have no desire to undertake linguistic analysis and solve the Chandidas-puzzle by distinguishing between the "real" Chandidas, Boru Chandidas, Dvija Chandidas, the Chandidas who worshipped [the goddess] Bashuli, or the Chandidas who loved a young woman. To me, there is only one Chandidas and one alone.'[58]

Again, overlooking for now the stridency of Sen's tone, it seems clear that sentiments or emotions were quite central to Sen's method of constituting the past. The past had to be made palpably present.[59] This is precisely what would be resisted by the new science

---

[56] D. C. Sen, *Bangabhasha o shahitya*, vol. 1, p. 121.

[57] D. C. Sen, *Bangabhasha o shahitya*, (Calcutta, 1901, 2d ed.), pp. 186–7.

[58] Dinesh Chandra Sen, *Bangabhasha o shahitya* (Calcutta[?]: Sanyal and Co., 1926[?], 6th ed.), pp. 213–4.

[59] There seems to be an interesting overlap—or maybe a homology— between this romantic way of collapsing the analytical distance between the

of history. It was not that the historian was not allowed any sentiments, but these could not be part of his or her method. If social-
scientific rationality was what was political, then the non-rational
could only be part of the personal. It could have a public life, but
not as part of one's method. This is best shown by contrasting Sen's
methods of approaching the past to those of the younger historian
Niharranjan Ray. Ray's magnum opus *Bangalir itihash: Adiparba* (A
History of the Bengali People: The First Phase), first published in
1949, is now considered a classic. As an individual, Ray appears to
have been as romantic a person as Sen. Indeed in explaining the genesis of his book, he writes a paragraph (in the preface) that is strongly
reminiscent of a certain passage in Dinesh Sen's autobiography. It
begins on this note: 'Whatever the amount of study, observation,
reflection, discussion and research that has gone into this book, it was
not a quest for knowledge that led me to write it.' Ray continued:

> The intoxicating, irrepressible and restless urges and the intense emotions
> of the vow of patriotism made me travel from one end of Bengal to the
> other in my early youth. In the peasant huts of this vast Bengal, at her river-
> ghats, in her paddyfields, in the shadow of her banyan trees, at the heart of
> her cities, on the sandbanks of the Padma, or on the crest of the waves of
> the Meghna—I saw a particular form of this country and its people and I
> loved it.... It was the inspiration of this love that made me start writing this
> book.... Ancient history is as true and alive for me as today's present. It is
> that live and true past, and not just a dead skeleton, which I have sought to
> capture in this book.[60]

---

past and the present and what is sometimes observed in studies of religious
practices. I have in mind Carolyn Dinshaw's stimulating discussion of 'queer
history'—'where past and present collapse in a now' connecting lives that are
only 'queerly co-extensive'. Dinshaw discusses the case of the medieval saint
Margery Kempe who literally treated Jesus' death 'as if he died this same
day' (Carolyn Dinshaw, 'Always Historicize? Margery Kempe Then and Now'
[unpub. ms.], 2003).
[60] Niharranjan Ray, *Bangalir itihash: Adiparba* (Calcutta: Dey's, 1993
[1949]), p. xix. The corresponding passage in Sen's autobiography reads:

> The sound of conch shells and bells every morning and evening, the sweet smell
> produced by burning of incense and sandalwood, the ever-emergent red colour
> of lotus flowers—it was as if they all filled up Bengal villages, their marketplaces,
> fields, ghats, and pathways, with an atmosphere of devotion to God. I began to

A romantic nationalism thus propelled Ray just as much as it had Sen in their respective endeavours. They both saw in the beauty of the Bengal countryside the 'home' of the Bengali spirit that romantics had celebrated in the songs and poems they wrote in the 1890s through the 1910s. Yet there was a profound difference between their methods. Sen's sentiments, as I have said, were also part of his academic method. The two could not be separated. Niharranjan Ray, however, clearly separated them. What he said in the preface was no doubt a part of his motivation for doing the research he did, but it was not a proclaimed or conscious part of his method of analysis. Ray began his book explaining why Bengali histories written by his predecessors such as Haraprasad Shastri, Akshaykumar Maitreya, Rakhaldas Bandyopadhyay, Ramaprasad Chanda, and others did not quite amount to a 'history of the Bengali people'. For a 'true introduction' (*jathartho porichoy*) to the history of the whole 'way of life' of Bengalis needed the application of a properly 'historical form of reasoning' (*itihasher jukti*) and a self-conscious framework of 'cause and effect relationships'.[61] Man was both a product and the creator, said Ray, of 'state, society, religion, art, literature, science, economic organisation and so on'.[62] Hence, the key to the past could not be just a sentimental apprehension of it. Sentiments had to be replaced by a sociological and a secular-humanist sensibility insofar as methods were concerned. When he uses poetry to enliven his discussion—as at the end of the section discussing the 'geographical destiny' (*bhougolik bhagyo*) of the Bengali people where he cites some lines by the poet Premendra Mitra—Ray takes care to distinguish between a historical fact and poetic fancy. Poetry lends flourish to his exposition, but it is not an inherent part of his method. 'This geographical destiny [of the Bengali people]', writes Ray quoting Mitra, 'has assumed a beautiful poetic form through the pen of a

---

consider the dust of every village of my motherland sacred. This was nothing like the [new-fangled] emotion of nationalism or patriotism on my part. Nor was it a feeling produced by simply copying the English. Truly did every particle of dust of this land make my tears flow. An indescribable feeling of attraction made me fall in love with the land of Bengal. (D. C. Sen, *Gharer katha o jugashahitya*, p. 120)

[61] Ray, *Bangalir itihash*, p. 5.

[62] Ray, *Bangalir itihash*, p. 5.

twentieth-century Bengali poet'.[63] But the 'beautiful poetic form' was
still poetry and not a 'fact'.

Ray's prose was thus part of a group of writings that inaugurated
the moment of social scientific history in the historiography of Bengali
identity. He himself showed an awareness of this. He writes:

> From towards the last third of the nineteenth century, beginnings were made
> in some parts of Europe—in Austria and Germany in particular but to some
> degree in France as well—in the study of the history of social development
> from a scientific point of view. Consequently, scholars everywhere have
> accepted that the larger social arrangements of different countries at different
> times depend on the mode of production of wealth and its distribution. Vari-
> eties of race, class, and social stratification grow up according to this mode.[64]

Was this a mild statement of certain Marxist principles? Perhaps. But it
was mild enough to be considered a general statement of a 'scientific'
approach to history by the doyen of Indian historians, Sir Jadunath
Sarkar, no Marxist himself. Blessing the book with a foreword, Sir
Jadunath made it clear that what made this book properly historical
were its attention to evidence and its focus on change and evolution.
He welcomed the idea of historical development that underlay the
book and praised its 'attempt to understand how the Bengali people
have gradually evolved into the modern-day Bengalis'.[65]

Arguments about sociological laws, about evidence and objectivity, about crafting—but not experiencing—the past eventually won
the day in Bengali debates about historical methods. Prabodhchandra
Sen's classic study of the history of Bengali historiography remarked
that the sense of the past that informed Bengali nationalists until about
the Swadeshi Movement (1905) had a dreamlike quality to it. Those
histories, said Sen, were inspired more by a 'dream-filled' (*shvapnomoy*)
vision of Bengal than a 'truth-filled' (*satyamoy*) one.[66] Dinesh Sen was
seen as one of the major practitioners of this genre. Acknowledging
his many qualities as a researcher, Prabodhchandra Sen found the following major fault in Sen's method: 'His litterateur-like proneness to

---

[63] Ray, *Bangalir itihash*, p. 71.

[64] Ray, *Bangalir itihash*, p. 8.

[65] Jadunath Sarkar, foreword to *Bangalir itihash*, p. x.

[66] Prabodhchandra Sen, *Banglar itihash-sadhana* (Calcutta: General Printers
and Publishers, 1953–4), p. 132.

being sentimental swamps the disinterested objectivity of the historian
in many places.' On the other hand, he praised Niharranjan Ray for
his capacity, precisely, to 'free' his methodological objectivity from 'the
lure of the sentiment of patriotism and other feelings'.[67]

In the end, Dinesh Sen conceded defeat. In 1935, a few years
before his death, an old and retired Sen published two very large
volumes entitled *Brihat banga* (Greater Bengal), a history of Bengali
culture from its mythical beginnings and its alleged spread to far
outside India. The book was badly received by the contemporary
critical public in Bengal. Sen's own preface to the book shows how
apologetically he now offered his writing to his readers, aware that
academic fashions had moved on. So had the politics of knowledge
changed that called such fashions into being. He realized that the
question of methods was a question of how one related to the larger
world. He could see that the talk about 'scientific' history bespoke
a certain sense of cosmopolitanism—a sense that one was part of
a global research community—that his older, once equally global
and cosmopolitan but now-discredited, romantic methods could no
longer evoke. 'I am not a lover of the world', he said now, 'I remain
hopelessly provincial'. 'If that makes someone think that I am not
suited to this age, that I am a [proverbial] frog-in-the-well left behind
by the ever-increasing and ever-progressing [surge of] civilisation,
then I will not protest for I am indeed that.' Sen was now forced
to recognize the disciplinary distinction between literature and history. 'I have spent my life with Bengali language and literature. I am
unknown in the field of history', he said. '[The new] professors [of
history] will find fault with me at every step.... Perhaps the language
of this book is not that of the scientific, judicious, disinterested historian.... This book, in particular, has not been written only with
the historians in mind.' The nation now was a profoundly unstable
category in his prose. Notice, for instance, within the space of the
same paragraph the figure of 'the ordinary people of Bengal' that
metamorphoses into 'Hindus'—a minority among the Bengalis, even
though Sen refers to them as the majority:

[67] P. Sen, *Banglar itihash-sadhana*, pp. 88, 135. See also Shyamali Sur's
discussion of romantic, nationalist histories in her *Oitihashik chinta o
jatiyotabaader unmesh: Bangla 1870–1912* (Calcutta: Progressive, 2002),
Chapter 3.

One of my aims is to arouse in the hearts of the ordinary people of Bengal a love for their own country. They will not be attracted to dry and arid research.... European writers generally pass in silence over the play of the supernatural in accounts of Christ's birth.... [But] they become overly scientific while discussing our history.... This kind of research only hurts the sharp sensitivities of the mute majority of our common people. But it behooves the Hindu writer to keep in mind the way the Hindu people look on the Tulasi plant or the iron bangle on the hands [of the married woman]. Otherwise the educated will get cut off from the rest of the community.[68]

Romantic Archives

I come to my final point. Archives, it seems to me, are politically constituted. Bengali literature, for someone like Sen, was a very special kind of archival resource with which to remake society. It had three characteristics. By self-consciously idealizing life, literature acted as a repository of time-tested virtues and values and thus furnished material for the making of the self. Second, by its very nature it tended to be popular and therefore national if not always democratic. And, finally, it was different from the cold facts of the history recorded in official documents, stone inscriptions, and coins in that by appealing to a continuity of emotional experience it defeated any attempt at an objectivist separation of the past from the present. However, it was not Sen's personal will that made this stance powerful when he first wrote *Bangabhasha o shahitya*. It was the romantic nationalism of the day that gave validity to his position and made literary endeavour an intrinsic part of a national project. It was similarly a change in the understanding of what was innately political (that is, in the best national interest) about knowledge—the rationality of social science procedures—that made Sen's method look quixotic, if not downright 'lunatic' (as his critics said), in the twentieth century.

The romantic sentiments of the Swadeshi period—once political and later merely personal—continued to live on as poetry, as precisely the expression of deep but personal emotions. A host of poets who rose to prominence between 1900 and 1920—among them Kalidas Ray, Jatindramohan Bagchi, Karunanidhan Bandyopadhyay, Kumudranjan

---

[68] Dinesh Chandra Sen, 'Preface', *Brihat banga* (Calcutta: Dey's, 1993 [1935]), pp. 30–3.

Mallik, and later, of course, Jasimuddin—found in the countryside an eternal Bengal to celebrate in their poetry.[69] Quite a few poems of this genre found their way into our school texts. One abiding theme of this poetry was a haunting desire on the part of poets to return in their future lives to the land of Bengal. How commonplace this senti-ment of return was may be judged from the opening lines of a popular love song of the 1940s: 'In a hundred years, may you and I return to a home in this very land.'[70] Poetry and songs thus remained critical to the transmission of romantic sentiments once forged in the workshop of nationalism of the late nineteenth and early twentieth centuries.

A critical nodal moment in this history of transmission of certain kinds of sentiments remains Jibanananda Das's book *Rupasi Bangla* (Bengal the Beautiful), a collection of poems composed in the early 1930s and published posthumously in the mid-1950s. Clinton Seely's sensitive study of Jibanananda Das, *A Poet Apart*, helps us to see the connection between the literary movement and sentiments that Dinesh Sen stood for in the 1890s and the 1910s and the poems on the subject of Bengal written by Das in the 1930s. The poems of *Rupasi Bangla* are famous for expressing the poet's desire to be (re) born in Bengal. This motif recurs through many of the sonnets: 'When I return to the banks of the Dhansiri, to this Bengal, / Not as a man, perhaps, but as a *salik* bird or white hawk.'[71] Notice how, in these lines, Bengal has a palpable presence. The poet could point to it as it were and say, '*this* Bengal'. But where was *this* Bengal to which Das yearned to return? It surely was not the Bengal of the realistic or 'sci-entific' historian or the geographer. '*This* Bengal' had the same kind of presence as Chandidas had for Dinesh Sen. In fact, the sense of Bengali history that marks these poems is in part the one that Dinesh Sen

[69] A discussion placing Jasimuddin's poetry in this context is to be found in Selima Khalek, *Jasimuddiner kabita: Alankar o chitraprakash* (Dhaka: Bangla Academy, 1993), Chapter 1.

[70] The song was written by Mohini Chaudhuri, a well-known songwriter of the period. The singer Juthika Roy recorded it to a tune composed by Kamal Dasgupta. See *Abismaraniya gitikar mohini chaudhuri*, ed. Pabitra Adhikari (Calcutta: Karuna Prakashani, 2000), p. 79.

[71] Quoted in Clinton Seely, *A Poet Apart: A Literary Biography of the Ben-gali Poet Jibanananda Das (1899–1954)* (Newark: University of Delaware Press, 1990), p. 92.

espoused. Further, research and interpretation of the kind pioneered by Sen had a critical role in fostering the imagination embedded in Das's poems. These poems are replete with references to 'folk' stories of the kind Dinesh Sen collected and to the medieval *mangal kavyas*, in particular to *chandi mangal* and *manasa mangal*, literary texts devoted to celebrating the powers of the folk goddesses Chandi and Manasa. The characters Chand and Behula from these kavyas and stories of their journeys live in an intimate relationship to the poetic sentiments expressed in *Rupasi Bangla*. Experience is indeed what fuses the past with the present into an eternal history. As Seely says: 'Chand from Champa and Behula establish a community of experience [with the poet], for back then they had seen Bengal's beauty just as the poet sees it now.'[72] A mythical sense of a continuous Bengali history helps Das to create a Bengali present. Seely writes:

> Jibanananda also refers to historical and mytho-historical figures: Ballal Sen, a king of ancient Bengal; Rajaballabh, whose glory was destroyed by the Kirtinasa river; Arjuna, from the *Mahabharata* epic; the Buddha and Confucius; the renowned medieval Bengali poets Mukundaram, Chandidas, Ramprasad, and Rayagunakar (Bharat Chandra Ray); and the man in whose memory Jibanananda had written one of his first poems, 'Deshabandhu' Chitta Ranjan Das.[73]

However, this was, of course, not a simple return of the spirit of Dinesh Chandra Sen. If Das's sonnets recuperated and rehearsed some of the sentiments underlying Sen's description of Bengal's pasts, they also displaced them on to a new context. For Das's enunciation of these sentiments had none of the nationalist, programmatic, and optimistic fervour of Dinesh Sen's exposition. These poems also carried an acutely historical sense of a twentieth-century 'crisis' in Bengali lives. It was as if by holding the historical and the non-historical together that Das could heal the wounds of the historical present. It also has to be noted that Das's sentiments remained personal. He never thought of this healing as a collective project:

> When the evening breeze from the Aswathha tree touches
> the blue forests of Bengal,
> I wander alone in the fields: it is as if the crisis in

[72] Seely, *A Poet Apart*, p. 93.
[73] Seely, *A Poet Apart*, p. 94–5.

Bengal's life
has ended today.[74]

It is interesting, however, that despite Das having been described as 'the most solitary poet' of Bengal, these poems, so distant from any properly historical or political sensibility, should, from time to time, enjoy a public-political life that Das himself never coveted. 'Certain readers', writes Seely, 'consider [*Bengal the Beautiful*] Jibanananda's most successful book. In 1971, during the Bangladesh liberation war, poems from this collection became viewed as expressions of the quintessential Bangladesh for which the Mukti Bahini ('freedom army') fought. Twice during the war's nine months, new editions of *Bengal the Beautiful* were published.'[75]

We do not know how Das's Muslim readers in Bangladesh read these poems during their liberation war. Did they read into his poems the folk-yet-Hindu literary allusions that filled them? Perhaps not. The return of Das may not have signalled the return of an interest in the Bengali literature of the so-called middle period. What, then, did return with Das in the 1970s, about forty years after these poems were written? An answer is suggested by an obscure poem by a not very well-known poet Narayan Sarkar, who penned the following poem in Calcutta in the tumultuous sixties. The poem was published in 1973 in a Bengali collection of contemporary revolutionary poetry. It was entitled, echoing Das, 'I Shall Return' and thus foretold a return of Jibanananda Das himself to a political context very different from that of his own time. Sarkar himself named this context. He described his poem as voicing the desire of those who had been killed by police during the 'recent [1964] food movement in [West] Bengal'. Here is the poem:

> I shall return again to this Bengal
> From the dark of sleep has called the Ichhamati [river]
> The soil is moist with our blood
> It is as if the Bhagirathi has drawn the outlines of a
> mother's kiss
> On the green, sad banks of Bengal wet from the waves of the
> Jalangi.
> Return I shall.

---

[74] Jibanananda Das, *Jibanananda Daser kabyagrantha* (Jibanananda Das's Books of Poetry), 2 vols (Calcutta: Bengal Publishers, 1981), vol. 1, 201.
[75] Seely, *A Poet Apart*, p. 97.

When the smell of paddy
Surrounds the taste of sun—and the Ichhamati
The Bhagirathi
The Jalangi
Of March
Wild with the offerings of life
Call like some eternal friend in the darkness of sleep
I shall return
'Smitten by Bengal's rivers and fields'.[76]

A political presence of the poetry of *Rupasi Bangla* speaks through
the entire body of this poem. The title quotes from the famous sonnet
by Das: 'When I return to the banks of the Dhansiri, to this Bengal.'
The Jalangi is one of the rivers mentioned in this sonnet that describes
Bengal as 'moistened by the Jalangi River's waves'. Expressions such as
'the taste of sun' are strongly reminiscent of Das's poetic idiom. And
the last sentence of the poem is a direct quotation from the same sonnet in *Rupasi Bangla*: 'When again I come, smitten by Bengal's rivers
and fields.'[77] Note how a political moment—the liberation war in
Bangladesh or the 1964 food movement in West Bengal—can bring
back a romantic access to a collective past, for the sentiments expressed
here are no longer merely personal. It is precisely through these sentiments that one inhabits a time that collapses the past and the present.
It is true that in Sarkar's poem there is no reference to characters from
Dinesh Sen's literary world, characters remembered in the lines of Das's
original sonnets. No talk here of Chand the merchant or of Behula
the truly chaste and devoted wife of medieval Bengal. Bengal here is
represented by the poetic names of her rivers—Jalangi, Bhagirathi, and
Ichhamati. The Bengali past itself combines with death in the image
of a dark depth from where the rivers, now constituting some kind of
primeval past, send forth their primeval call. That call does not belong
to the past. It comes from the future, a future that at the same time is a
return. The martyrs will return from an ancient darkness, the poet tells
us, when they hear the call.

Bengali poetry thus, I suggest, acts as the place where a collective
memory of a now-discredited romantic sense of the political—the

---

[76] Narayan Sarkar, 'Abar ashiba phire', in *He swadesh agnimoy swadesh*, ed.
Kamalesh Sen (Calcutta: New Book Center, 1973), p. 60.

[77] Quoted in Seely, *A Poet Apart*, p. 93.

sense that once enabled Dinesh Sen to look on his history of Bengali literature as a nationalist, that is, political, exercise—is archived. But, in likening this historical process of transmission of sentiments to the process of archiving, I do not mean to say that this archive is simply there in any objective sense for us to make use of it. It is, in that sense, not the archive the historian usually draws on in writing exact and accurate narratives of the past. Nor is it an archive in a metaphorical sense. Bengalis on both sides of the national divide unwittingly make a political archive of their romantic legacy only in the process of their involvement in actual political struggles. Otherwise, the legacy is simply there, as printed words, as aesthetics, as historical monuments to Bengali romanticism, once alive but now dead and cold. In this mode, they can only be revived as merely one's personal sentiments. To proclaim an individual sentiment as something political would indeed be sentimentalism. It is only during 'mass' political struggles—be it the freedom struggle in Bangladesh, the Naxalite movement in West Bengal, or the Swadeshi Movement that desired but failed to mobilize the masses—that the legacy of the romantic moment of our fraught nationalism, mediated by a long line of Bengali poets, may come back to haunt our own political sentiments. When such haunting happens, our being political can no longer be reduced to any one understanding of what it means to be political. Both romantic and social science imaginations jostle in that space.

The legacy of romantic nationalism, however, cannot mean yet another quest for a Bengali identity. As I have tried to show, there never was a stable Bengali identity. A quest today for the Behulas and the Kalketus of yore can only come to grief. The question is: What politics can we reconstitute out of our romantic investment in the language? The politics I have in mind, however, is not programmatic. The making of a romantic literary legacy into a political archive is not something we can will into being. Romantic thoughts no longer furnish our analytical frameworks, but the inheritance of romanticism is built into the Bengali language. Our everyday and unavoidable transactions with the poetry of the language may thus be compared to a practice of vigilant waiting—waiting actively for the return of the moment of a political yield. This vigilant and active waiting can itself be political—listen to the romantic voice of a Bengali communist poet who captures its spirit:

This condition of life
is not for the whole year—
only the few months when it rains.
The blazing fire of the dry wood
will cook rice in no time.
And
whatever is there
will come back into view
sharp and clear.
When the rains depart
we will put out in the sun
everything that is wet
woodchips and all.
Put out in the sun
we shall
even our hearts.[78]

[78] Shubhas Mukhopadhyay, 'Rode Debo', in *Shubhas Mukhopadhyayer srestha kobita* (Calcutta: Dey's, 1976), pp. 116–17.

7

READING FANON
What Use Is Utopian Thought?*

Is there any one political–intellectual problem that defines the twentieth century? Of course, a century is a long span of time marked by many different developments. Yet certain problems sometimes come to the fore. We can think of the European eighteenth century as a global period that saw France and Britain join Portugal, Spain, and the Netherlands as founders of modern empires, and as a period of Enlightenment that powerfully upheld an abstract idea of human equality. It was also, ironically, a period that overlooked the problem of slavery and the question of discrimination against women. The nineteenth century—some very important critics (among whom we have to count Nietzsche) notwithstanding—concluded on a high note of progress, leaving to the peoples of less industrialized and colonized nations the legacies of Marxism and liberalism as the two greatest gifts of European political thought. How would one see the global history of the twentieth century? From what developments of the twentieth century shall we derive our resources to deal with the future?

* The author is grateful to Professor Jörn Rüsen for the original invitation to present this paper at a conference he organized in Essen in 2006 and to discussions with both Professor Rüsen and other participants in the seminar. An earlier version of this chapter appeared in a book published in honour of Alf Luedtke: Belinda Davis, Thomas Lindenberger, Michael Wildt, eds, *Alltag, Erfahrung, Eigensinn: Historisch-anthropologische Erkundungen* (Frankfurt and New York: Campus Verlag, 2008), pp. 74–90.

There could no doubt be more than one answer to this question. Let me begin with one that we have already been given. 'The problem of the twentieth century', wrote the great African American thinker W. E. B. Du Bois, peering into the future just as the century began, 'is the problem of the color-line'.[1] He was prescient in saying this. Du Bois' colour line ran right through the colonial divide in the first 50 or 60 years of the century (or longer in the case of South Africa) and through the lives of those whose ancestors had lived through Atlantic systems of slavery. In Du Bois's words, the colour line concerned 'the relation of the darker to the lighter races of men in Asia and Africa, in America and the islands of the sea'.[2] The same line also divided the indigenous peoples from their white settler-colonial rulers and, as we know, assumed a vicious form in the biological racism of the Nazis. Even when it did not assume the menacingly virulent form of the Nazi imagination, biological racism or varieties of social Darwinism underpinned administrative policies in European colonies. Cultural and historical differences were often used by European colonizers to make subordinated peoples look like inferior and deprived versions of humanity. There were, of course, contrary and anti-imperial voices in Europe—Sankar Muthu's book on the Enlightenment comes to mind—but they usually did not set the tone of policy as European empires consolidated themselves.[3]

Du Bois, however, also pointed to a more positive side of the colour line. He said that 'the characteristic of our age' was 'the contact of European civilization with the world's underdeveloped peoples'. It was true that much of this contact, as he put it, was 'not pleasant to look back upon'. 'War, murder, slavery, extermination, and debauchery,—this has again and again been the result of carrying civilization and the blessed gospel to the isles of the sea and the heathen without the law.'[4] But the very fact of close contact between Europeans and others in large numbers and in everyday life also opened up new human opportunities that, Du Bois hoped, would be taken up by leaders in the

[1] W. E. B. Du Bois, 'Of the Dawn of Freedom', in his *The Souls of the Black Folk* (New York: Penguin Books, 1989; first pub. 1903), p. 13.

[2] Du Bois, 'Of the Dawn of Freedom', p. 13.

[3] Sankar Muthu, *Enlightenment against Empire* (Princeton, NJ: Princeton University Press, 2003).

[4] W. E. B. Du Bois, 'Of the Sons of Master and Men', in *The Souls of Black Folk*, p. 133.

twentieth century. Du Bois's words were prescient again. They powerfully expressed a certain humanism of the oppressed while perhaps
reflecting at the same time certain nineteenth-century ideas about evolution and civilizational hierarchies. There were even some faint echoes
of Nietzsche in the association he made between nobility and strength.
This is what he said:

> It is, then, the strife of all honorable men of the twentieth century to see
> that in the future competition of races the survival of the fittest shall mean
> the triumph of the good, the beautiful, and the true; that we may be able to
> preserve for future civilization all that is really fine and noble and strong, and
> not continue to put premium on greed and impudence and cruelty.[5]

To overcome the colour line and preserve for humanity all that was
good, beautiful, and true is how Du Bois posed the task for his time.
One can look on Mahatma Gandhi, Martin Luther King Jr, and Nelson
Mandela as men who embodied, howsoever partially, the twentieth
century's realization of Du Bois' dream.

Our times are different. They are different in two principal ways.
First of all, the colour line does not quite run in the way it did in colonial, Nazi, or apartheid regimes. 'Racism' as an ideological belief in a
hierarchy of biological races has lost its coherence and has very few
followers today, but the word is still used to denote the multitude of
ways in which human beings are inferiorized, marginalized, demeaned,
threatened, excluded, and dehumanized on the basis of the way they
look or on the basis of a devalorization of their group identity. As the
philosopher Étienne Balibar has put it: on one hand, 'racism' no longer
really exists and, on the other, subtle forms of racial profiling and discrimination proliferate. It is not surprising, as Professor Balibar explained
in a recent lecture he gave at the University of Chicago, that the riots of
November 2005 by the youth of North African descent in the suburbs
of Paris had something to do with forms of policing and administration
that were copied directly from France's colonial practices.[6]

The second big difference that marks the twenty-first century apart
from the twentieth is in the way discussions of globalization now have
to take into account another global phenomenon: climate change or
global warming. One could risk the proposition that if the question of

---

[5] Bois, 'Of the Sons of Master and Men', p. 134.
[6] Étienne Balibar, lecture given at the University of Chicago in Spring 2006.

the twentieth century was the colour-line, the question of this century will be the environment. Now, the literature on globalization and that of global warming view the human being in rather different ways. The former views the human being as endowed with cultural and historical differences; so major questions in globalization analyses turn around the issue of what to do and how to understand differences between humans (hence, the emphases on toleration, cosmopolitanism, cross-cultural conversation, and so on). The scientific literature on global warming, on the other hand, often views humans as already always constituted as one, as members perhaps of a species that through its simultaneous coexistence on the planet and its shared, though uneven and unequal, search for the good life has degraded its own biosphere and the general environment.[7]

In spite of this important difference, however, it is my submission that policies of global strategies for mitigating the effects of climate change will have to take into account sentiments borne out of anti-colonial struggles in many parts of the world—witness how both India and China, in their bargaining with Western nations over measures to be adopted to fight global warming, keep harping on the historical self-interestedness of the Western nations. So the literature on globalization will remain relevant even as we begin to accept our collective responsibility in creating environmental problems that affect us on a planetary scale. It is because they see the world still divided between the West and the rest, that China and India put the stress on seeing this collective and shared responsibility as 'differentiated'. Let me repeat, then, a point Balibar has made on several occasions.[8] We live in a world that is postcolonial in two senses. We have all been profoundly affected by the waves of decolonization that shook the latter half of the twentieth century. And, increasingly, movements of people in large numbers across the world—mainly from the South to the North, propelled by all kinds of crises, ranging from the political to the environmental—ensures that most developed countries today have significant numbers of people from parts of the

[7] See Dipesh Chakrabarty, 'The Climate of History: Four Theses', *Critical Inquiry* (Winter 2009): 197–222 (reprinted in this volume).

[8] Étienne Balibar, 'Europe: Provincial, Common, Universal', unpublished paper presented at the Consortium of Humanities Centers and Institutes Annual Meeting, 17–18 June 2005, University of Utrecht, The Netherlands; and Etienne Balibar, 'Europe: An "Unimagined Frontier of Democracy"', *Diacritics* (Fall–Winter 2003): 37–44.

world previously colonized by European powers. The question of what to do with cultural and historical differences between human groups—to which what is called racism is merely a default response—only becomes more insistent as we enter a postcolonial world in which more people move around from one place to another as migrants and refugees, legal or illegal, skilled or unskilled; a world in which multinational and global or regional agencies, whether private or governmental, supplement the nation state; an age in which even the phenomenon of so-called terrorism cannot but be a multicultural and multinational enterprise. Given what the United Nations projects to be the world's population growth in the next four decades—a one and a half times increase to nine billion is their median projection—and the ageing populations of the richer countries, one can safely predict that this will see further large-scale population movements in the world from the South to the North. Climate change will contribute to the process. So the problems of global warming will have to be dealt with in a world that has also been shaped by the processes and cultural politics of globalization.

The globalized world is what we inhabit: connected, fluvial, and 'flat' and crowded, as the Indian software entrepreneur Nandan Nilekani put it and as the expression has been adopted by the *New York Times* columnist Thomas Friedman.[9] On the one hand, this is an exciting world full of human possibilities as we increasingly come into contact with people who are not like ourselves. It should promote an ethos of cosmopolitanism throughout the world, whether officially so-called or not. This could be a world that actually promoted more human toleration and understanding by generating identifications that challenged and crossed national boundaries. On the other hand, the presence of cultural differences could also produce more prejudice and fear. One powerful version of this fear that has acquired some notoriety is, of course, Huntington's thesis about the clash of civilizations. Another has been the fear of refugees and immigrants (legal and illegal) in many countries of the Western democracies. Besides, as Foucault pointed out in his lectures at Collège de France in 1976—published in English under the title *'Society Must be Defended'* —the ways modern societies manage populations on a large scale (methods that Foucault called Regulation in order to distinguish them

---

[9] See Thomas L. Friedman, *The World Is Flat: A Brief History of the Twenty-First Century* (New York: Farrar, Strauss and Giroux, 2006), pp. 4–8.

from his idea of Discipline) undermine liberal principles of government.[10] Governments have never officially subscribed to the Huntington thesis, with even President Bush acknowledging that civilizations, including the Islamic one, are always internally plural and contradictory. But it is clear that as Western governments necessarily become more security-minded in the fight against ill-defined and seemingly interminable forces of terror, they adopt 'emergency' measures that both undercut civil liberties and are deployed at the same time to control immigration as well. Given the nature of modern 'terrorism', this is an emergency with no end in sight!

When Hannah Arendt wrote *The Human Condition* in the late 1950s, she did so, as she put it, from 'the vantage point of our newest experiences and our most recent fears'.[11] At the end of the twentieth century, globalization, I submit, became simultaneously a site of our 'newest experiences and our most recent fears' about fellow human beings. (I leave aside for the moment the kind of experiences and alarmed reactions global warming has given rise to.) It is, therefore, all the more urgent that we devote our collective attention to questions of humanism and to the problem of how to think about and relate to—or even converse across—cultural and historical differences.

Globalization often appears as a 'blind force' in people's lives making them a 'victim' of it. Yet if we are to participate, however vicariously, in some sense of having agency over its processes, we need to be able to spell out visions of humanity that propel such a movement. Questions abound. Will globalization lead to one global culture that the media will both mould and sell? Will globalization mean that all our claims to cultural differences will survive only if we can make such differences into marketable commodities so that the 'local' becomes merely an inflection of global capitalism? Or will globalization lead to the emergence of a universal humanism that is enriched by numerous particulars? The time has come for the world to produce a new charter of humanism, now that the nation state is no longer the exclusive repository of cultural difference. The problem, if anything, is accentuated by the emergent crisis of climate change, for we cannot strategically become 'one' (which is what

---

[10] Michel Foucault, *'Society Must be Defended': Lectures at Collège de France*, trans. David Macey (New York: Picador, 2003).

[11] Hannah Arendt, *The Human Condition* (Chicago: University of Chicago Press, 1998 [1958]), p. 5.

we in part need to do to synchronize human responses to questions of global warming) if our claims to difference go unrecognized.

How do we find those moments in human history when human beings have desired togetherness without their differences being made into excuses for domination? I want to begin by suggesting that one exemplary archive of such thought would be the writings of anti-colonial and anti-imperial thinkers of the twentieth century. These were people deeply engaged with the traditions that made Europe modern and who yet knew first-hand the exclusionary tendencies of the humanism that European colonizers preached to the colonized. These thinkers felt compelled to consider afresh the problem of being human and to reflect on the need for a new kind of humanist charter as part of their effort to build a world in which the domination of humans by humans would be finished for once and for all. This was utopian thought to be sure—for I am enough of a Nietzschean to grant the will to power that animates human existence in everyday life—but a utopian thought that was badly needed. For there could not be any modern anti-colonial movement without utopian dreams of a world without domination; it was such utopian dreams that one hurled at the face of one's enemy, the colonial masters. The utopian nature of anti-colonial thought is also exposed in the fact that no ex-colonial nation, on independence, has ever kept the promise it made with itself while fighting the indignity of colonial rule. Postcolonial states and nations have often repeated the sins of colonial rule with respect to their own populations.[12] Yet anti-colonial, utopian humanism remains valuable as an archive precisely because this humanism turns around certain axes—the universal versus the particular, the ideal versus the pragmatic, the past as a resource (tradition, as in the hands of a Tagore or Gandhi) versus the need to overcome the past— that often act as organizing themes for contemporary debates as well.

Anti-colonial Humanism

My case in point is the anti-colonial humanism of Frantz Fanon and of Negritude thinkers such as Leopold Senghor and Aimé Césaire. I choose them for a particular reason. When I read about Fanon's and

---

[12] See my 'Introduction' to Dipesh Chakrabarty, Rochona Majumdar, and Andrew Sartori, eds, *From the Colonial to the Postcolonial: India and Pakistan in Transition* (New Delhi: Oxford University Press, 2007).

Césaire's and Senghor's restless spirit in their struggle against the colonizing humanism of the ruling race they encountered, and I reconsider my own Indian background—and my background in Indian history—I realize that colonial rule was not the same everywhere, nor were the compulsions of the race-dynamic the same. A Gandhi or a Tagore or a Nehru—the three most universalist and yet profoundly Indian anticolonial thinkers I can recall immediately—never theorized race with the intensity of Negritude writers or writers in the African American diaspora. It was not that Indians did not come across incidents of unpleasant and extreme British arrogance. But in their experience of colonial rule, racism remained episodic rather than something constitutive of colonial relations of power. Readers of Gandhi's autobiography will notice how often in South Africa he used to think of law as a weapon against racism. Perhaps the low castes—in particular the so-called untouchable groups—experienced something like racism but that was at the hands of other Indians. The British did not oppress the 'middle class' they created in India in quite in the same way as the French did the 'natives' in Francophone Africa or the Caribbean islands, so we bring to today's questions somewhat different legacies when we argue from the experience of colonial rule in India. A Fanon or a Senghor or a Césaire had to purchase their universal humanism at a price that anti-colonial Indians perhaps never had to pay.

Utopian thought is unrealizable by definition. In that sense it always fails. Fanon's thoughts are interesting because his is a rich and instructive case of failure. Fanon, who was born in Martinique in 1925 and who died in a Washington hospital in the United States in 1961, was a product and prisoner of European thought. Indeed, it is impossible to think of his works without reference to the Parisian milieu of Marxism, existentialism, and psychiatry of the 1940s and the 1950s. But he was also someone who burned with a spirit of rebellion against the way European colonial rule and its attendant racism showed up what was problematic in the colonizing humanism of Europeans. As he declaimed, angrily and with some rhetorical liberties, asking for a new beginning to human history: 'Leave this Europe where they are never done talking of man, yet murder men everywhere they find them.'[13] But where would one go, leaving 'this'

---

[13] Frantz Fanon, *The Wretched of the Earth*, trans. Constance Farrington (New York: Grove Press, 1963), p. 311.

Europe? Not back to a blackness that had been proclaimed by Fanon's mentors such as Leopold Sédar Senghor (1906–2001), the Senegalese poet and intellectual and later president of the country, and Aimé Césaire (1913–2008), the poet who was once Fanon's teacher in Martinique and was later to be the mayor of Fort de France and a deputy to the French parliament, both of them among the foremost creators of the Negritude movement in Paris in the 1930s and the 1940s. That option did not work for Fanon and we will soon see why. For him, there was nowhere to go but to create a new beginning with European thought outside of Europe, to rescue from Europeans their heritage of the abstract humanism of the Enlightenment—the human who is the subject of the idea of human rights as spelled out at the end of the eighteenth century—and make that everybody's heritage everywhere. Fanon was never a nationalist and never failed to acknowledge what one owed to Europe: 'All the elements of a solution to the great problems of humanity have, at different times, existed in European thought.' The problem was that the 'action of European men has not carried out the mission which fell to them'.[14] America was no alternative model either, for its institution of slavery mocked at every step its loyalty to the values of the Enlightenment:

> Two centuries ago, a former European colony decided to catch up with Europe. It succeeded so well that the United States of America became a monster, in which the taints, the sickness, and the inhumanity of Europe have grown to appalling dimensions.[15]

Hence the option before the Third World—for Fanon wrote at a time when this concept still held ground—could not be that of catching up with Europe or becoming like America (that is, modernization programmes). The choice, according to Fanon, was profoundly new and yet in a deep sense connected to Europe:

> Let us create the whole man, whom Europe has been incapable of bringing to triumphant birth.... No, there is no question of return to Nature. It is simply a concrete question of not dragging men toward mutilation.... No, we do not want to catch up with anyone. What we want to do is to go forward all the time, night and day, in the company of Man, in the company of all men.... It is a question of the Third World starting a new history of Man, a history which will have regard to the sometimes prodigious theses which

[14] Fanon, *The Wretched of the Earth*, p. 314.
[15] Fanon, *The Wretched of the Earth* , p. 313.

Europe has put forward, but which will also not forget Europe's crimes, of which the most horrible was committed in the heart of man.[16]

The target of Fanon's new universalism was not merely the failed application of universalist thought by European colonists who always replaced the abstract figure of the human or man by that of the white man, saying to the Native, 'be like me!' and thus mistaking sameness for equality and setting up the never-ending game of the 'native' always having to catch up (the French called it 'assimilation') with the European.[17] Fanon was disagreeing with his mentors as well—Césaire and Senghor. Both Senghor and Césaire—deeply immersed in Parisian debates to do with Hegel and dialectics, Heidegger and existentialism, Breton and surrealism—rejected the French republican version of colonial humanism. The French, as is well known, granted colonized people French nationality without full citizenship that they advocated only for a tiny native elite, depending on their perceived stage of evolution. Alternatively, as Gary Wilder has shown in his book on French cultural policies in their colonial territories, 'educated elites were supposed to be those exceptional natives who had become autonomous individuals'. 'Yet they were identified as incipient individuals who were never yet ready to assume full citizenship rights because of the irreducible residue of African culture they supposedly could not transcend.' Wilder thus characterizes the imperatives of what he calls colonial (and official) humanism as 'individualism without individuality, collectivity without collectivism, citizenship without culture, nationality without citizenship, training without civil society'.[18]

This was a humanism that belittled the colonized. Senghor and Césaire were right to reject it. Instead, they used their poetic gifts and their affiliations with a variety of aesthetic movements—black literature coming out of the African American diaspora, existentialism, French and German colonial ethnography, surrealism, and Marxism—to develop a poetic diction that emphasized their refusal to be assimilated into French universalist ideas by exploring, creatively, the different dimensions of

---

[16] Fanon, *The Wretched of the Earth*, pp. 313–15.

[17] See the excellent discussion in Gary Wilder, *The French Imperial Nation-State: Negritude and Colonial Humanism* (Chicago: University of Chicago Press, 2005), Part 2.

[18] Wilder, *The French Imperial Nation-State*, pp. 133–5, 143.

their blackness and African roots. It was as if they declared a war of the particular against the universal. The result was the famous Negritude movement that both invigorated and disturbed many black intellectuals including Fanon and, later, Wole Soyinka, who once famously asked, in criticism and banter, 'Does the Tiger need to display its Tigritude?'

There has been much written on the works of Negritude writers and on Senghor and Césaire specifically and I do not intend to revisit that literature here. What is of interest to me is the fact that this war of the particular against the universal was not anti-universal in itself. Césaire and Senghor were definitely trying to resist the French imperial attempt to assimilate them into a Frenchness that for the colonized could only be an instrument of exclusion and oppression. They would therefore—and by way of claiming their roots—seek to introduce into their works images and sounds of an Africa they expressed nostalgia for: the Africa of sensuality, of nights where the tom-tom beat out its rhythms to the 'music of Koras and the Balaphon', and of villages that did not aim to expand, occupy, and civilize the land of others. As Senghor wrote in one of his poems:

> At the bend in the road the river, blue by the cool September meadows.
> A paradise protecting from fever a child who eyes are bright like two Swords
> Paradise my African childhood, protecting innocence from Europe.[19]

Or consider these lines from Césaire's celebrated *Notes on the Return to One's Land of Birth*—immortal monuments to anti-colonial criticism of the Europe that saw in its worldly power to subjugate others the proof its 'superior' civilization:

> Eia for those who have never invented anything
> for those who never explored anything
> for those who never conquered anything
> but yield, captivated to the essence of all things
> ignorant of surfaces but captivated by the motion of all things
> indifferent to conquering, but playing the game of the world.[20]

[19] Senghor cited in Linn Cary Mehta, 'Poetry and Decolonization: Tagore, Yeats, Senghor, Césaire, and Neruda, 1914–1950', PhD dissertation, Columbia University, 2004, p. 326.

[20] Césaire's *Cahier d'un retour au pays natal* (1939, begun 1936) cited in Wilder, *The French Imperial Nation-State*, pp. 287–8.

This turning back to Africa or blackness—a 'will to particularism', as he once called it—was something Fanon could never accept.[21] For one thing, he thought that the Negritude movement papered over all that divided Africans from Africans or the African from the African American or the African American from the black people of the Antilles.[22] But more to the point, he believed that the black peoples of colonial Africa and even those of America and the Caribbean islands had had their pasts so changed by the colonial impact that there was no way of returning to a pre-colonial past escaping Europeans' representations of it: 'Colonialism is not satisfied merely holding a people in its grip.... By a kind of perverted logic, it turns to the past of the oppressed people, and distorts, disfigures, and destroys it'.[23] There was nothing to be found in claiming the colour line for oneself:

> The Negro problem does not resolve itself into the problem of Negroes living among white men but rather of Negroes exploited, enslaved, despised by a colonialist, capitalist society that is only accidentally white.[24]

Or as he put it differently in the same text: 'The discovery of the existence of a Negro civilization in the fifteenth century confers no patent of humanity on me. Like it or not, the past can in no way guide me in the present moment.[25]

Fanon's description of Negritude poetry as a 'will to particularism' was at the very least a misreading of what Césaire and Senghor and their comrades intended to achieve. It is true, as Fanon charged, that Senghor or Césaire owed their romanticism of Africa to the sympathies of colonial ethnography. The German Africanist and ethnologist Leo Frobenius, whose books were quickly translated into French, had a great influence on Senghor, for instance. Senghor actually wrote a foreword to a Frobenius anthology in 1973 and thus remembered his impact:

> I still have before me ... the copy of the *Histoire de la Civilisation Africaine* on the third page of which Césaire wrote: 'décembre 1936.' ... I was intellectually on familiar terms with the greatest Africanists and above

---

[21] Fanon, *The Wretched of the Earth*, p. 239.

[22] Fanon, *The Wretched of the Earth*, the chapter 'National Culture'.

[23] Fanon, *The Wretched of the Earth*, p. 210.

[24] Frantz Fanon, *Black Skin, White Masks*, trans. Charles Lam Markmann (London: Paladin, 1970 [1952]), p. 144.

[25] Fanon, *Black Skin, White Masks*, p. 160.

all the ethnologists and the linguists. But suddenly, like a thunderclap—Frobenius! All the history and pre-history of Africa were illuminated, to their very depths. And we still carry the mark of the master in our minds and spirits, like a form of tattooing carried out in the initiation ceremonies in the sacred grove. We knew by heart Chapter II of the first book of the History, entitled 'What Does Africa Mean to Us?', a chapter adorned with lapidary phrases such as this: 'The idea of the 'barbarous Negro' is a European invention, which in turn dominated Europe until the beginning of this century'.[26]

So Fanon was right: the past Senghor and Césaire related to was already a creation of European Africanists. But where Fanon misread the intention of Senghor and Césaire was in not recognizing that they also were looking for a universal humanism but through a different path. As Senghor once put it: 'To be nègre is to recover what is human beneath the rust of what is artificial and of "human conventions."'[27] A lecture Senghor gave at the Dakar Chamber of Commerce on 8 September 1937 sought to demonstrate 'that universal humanism, when pushed to its logical limit, necessarily leads to a spatiotemporally specific cultural humanism'.[28] And he was clear that he was not looking for any 'authentic African culture': 'Our milieu is no longer West Africa, it is also French, it is international; we should say, it is Afro-French.' Implying 'that the universal human being always and only exists in culturally mediated forms', he rejected, as Wilder puts it, both 'the universalizing racism of the civilizing mission and the particularizing racism of the white supremacists'.[29] In fact, the first volume of his collected works was called Liberté: Négritude et humanisme (Liberty: Negritude and Humanism). He claimed that the book was a 'cornerstone in the edification of the Civilization of the Universal, which will be the common work of all races, of all different civilizations.... It has been enriched by the contribution of European civilization, which it has likewise enriched.... Negritude is therefore not a racism ... In truth, Negritude is a Humanism.'[30]

The same could be said of Césaire whose Notes included the prayer: 'Preserve me from all hatred/ do not make me into that man of hatred for

---

26 Cited in Mehta, 'Poetry and Decolonization', p. 301.
27 Senghor cited in Wilder, The French Imperial Nation-State, pp. 188–9.
28 Senghor cited in Wilder, The French Imperial Nation-State, p. 235.
29 Senghor cited in Wilder, The French Imperial Nation-State, p. 241.
30 Senghor cited in Wilder, The French Imperial Nation-State, p. 250.

whom I only feel hatred / for entrenched as I am in this unique race ... that what I want is universal hunger / for universal thirst.'[31] In an interview with René Depestre, Césaire added: 'My will to be rooted is ferocious. Hegel once wrote that the universal is not the negation of the particular, because one moves toward the universal through a deepening of the particular.' And in a famous letter in 1956 to Maurice Thorez, on the occasion of the resignation of his membership of the French Communist Party, Césaire remarked: 'Provincialism? Not at all. I do not enclose myself in a narrow particularism. But nor do I want to lose myself in a lifeless universalism. There are two ways to lose oneself: through walled segregation within the particular and through dilution within the universal. My conception of the universal is of a universal enriched by every particular.'[32] Césaire was intensely aware of the utopian nature of his project and that is why he found in poetry an effective resolution of the universal and the particular. In opposition to Sartre and others who thought the French language could not be an effective vehicle for the expression of Africanness or blackness, Césaire said in an interview published in 1978:

> I am not a prisoner of the French language. I try and have always wanted to *bend* French. That's why I have had a strong affection for Mallarmé, because he has shown me ... that language at bottom is arbitrary. It is not a natural phenomenon.... My effort has been to bend the French language, to transform it in order to express, let us say, 'this self, this black, creole, Martinican, West Indian self.' That is why I am much more interested in poetry than in prose, precisely to the extent that the poet creates his language.... I re-create a language that is not French. If the French rediscover their language in mine, well, that's their affair.[33]

As is well known, what prompted Fanon's critique of Negritude was Sartre's gloss on Negritude in his introduction entitled 'Black Orpheus' to Senghor's 1948 collection of Negritude poetry. Sartre described Negritude as 'a temporary "racist anti-racism" that would

---

[31] Senghor cited in Wilder, *The French Imperial Nation-State*, p. 288.

[32] Senghor cited in Wilder, *The French Imperial Nation-State*, p. 290.

[33] See Aimé Césaire, *Non-vicious Circle: Twenty Poems of Aimé Césaire*, trans. and introduced by Gregson Davis (Stanford, CA: Stanford University Press, 1984), p. 14. A related but different politics of the French language is present in the writings of Édouard Glissant. See his *Poetics of Relation*, trans. Betsy Wing (Ann Arbor: The University of Michigan Press, 1997 [1990]).

be transcended by the dialectic of history'.[34] Fanon said to his friends: 'The generation of young black poets has received a blow they will not recover from.'[35] That blow, one feels, shaped much of the argument in *Black Skin, White Masks*. Fanon now felt that 'every hand was a losing hand'. 'I wanted to be typically Negro—it was no longer possible. I wanted to be white—it was a joke.'[36] Sartre had made a 'minor dialectic' of Negritude in the larger Hegelian schema of world transformation. The Negro's 'anti-racist racism' was only a temporary phenomenon soon to be superseded by the coming of a universal humanist consciousness: 'Beyond the black-skinned men of his race it is the battle of the world proletariat that is his song.'[37] Fanon decided that the only way open to him was to struggle for a completely new universal, not as a black man—for he only happened to be black—and not even as a historical man descended from slaves ('I am not the slave of the Slavery that dehumanized my ancestors'). 'The Negro is not.', he wrote, putting a deliberate full stop after 'not' and starting a new sentence: 'Any more than the white man.' 'There is no Negro mission; there is no white burden.'[38] What there was, was the Enlightenment mission of valuing the abstract human being of human rights, someone who is entitled to our civility long before we have in any way placed him or her in any historical or social context.[39] But this was precisely the mission that the white man, self-absorbed in his arrogant sense of supremacy, was not able to carry out. How would the oppressed man of colour keep that pledge to the Enlightenment? This is where Fanon mobilized the rhetorical power of the figure of redemptive violence and called for an act of complete volition by which, at one stroke, to leap out of history:

> No attempt must be made to encase man, for it is his destiny to be set free. The body of history does not determine a single one of my actions.

[34] David Macey, *Frantz Fanon: A Biography* (New York: Picador, 2000), p. 187.

[35] Fanon, *Black Skin, White Masks*, p. 94.

[36] Fanon, *Black Skin, White Masks*, pp. 93–4.

[37] Sartre quoted in Fanon, *Black Skin, White Masks*, p. 94.

[38] Fanon, *Black Skin, White Masks*, pp. 163–5.

[39] Julia Kristeva's discussion of the French declaration of civil and human rights in *Strangers to Ourselves*, trans. Leon Roudiez (New York: Columbia University Press, 1991).

I am my own foundation.
And it is by going beyond the historical, instrumental hypothesis that I will
initiate the cycle of my freedom.

...

I, the man of colour, want only this:
... That the enslavement of man by man cease for ever.... That it be possible
for me to discover and to love man, wherever he may be.

...

My final prayer:
O my body, make of me always a man who questions![40]

Fanon as Heritage

Let me draw some lessons from the story I have recounted in this essay.
We have three positions on humanism here. First, Sartre's in his 'Black
Orpheus' where he wanted to say that the Negritude emphasis on
blackness and race—on the particular, say—was a temporary recourse
to anti-racist racism, soon to be sublated into a superior term of history's dialectic, universal proletarian consciousness. Fanon's biographer,
David Macey, has pointed out what was problematic about this position: 'Sartre falls into a trap of his own making, and he describes that
very trap in his *Réflexions* when speaks of the "democrat's" inability to
recognize the Jew in the assertion of his Jewishness and in his insistence
on the need to see him [the Jew] as a universal.'[41] Then there was
Frantz Fanon's position that called for an entirely new historical stab at
Enlightenment humanism, except that it was a task that now belonged
to anti-colonial people of colour. But the creation of this universal called
for something like a violent action of the will, akin to jumping out of
one's own skin. It has never been realized in the world and cannot
be, for it is extreme in its deliberate inattention to history. It is a programme for violence that implodes from within.[42] The third position
is that of Césaire's or Senghor's that does look for a path to universal
humanism but a universal that will never be able to fold completely
into itself—and thereby subsume in a Hegelian way—any particular

---

[40] Fanon, *Black Skin, White Masks*, pp. 164–5.

[41] Macey, *Frantz Fanon*, p. 187. Macey explains that by 'democrat' Sartre
meant 'wooly liberal'.

[42] None of this, however, denies the poetic appeal of Sartre's or Fanon's
universals or their capacity to seem apt in certain specific circumstances.

that enriches it. The Jew will be allowed his assertion of Jewishness as will be the Muslim his Muslimness, so long as the assertion of the particular does not aim to destroy the universal.

The question is: What is the use of this remembrance? For it may be said against my invocation of the familiar names of Fanon, Césaire, or Senghor that they, in turn, remind us of the radicalism of the sixties, forms of utopian thinking that may appear useless in the face of a world in which capitalist globalization and domination seem inexorable. Today's tasks, it may be said, ought to be humbler and pragmatic, and not echo the seductive but powerless dreams of these anti-colonial thinkers. But what use, one might counter, is a pragmatism the logic of which amounts to simple capitulation to that forces one once set out to fight? Should one not instead try and develop pragmatisms that rework and recall—in however fragmented and practical a manner— the idealisms of the past that once sought to change the world, lock, stock, and barrel? Let me give a concrete example of this phenomenon from postcolonial writing. Salman Rushdie's subversion of the English language from within may seem pragmatic and practical without being driven by a revolutionary or totalizing intent. But can one deny that it stands on the shoulders of the efforts of anti-colonial writers such as Césaire whose desire to 'bend French' arose out of a desire for total anti-colonial autonomy?

Our indebtedness to the sixties is not simply a historical one for in that case it could be a 'bad debt' that we may not ever be able to— or even want to—repay in an age when Foucault and a host of other thinkers have made us suspicious of all universals that not only seem utopian at best but even more dangerously like so many ruses of power at worst. Since no universal humanism, Hegelian, Marxian, or Fanonian or even that of a Senghor or Cesaire, appears to interrupt with the force of necessity any of the pure contingency of events that constitute globalization and global warming, one might argue that all we have left is the endless procession of one contingency meeting another to create the unavoidable and conflicted space of history within which we find ourselves. These conflicts of contingencies admit of no metanarratives. We should better be practical, it would be argued.

Yet being practical and pragmatic by itself never bridges the gap between what is and what ought to be in human affairs. Our normative visions of history are always utopian. The idea that the normative or the reasonable will realize itself in history through some kind of 'cunning of reason' does not any longer inspire confidence. But if we did not keep alive some form of political activism around what ought to be in human affairs, what intellectual resources would we have to draw upon when, suddenly and contingently, a moment of necessity erupts in human history? Take the case of global warming, which I mentioned at the beginning of this chapter. We all know what ought to happen: nations need to come together and act concertedly in the name of humanity to drastically and immediately reduce our greenhouse gas emissions. While this 'ought' position is known and accepted on all hands, contingent, everyday, practical politics is caught up in questions of responsibility and 'climate justice' and in the talk about the 'West and the rest' divide, while we all acknowledge the biosphere to be common to all humans. There is no straight path from the everyday and the realm of the possible to the realm of what ought to be. The talk of humanity in everyday politics sounds either self-interested or naïve and vapid. How do we think about the connection here between the contingency and necessity?

Here, in conclusion, it may be useful to introduce the idea of the *clinamen*, which Cesare Casarino, in a recent essay that meditates on Pasolini's poems on Gramsci, has excavated from the work of the late Louis Althusser. Althusser said, invoking the idea of the clinamen as found in the atomistic materialism of Democritean and Epicurean philosophies: 'Rather than thinking of contingency as a modality of necessity [that is, the realization of a universal] or as an exception to necessity, one ought to think of necessity as the becoming-necessary of the encounter of contingencies.'[43] The clinamen in ancient Greek philosophy, explains Casarino, 'is that inclination or curve in the free fall of the atoms that ultimately causes them to collide with one another, thereby begetting the world'. It marks, Casarino glosses further, 'that bending force which produced contingency and necessity as immanent to one another rather than producing one as transcendent with respect

[43] Louis Althusser, 'Une philosophie pour le marxisme: 'La ligne de Démocrite', in *Sur la philosophie* (Paris: Gallimard, 1994), p. 42, translated in Cesare Casarino, 'The Southern Answer: Pasolini, Universalism, Decolonization', *Critical Inquiry* 36, no. 4 (Summer 2010): 673–96.

to the other, that force which produces the world of necessity as the becoming-necessary of the contingent encounters of atoms'.[44]

Obviously, we do not have to take ancient Greek physics seriously. It is the image of contingencies bringing into being—through their own contingent encounters—the necessary moment of the universal that concerns us here. Normal, everyday politics maintains a gap between what seems practical and pragmatic and what ought to be. Utopian thought leaps across the gap between the contingent and the necessary, between what is in the realm of the everyday and what ought to be. By itself such thought cannot produce the necessity it speaks to. But the clinamen of the ancient Greek imagination—that curve in the free fall of contingencies that brought atoms together to create the becoming-necessary of the contingent—may indeed operate in human affairs. One day, the contingencies may indeed collide in such a way as to make the question of acting in the name of humanity a necessary question, so deep and urgent may indeed be our sense of the crisis. To keep alive utopian thought is to keep alive the possibility of a politics that can supplement—not displace—the politics of the possible.

That is why we need to remember the universal humanism of a Fanon or a Senghor—the universalism of the oppressed. This act of simultaneously nurturing that which ought to be while both engaging that which is and waiting for the moment of the becoming-necessary of the contingent may be likened to a certain kind of work: the work of keeping the powder dry for the day we need it.

44 Casarino, 'The Southern Question'.

II

THE PLANETARY HUMAN

8

THE CLIMATE OF HISTORY
Four Theses*

The current planetary crisis of climate change or global warming elicits a variety of responses in individuals, groups, and governments, ranging from denial, disconnect, and indifference to a spirit of engagement and activism of varying kinds and degrees. These responses saturate our sense of the now. Alan Weisman's best-selling book *The World without Us* suggests a thought experiment as a way of experiencing our present: 'Suppose that the worst has happened. Human extinction is a fait accompli.... Picture a world from which we all suddenly vanished.... Might we have left some faint, enduring mark on the universe? ... Is it possible that, instead of heaving a huge biological sigh of relief, the world without us would miss us?'[1] I am drawn to Weisman's experiment as it tellingly demonstrates how the current crisis can precipitate a sense of the present that disconnects the future from the past by putting such a future beyond the grasp of historical sensibility. The

* Edited from *Critical Inquiry* 35, no. 2 (Winter 2009): 197–222. This essay is dedicated to the memory of Greg Dening. Thanks are due to Lauren Berlant, James Chandler, Carlo Ginzburg, Tom Mitchell, Sheldon Pollock, Bill Brown, Françoise Meltzer, Debjani Ganguly, Ian Hunter, Julia A. Thomas, and Rochona Majumdar for critical comments on an earlier draft. I wrote the first version of this essay in Bengali for a journal in Calcutta and remain grateful to its editor, Asok Sen, for encouraging me to work on this topic.
[1] Alan Weisman, *The World without Us* (New York: Thomas Dunne/St. Martin's Press, 2007), pp. 3–5.

discipline of history exists on the assumption that our past, present, and future are connected by a certain continuity of human experience. We normally envisage the future with the help of the same faculty that allows us to picture the past. Weisman's thought experiment illustrates the historicist paradox that inhabits contemporary moods of anxiety and concern about the finitude of humanity. To go along with Weisman's experiment, we have to insert ourselves into a future 'without us' in order to be able to visualize it. Thus, our usual historical practices for visualizing times, past and future, times inaccessible to us personally—the exercise of historical understanding—are thrown into a deep contradiction and confusion. Weisman's experiment indicates how such confusion follows from our contemporary sense of the present insofar as that present gives rise to concerns about our future. Our historical sense of the present, in Weisman's version, has thus become deeply destructive of our general sense of history.

I will return to Weisman's experiment in the last part of this chapter. There is much in the debate on climate change that should be of interest to those involved in contemporary discussions about history. For as the idea gains ground that the grave environmental risks of global warming have to do with excessive accumulation in the atmosphere of greenhouse gases produced mainly through the burning of fossil fuel and the industrialized use of animal stock by human beings, certain scientific propositions have come into circulation in the public domain that have profound, even transformative, implications for how we think about human history or about what the historian C. A. Bayly recently called 'the birth of the modern world'.[2] Indeed, what scientists have said about climate change challenges not only the ideas about the human that usually sustain the discipline of history but also the analytic strategies that postcolonial and post-imperial historians have deployed in the last two decades in response to the post-war scenario of decolonization and globalization.

In what follows, I present some responses to the contemporary crisis from a historian's point of view. However, a word about my own relationship to the literature on climate change—and indeed to the crisis itself—may be in order. I am a practicing historian with a strong interest

[2] See C. A. Bayly, *The Birth of the Modern World, 1780–1914: Global Connections and Comparisons* (Malden, MA: Blackwell, 2004).

in the nature of history as a form of knowledge, and my relationship to the science of global warming is derived, at some remove, from what scientists and other informed writers have written for the education of the general public. Scientific studies of global warming are often said to have originated with the discoveries of the Swedish scientist Svante Arrhenius in the 1890s, but self-conscious discussions of global warming in the public realm began in the late 1980s and early 1990s, the same period in which social scientists and humanists began to discuss globalization.[3] However, these discussions have so far run parallel to each other. While globalization, once recognized, was of immediate interest to humanists and social scientists, global warming, in spite of a good number of books published in the 1990s, did not become a public concern until the 2000s. The reasons are not far to seek. As early as 1988, James Hansen, the director of NASA's Goddard Institute of Space Studies, told a Senate committee about global warming and later remarked to a group of reporters on the same day: 'It's time to stop waffling ... and say that the greenhouse effect is here and is affecting our climate.'[4] But governments, beholden to special interests and wary of political costs, would not listen. George H. W. Bush, then the president of the United States, famously quipped that he was going to fight the greenhouse effect with the 'White House effect'.[5] The situation changed in the 2000s when the warnings became dire, and the signs of the crisis—such as the drought in Australia, frequent cyclones and brush fires, crop failures in many parts of the world, the melting of Himalayan and other mountain glaciers and of the polar ice caps, and the increasing acidity of the seas and the damage to the food chain— became politically and economically inescapable. Added to this were

[3] The prehistory of the science of global warming going back to nineteenth-century European scientists such as Joseph Fourier, Louis Agassiz, and Arrhenius is recounted in many popular publications. See, for example, the book by Bert Bolin, the chairman of the UN's Intergovernmental Panel on Climate Change (1988–97), *A History of the Science and Politics of Climate Change: The Role of the Intergovernmental Panel on Climate Change* (Cambridge: Cambridge University Press, 2007), pt 1.

[4] Quoted in Mark Bowen, *Censoring Science: Inside the Political Attack on Dr. James Hansen and the Truth of Global Warming* (New York: Dutton, 2008), p. 1.

[5] Quoted in Bowen, *Censoring Science*, p. 228. See also Bill McKibben, 'Too Hot to Handle: Recent Efforts to Censor Jim Hansen', *Boston Globe*, 5 February 2006, p. E1.

growing concerns, voiced by many, about the rapid destruction of other species and about the global footprint of a human population poised to pass the nine billion mark by 2050.[6]

As the crisis gathered momentum in the last few years, I realized that all my readings in theories of globalization, Marxist analysis of capital, subaltern studies, and postcolonial criticism over the last 25 years, while enormously useful in studying globalization, had not really prepared me for making sense of this planetary conjuncture within which humanity finds itself today. The change of mood in globalization analysis may be seen by comparing Giovanni Arrighi's masterful history of world capitalism, The Long Twentieth Century (1994), with his more recent Adam Smith in Beijing (2007), which, among other things, seeks to understand the implications of the economic rise of China. The first book, a long meditation on the chaos internal to capitalist economies, ends with the thought of capitalism burning up humanity 'in the horrors (or glories) of the escalating violence that has accompanied the liquidation of the Cold War world order'. It is clear that the heat that burns the world in Arrighi's narrative comes from the engine of capitalism and not from global warming. By the time Arrighi comes to write Adam Smith in Beijing, however, he is much more concerned with the question of ecological limits to capitalism. That theme provides the concluding note of the book, suggesting the distance that a critic such as Arrighi has travelled in the thirteen years that separate the publication of the two books.[7] If, indeed, globalization and global warming are born of overlapping processes, the question is how we bring them together in our understanding of the world.

Not being a scientist myself, I also make a fundamental assumption about the science of climate change. I assume the science to be right in its broad outlines. I thus assume that the views expressed particularly in the 2007 Fourth Assessment Report of the Intergovernmental Panel on Climate Change of the United Nations, in the Stern Review, and

---

[6] See, for example, Walter K. Dodds, Humanity's Footprint: Momentum, Impact, and Our Global Environment (New York: Columbia University Press, 2008), pp. 11–62.

[7] Giovanni Arrighi, The Long Twentieth Century: Money, Power, and the Origins of Our Times (London: Verso, 2006 [1994]), p. 356; see Giovanni Arrighi, Adam Smith in Beijing: Lineages of the Twenty-First Century (London: Verso, 2007), pp. 227–389.

in the many books that have been published recently by scientists and scholars seeking to explain the science of global warming leave me with enough rational ground for accepting, unless the scientific consensus shifts in a major way, that there is a large measure of truth to the anthropogenic theories of climate change.[8] For this position, I depend on observations such as the following one reported by Naomi Oreskes, a historian of science at the University of California, San Diego. Upon examining the abstracts of 928 papers on global warming published in specialized peer-reviewed scientific journals between 1993 and 2003, Oreskes found that not a single one sought to refute the 'consensus' among scientists 'over the reality of human-induced climate change'. There is disagreement over the amount and direction of change. But 'virtually all professional climate scientists', writes Oreskes, 'agree on the reality of human-induced climate change, but debate continues on tempo and mode'.[9] Indeed, in what I have read so far, I have not seen any reason yet for remaining a global-warming sceptic.

The scientific consensus around the proposition that the present crisis of climate change is man-made forms the basis of what I have to

---

[8] An indication of the growing popularity of the topic is the number of books published in the last four years with the aim of educating the general reading public about the nature of the crisis. Here is a brief list of some of the most recent titles that inform this essay: Mark Maslin, *Global Warming: A Very Short Introduction* (Oxford: Oxford University Press, 2004); Tim Flannery, *The Weather Makers: The History and Future Impact of Climate Change* (Melbourne: Text Publishing, 2005); David Archer, *Global Warming: Understanding the Forecast* (Malden, MA: Blackwell, 2007); Kelly Knauer, ed., *Global Warming* (New York: Time Books, 2007); Mark Lynas, *Six Degrees: Our Future on a Hotter Planet* (Washington, D.C.: National Geographic, 2008); William H. Calvin, *Global Fever: How to Treat Climate Change* (Chicago: University of Chicago Press, 2008); James Hansen, 'Climate Catastrophe', *New Scientist* (28 July–3 August 2007): 30–4; James Hansen et al., 'Dangerous Human-Made Interference with Climate: A GISS ModelE Study', *Atmospheric Chemistry and Physics* 7, no. 9 (2007): 2287–312; and James Hansen et al., 'Climate Change and Trace Gases', *Philosophical Transactions of the Royal Society* (15 July 2007): 1925–54. See also Nicholas Stern, *The Economics of Climate Change: The 'Stern Review'* (Cambridge: Cambridge University Press, 2007).

[9] Naomi Oreskes, 'The Scientific Consensus on Climate Change: How Do We Know We're Not Wrong?', in *Climate Change: What It Means for Us, Our Children, and Our Grandchildren*, ed. Joseph F. C. Dimento and Pamela Doughman (Cambridge, MA: MIT Press, 2007), pp. 73, 74.

say here. In the interest of clarity and focus, I present my propositions in the form of four theses. The last three theses follow from the first one. I begin with the proposition that anthropogenic explanations of climate change spell the collapse of the age-old humanist distinction between natural history and human history and end by returning to the question I opened with: How does the crisis of climate change appeal to our sense of human universals while challenging at the same time our capacity for historical understanding?

Thesis I: Anthropogenic Explanations of Climate Change Spell the Collapse of the Age-old Humanist Distinction between Natural History and Human History

Philosophers and students of history have often displayed a conscious tendency to separate human history—or the story of human affairs, as R. G. Collingwood put it—from natural history, sometimes proceeding even to deny that nature could ever have history quite in the same way humans have it. This practice itself has a long and rich past of which, for reasons of space and personal limitations, I can only provide a very provisional, thumbnail, and somewhat arbitrary sketch.[10]

We could begin with the old Viconian–Hobbesian idea that we, humans, could have proper knowledge of only civil and political institutions because we made them, while nature remains God's work and ultimately inscrutable to man. 'The true is identical with the created: *verum ipsum factum*' is how Croce summarized Vico's famous dictum.[11] Vico scholars have sometimes protested that Vico did not make such a drastic separation between the natural and the human sciences as Croce and others read into his writings, but even they admit that such a reading is widespread.[12]

[10] A long history of this distinction is traced in Paolo Rossi, *The Dark Abyss of Time: The History of the Earth and the History of Nations from Hooke to Vico*, trans. Lydia G. Cochrane (Chicago: University of Chicago Press, 1984 [1979]).

[11] Benedetto Croce, *The Philosophy of Giambattista Vico*, trans. R. G. Collingwood (New Brunswick, NJ: Transaction Publishers, 2002 [1913]), p. 5. Carlo Ginzburg has alerted me to problems with Collingwood's translation.

[12] See the discussion in Perez Zagorin, 'Vico's Theory of Knowledge: A Critique', *Philosophical Quarterly* 34 (January 1984): 15–30.

This Viconian understanding was to become a part of the historian's common sense in the nineteenth and twentieth centuries. It made its way into Marx's famous utterance that 'men make their own history, but they do not make it just as they please' and into the title of the Marxist archaeologist V. Gordon Childe's well-known book, *Man Makes Himself.*[13] Croce seems to have been a major source of this distinction in the second half of the twentieth century through his influence on 'the lonely Oxford historicist' Collingwood who, in turn, deeply influenced E. H. Carr's 1961 book *What Is History?*, which is still perhaps one of the best-selling books on the historian's craft.[14] Croce's thoughts, one could say, unbeknown to his legatees and with unforeseeable modifications, have triumphed in our understanding of history in the postcolonial age. Behind Croce and his adaptations of Hegel and hidden in Croce's creative misreading of his predecessors stands the more distant and foundational figure of Vico.[15] The connections here, again, are many and complex. Suffice it to say for now that Croce's 1911 book, *La filosofia di Giambattista Vico*, dedicated, significantly, to Wilhelm Windelband, was translated into English in 1913 by none other than Collingwood, who was an admirer, if not a follower, of the Italian master.

However, Collingwood's own argument for separating natural history from human ones developed its own inflections, while running,

---

[13] Karl Marx, 'The Eighteenth Brumaire of Louis Bonaparte', in Marx and Frederick Engels, *Selected Works* (Moscow: Progress Publishers, 1969), vol. 1, p. 398. See V. Gordon Childe, *Man Makes Himself* (London: Watts, 1941). Indeed Althusser's revolt in the 1960s against humanism in Marx was in part a jihad against the remnants of Vico in the savant's texts; see Étienne Balibar, personal communication to author, 1 December 2007. I am grateful to Ian Bedford for drawing my attention to complexities in Marx's connections to Vico.

[14] David Roberts describes Collingwood as 'the lonely Oxford historicist … ', in important respects a follower of Croce's' (David D. Roberts, *Benedetto Croce and the Uses of Historicism* [Berkeley: University of California Press, 1987], p. 325).

[15] On Croce's misreading of Vico, see the discussion in general in Cecilia Miller, *Giambattista Vico: Imagination and Historical Knowledge* (Basingstoke: Palgrave Macmillan, 1993), and James C. Morrison, 'Vico's Principle of Verum is Factum and the Problem of Historicism', *Journal of the History of Ideas* 39 (October–December 1978): 579–95.

one might say, still on broadly Viconian lines as interpreted by Croce. Nature, Collingwood remarked, has no 'inside'. 'In the case of nature, this distinction between the outside and the inside of an event does not arise. The events of nature are mere events, not the acts of agents whose thought the scientist endeavours to trace.' Hence, 'all history properly so called is the history of human affairs'. The historian's job is 'to think himself into [an] action, to discern the thought of its agent'. A distinction, therefore, has 'to be made between historical and non-historical human actions.... So far as man's conduct is determined by what may be called his animal nature, his impulses and appetites, it is non-historical; the process of those activities is a natural process.' Thus, says Collingwood, 'the historian is not interested in the fact that men eat and sleep and make love and thus satisfy their natural appetites; but he is interested in the social customs which they create by their thought as a framework within which these appetites find satisfaction in ways sanctioned by convention and morality'. Only the history of the social construction of the body, not the history of the body as such, can be studied. By splitting the human into the natural and the social or cultural, Collingwood saw no need to bring the two together.[16]

In discussing Croce's 1893 essay 'History Subsumed under the Concept of Art', Collingwood wrote: 'Croce, by denying [the German idea] that history was a science at all, cut himself at one blow loose from naturalism, and set his face towards an idea of history as something radically different from nature.'[17] David Roberts gives a fuller account of the more mature position in Croce. Croce drew on the writings of Ernst Mach and Henri Poincaré to argue that 'the concepts of the natural sciences are human constructs elaborated for human purposes'. 'When we peer into nature', he said, 'we find only ourselves'. We do not 'understand ourselves best as part of the natural world'. So, as Roberts puts it: 'Croce proclaimed that there is no world but the human world, then took over the central doctrine of Vico that we can know the human world because we have made it.' For Croce, then, all material objects were subsumed into human thought. No rocks, for example, existed in themselves. Croce's idealism, Roberts explains,

[16] R. G. Collingwood, *The Idea of History* (New York: Oxford University Press, 1976 [1946]), pp. 212–14, 216.

[17] Collingwood, *Idea of History*, p. 193.

'does not mean that rocks, for example, "don't exist" without human beings to think them. Apart from human concern and language, they neither exist nor do not exist, since "exist" is a human concept that has meaning only within a context of human concerns and purposes.'[18] Both Croce and Collingwood would thus enfold human history and nature, to the extent that the latter could be said to have history, into purposive human action. What exists beyond that does not 'exist' because it does not exist for humans in any meaningful sense.

In the twentieth century, however, other arguments, more sociological or materialist, have existed alongside the Viconian one. They too have continued to justify the separation of human from natural history. One influential, though perhaps infamous, example would be the booklet on the Marxist philosophy of history that Stalin published in 1938, *Dialectical and Historical Materialism*. This is how Stalin put the problem:

> Geographical environment is unquestionably one of the constant and indispensable conditions of development of society and, of course, … [it] accelerates or retards its development. But its influence is not the determining influence, inasmuch as the changes and development of society proceed at an incomparably faster rate than the changes and development of geographical environment. In the space of 3000 years three different social systems have been successfully superseded in Europe: the primitive communal system, the slave system and the feudal system…. Yet during this period geographical conditions in Europe have either not changed at all, or have changed so slightly that geography takes no note of them. And that is quite natural. Changes in geographical environment of any importance require millions of years, whereas a few hundred or a couple of thousand years are enough for even very important changes in the system of human society.[19]

For all its dogmatic and formulaic tone, Stalin's passage captures an assumption perhaps common to historians of the mid-twentieth century: man's environment did change but changed so slowly as to make the history of man's relation to his environment almost timeless and thus not a subject of historiography at all. Even when Fernand Braudel rebelled against the state of the discipline of history as he found it

---

[18] David D. Roberts, *Benedetto Croce and the Uses of Historicism*, pp. 59, 60, 62.

[19] Joseph Stalin, *Dialectical and Historical Materialism* (1938), available at www.marxists.org/reference/archive/stalin/works/1938/09.html (last accessed on 30 May 2018).

in the late 1930s and proclaimed his rebellion later in 1949 through
his great book *The Mediterranean*, it was clear that he rebelled mainly
against historians who treated the environment simply as a silent and
passive backdrop to their historical narratives, something dealt with
in the introductory chapter but forgotten thereafter, as if, as Braudel
put it, 'the flowers did not come back every spring, the flocks of sheep
migrate every year, or the ships sail on a real sea that changes with the
seasons'. In composing *The Mediterranean*, Braudel wanted to write a
history in which the seasons—'a history of constant repetition, ever-
recurring cycles'—and other recurrences in nature played an active
role in moulding human actions.[20] The environment, in that sense, had
an agentive presence in Braudel's pages, but the idea that nature was
mainly repetitive had a long and ancient history in European thought,
as Gadamer showed in his discussion of Johann Gustav Droysen.[21]
Braudel's position was no doubt a great advance over the kind of
nature-as-a-backdrop argument that Stalin developed. But it shared a
fundamental assumption, too, with the stance adopted by Stalin: the
history of 'man's relationship to the environment' was so slow as to be
'almost timeless'.[22] In today's climatologists' terms, we could say that
Stalin and Braudel and others who thought thus did not have available
to them the idea, now widespread in the literature on global warming,
that the climate, and hence the overall environment, can sometimes
reach a tipping point at which this slow and apparently timeless backdrop for human actions transforms itself with a speed that can only
spell disaster for human beings.

If Braudel, to some degree, made a breach in the binary of natural/
human history, one could say that the rise of environmental history in

---

[20] Fernand Braudel, 'Preface to the First Edition', *The Mediterranean and the
Mediterranean World in the Age of Philip II*, trans. Siân Reynolds, 2 vols (London:
Harper Collins, 1972 [1949]), vol. 1, p. 20. See also Peter Burke, *The French
Historical Revolution: The 'Annales' School, 1929–89* (Stanford, CA: Stanford
University Press, 1990), pp. 32–64.

[21] See Hans-Georg Gadamer, *Truth and Method*, trans. Joel Weinsheimer
and Donald G. Marshall (London: Continuum, 1988 [1975; 1979], 2nd ed.),
pp. 214–18. See also Bonnie G. Smith, 'Gender and the Practices of Scientific History: The Seminar and Archival Research in the Nineteenth Century',
American Historical Review 100 (October 1995): 1150–76.

[22] Braudel, 'Preface to the First Edition', p. 20.

the late twentieth century made the breach wider. It could even be argued that environmental historians have sometimes indeed progressed towards producing what could be called natural histories of man. But there is a very important difference between the understanding of the human being that these histories have been based on and the agency of the human now being proposed by scientists writing on climate change. Simply put, environmental history, where it was not straightforwardly cultural, social, or economic history, looked upon human beings as biological agents. Alfred Crosby Jr, whose book *The Columbian Exchange* did much to pioneer the 'new' environmental histories in the early 1970s, put the point thus in his original preface: 'Man is a biological entity before he is a Roman Catholic or a capitalist or anything else.'[23] The recent book by Daniel Lord Smail, *On Deep History and the Brain*, is adventurous in attempting to connect knowledge gained from evolutionary and neurosciences with human histories. Smail's book pursues possible connections between biology and culture—between the history of the human brain and cultural history, in particular—while being always sensitive to the limits of biological reasoning. But it is the history of human biology and not any recent theses about the newly acquired geological agency of humans that concerns Smail.[24]

Scholars writing on the current climate-change crisis are indeed saying something significantly different from what environmental historians have said so far. In unwittingly destroying the artificial but time-honoured distinction between natural and human histories, climate scientists posit that the human being has become something much larger than the simple biological agent that he or she always has been. Humans now wield a geological force. As Oreskes puts it: 'To deny that global warming is real is precisely to deny that humans have become geological agents, changing the most basic physical processes of the earth.'

> For centuries, [Oreskes continues] scientists thought that earth processes were so large and powerful that nothing we could do could change them. This was a basic tenet of geological science: that human chronologies were

---

[23] Alfred W. Crosby, Jr, *The Columbian Exchange: Biological and Cultural Consequences of 1492* (Westport, CT: Praeger, 2003 [1972]), p. xxv.

[24] See Daniel Lord Smail, *On Deep History and the Brain* (Berkeley: University of California Press, 2008), pp. 74–189.

insignificant compared with the vastness of geological time; that human activities were insignificant compared with the force of geological processes. And once they were. But no more. There are now so many of us cutting down so many trees and burning so many billions of tons of fossil fuels that we have indeed become geological agents. We have changed the chemistry of our atmosphere, causing sea level to rise, ice to melt, and climate to change. There is no reason to think otherwise.[25]

Biological agents and geological agents—two different names with very different consequences. Environmental history, to go by Crosby's masterful survey of the origins and the state of the field in 1995, has much to do with biology and geography but hardly ever imagined human impact on the planet on a geological scale. It was still a vision of man 'as a prisoner of climate', as Crosby put it quoting Braudel, and not of man as the maker of it.[26] To call human beings geological agents is to scale up our imagination of the human. Humans are biological agents, both collectively and as individuals. They have always been so. There was no point in human history when humans were not biological agents. But we can become geological agents only historically and collectively, that is, when we have reached numbers and invented technologies that are on a scale large enough to have an impact on the planet itself. To call ourselves geological agents is to attribute to us a force on the same scale as that released at other times when there has been a mass extinction of species. We seem to be currently going through that kind of a period. The current 'rate in the loss of species diversity', specialists argue, 'is similar in intensity to the event around 65 million years ago which wiped out the dinosaurs'.[27] Our footprint was not always that large. Humans began to acquire this agency only since the Industrial Revolution, but the process really picked up in the

[25] Oreskes, 'The Scientific Consensus', p. 93.

[26] Alfred W. Crosby Jr, 'The Past and Present of Environmental History', *American Historical Review* 100 (October 1995): 1185.

[27] Will Steffen, director of the Centre for Resource and Environmental Studies at the Australian National University, quoted in 'Humans Creating New 'Geological Age', *The Australian*, 31 (March 2008), available at https://www.theage.com.au/news/environment/humans-creating-a-new-geological-age/2008/03/31/1206850741327.html (last accessed on 30 May 2018). Steffen's reference was the Millennium Ecosystem Assessment Report of 2005. See also Neil Shubin, 'The Disappearance of Species', *Bulletin of the American Academy of Arts and Sciences* 61 (Spring 2008): 17–19.

second half of the twentieth century. Humans have become geological agents very recently in human history. In that sense, we can say that it is only very recently that the distinction between human and natural histories—much of which had been preserved even in environmental histories that saw the two entities in interaction—has begun to collapse. For it is no longer a question simply of man having an interactive relation with nature; this humans have always had, or at least that is how man has been imagined in a large part of what is generally called the Western tradition.[28] Now it is being claimed that humans are a force of nature in the geological sense. A fundamental assumption of Western (and now universal) political thought has come undone in this crisis.[29]

Thesis 2: The Idea of the Anthropocene, the New Geological Epoch When Humans Exist as a Geological Force, Severely Qualifies Humanist Histories of Modernity/Globalization

How to combine human cultural and historical diversity with human freedom has formed one of the key underlying questions of human histories written of the period from 1750 to the years of present-day globalization. Diversity, as Gadamer pointed out with reference to Leopold von Ranke, was itself a figure of freedom in the historian's imagination of the historical process.[30] *Freedom* has, of course, meant different things at different times, ranging from ideas of human and citizens' rights to those of decolonization and self-rule. Freedom, one could say, is a blanket category for diverse imaginations of human

[28] Bill McKibben's argument about the 'end of nature' implied the end of nature as 'a separate realm that had always served to make us feel smaller' (Bill McKibben, *The End of Nature* [New York: Random House, 2006 (1989)], p. xxii).

[29] Bruno Latour's *Politics of Nature: How to Bring the Sciences into Democracy*, trans. Catherine Porter (Cambridge, MA: Harvard University Press, 2004 [1999]), written before the intensification of the debate on global warming, calls into question the entire tradition of organizing the idea of politics around the assumption of a separate realm of nature and points to the problems that this assumption poses for contemporary questions of democracy.

[30] Gadamer, *Truth and Method*, p. 206: The historian 'knows that everything could have been different, and every acting individual could have acted differently'.

autonomy and sovereignty. Looking at the works of Kant, Hegel, or Marx; nineteenth-century ideas of progress and class struggle; the struggle against slavery; the Russian and Chinese Revolutions; the resistance to Nazism and Fascism; the decolonization movements of the 1950s and 1960s and the revolutions in Cuba and Vietnam; the evolution and explosion of the rights discourse; the fight for civil rights for African Americans, indigenous peoples, Indian Dalits, and other minorities; down to the kind of arguments that, say, Amartya Sen put forward in his book *Development as Freedom*, one could say that freedom has been the most important motif of written accounts of human history of these 250 years. Of course, as I have already noted, freedom has not always carried the same meaning for everyone. Francis Fukuyama's understanding of freedom would be significantly different from that of Sen. But this semantic capaciousness of the word only speaks to its rhetorical power.

In no discussion of freedom in the period since the Enlightenment was there ever any awareness of the geological agency that human beings were acquiring at the same time as and through processes closely linked to their acquisition of freedom. Philosophers of freedom were mainly, and understandably, concerned with how humans would escape the injustice, oppression, inequality, or even uniformity foisted on them by other humans or human-made systems. Geological time and the chronology of human histories remained unrelated. This distance between the two calendars, as we have seen, is what climate scientists now claim has collapsed. The period I have mentioned, from 1750 to now, is also the time when human beings switched from wood and other renewable fuels to large-scale use of fossil fuel—first coal and then oil and gas. The mansion of modern freedoms stands on an ever-expanding base of fossil fuel use. Most of our freedoms so far have been energy-intensive. The period of human history usually associated with what we today think of as the institutions of civilization—the beginnings of agriculture, the founding of cities, the rise of the religions we know, the invention of writing—began about 10,000 years ago, as the planet moved from one geological period, the last ice age or the Pleistocene, to the more recent and warmer Holocene. The Holocene is the period we are supposed to be in; but the possibility of anthropogenic climate change has raised the question of its termination. Now that humans—thanks to our numbers, the burning of fossil fuel, and other related activities—have become a geological agent on the planet, some scientists have proposed that we recognize the beginning of a new geological era, one in which humans act as a main determinant of the environment of the planet. The name they have coined for this new geological age is Anthropocene. The proposal was first made by the Nobel-winning chemist Paul J. Crutzen and his collaborator, a marine science specialist, Eugene F. Stoermer. In a short statement published in 2000, they said: 'Considering ... [the] major and still growing impacts of human activities on earth and atmosphere, and at all, including global, scales, it seems to us more than appropriate to emphasize the central role of mankind in geology and ecology by proposing to use the term "anthropocene" for the current geological epoch.'[31] Crutzen elaborated on the proposal in a short piece published in *Nature* in 2002:

> For the past three centuries, the effects of humans on the global environment have escalated. Because of these anthropogenic emissions of carbon dioxide, global climate may depart significantly from natural behaviour for many millennia to come. It seems appropriate to assign the term 'Anthropocene' to the present, ... human-dominated, geological epoch, supplementing the Holocene—the warm period of the past 10–12 millennia. The Anthropocene could be said to have started in the latter part of the eighteenth century, when analyses of air trapped in polar ice showed the beginning of growing global concentrations of carbon dioxide and methane. This date also happens to coincide with James Watt's design of the steam engine in 1784.[32]

It is, of course, true that Crutzen's saying so does not make the Anthropocene an officially accepted geologic period. As Mike Davis comments, 'in geology, as in biology or history, periodization is a complex, controversial art', involving, always, vigorous debates and contestation.[33] The name Holocene for 'the post-glacial geological epoch of the past ten to twelve thousand years'[34], for example, gained no immediate acceptance when proposed—apparently by Sir Charles Lyell—in 1833. The International Geological Congress

---

[31] Paul J. Crutzen and Eugene F. Stoermer, 'The Anthropocene', *IGBP* [International Geosphere-Biosphere Programme] *Newsletter* 41 (2000): 17.

[32] Paul J. Crutzen, 'Geology of Mankind', *Nature* (3 January 2002), p. 23.

[33] Mike Davis, 'Living on the Ice Shelf: Humanity's Meltdown', 26 June 2008, available at tomdispatch.com/post/174949 (last accessed on 30 May 2018). I am grateful to Lauren Berlant for bringing this essay to my attention.

[34] Crutzen and Stoermer, 'The Anthropocene', p. 17.

officially adopted the name at their meeting in Bologna after about 50 years, in 1885.[35] The same goes for the Anthropocene. Scientists have engaged Crutzen and his colleagues on the question of when exactly the Anthropocene may have begun. But the February 2008 newsletter of the Geological Society of America, *GSA Today*, opens with a statement signed by the members of the Stratigraphy Commission of the Geological Society of London accepting Crutzen's definition and dating of the Anthropocene.[36] Adopting a 'conservative' approach, they conclude: 'Sufficient evidence has emerged of stratigraphically significant change (both elapsed and imminent) for recognition of the Anthropocene—currently a vivid yet informal metaphor of global environmental change—as a new geological epoch to be considered for formalization by international discussion.'[37] There is increasing evidence that the term is gradually winning acceptance among social scientists as well.[38]

So, has the period from 1750 to now been one of freedom or that of the Anthropocene? Is the Anthropocene a critique of the narratives of freedom? Is the geological agency of humans the price we pay for the pursuit of freedom? In some ways, yes. As Edward O. Wilson said in his *The Future of Life*: 'Humanity has so far played the role of planetary killer, concerned only with its own short-term survival. We have cut much of the heart out of biodiversity.... If Emi, the Sumatran rhino could speak, she might tell us that the twenty-first century is thus far no

[35] Crutzen and Stoermer, 'The Anthropocene', p. 17.

[36] See William F. Ruddiman, 'The Anthropogenic Greenhouse Era Began Thousands of Years Ago', *Climatic Change* 61, no. 3 (2003): 261–93; Paul J. Crutzen and Eugene F. Stoermer, 'How Long Have We Been in the Anthropocene Era?' *Climatic Change* 61, no. 3 (2003): 251–57; and Jan Zalasiewicz et al., 'Are We Now Living in the Anthropocene?' *GSA Today* 18 (February 2008): 4–8. I am grateful to Neptune Srimal for this reference.

[37] Zalasiewicz et al., 'Are We Now Living in the Anthropocene?', p. 7. Davis described the London Society as 'the world's oldest association of Earth scientists, founded in 1807' (Davis, 'Living on the Ice Shelf').

[38] See, for instance, Libby Robin and Steffen, 'History for the Anthropocene', *History Compass* 5, no. 5 (2007): 1694–1719, and Jeffrey D. Sachs, 'The Anthropocene', in Jeffrey D. Sachs, *Common Wealth: Economics for a Crowded Planet* (New York: Penguin, 2008), pp. 57–82. Thanks to Debjani Ganguly for drawing my attention to the essay by Robin and Steffen, and to Robin for sharing it with me.

exception.'[39] But the relation between Enlightenment themes of freedom and the collapsing of human and geological chronologies seems more complicated and contradictory than a simple binary would allow. It is true that human beings have tumbled into being a geological agent through our own decisions. The Anthropocene, one might say, has been an unintended consequence of human choices. But it is also clear that for humans any thought of the way out of our current predicament cannot but refer to the idea of deploying reason in global, collective life. As Wilson put it: 'We know more about the problem now.... We know what to do.'[40] Or, to quote Crutzen and Stoermer again:

> Mankind will remain a major geological force for many millennia, maybe millions of years, to come. To develop a world-wide accepted strategy leading to sustainability of ecosystems against human-induced stresses will be one of the great future tasks of mankind, requiring intensive research efforts and wise application of knowledge thus acquired.... An exciting, but also difficult and daunting task lies ahead of the global research and engineering community to guide mankind towards global, sustainable, environmental management.[41]

Logically, then, in the era of the Anthropocene, we need the Enlightenment (that is, reason) even more than in the past. There is one consideration though that qualifies this optimism about the role of reason and that has to do with the most common shape that freedom takes in human societies: politics. Politics has never been based on reason alone. And politics in the age of the masses and in a world already complicated by sharp inequalities between and inside nations is something no one can control. 'Sheer demographic momentum', writes Davis,

> will increase the world's urban population by 3 billion people over the next 40 years (90% of them in poor cities), and no one—absolutely no one [including, one might say, scholars on the Left]—has a clue how a planet of slums, with growing food and energy crises, will accommodate their biological survival, much less their inevitable aspirations to basic happiness and dignity.[42]

[39] Edward O. Wilson, *The Future of Life* (New York: Alfred A. Knopf, 2002), p. 102.

[40] Wilson, *The Future of Life*, p. 102.

[41] Crutzen and Stoermer, 'The Anthropocene', p. 18.

[42] Davis, 'Living on the Ice Shelf'.

It is not surprising then that the crisis of climate change should produce anxieties precisely around futures that we cannot visualize. Scientists' hope that reason will guide us out of the present predicament is reminiscent of the social opposition between the myth of science and the actual politics of the sciences that Bruno Latour discusses in his *Politics of Nature*.[43] Bereft of any sense of politics, Wilson can only articulate his sense of practicality as a philosopher's hope mixed with anxiety: 'Perhaps we will act in time.'[44] Yet the very science of global warming produces, of necessity, political imperatives. Tim Flannery's book, for instance, raises the dark prospects of an 'Orwellian nightmare' in a chapter entitled '2084: The Carbon Dictatorship?'[45] Mark Maslin concludes his book with some gloomy thoughts: 'It is unlikely that global politics will solve global warming. Technofixes are dangerous or cause problems as bad as the ones they are aimed at fixing.... [Global warming] requires nations and regions to plan for the next 50 years, something that most societies are unable to do because of the very short-term nature of politics.' His recommendation, 'we must prepare for the worst and adapt', coupled with Davis's observations about the coming 'planet of slums' places the question of human freedom under the cloud of the Anthropocene.[46]

Thesis 3: The Geological Hypothesis Regarding the Anthropocene Requires Us to Put Global Histories of Capital in Conversation with the Species History of Humans

Analytic frameworks engaging questions of freedom by way of critiques of capitalist globalization have not, in any way, become obsolete in the age of climate change. If anything, as Davis shows, climate change may well end up accentuating all the inequities of the capitalist world order if the interests of the poor and vulnerable

---

[43] See Latour, *Politics of Nature*.

[44] Wilson, *The Future of Life*, p. 102.

[45] Flannery, *The Weather Makers*, p. xiv.

[46] Maslin, *Global Warming*, p. 147. For a discussion of how fossil fuels created both the possibilities for and the limits of democracy in the twentieth century, see Timothy Mitchell, 'Carbon Democracy', forthcoming in *Economy and Society*. I am grateful to Mitchell for letting me cite this unpublished paper.

are neglected.[47] Capitalist globalization exists, so should its critiques. But these critiques do not give us an adequate hold on human history once we accept that the crisis of climate change is here with us and may exist as part of this planet for much longer than capitalism or long after capitalism has undergone many more historic mutations. The problematic of globalization allows us to read climate change only as a crisis of capitalist management. While there is no denying that climate change has profoundly to do with the history of capital, a critique that is only a critique of capital is not sufficient for addressing questions relating to human history once the crisis of climate change has been acknowledged and the Anthropocene has begun to loom on the horizon of our present. The geologic now of the Anthropocene has become entangled with the now of human history.

Scholars who study human beings in relation to the crisis of climate change and other ecological problems emerging on a world scale make a distinction between the recorded history of human beings and their deep history. Recorded history refers, very broadly, to the 10,000 years that have passed since the invention of agriculture but more usually to the last 4,000 years or so for which written records exist. Historians of modernity and 'early modernity' usually move in the archives of the last 400 years. The history of humans that goes beyond these years of written records constitutes what other students of human pasts—not professional historians—call deep history. As Wilson, one of the main proponents of this distinction, writes: 'Human behavior is seen as the product not just of recorded history, ten thousand years recent, but of deep history, the combined genetic and cultural changes that created humanity over hundreds of [thousands of] years.'[48] It, of course, goes to the credit of Smail that he has attempted to explain to professional historians the intellectual appeal of deep history.[49]

Without such knowledge of the deep history of humanity it would be difficult to arrive at a secular understanding of why climate change constitutes a crisis for humans. Geologists and climate scientists may explain why the current phase of global warming—as distinct from

---

[47] Davis, 'Living on the Ice Shelf'.

[48] Edward O. Wilson, *In Search of Nature* (Washington, D.C.: Island, 1996), pp. ix–x.

[49] See Smail, *On Deep History and the Brain*.

the warming of the planet that has happened before—is anthropogenic in nature, but the ensuing crisis for humans is not understandable unless one works out the consequences of that warming. The consequences make sense only if we think of humans as a form of life and look on human history as part of the history of life on this planet. For, ultimately, what the warming of the planet threatens is not the geological planet itself but the very conditions, both biological and geological, on which the survival of human life as developed in the Holocene period depends.

The word that scholars such as Wilson or Crutzen use to designate life in the human form—and in other living forms—is species. They speak of the human being as a species and find that category useful in thinking about the nature of the current crisis. It is a word that will never occur in any standard history or political–economic analysis of globalization by scholars on the Left, for the analysis of globalization refers, for good reasons, only to the recent and recorded history of humans. Species thinking, on the other hand, is connected to the enterprise of deep history. Further, Wilson and Crutzen actually find such thinking essential to visualizing human well-being. As Wilson writes: 'We need this longer view ... not only to understand our species but more firmly to secure its future.'[50] The task of placing, historically, the crisis of climate change thus requires us to bring together intellectual formations that are somewhat in tension with each other: the planetary and the global; deep and recorded histories; species thinking and critiques of capital.

In saying this, I work somewhat against the grain of historians' thinking on globalization and world history. In a landmark essay published in 1995 and entitled 'World History in a Global Age', Michael Geyer and Charles Bright wrote: 'At the end of the twentieth century, we encounter, not a universalizing and single modernity but an integrated world of multiple and multiplying modernities.' 'As far as world history is concerned', they said, 'there is no universalizing spirit.... There are, instead, many very specific, very material and pragmatic practices that await critical reflection and historical study.' Yet, thanks to global connections forged by trade, empires, and capitalism, 'we confront a startling new condition: humanity, which has

---

[50] Wilson, *In Search of Nature*, p. x.

been the subject of world history for many centuries and civilizations, has now come into the purview of all human beings. This humanity is extremely polarized into rich and poor.'[51] This humanity, Geyer and Bright imply in the spirit of the philosophies of difference, is not one. It does not, they write, 'form a single homogenous civilization'. 'Neither is this humanity any longer a mere species or a natural condition.' 'For the first time', they say, with some existentialist flourish, 'we as human beings collectively constitute ourselves and, hence, are responsible for ourselves'.[52] Clearly, the scientists who advocate the idea of the Anthropocene are saying something quite the contrary. They argue that because humans constitute a particular kind of species they can, in the process of dominating other species, acquire the status of a geologic force. Humans, in other words, have become a natural condition, at least today. How do we create a conversation between these two positions?

It is understandable that the biological-sounding talk of species should worry historians. They feel concerned about their finely honed sense of contingency and freedom in human affairs having to cede ground to a more deterministic view of the world. Besides, there are always, as Smail recognizes, dangerous historical examples of the political use of biology.[53] The idea of species, it is feared, in addition, may introduce a powerful degree of essentialism in our understanding of humans. I will return to the question of contingency later in this section, but, on the issue of essentialism, Smail helpfully points out why species cannot be thought of in essentialist terms:

Species, according to Darwin, are not fixed entities with natural essences imbued in them by the Creator.... Natural selection does not homogenize the individuals of a species.... Given this state of affairs, the search for a normal ... nature and body type [of any particular species] is futile. And so it goes for the equally futile quest to identify 'human nature'. Here, as in so many areas, biology and cultural studies are fundamentally congruent.[54]

[51] Michael Geyer and Charles Bright, 'World History in a Global Age', *American Historical Review* 100 (October 1995): 1058–9.
[52] Geyer and Bright, 'World History in a Global Age', p. 1059.
[53] See Smail, *On Deep History and the Brain*, p. 124.
[54] Smail, *On Deep History and the Brain*, pp. 124–5.

It is clear that different academic disciplines position their practitioners differently with regard to the question of how to view the human being. All disciplines have to create their objects of study. If medicine or biology reduces the human to a certain specific understanding of him or her, humanist historians often do not realize that the protagonists of their stories—persons—are reductions, too. Absent personhood, there is no human subject of history. That is why Derrida earned the wrath of Foucault by pointing out that any desire to enable or allow madness itself to speak in a history of madness would be 'the maddest aspect' of the project.[55] An object of critical importance to humanists of all traditions, personhood is nevertheless no less of a reduction of or an abstraction from the embodied and whole human being than, say, the human skeleton discussed in an anatomy class.

The crisis of climate change calls on academics to rise above their disciplinary prejudices, for it is a crisis of many dimensions. In that context, it is interesting to observe the role that the category of species has begun to play among scholars, including economists, who have already gone further than historians in investigating and explaining the nature of this crisis. The economist Jeffrey Sachs's book *Common Wealth*, meant for the educated but lay public, uses the idea of species as central to its argument and devotes a whole chapter to the Anthropocene.[56] In fact, the scholar from whom Sachs solicited a foreword for his book was none other than Edward Wilson. The concept of species plays a quasi-Hegelian role in Wilson's foreword in the same way as the multitude or the masses in Marxist writings. If Marxists of various hues have at different times thought that the good of humanity lay in the prospect of the oppressed or the multitude realizing their own global unity through a process of coming into self-consciousness, Wilson pins his hope on the unity possible through our collective self-recognition as a species: 'Humanity has consumed or transformed enough of Earth's irreplaceable resources to be in better shape than ever before. We are smart enough and now, one hopes, well informed enough to

---

[55] Jacques Derrida, 'Cogito and the History of Madness', in *Writing and Difference*, trans. Alan Bass (Chicago: University of Chicago Press, 1978), p. 34.

[56] See Sachs, *Common Wealth*, pp. 57–82.

achieve self-understanding as a unified species.... We will be wise to
look on ourselves as a species.'[57]

Yet doubts linger about the use of the idea of species in the
context of climate change, and it would be good to deal with one
that can easily arise among critics on the Left. One could object,
for instance, that all the anthropogenic factors contributing to global
warming—the burning of fossil fuel, industrialization of animal
stock, the clearing of tropical and other forests, and so on—are after
all part of a larger story: the unfolding of capitalism in the West
and the imperial or quasi-imperial domination by the West of the
rest of the world. It is from that recent history of the West that the
elite of China, Japan, India, Russia, and Brazil have drawn inspiration in attempting to develop their own trajectories towards superpower politics and global domination through capitalist economic,
technological, and military might. If this is broadly true, then does
not the talk of species or mankind simply serve to hide the reality
of capitalist production and the logic of imperial—formal, informal,
or machinic in a Deleuzian sense—domination that it fosters? Why
should one include the poor of the world—whose carbon footprint
is small anyway—by the use of such all-inclusive terms as 'species' or
'mankind' when the blame for the current crisis should be squarely
laid at the door of the rich nations in the first place and of the richer
classes in the poorer ones?

We need to stay with this question a little longer; otherwise the
difference between the present historiography of globalization and
the historiography demanded by anthropogenic theories of climate
change will not be clear to us. Though some scientists would want to
date the Anthropocene from the time agriculture was invented, my
readings mostly suggest that our falling into the Anthropocene was
neither an ancient nor an inevitable happening. Human civilization
surely did not begin on the condition that, one day in his history, man
would have to shift from wood to coal and from coal to petroleum
and gas. That there was much historical contingency in the transition
from wood to coal as the main source of energy has been demonstrated powerfully by Kenneth Pomeranz in his path-breaking book

[57] Wilson, foreword to Sachs, *Common Wealth*, p. xii. Students of Marx may
be reminded here of the use of the category 'species being' by the young Marx.

The Great Divergence.[58] Coincidences and historical accidents similarly litter the stories of the 'discovery' of oil, of the oil tycoons, and of the automobile industry as they do any other histories.[59] Capitalist societies themselves have not remained the same since the beginning of capitalism.[60] Human population, too, has dramatically increased since the Second World War. India alone is now more than three times more populous than at independence in 1947. Clearly, nobody is in a position to claim that there is something inherent to the human species that has pushed us finally into the Anthropocene. We have stumbled into it. The way to it was no doubt through industrial civilization. (I do not make a distinction here between the capitalist and socialist societies we have had so far, for there was never any principled difference in their use of fossil fuel.)

If the industrial way of life was what got us into this crisis, then the question is, why think in terms of species, surely a category that belongs to a much longer history? Why could not the narrative of capitalism—and hence its critique—be sufficient as a framework for interrogating the history of climate change and understanding its consequences? It seems true that the crisis of climate change has been necessitated by the high-energy-consuming models of society that capitalist industrialization has created and promoted, but the current crisis has brought into view certain other conditions for the existence of life in the human form that have no intrinsic connection to the logics of capitalist, nationalist, or socialist identities. They are connected rather to the history of life on this planet, the way different life forms connect to one another, and the way the mass extinction of one species could spell danger for another. Without such a history of life, the crisis of climate change has no human 'meaning'. For, as I have said before, it is not a crisis for the inorganic planet in any meaningful sense.

[58] See Kenneth Pomeranz, *The Great Divergence: China, Europe, and the Making of the Modern World Economy* (Princeton, NJ: Princeton University Press, 2000).

[59] See Mitchell, 'Carbon Democracy'. See also Edwin Black, *Internal Combustion: How Corporations and Governments Addicted the World to Oil and Derailed the Alternatives* (New York: St. Martin's Griffin, 2006).

[60] Arrighi's *The Long Twentieth Century* is a good guide to these fluctuations in the fortunes of capitalism.

In other words, the industrial way of life has acted much like the rabbit hole in Alice's story; we have slid into a state of things that forces on us a recognition of some of the parametric (that is, boundary) conditions for the existence of institutions central to our idea of modernity and the meanings we derive from them. Let me explain. Take the case of the so-called agricultural revolution of 10,000 years ago. It was not just an expression of human inventiveness. It was made possible by certain changes in the amount of carbon dioxide in the atmosphere, a certain stability of the climate, and a degree of warming of the planet that followed the end of the Ice Age (the Pleistocene era)—things over which human beings had no control. 'There can be little doubt', writes one of the editors of *Humans at the End of the Ice Age*, 'that the basic phenomenon—the waning of the Ice Age—was the result of the Milankovitch phenomena: the orbital and tilt relationships between the Earth and the Sun'.[61] The temperature of the planet stabilized within a zone that allowed grass to grow. Barley and wheat are among the oldest of such grasses. Without this lucky 'long summer' or what one climate scientist has called an 'extraordinary' 'fluke' of nature in the history of the planet, our industrial–agricultural way of life would not have been possible.[62] In other words, whatever our socio-economic and technological choices, whatever the rights we wish to celebrate as our freedom, we cannot afford to destabilize conditions (such as the temperature zone in which the planet exists) that work like boundary parameters of human existence. These parameters are independent of capitalism or socialism. They have been stable for much longer than the histories of these institutions and have allowed human beings to become the dominant species on earth. Unfortunately, we have now ourselves become a geological agent disturbing these parametric conditions needed for our own existence.

This is not to deny the historical role that the richer and mainly Western nations of the world have played in emitting greenhouse gases. To speak of species thinking is not to resist the politics of 'common but differentiated responsibility' that China, India, and other developing

[61] Lawrence Guy Straus, 'The World at the End of the Last Ice Age', in *Humans at the End of the Ice Age: The Archaeology of the Pleistocene-Holocene Transition*, ed. Lawrence Guy Straus et al. (New York: Plenum, 1996), p. 5.
[62] Flannery, *The Weather Makers*, pp. 63, 64.

countries seem keen to pursue when it comes to reducing greenhouse gas emissions.[63] Whether we blame climate change on those who are retrospectively guilty—that is, blame the West for their past performance—or those who are prospectively guilty (China has just surpassed the United States as the largest emitter of carbon dioxide, though not on a per capita basis) is a question that is tied no doubt to the histories of capitalism and modernization.[64] But scientists' discovery of the fact that human beings have in the process become a geological agent points to a shared catastrophe that we have all fallen into. Here is how Crutzen and Stoermer describe that catastrophe:

> The expansion of mankind ... has been astounding.... During the past 3 centuries human population increased tenfold to 6000 million, accompanied e.g. by a growth in cattle population to 1400 million (about one cow per average size family).... In a few generations mankind is exhausting the fossil fuels that were generated over several hundred million years. The release of SO_2 ... to the atmosphere by coal and oil burning, is at least two times larger than the sum of all natural emissions ...; more than half of all accessible fresh water is used by mankind; human activity has increased the species extinction rate by thousand to ten thousand fold in the tropical rain forests.... Furthermore, mankind releases many toxic substances in the environment.... The effects documented include modification of the geochemical cycle in large freshwater systems and occur in systems remote from primary sources.[65]

Explaining this catastrophe calls for a conversation between disciplines and between recorded and deep histories of human beings in the same way that the agricultural revolution of 10,000 years ago could not be explained except through a convergence of three disciplines: geology, archaeology, and history.[66]

---

[63] Ashish Kothari, 'The Reality of Climate Injustice', *The Hindu*, 18 November 2007, available at www.hinduonnet.com/thehindu/mag/2007/11/18/stories/2007111850020100.html (last accessed on 30 May 2018).

[64] I have borrowed the idea of 'retrospective' and 'prospective' guilt from a discussion led at the Franke Institute for the Humanities by Peter Singer during the Chicago Humanities Festival, November 2007.

[65] Crutzen and Stoermer, 'The Anthropocene', p. 17.

[66] See Colin Tudge, *Neanderthals, Bandits, and Farmers: How Agriculture Really Began* (New Haven, CT: Yale University Press, 1999), pp. 35–6.

Scientists such as Wilson or Crutzen may be politically naïve in not recognizing that reason may not be all that guides us in our effective collective choices—in other words, we may collectively end up making some unreasonable choices—but I find it interesting and symptomatic that they speak the language of the Enlightenment. They are not necessarily anti-capitalist scholars, and yet clearly they are not for business-as-usual capitalism either. They see knowledge and reason providing humans not only a way out of this present crisis but a way of keeping us out of harm's way in the future. Wilson, for example, speaks of devising a 'wiser use of resources' in a manner that sounds distinctly Kantian.[67] But the knowledge in question is the knowledge of humans as a species, a species dependent on other species for its own existence, a part of the general history of life. Changing the climate, increasingly not only the average temperature of the planet but also the acidity and the level of the oceans, and destroying the food chain are actions that cannot be in the interest of our lives. These parametric conditions hold irrespective of our political choices. It is therefore impossible to understand global warming as a crisis without engaging the propositions put forward by these scientists. At the same time, the story of capital, the contingent history of our falling into the Anthropocene, cannot be denied by recourse to the idea of species, for the Anthropocene would not have been possible, even as a theory, without the history of industrialization. How do we hold the two together as we think the history of the world since the Enlightenment? How do we relate to a universal history of life—to universal thought, that is—while retaining what is of obvious value in our postcolonial suspicion of the universal? The crisis of climate change calls for thinking simultaneously on both registers, to mix together the immiscible chronologies of capital and species history. This combination, however, stretches, in quite fundamental ways, the very idea of historical understanding.

Thesis 4: The Cross-Hatching of Species History and the History of Capital Is a Process of Probing the Limits of Historical Understanding

Historical understanding, one could say following the Diltheyan tradition, entails critical thinking that makes an appeal to some generic

---

[67] Wilson, *In Search of Nature*, p. 199.

ideas about human experience. As Gadamer pointed out, Dilthey saw 'the individual's private world of experience as the starting point for an expansion that, in a living transposition, fills out the narrowness and fortuitousness of his private experience with the infinity of what is available by re-experiencing the historical world'. 'Historical consciousness', in this tradition, is thus 'a mode of self-knowledge' garnered through critical reflections on one's own and others' (historical actors') experiences.[68] Humanist histories of capitalism will always admit of something called the experience of capitalism. E. P. Thompson's brilliant attempt to reconstruct working-class experience of capitalist labour, for instance, does not make sense without that assumption.[69] Humanist histories are histories that produce meaning through an appeal to our capacity not only to reconstruct but, as Collingwood would have said, but also to re-enact in our own minds the experience of the past.

When Wilson then recommends in the interest of our collective future that we achieve self-understanding as a species, the statement does not correspond to any historical way of understanding and connecting pasts with futures through the assumption of there being an element of continuity to human experience (see Gadamer's point mentioned earlier). Who is the we? We humans never experience ourselves as a species. We can only intellectually comprehend or infer the existence of the human species but never experience it as such. There could be no phenomenology of us as a species. Even if we were to emotionally identify with a word like mankind, we would not know what being a species is, for, in species history, humans are only an instance of the concept species as indeed would be any other life form. But one never experiences being a concept.

The discussion about the crisis of climate change can thus produce affect and knowledge about collective human pasts and futures that work at the limits of historical understanding. We experience specific effects of the crisis but not the whole phenomenon. Do we then say, with Geyer and Bright, that 'humanity no longer comes into being

[68] Gadamer, *Truth and Method*, pp. 232, 234. See also Michael Ermarth, *Wilhelm Dilthey: The Critique of Historical Reason* (Chicago: University of Chicago Press, 1978), pp. 310–22.

[69] See E. P. Thompson, *The Making of the English Working Class* (Harmondsworth: Penguin, 1963).

through "thought"'[70] or say with Foucault that 'the human being no longer has any history'?[71] Geyer and Bright go on to write in a Foucaultian spirit: 'Its [world history's] task is to make transparent the lineaments of power, underpinned by information, that compress humanity into a single humankind.'[72]

This critique that sees humanity as an effect of power is, of course, valuable for all the hermeneutics of suspicion that it has taught postcolonial scholarship. It is an effective critical tool in dealing with national and global formations of domination. But I do not find it adequate in dealing with the crisis of global warming. First, inchoate figures of us all and other imaginings of humanity invariably haunt our sense of the current crisis. How else would one understand the title of Weisman's book *The World Without Us* or the appeal of his brilliant though impossible attempt to depict the experience of New York after we are gone![73] Second, the wall between human and natural history has been breached. We may not experience ourselves as a geological agent, but we appear to have become one at the level of the species. And without that knowledge that defies historical understanding there is no making sense of the current crisis that affects us all. Climate change, refracted through global capital, will no doubt accentuate the logic of inequality that runs through the rule of capital; some people will no doubt gain temporarily at the expense of others. But the whole crisis cannot be reduced to a story of capitalism. Unlike in the crises of capitalism, there are no lifeboats here for the rich and the privileged (witness the drought in Australia or recent fires in the wealthy neighbourhoods of California). The anxiety global warming gives rise to is reminiscent of the days when many feared a global nuclear war. But there is a very important difference. A nuclear war would have been a conscious decision on the part of the powers that be. Climate change is an unintended consequence of human actions and shows, only through scientific analysis, the effects of our actions as a species. Species may indeed be the name of a placeholder for an emergent, new universal

---

[70] Geyer and Bright, 'World History in a Global Age', p. 1060.

[71] Michel Foucault, *The Order of Things: An Archaeology of Human Knowledge*, trans. pub. (New York: Pantheon, 1973 [1966]), p. 368.

[72] Geyer and Bright, 'World History in a Global Age', p. 1060.

[73] See Weisman, *The World without Us*, pp. 25–8.

history of humans that flashes up in the moment of the danger that is climate change. But we can never understand this universal. It is not a Hegelian universal arising dialectically out of the movement of history, or a universal of capital brought forth by the present crisis. Geyer and Bright are right to reject those two varieties of the universal. Yet climate change poses for us a question of a human collectivity, an us, pointing to a figure of the universal that escapes our capacity to experience the world. It is more like a universal that arises from a shared sense of a catastrophe. It calls for a global approach to politics without the myth of a global identity, for, unlike a Hegelian universal, it cannot subsume particularities. We may provisionally call it a 'negative universal history'.[74]

[74] I am grateful to Antonio Y. Vasquez-Arroyo for sharing with me his unpublished paper 'Universal History Disavowed: On Critical Theory and Post-colonialism', where he has tried to develop this concept of negative universal history on the basis of his reading of Theodor Adorno and Walter Benjamin.

9

ON SOME RIFTS IN CONTEMPORARY THINKING ON CLIMATE CHANGE*

'Life is understood backwards but must be lived forwards.'

—Søren Kierkegaard

The name 'Anthropocene' coined by Paul Crutzen in 2000 has become popular in both scientific and non-scientific circles. In strictly geological terms, however, it has no formal status yet. Whether or not we are living through a time that future or alien geologists could describe as producing ample stratigraphic and other signals of significant human modification of the planet to warrant such a name remains an open question to be decided by relevant scientists and by such respected bodies as the International Commission on Stratigraphy.[1] But the term has also come to communicate a general sense of the domination of the planet by the human species. Depending on how one understands

---

* Published in French as 'Quelques failles dans la pensée sur le changement climatique', in De l'univers clos au monde infini, ed. Émilie Hache (Paris: Éditions Dehors, 2014), pp. 107–46

[1] See J. Zalasiewicz, P. J. Crutzen, and W. Steffen, 'The Anthropocene', in The Geologic Time Scale 2012, ed. Felix Gradstein et al. (Atlanta, GA: Elsevier, 2013), pp. 1033–40, and Jan Zalasiewicz, 'The Human Touch', The Paleontology Newsletter 82 (March 2013): 23–31. See also the discussion between Bernd M. Scherer and Jan Zalasiewicz available on YouTube at http://www.youtube.com/watch?v=AcHCRPte67s, posted on 26 January 2013 and accessed on 12 September 2013.

the term 'Anthropocene', the answer to the question as to when such a period may have begun varies.

What concerns me here is a more limited proposition that seems to have received a general acceptance among climate scientists. This is the idea that we are living through a time when humans collectively, thanks to their profligate use of fossil fuel, act with the power of a geophysical force—that is, with the power that would normally belong to some enormous geophysical agency such as shifts in tectonic plates or major volcanic eruptions or a strike by an asteroid—to determine the climate of the planet as a whole. As a student of human history, I cannot but notice the irony of all this. Human beings all over the world owe their freedom from use of massive forced labour—as was needed, say, to build ancient or early modern monumental structures—to the discovery and availability of cheap energy in the shape of fossil fuels. The relationship between the theme of freedom celebrated in much of the history of modern humans and energy based on fossil-fuel sources is deep and real. Critics of the human use of fossil fuel acknowledge this. 'Fossil fuel energy, and only fossil fuel energy, made it possible to break with the old agrarian pattern and construct the industrial world', writes the 'peak oil theorist' John Michael Greer.[2] The historians John and William McNeill put the point forcefully, though a little problematically (in that modern forms of slavery actually coexisted with widespread use of fossil fuel):

> What the harnessing of fossil fuels achieved in the sphere of work itself—a historic liberation from muscular toil—abolition achieved in the social sphere. They were connected events and roughly simultaneous. The use of inanimate energy gradually made labor less scarce, and forced labor less appealing.... Worldwide currents of demographic growth, industrialization and energy use, and egalitarian morality all flowed together to refashion the human condition.[3]

It then has to be one of the profoundest ironies of the same history that the increasing use of such energy should have now transformed

---

[2] John Michael Greer, 'Progress vs. Apocalypse', in *The Energy Reader*, ed. Tom Butler, Daniel Lerch, and George Wuerthner (Sausalito, CA: Foundation for Deep Ecology, 2012), p. 97.

[3] J. R. McNeill and William H. McNeill, *The Human Web: A Bird's-Eye View of World History* (New York: W. W. Norton, 2003), p. 258.

our collective image in our own eyes from that of an autonomous, if not sovereign, purposeful, and freedom-seeking agency to that of a physical force, the sheer capacity to produce pull or push on an object by interacting with it as merely another object. A geological force has no sense of purpose or sovereignty. Humans have clearly embroiled themselves in histories much larger than their 'own'. Interfering with the glacial–interglacial cycle of the earth is probably a lot more than what pioneers of fossil fuel energy bargained for. This very sense of irony is expressed when, in his book *Storms for My Grandchildren*, the famous NASA scientist James Hansen calls anthropogenic global warming a 'Faustian bargain'.[4]

The climate crisis brings into view the collision—or the running up against one another—of three histories that, from the point of view of human history, are normally assumed to be working at such different and distinct paces that they are treated as processes separate from one another for all practical purposes: the history of the earth system, the history of life including that of human evolution on the planet, and the more recent history of the industrial civilization (for many, capitalism). Humans now unintentionally straddle these three histories that operate on different scales and at different speeds.

Humans have interfered with the glacial–interglacial cycle of the planet—which normally completes itself over 130,000 or so years—so much so that we have effectively put off the next ice age. Thus, Curt Stager in his book *Deep Future* remarks: 'Not only have we warmed the world during this century with our carbon emissions; we've also stopped the next ice age in its tracks.'[5] The paleo-climatologist David Archer agrees: 'The fossil fuel era may stave off the next ice age, which was due in 50,000 years but may now be delayed for 500,000 years.'[6] The point is echoed elsewhere by Bill McGuire: '...So great are the quantities of carbon dioxide we are pumping into the atmo-

[4] James Hansen, *Storms for My Grandchildren: The Truth About the Coming Climate Catastrophe and Our Last Chance to Save Humanity* (New York: Bloomsbury, 2009), Chapter 6.

[5] Curt Stager, *Deep Future: The Next 100,000 Years of Life on Earth* (New York: St Martin's Press, 2011), p. 26. Thanks to Clive Hamilton for drawing my attention to Stager's book.

[6] David Archer, *The Global Carbon Cycle* (Princeton, NJ: Princeton University Press, 2010), p. 136.

sphere that we may skip anything from the next glaciation to the next five.'[7] If this is true, then it clearly marks a significant departure from the usual scientific understanding of the environmental role of humans summarized as follows by the respected energy and environmental historian Vaclav Smil: 'The fundamental variables that ... are the primary governors of climate ... are *absolutely beyond* any human influences.... Nor can there be ever any human control of the fundamental planet-forming processes of plate tectonics that govern climate by redistributing land masses and the oceans ... or that generate volcanic eruptions and earthquakes.'[8] What Smil says has obviously held for most of human history, yet the proposition about anthropogenic climate change is precisely that humans have *now* unwittingly acquired a capacity to change the climate of the whole planet, something that has so far belonged to forces operating on scales unimaginable for those not used to thinking in geological terms. Even earthquakes and movements in the planet's crust, as Bill McGuire shows in his book *Waking the Giant*, have been influenced in geological times by climate changes that affected the thickness of ice on earth and raised sea levels, and there is no reason why human-induced climate change would not have similar effects.[9]

Archer further explains that we do not know what impact the putting off of the next or next several ice age(s) could have on the planet's thermostat, the carbon cycle, that completes itself over a million years during which time the planet alternates between a hothouse condition (no polar ice) and an icehouse condition (something that we are currently in) and that, under certain circumstances, can amplify the effects of the glacial–interglacial cycle though, over its lifetime, it maintains a CO_2 balance for the planet. In Archer's words: 'The carbon cycle on time scales of glacial/interglacial cycles seems to have a different character than it does on million-year time scales. Here it tends to amplify climate changes driven by orbital forcing.'[10]

---

[7] Bill McGuire, *Waking the Giant: How a Changing Climate Triggers Earthquakes, Tsunamis, and Volcanoes* (New York and Oxford: Oxford University Press, 2012), p. 65.

[8] Vaclav Smil, *Harvesting the Biosphere: What We Have Taken from Nature* (Cambridge, MA: The MIT Press, 2013), pp. 240–1 (emphasis added).

[9] McGuire, *Waking the Giant*, pp. 98, 158–9, 221 and passim.

[10] Archer, *Global Carbon Cycle*, p. 57.

Paleo-climatologists tell a very long history when it comes to explaining the significance of anthropogenic global warming. There is, first of all, the question of evidence. Ice-core samples of ancient air—more than 600,000 years old—have been critical in establishing the anthropogenic nature of the current warming.[11] There are, besides, paleoclimatic records of the past in fossils and other geological materials. In his lucid book on the oil industry's response—not always or uniformly negative—to the climate crisis, the geologist and oil-industry advisor Bryan Lovell writes that the group within the industry that supplied it with compelling evidence of the serious challenge that greenhouse gas emissions posed to the future of humanity were geologists who could read deep climate histories buried in sedimentary rocks to see the effects of 'a dramatic warming event that took place 55 million years ago'. In the literature, this is known as the PETM, the late Paleocene–Eocene Thermal Maximum.

> Comparison of the volume of carbon released to the atmosphere [then] … and the volume we are now releasing ourselves strongly suggests that we are indeed facing a major global challenge. We are in danger of repeating that 55 million-year-old global warming event, which disrupted earth over 100,000 years. That event took place long before *Homo Sapiens* were around to light so much as a campfire.[12]

How far the arc of the geological history explaining the present climate crisis projects into the future may be quickly seen from the very subtitle of a recent book authored by the Chicago geophysicist David Archer. This book called *The Long Thaw* has the following for its subtitle: *How Humans Are Changing the Next 100,000 Years of Earth's Climate*.[13] 'Mankind is becoming a force in climate comparable to the orbital variations that drive glacial cycles', writes Archer.[14] He continues:

[11] Susan Solomon et al., eds, *Climate Change 2007: The Physical Science Basis* (Contribution to the Working Group I to the Fourth Assessment Report of the Intergovernmental Panel on Climate Change) (Cambridge: Cambridge University Press, 2009; first pub. 2007), p. 446, Box 6.2.

[12] Bryan Lovell, *Challenged By Carbon: The Oil Industry and Climate Change* (Cambridge: Cambridge University Press, 2010), p. xi.

[13] David Archer, *The Long Thaw: How Humans Are Changing the Next 100,000 Years of Earth's Climate* (Princeton, NJ: Princeton University Press, 2009).

[14] Archer, *The Long Thaw*, p. 6.

The long lifetime of fossil fuel CO_2 creates a sense of fleeting folly about the use of fossil fuels as an energy source. Our fossil fuel deposits, 100 million years old, could be gone in a few centuries, leaving climate impacts that will last for hundreds of millennia. The lifetime of fossil fuel CO_2 in the atmosphere is a few centuries, plus 25% that lasts essentially for ever.[15]

The carbon cycle of the earth—as Archer explains in his short book on the subject and as Curt Stager repeats in his *Deep Future*—will eventually clean up the excess CO_2 we put out in the atmosphere but it works on an inhumanly long timescale.[16] 'The funny thing about the carbon cycle', writes Archer,

> is that the same carbon-cycle machinery both stabilizes the climate (on million-year time scale) and perturbs it (on glacial time scales). It would be analogous to some erratic fault in the surface, driving the house to warm up and cool down, while the thermostat tries to control the temperature of the house by regulating the furnace as best as it can. Time to call the furnace guy![17]

The climate crisis thus produces problems that we ponder over on very different and incompatible scales of time. Policy specialists think in terms of years, decades, at most centuries while politicians in democracies think in terms of their electoral cycles. Understanding what anthropogenic climate change is and how long its effects may last calls for thinking on very large scales, scales that defy the usual measures of time that inform human affairs. Archer goes to the heart of the problem here when he acknowledges that the million-year timescale of the planet's carbon cycle is 'irrelevant for political considerations of climate change on human time scales'. Yet, he insists, it remains relevant to any understanding of anthropogenic climate change since 'ultimately global warming will last for as long as it takes these slow processes to act'.[18]

Events—or more properly a cascade of events, which is what climate change is—conceived on such very large scales do not lend themselves easily to policymaking or activism. Yet 'What can we do about climate change?' remains an urgent and insistent question that understandably informs everything we write about the problem. However, when we

[15] Archer, *The Long Thaw*, p. 11.
[16] Stager, *Deep Future*, Chapter 2.
[17] Archer, *Global Carbon Cycle*, p. 20.
[18] Archer, *Global Carbon Cycle*, p. 21.

think of ourselves through this figure of sovereignty (and not as a geo-physical force!)—'what can *we* do?'—we naturally think on timescales that are human, the next 5, 50, or a 100 years. The language through which we speak of the climate crisis is shot through with this problem of human and inhuman or non-human scales of time. Take the most ubiquitous distinction we make in our everyday prose between non-renewable sources of energy and the 'renewables'. Fossil fuels we consider non-renewable on our terms but, as Bryan Lovell points out, fossil fuels are indeed renewable if only we think of them on a scale that is (in his terms) 'inhuman': 'Two hundred million years from now, a form of life requiring abundant oil for some purpose should find that plenty has formed since our own times.'[19]

Significant gaps between cognition and action thus open up in the existing literature on the climate problem between what we scientifically know about it—the vastness of its non-human or inhuman scale, for instance—and how we think about it when we treat it as a problem to be handled by the human means at our disposal. The latter have been developed for addressing problems we face on familiar scales of time. I call these gaps or openings in the landscape of our thoughts 'rifts' because they are like fault lines on a seemingly continuous surface: we have to keep crossing or straddling them as we think or speak of climate change. They inject a certain degree of contradictoriness in our thinking for we are being asked to think on different scales at once.

I want to discuss here three such rifts: the various regimes of probability that govern our everyday lives in modern economies now having to be supplemented by our knowledge of the radical uncertainty (of the climate); the story of our necessarily divided human lives having to be supplemented by the story of our collective life as a species, a dominant species, on the planet; and having to wrestle with our inevitably anthropocentric thinking in order to supplement it with forms of disposition towards the planet that do not put humans first. We have not yet overcome these dilemmas to settle decidedly on any one side of them. They remain as rifts.

In the rest of this chapter, I will discuss and elaborate on these rifts.

---

[19] Lovell, *Challenged By Carbon*, p. 75.

Probability and Radical Uncertainty

Modern life is ruled by regimes of probabilistic thinking. From evaluating lives for actuarial ends to the working of money and stock markets, we manage our societies by calculating risks and assigning probability values to them.[20] 'Economics', writes Charles S. Pearson in his book *Economics and the Challenge of Global Warming*, 'often makes a distinction between risk, where probabilities of outcomes are known, and uncertainty, where probabilities are not known and perhaps unknowable'.[21] This is surely one reason why economics as a discipline has emerged as the major art of social management today.[22] There is, therefore, an understandable tendency in both climate justice and climate policy literature—the latter dominated by economists or law scholars who think like economists—to focus not so much on what paleo-climatologists or geophysicists who study planetary climate historically have to say about climate change but rather on what we might call the physics of global warming that often presents a predictable, static set of relationships of probability and proportion: if the share of greenhouse gases in the atmosphere goes up by X, then the probability of the earth's average surface temperature going up by so much is Y.[23]

Such a way of thinking assumes a kind of stability or predictability—however probabilistic it may be—on the part of a warming atmosphere

[20] A thoughtful series of essays connecting public perceptions of risks and their management through statistical analyses and political and legal regulation is to be had in Cass R. Sunstein, *Risk and Reason: Safety, Law, and the Environment* (Cambridge: Cambridge University Press, 2002).

[21] Charles S. Pearson, *Economics and the Challenge of Global Warming* (Cambridge: Cambridge University Press, 2011), p. 25n6.

[22] A classic text on this topic is Frank Knight, *Risk, Uncertainty, and Profit* (Boston and New York: Houghton Mifflin Company, 1921). Knight would have objected to my use of the word 'art' with regard to the discipline of economics for he considered it to be part of the sciences. He begins the book with the statement: 'Economics, or more properly theoretical economics, is the only one of the social sciences which has aspired to the distinction of an exact science' (p. 1), while praising physics for securing 'our present marvelous mastery over the forces of nature' (p. 5).

[23] See, for example, the chart reproduced in Nicholas Stern, ed., *The Economics of Climate Change: The Stern Review* (Cambridge: Cambridge University Press, 2006), p. 200. See also Eric A. Posner and David Wisebach, *Climate Change Justice* (Princeton, NJ: Princeton University Press, 2010), Chapter 2.

that paleo-climatologists, focused more on the greater danger of tipping points, often do not assume. This is not because policy-thinkers are not concerned about the dangers of climate change; nor because they are ignorant of the profoundly non-linear nature of the relationship between greenhouse gases and rise in the planet's average surface temperature. They clearly are. But their methods are such that they appear to hold or bracket climate change as a broadly known variable (converting its uncertainties into risks that have been acknowledged and evaluated) while working out options that humans can create for themselves striving together or even wrangling among themselves. The world climate system, in other words, has no significant capacity to be a 'wild card' in their calculations in so far as they can make policy-prescriptions; it is there in a relatively predictable form to be managed by human ingenuity and political mobilization.

The rhetoric of the climate scientists, on the other hand, in what they write to persuade the public is often remarkably vitalist: in explaining the danger of anthropogenic climate change, they often resort to a language that portrays the climate system as a living organism. There is not only the famous case of the British geochemist James Lovelock comparing the life-system on the planet to a single living organism that he christened Gaia—a point that even the 'sober' paleo-climatologist David Archer accommodates in his primer on the global carbon cycle as a fair but 'philosophical definition'.[24] Archer himself describes the 'carbon cycle of the Earth' as 'alive'.[25] The image of climate as a temperamental 'animal' also inhabits the language of the environmental scientist Wallace (Wally) Broecker who in a book co-authored with Robert Kunzig thus describes his studies:

> Every now and then,... nature has decided to give a good swift kick to the climate beast. And the beast has responded, as beasts will—violently and a little unpredictably. Computer models ... [are] certainly a valid approach. But studying how the beast has responded in the past under stress is another way to prepare ourselves for what might happen as we take a whack at it ourselves. That's the idea that has obsessed Broecker

[24] Archer, *Global Carbon Cycle*, p. 22. Lovelock himself defends the 'concept' of Gaia at least as a metaphor. See James Lovelock, *The Vanishing Face of Gaia: A Final Warning* (New York: Basic Books, 2009), p. 13.

[25] Archer, *Global Carbon Cycle*, p. 1.

for the past twenty-five years, and with each passing year it has come to seem more urgent.[26]

Or notice how James Hansen uses the word 'lethargy' in explaining climate change in his aforementioned book *Storms of My Grandchildren*: 'The speed of glacial-interglacial change is dictated by 20,000-, 40,000-, and 100,000-year time scales for changes of Earth's orbit—but this does not mean that climate change is inherently *that* lethargic. On the contrary, human-made climate-forcing, by paleoclimate standards, is large and changes in decades, not tens of thousands of years.'[27] The vitalism of this prose does not arise because climate scientists are less 'scientific' than economists and policymakers. The vitalist metaphors issue from climate scientists' anxiousness to communicate and underscore two points about earth's climate: that its too many uncertainties cannot ever be completely tamed by existing human knowledge and hence the inherent unpredictability of its exact 'tipping points'. As David Archer puts it: 'The IPCC forecast for climate change in the coming century is for a generally smooth increase in temperature.... However, actual climate changes in the past have tended to be abrupt.... [C]limate models ... for the most part are unable to simulate the flip flops in the past climate record very well.'[28]

It is in fact this sense of a 'climate beast' that is missing from both the literature inspired by economics and that inspired by political commitments on the left. The moral philosopher John Broome, a lead author of the Working Group III of the Intergovernmental Panel on Climate Change (IPCC) and himself an economist-turned-philosopher, looks forward to a future where climate models continually improve to 'narrow' the probabilities that 'should be assigned to various possibilities'. For economic reasoning to have a better grasp of the world, 'detailed information about probabilities' is needed and, adds Broome, 'we are waiting for it to be supplied by scientists'.[29] But this may be

[26] Wallace S. Broecker and Robert Kunzig, *Fixing Climate: What Past Climate Changes Reveal about the Current Threat—And How to Counter It* (New York: Hill and Wang, 2008), p. 100.

[27] Hansen, *Storms of My Grandchildren*, p. 71.

[28] Archer, *The Long Thaw*, p. 95.

[29] John Broome, *Climate Matters: Ethics in a Warming World* (New York: W. W. Norton, 2012), p. 129.

to misunderstand the nature of the planet's climate and that of the models humans make of it. Climate uncertainties may not always be like measurable risks. 'Do we really need to know more than we know now about how much the Earth will warm? *Can* we know more?', asks Paul Edwards rhetorically in his book on the history of climate models, *A Vast Machine.* 'It is virtually certain that CO_2 concentrations will reach 550 ppm (the doubling point) sometime in the middle of this century' and the planet 'will certainly overshoot CO_2 doubling.' He reports climate scientists as engaged in the speculation 'that *we will probably never get a more exact estimate than we already have*'.[30]

The reasoning behind Edwards's statement is relevant to my argument. 'If engineers are sociologists', says Edwards, 'then climate scientists are historians'. Like historians, 'every generation of climate scientists revisit the same data, the same events—digging through the archives to ferret out new evidence, correct some previous interpretation', and so on. And 'just as with human history, we will never get a single, unshakable narrative of the global climate's past. Instead we get different versions of the atmosphere …, convergent yet never identical.'[31] Moreover, 'all of today's analyses are based on the climate we have experienced in historical time'. 'Once the world has warmed by 4°C', he quotes scientists Myles Allen and David Frame, 'conditions will be so different from anything we can observe today (and still more different from the last ice age) that it is inherently hard to say when the warming will stop'. Their point, Edwards explains, is this: it is not only that we do not know if 'there is some "safe" level of greenhouse gases that would "stabilize" the climate' for humans; thanks to anthropogenic global warming, we may 'never' be in a position to find out whether such a point of stabilization can exist in human timescales.[32]

The first rift that I speak of organizes itself around the question of the tipping point of the climate, a point beyond which global warming could be catastrophic for humans. That such a possibility exists is not in doubt. Paleo-climatologists know that the planet has undergone such warming in the geological past (as in the case of the PETM event). But

[30] Paul N. Edwards, *A Vast Machine: Computer Models, Climate Data, and the Politics of Global Warming* (Cambridge, MA: The MIT Press, 2010), pp. 438–9.

[31] Edwards, *A Vast Machine*, p. 431.

[32] Edwards, *A Vast Machine*, p. 439.

we cannot predict how quickly such a point could arrive. It remains an uncertainty, not amenable to the usual cost-benefit analyses that are a necessary part of risk-management strategies. As Pearson explains, 'BC [benefit-cost analysis] is not well suited to making catastrophe policy' and acknowledges that the 'special features that distinguish uncertainty in global warming are the presence of non-linearities, thresholds and potential tipping points, irreversibilities, and the long time horizon' that make 'projections of technology, economic structure, preferences and a host of other variables 100 years from now increasingly questionable'.[33] 'The implication of uncertainty, thresholds, tipping points', he writes, 'is that we should take a precautionary principle', that is, 'avoid taking steps today that lead to irreversible changes'.[34] But 'the precautionary principle', as Sunstein explains, also involves cost-benefit analysis and some estimation of probability: 'Certainly we should acknowledge that a small probability (say, 1 in 100,000) of serious harm (say, 100,000 deaths) deserves extremely serious attention ["better safe than sorry"].'[35] But we simply do not know the probability of the tipping point being reached over the next several decades or by 2100, for the tipping point would be a function of the rise in global temperature and multiple, unpredictable amplifying feedback loops working together. Under the circumstances, the one principle that the climate scientist James Hansen recommends to policy-thinkers concerns the use of coal as a fuel. He writes: 'If we want to solve the climate problem, we must phase out our coal emissions. Period.'[36] Not quite a 'precautionary principle' but what in the literature on risks would be known as 'the maximum principle': 'choose the policy with the best worst-case outcome'.[37] But this would seem unacceptable to governments and businesses around the world, for without coal, which China and India are still dependent on to a large degree (68–70 per cent of their energy supply), how would the majority of the world's poor be lifted out of poverty in the next few decades and thus equipped to adapt to the impact of climate change? Or, would the world scrambling to avoid the

---

[33] Pearson, *Economics and the Challenge of Global Warming*, pp. 26, 31.

[34] Pearson, *Economics and the Challenge of Global Warming*, p. 30.

[35] Sunstein, *Risk and Reason*, p. 103.

[36] Hansen, *Storms of My Grandchildren*, p. 176.

[37] See Sunstein, *Risk and Reason*, p. 129n40.

tipping point of the climate make the global economy itself tip over and cause untold human misery? Thus, would avoiding 'the harm' itself do more harm, especially as we do not know the probability of reaching the tipping point in the coming few decades?—this is the dilemma that goes with the application here of the precautionary or the maximum principle, as both Sunstein and Pearson explain.[38] It is not surprising that the philosopher Stephen Gardiner's chapter on 'cost-benefit' analyses in the context of climate change should be named 'Cost Benefit Paralysis!'[39]

At the heart of this rift is the question of scale. On the much more extended canvas on which they place the history of the planet, paleo-climatologists see climatic tipping points and species extinction as perfectly repeatable phenomena, irrespective of whether or not we can model for them. Our strategies of risk-management, however, arise from more short-term calculations of costs and their probabilities. The climate crisis requires us to move back and forth between thinking on these different scales all at once.

Our Divided Lives as Humans and Our Collective Life as a Dominant Species

Climate change gives rise to large and diverse issues of justice: justice between generations, between small island nations and the polluting countries (both past and prospective), between developed, industrialized nations (historically responsible for most emissions) and the newly industrializing ones, on questions of per capita emissions, and so on. There are good reasons why questions of justice arise but,

[38] Pearson, *Economics and the Challenge of Global Warming*, p. xx, and Sunstein, *Risk and Reason*, p. 129, acknowledge that 'the worst-case scenario involving global warming' calls for the application of the 'maximum principle' and yet recommends 'the cap and trade' system—which assumes a gradual transition to renewables—as 'it seems to be the most promising, in part because it is so much less expensive than the alternatives'. This amounts to replacing the maximum principle by the precautionary one. We can only infer how little understood the challenge of global warming-related 'uncertainty' was among scholars who assumed that the usual strategies of risk-management would be an adequate response to the problem.

[39] Stephen M. Gardiner, *A Perfect Moral Storm: The Ethical Tragedy of Climate Change* (Oxford and New York: Oxford University Press, 2011), Chapter 8.

leaving aside the question of intergenerational ethics that concerns the future, we should be clear that anthropogenic climate change is not inherently—or logically—a problem of past or accumulated intra-human injustice though, considered historically, it does entail some crucial justice issues, for only a few nations (some twelve or fourteen) and a fragment of humanity (about one-fifth) are historically responsible for most of the emissions of greenhouse gases so far. But imagine a counter-factual reality of a world in terms of income distribution both between and inside nations: imagine that Trotsky, for example, had won the debate with Stalin after the Bolshevik Revolution so that the revolution was successfully exported to every part of the world and the Soviets were not restricted by the Stalinist principle of building 'socialism in one country'. Suppose we had socialist prosperity in every nation but that the prosperity was based on current technology, population levels, and the exploitation of fossil fuel. The world would have undoubtedly been more egalitarian and just—at least in terms of distribution of income and wealth—but the climate crisis would have been worse! Our collective carbon footprint would have only been larger—for the poor do not consume much and contribute little to the production of greenhouse gases—and the climate change crisis would have been on us much sooner and in a much more drastic way. It is, ironically, thanks to the poor—that is, to the fact that development *is* uneven and unfair—that we do not put out even larger quantities of greenhouse gases into the biosphere than we actually do. Thus, logically speaking, the climate crisis is not inherently a result of economic inequalities—it is really a matter of the quantity of greenhouses gases we put out into the atmosphere that in itself is indifferent to human dramas. Those who connect climate change exclusively to historical origins/formations of income inequalities in the modern world raise valid questions about historical inequalities; but a reduction of the problem of climate change to that of capitalism (folded into the histories of modern European expansion and empires) only blinds us to questions of human agency that climate scientists—working with visions of pasts and futures on much larger scales—often bring to the fore: our agency as a species or a geophysical force over a period of time much longer than that of capitalism. If we see climate change primarily as a symptom of what is wrong with the capitalist mode of production, then all talk of a 'human-induced climate change' can only come under suspicion, for the word 'human' will then sound like a fig leaf with which to hide the venality of the consumption practices of the exploiting nations and classes. This analytical strategy is ultimately blind to the intertwining of human histories with the larger history of the planet and of our place in that history.

Peter Newell, a professor of international development at the University of East Anglia, and Matthew Paterson, a professor of political science at the University of Ottawa, express just such a sense of discomfiture about the use of the word 'human' in the expression 'human-induced climate change' in their recent book, *Climate Capitalism.* 'Behind the cosy language used to describe climate change as a common threat to all humankind,' they write, 'it is clear that some people and countries contribute to it disproportionately, while other bear the brunt of its effects'. 'What makes it a particularly tricky issue to address', they go on to say, 'is that it is the people that will suffer most that currently contribute least to the problem, i.e. the poor in the developing world. Despite often being talked about as a scientific question, climate change is *first and foremost a* deeply political and moral issue.'[40] Sunita Narain, director of the Centre for Science and Environment in Delhi, remarks in her endorsement of the book: 'Climate Change we know is intrinsically linked to the model of economic growth in the world.'[41] The climate crisis, write John Bellamy Foster, Brett Clark, and Richard York in their thoughtful book, *The Ecological Rift*, is 'at bottom, the product of a social rift: the domination of human being by human being. The driving force is a society based on class, inequality, and acquisition without end.'[42]

A very similar position was put forward in 2009 when the Department of Economic and Social Affairs of the United Nations published a report carrying the title *Promoting Development and Saving*

[40] Peter Newell and Matthew Paterson, *Climate Capitalism: Global Warming and the Transformation of the Global Economy* (Cambridge: Cambridge University Press, 2010), p. 7 (emphasis added).

[41] Sunita Narain, cover endorsement for Newell and Paterson, *Climate Capitalism.*

[42] John Bellamy Foster, Brett Clark, and Richard York, *The Ecological Rift: Capitalism's War on Earth* (New York: Monthly Review Press, 2010), p. 47.

the Planet.[43] In signing off the report, Mr Sha Zukang, the then United Nations undersecretary general for economic and social affairs, wrote: 'The climate crisis is the result of the very uneven pattern of economic development that evolved over the past two centuries, which allowed today's rich countries to attain their current levels of income, in part through not having to account for the environmental damage now threatening the lives and livelihoods of others.'[44] Characterizing climate change as a 'development challenge', Sha Zukang went on to remark how a certain deficit of trust marks the attitude of the non-Western countries towards the West.[45] The report actually expanded on his point: 'How developing countries can achieve catch-up growth and economic convergence in a carbon-constrained world and what the advanced countries must do to relieve these concerns have become leading questions for policy makers at the national and international levels.'[46]

The original formulation of this position, to the best of my knowledge, goes back to 1991 when two well-known and respected Indian environmental activists, the late Anil Agarwal and Sunita Narain (whom we have already met), authored a booklet titled *Global Warming in an Unequal World: A Case of Environmental Colonialism* published by their organization, the Centre for Science and Environment, in Delhi.[47] This booklet did much to generate the idea of 'shared but differentiated responsibilities' and the tendency to argue from figures of per capita emissions of greenhouse gases that became popular as part of the Kyoto Protocol. Agarwal and Narain's immediate provocation for writing this book was the publication of a report by the World Resources Institute the year before. 'The idea', wrote Agarwal and Naraian, 'that developing countries like India and China must share the blame for heating up the earth and destabilizing the climate, as espoused in a recent study published in the United

[43] *Promoting Development and Saving the Planet* (New York: United Nations, 2009).

[44] *Promoting Development*, p. vii.

[45] *Promoting Development*, p. xviii.

[46] *Promoting Development*, p. 3.

[47] Anil Agarwal and Sunita Narain, *Global Warming in an Unequal World: A Case of Environmental Colonialism* (Delhi: Centre for Science and Environment, 1991).

States by the World Resources Institute in collaboration with the United Nations, is an excellent example of *environmental colonialism'*. They continued:

> *A detailed look at the data presented by WRI itself leads to the conclusion that India and China cannot be held responsible even for a single kg of carbon dioxide or methane that is accumulating in the earth's atmosphere.... The accumulation is mainly the result of the gargantuan consumption of the developed countries, particularly the United States.*[48]

Making a distinction between 'the "survival emissions" of the poor ... [and] the "luxury emissions" of the rich', and building from the argument that the natural carbon sinks—such as the oceans—were part of the global commons and hence best distributed between nations by applying the principle of equal access on a per capita basis, Agarwal and Narain proceeded to expand on their visions of 'sustainable development': 'In a world that aspires to such lofty ideals like global justice, equity, and sustainability, this vital global common should be shared equally on a per capita basis.'[49]

What thus distinguishes this history of 'anthropogenic global warming' from that put forward by climate scientists is the suspicion, from this particular 'climate justice' position, of any talk of a common 'humanity' being responsible for the situation we find ourselves in. Agarwal and Narain were thus extremely sceptical of what they saw as the 'one world-ism' of Gus Speth—James Gustave Speth, an environmental lawyer and Yale academic—who was the founder-director of the World Resources Institute and who claimed that 'the new information means that industrial and developing countries must work together to begin to reduce emissions of greenhouse gases and we need a new era of environmental cooperation'. Agarwal and Narain retorted: 'Just what kind of politics or morality is this which masquerades in the name of "one worldism" and "high minded internationalism?"' 'Third World environmentalists', they warned, 'must not get taken for a ride by this highly partisan "one worldism"'.[50]

---

[48] World Resources Institute, *World Resources 1990–91: A Guide to the Global Environment* (New York: Oxford University Press, 1990), cited in Agarwal and Narain, *Global Warming*, p. 1 (emphasis in the original).

[49] Agarwal and Narain, *Global Warming in an Unequal World*, pp. 2, 13.

[50] Agarwal and Narain, *Global Warming in an Unequal World*, pp. 3, 5.

Clearly, the roots of the suspicion of this use of the category 'humanity' go back to the 'Third World'-ist sentiments of the 1950s and 1960s, years that saw struggles to decolonize the world. The solution that Agarwal and Narain recommended had this Third Worldist politics written all over it and they recognized it as such: the 'rich and powerful consumers of the world ... [should pay] ... the true cost of their consumption. *That is not an economic issue but an intensely political one*'.[51] And the leadership for this politics, in their view, required a united bloc of the leaders of the Third World nations, as otherwise for the poor 'this will remain a harsh and vicious world which is not prepared to give them a fair place'.[52] One could say, in parenthesis, that much of the recent climate change policy debate in India vis-à-vis the Copenhagen conference revolved implicitly around this question of the extent to which India or China could continue to play the 'Third World' card while also aspiring to be major players in the global economy and ignoring effectively the precarious situations in which smaller nations such as the Maldives or Samoa find themselves.[53]

This suspicion of the category 'human' is of a postcolonial variety. Given the predatory history of nations, in particular the Western nations, in the last 500 years, one cannot simply dismiss the suspicion. It will remain a part of the landscape of negotiations around climate change. But the argument presented is not without some problems. The real elephant in the room is the question of population. The 'problem' of population, while due surely in part to modern medicine, public health measures, eradication of epidemics, the use of artificial fertilizers, and so on, cannot be attributed in any straightforward way to a logic of a predatory and capitalist West, for neither China nor India pursued unbridled capitalism while their populations exploded.

[51] Agarwal and Narain, *Global Warming in an Unequal World*, p. 24 (emphasis in the original).

[52] Agarwal and Narain, *Global Warming in an Unequal World*, p. 25.

[53] Incidentally, Agarwal and Narain's 'Third Worldism' and the smaller island nations' concerns about the implications of global warming and the consequent rise in sea levels date from the same period, the early 1990s. See Robert Chase and Joeli Veitayaki, *Implications of Climate Change and Sea Level Rise for Western Samoa: Report of a Preparatory Mission* (Apia, Western Samoa: December 1992), available at http://202.4.49.29/att/IRC/eCOPIES/Countries/Samoa/74.pdf (last accessed on 24 April 2010).

In the fact, the issue of population as it relates to climate change gets both acknowledged and disavowed in the per capita figures that often underlie these arguments for 'climate justice'. If India had been more successful with population control or with economic development, the per capita emission figures would have been higher (that the richer classes in India want to emulate Western styles and standards of consumption would be obvious to any observer). Indeed the Indian minister in charge of the Environment and Forests, Mr Jairam Ramesh, said as much in an address to the Indian Parliament in 2009: 'Per-capita is an accident of history. It so happened that we could not control our population.'[54]

Yet population remains a very important factor in how the climate crisis plays out. For without their having such large populations that the Chinese and Indian governments legitimately desire to 'pull out of poverty', they would not be building so many coal-fired power stations every year. The Indian government is fond of quoting Gandhi on the present environmental crisis: 'The earth [*prithvi*] provides enough to satisfy every man's need but not enough for every man's greed.'[55] Yet 'greed' and 'need' become indistinguishable from each other in

[54] See Navroj K. Dubash, ed., *Handbook of Climate Change and India: Development, Politics and Governance* (New Delhi: Oxford University Press, 2012), p. 238. See also the paper by D. Raghunandan in this book where he argues that this 'climate justice' position that India championed at many international forums on climate change was informed more by 'geopolitical assessments' than by any 'deep scientific understanding' (pp. 172–3).

[55] Gandhi is supposed to have said this in Hindi in 1947 to his secretary Pyarelal Nayyar who reproduced it in his book, *Mahatma Gandhi—The Last Phase*, 2 vols (Ahmedabad: Navajivan Publishing House, 1956–8). There is a good discussion of the saying in Y. P. Anand and Mark Lindley's paper 'Gandhi on providence and greed' available on the internet at http://www.academia.edu/303042/Gandhi_on_providence_and_greed (last accessed on 13 September 2013). Anand and Lindley say that Gandhi was influenced by the work of J. C. Kumarappa, in turn a Gandhian economist to whose book *Economy of Permanence* (1945) Gandhi had contributed a preface. Interestingly, India's *National Action Plan on Climate Change* misquotes Gandhi's dictum as saying 'The earth has enough resources to meet people's needs but will never have enough to satisfy people's greed', thus missing the emphasis that Gandhi typically put on the individual's sense of moral responsibility. See Government of India's *National Action Plan on Climate Change* (p. 1) available at http://pmindia.gov.in/climate_change_english.pdf (last accessed on 12 September 2013).

arguments in defence of continued use of coal, the worst offender among fossil fuels. India and China want coal; Australia and other countries want to export it. It is still the cheapest variety of fossil fuel. In 2011, reports the *New York Times*, 'coal represented 30 per cent of world energy' and that was 'the highest share it [had] had since 1969'. Coal use was expected to increase by 50 per cent by 2035 bringing enormous export opportunities to companies in South America. 'American coal companies', remarked the report in the *Times*, 'badly want to export coal from the country's most productive mines in the Powder River Basin in Wyoming and Montana' as they saw that in the longer term, thanks to China and India, coal's future seemed 'bright—mainly because it is cheaper than its competitors'.[56] This vast market for coal would not have come about without China and India justifying the use of coal by referring to the needs of their poor.

Population is also a problem because the total size and distribution of humanity matters in how the climate crisis unfolds, particularly with regards to species extinction. There is the widely accepted point that humans have been putting pressures on other species for quite some time now; I do not need to belabour it. Indeed the war between humans and animals such as the rhinoceros, elephants, monkeys, and big cats may be seen every day in many Indian cities and villages. That we have consumed many varieties of marine life out of existence is also generally accepted. Ocean acidification threatens the lives of many species.[57] And, clearly, as many have pointed out, the exponential growth of human population in the twentieth century has generally had much to do with fossil fuels through the use of artificial fertilizers, pesticides, and pumps for irrigation.[58]

But there is another reason why the history of human evolution and the total number of human beings today matter when we get to the question of species survival as the planet warms. One way that species threatened by global warming will try to survive is by migrating to areas more conducive to their existence. This is how they have survived past changes in the climatic conditions of the planet. But now there are so

[56] 'With China and India Ravenous for Energy, Coal's Future Seems Assured', *New York Times*, 13 November 2012, p. B6.

[57] On all this, see Hansen, *Storms of My Grandchildren*.

[58] See Smil, *Harvesting the Biosphere*, p. 221; Butler, Lerch, and Wuerthner, eds, *The Energy Reader*, pp. 11–12.

many of us and we are so widespread on this planet that we stand in the way. Curt Stager puts it clearly:

> Even if we take a relatively moderate emissions path into the future and thereby hope to avoid destroying the last polar and alpine refugees, warming on the scale [expected] … will still nudge many species toward higher latitudes and elevation. In the past, species could simply move … but this time they'll be trapped within the confines of habitats that are mostly immobilized by our presence.… As the Anthropocene warming rises toward its as yet unspecified peak, our long-suffering biotic neighbors face a situation that they have never encountered before in the long, dramatic history of ice ages and interglacials. They can't move because we're standing in their way.[59]

The irony of the point runs deeper. The spread of human groups throughout the world—the Pacific islands were the last to be settled by around 3,500 BP—and their growth in the age of industrial civilization now makes it difficult for human climate refugees to move to safer and more inhabitable climes.[60] Other humans will stand in their way. Burton Richter, the Nobel-winning physicist from Stanford who now interests himself in climate matters, puts the point thus:

> We [humans] were able to adapt to [climate] change in the past … but there were tens of thousands of years to each swing compared with only hundreds of years for the earth to heat up this time. The slow pace of change gave the relatively small population back then time to move, and this is what it did during the many temperature swings of the past, including the ice ages. The population now is too big to move *en masse*, so we had better do our best to limit the damage we are causing.[61]

The history of population thus belongs to two histories at once: the very short-term history of the industrial way of life—of modern medicine, technology, and fossil fuels (fertilizers, pesticides, irrigation)—that

---

[59] Stager, *Deep Future*, pp. 62, 66. See also the discussion in Hansen, *Storms of My Grandchildren*, pp. 145–6.

[60] Michael Denny and Lisa Matisoo-Smith, 'Rethinking Polynesian Origins: Human Settlement of the Pacific', LENScience Senior Biology Seminar Series, Alan Wilson Centre, The University of Otago, available at https://docs.google.com/viewer?a=v&q=cache:zksQjlwnN9sJ:lens.auckland.ac.nz/images/3/31/Pacific_Migration_Seminar_Paper.pdf (last accessed on 4 January 2013).

[61] Burton Richter, *Beyond Smoke and Mirrors: Climate Change and Energy in the 21st Century* (Cambridge: Cambridge University Press, 2010), p. 2.

accompanied and enabled the growth in our numbers; and the much, much longer-term deep history of our species, the history through which we have evolved to be the dominant species of the planet, spreading all over it and now threatening the existence of many other life forms. The poor participate in that shared history of human evolution just as much as the rich do. The per capita emission figures, while useful in making a necessary and corrective political point in the debates on climate change, hide that larger history. But 'population' is clearly a category that conjoins the two histories together.

Between Anthropocentrism and Enlightened Anthropocentrism

Just because the climate crisis reveals the sudden coming together—the enjambment, if you will—of the usually separated syntactic orders of recorded and deep histories of the human kind, of species history, and the history of the earth systems, revealing the deep connections through which the planet's carbon cycle and life interact with each other and so on, it does not mean that this knowledge will stop humans from pursuing, with vigour and vengeance, our all too human ambitions and squabbles that unite and divide us at the same time.[62] However much we speak of a human-induced climate change, humanity will remain a category of thought, even an ideal of political horizons, but perhaps never become a unified political agent acting in ways that are unjust to none. Evolutionary biologists who explain how deeply evolved our instincts of cooperation are also explain how hardwired is our tribalism or what Edward O. Wilson calls 'the instinct to defend the nest'.[63] Our

---

[62] Lovelock writes thus of the connection between life and the atmosphere: 'The oxygen of the atmosphere is almost wholly the product of photosynthetic organisms, and without it there would be no animals or invertebrates, nor would we burn fuels and so add carbon dioxide to the air.... Organisms adapted not to [a] static world ... but to a dynamic world built by the organisms themselves' (Lovelock, *The Vanishing Face*, p. 48). On the role that life has played in making the earth habitable, see also the discussion in Raymond T. Pierrehumbert, *Principles of Planetary Climate* (Cambridge: Cambridge University Press, 2010), pp. 10–14. Pierrehumbert comments: 'The book is far from closed on the Habitability Problem' (p. 14). See also note 67 given later.

[63] E. O. Wilson, *The Social Conquest of Earth* (New York: W. W. Norton, 2012).

being social is perhaps predicated, in evolutionary terms, on our being divided as well: much early socialization happened in small bands of humans that fought one another, and that that trait remains coded in our evolutionary make-up.

In their fascinating paper on 'The Anthropocene', Will Steffen, Paul Crutzen, and John McNeill have drawn our attention to what they call—after Polyani, I assume—the period of 'The Great Acceleration' in human history, c.1945–2015, when global figures for population, real gross domestic products, foreign direct investment, damming of rivers, water use, fertilizer consumption, urban population, paper consumption, transport motor vehicles, telephones, international tourism, and McDonald's restaurants (yes!), all began to increase dramatically, in an exponential fashion.[64] This period, they suggest, could be a strong candidate for an answer to the question as to when did the Anthropocene begin. While the Anthropocene may stand for all the climate problems we face today collectively, as a historian of human affairs it is impossible for me not to notice that this period of so-called great acceleration is also the period of great decolonization in countries that had been dominated by European imperial powers and that made a move towards modernization (the damming of rivers, for instance) over the ensuing decades and, with the globalization of the last twenty years, towards a certain degree of democratization of consumption as well. As a historian, I cannot ignore the fact that 'the great acceleration' included the production and consumption of consumer durables—such as the refrigerator and the washing machine—in Western households that were touted as 'emancipatory' for women.[65] Nor can I forget the pride with which today the most ordinary and poor Indian citizen now possesses his or her smartphone or a fake and cheap substitute.[66] The lurch into the Anthropocene has also been globally the story of some long-anticipated social justice as well.

[64] Will Steffen, Paul J. Crutzen, and John R. McNeill, 'The Anthropocene: Are Humans Now Overwhelming the Great Forces of Nature [?]', *AMBIO: A Journal of the Human Evolution* 36, no. 8 (2007): 614–21.

[65] For an Australian example of this, see Lesley Johnson, *The Modern Girl: Childhood and Growing Up* (Sydney: Allen and Unwin, 1993).

[66] See Robin Jeffrey and Assa Doron, *The Great Indian Phone Book: How Cheap Mobile Phones Change Politics and Daily Lives* (London: Hurst, 2013).

Social justice projects, however, are usually very human-centred, for the human has been at the centre of political thought, and when we look at the world politically, it is human welfare that emerges as our primary concern even though recent environmentalist cautions have led to some questioning of this stance. Paleo-climatologists writing on global warming, however, move away from such an anthropocentric outlook on the world and invariably invite us to take a longer-term view of the planet; they emphasize the role of life in the maintenance of the earth's climate and raise questions about where humanity might be assigned a place in that larger story.[67] But there is also the discourse of modernization—a human-centric discourse. Capitalist economies in particular work on anthropocentric principles more intensely than did feudal or rural economies or those based predominantly on cultivation by peasants or farming families. Consumption-driven mass economies perhaps strengthen anthropocentric tendencies of thought to even higher degrees.

The result has been a near-complete human appropriation of the biosphere. Jan Zalasiewicz quotes some sobering statistics from the researches of Vaclav Smil:

> Smil has taken our measure from the most objective criterion of all: collective weight. Considered simply as body mass ... we now bulk up to about a third of terrestrial vertebrate body mass on Earth. Most of the other two-thirds, by the same measure, comprise what we keep to eat: cows, pigs, sheep and such. Something under 5% and perhaps as little as 3% is now made of the genuinely wild animals—the cheetahs, elephants,

---

[67] Lovelock's idea that life plays a role in its own maintenance on the planet not only enjoys wide appeal—see, for instance, William Ophul's *Plato's Revenge: Politics in the Age of Ecology* (Cambridge, MA: MIT Press, 2011), pp. 34–36, 65—but has also received a fascinating and rigorous critique in Toby Tirell's *On Gaia* (Princeton, NJ: Princeton University Press, 2013). But see also Doug Macdougall, *Why Geology Matters: Decoding the Past, Anticipating the Future* (Berkeley: University of California Press, 2011), pp. xi, 171, 251:

> Organic life itself, once formed, becomes a determinant of the non-organic world: bacterial work contributes to the carbon cycle, even mineral-formation is biologically mediated.... Once photosynthesizing plants gained a foothold and began to oxygenate the atmosphere and oceans, a whole new array of oxide materials appeared at the Earth's surface. The increase in mineral numbers is irreversible; we can never go back to the sixty or so that existed before planet formation.

antelopes and the like.... Earlier in the Quaternary [the last two million years], ... humans were just one of some 350 large ... vertebrate species....

'Given the precipitate drop in the numbers of wild vertebrates, one might imagine that vertebrate biomass as a whole has gone down', writes Zalasiewicz, and comments:

> Well, no.... Humans have become very good at, firstly, increasing the rate of vegetable growth, by conjuring nitrogen from the air and phosphorus from the ground, and then directing that extra growth towards its brief stopover in our captive beasts, and thence, to us.... the total vertebrate biomass has increased by something approaching an order of magnitude above "natural" levels.

Zalasiewicz himself remarks: 'Staggering, isn't it?'[68]

This brings me to my third rift in the literature on climate change. How do we reconcile our anthropocentric human concerns with justice and welfare with the knowledge of our having become a dominant species whose existence produces stress not only for humans and other forms of life but for the climate system of the planet as a whole?

Here again we encounter very different and opposed moods in the literature. There are those who acknowledge the deleterious impact of humans on their environment and yet find the solution to global warming in some understanding of the specialness of humans, usually in some form or other of human ingenuity. Mark Lynas, for instance, a climate change journalist, literally exhorts humans to become the 'god species' in his book by that name by cheerily adopting geoengineering as way to solve or manage the problem of climate change. 'Can humanity manage the planet—and itself—towards [the] transition to sustainability?' he asks. His answer: 'Grounds for optimism are at least as strong as the grounds for pessimism, and only optimism can give us motivation and passion we will need to succeed.... The truth is that global environmental problems are soluble. Let us go forward and solve

---

[68] Zalasiewicz, 'The Human Touch', p. 2. While Zalasiewicz's summary of Smil's researches is extremely helpful, it should be remembered most of Smil's effort in *Harvesting the Biosphere* is directed at reminding the reader of the methodological challenges involved in measuring the changes reported on here and how approximate and provisional the relevant numbers are.

them.'[69] Erle Ellis, a geographer at the University of Maryland, writes in the *New York Times* of 13 September 2013 that the idea that 'humans must live within the natural environmental limits of our planet denies the reality of our entire history, and most likely the future.... The only limits to creating a planet that future generations will be proud of are our imaginations and our social systems. In moving towards a better Anthropocene, the environment will be what we make it.' In fact, he calls *this* 'the science of the Anthropocene'.[70]

Lynas's and Ellis's propositions are not only about human specialness but also about our special claims on the planet. At the opposite end of the spectrum are scientists who advise otherwise and place the human in no special relation to the biosphere. It is possible that their triumphal optimism is, in Lauren Berlant's sense of the term, cruel: 'A relation of cruel optimism exists when something you desire is actually an obstacle to your flourishing.'[71] Clive Hamilton's book, *Earthmasters*, on the pitfalls of geoengineering, for example, powerfully argues how geoengineering could indeed endanger human flourishing.[72] Vaclav Smil concludes his massively researched book, *Harvesting the Biosphere*, with these cautionary words: 'If billions of poor people in low-income countries were to claim even half the current per capita harvests prevailing in affluent economies, too little of the Earth's primary production would be left in its more or less natural state, and very little would remain for mammalian species other than ours.'[73] The paleo-climatologist David Archer also begins *The Long Thaw* on a completely different note. Science, Archer thinks, is humbling for humans for it does not hold up the case for human specialness. It

[69] Mark Lynas, *The God Species: How the Planet Can Survive the Age of Humans* (London: Fourth Estate, 2011), pp. 243–4.

[70] Erle C. Ellis, 'Overpopulation is Not the Problem', *New York Times*, 13 September 2013.

[71] Lauren Berlant, *Cruel Optimism* (Durham, NC: Duke University Press, 2011), pp. 1, 24.

[72] Clive Hamilton, *Earthmasters: The Dawn of the Age of Climate Engineering* (New Haven and London: Yale University Press, 2013). Pierrehumbert's opinions on 'geoengineering fixes' are also clear: 'They are a rather desperate and alarming prospect as a solution to global warming, since they offset a climate forcing lasting a thousand years or more with a fix requiring more or less annual maintenance if catastrophe is not to strike' (*Planetary Climate*, p. 67).

[73] Smil, *Harvesting the Biosphere*, p. 252.

rather tells us we are not 'biologically "special"'—'we are descended from monkeys, and they from even humbler origins'. 'Geological evidence', he further writes, 'tells us that the world is much older than we are, and there's no evidence that it was created especially for us. This is all very humbling.'[74]

The idea that humans are special has, of course, a long history. We should perhaps speak of 'anthropocentrisms' in the plural here. There is, for instance, a long line of thinking—from religions that came long after humans established the first urban centres of civilization and created the idea of a transcendental God through to the modern social sciences—that has humans positioned as facing the rest of the world, as nature. These later religions are in strong contrast, it seems, with the much more ancient religions of hunting-gathering peoples (I think here of the Australian Aboriginals and their stories) that often saw humans as part of animal life (as though we were part of the 'Animal Planet' show and not simply watching it from outside the idiot box). The humans were not necessarily special in these ancient religions: they ate and got eaten in the same way that other animals did. They were part of life.[75] The very idea of a transcendental God saw humans in a special relationship to the Creator and to his creation, the world.

This point needs a separate and longer discussion but for a completely random and arbitrary—arbitrary, for I could have chosen examples from other religious traditions including Hinduism—instance of this for now consider the following remarks from Fazlur Rahman, the noted scholar of Islam who taught at the University of Chicago. By way of explaining the term *qadar*—meaning both 'power and measuring out'—that the Quran uses in close association with another word, *amr*, meaning 'command' to express the nature of God, Rahman remarks thus on God's relationship to man as mediated through nature:

[74] Archer, *The Long Thaw*, pp. 1–2.

[75] Cf. Emile Durkheim, *The Elementary Forms of Religious Life*, trans. Joseph Ward Swain (London: George Allen and Unwin, 1982 [1915]), pp. 134, 139. In determining 'the place of man in the scheme of religious things' in his discussion of totemistic beliefs, Durkheim was clear that totemism pointed to the 'double nature' of man: 'Two beings co-exist within him: a man and an animal.' And again: 'We must be careful not to consider totemism a sort of animal worship.... Their [men and their totems'] relations are rather those of two things who are on the same level and of equal value.'

The all-powerful, purposeful, and merciful God … 'measured out' everything, bestowing upon everything the right range of potentialities, its laws
of behavior, in sum, its character. This measuring on the one hand ensures
the orderliness of nature and on the other expresses the most fundamental,
unbridgeable difference between the nature of God and the nature of man:
the Creator's measuring implies an infinitude wherein no measured creature
… can share.

This is why 'nature does not and cannot disobey God's commands
[amr] and cannot violate natural laws'.[76] While this enjoins very clearly
that man must not play God, it does not mean, as Rahman clarifies,
that 'man cannot discover the laws and exploit it for human benefit'.[77]
God is kind because he has stocked the world with provisions for us![78]
Environmentalists, similarly, have long cited a verse in the Genesis in
which the Lord says '[let men] have dominion … over all the earth, and
over every creeping thing that creeps on earth' and enjoins man to 'be
fruitful and multiply and fill the earth and subdue it'.[79]

We get the same thought in secular and unvarnished prose in the
Oxford moral philosopher John Broome's thoughts on 'ethics in a
warming world', and the sources of his thinking are clearly not in Islam.
In a section entitled 'What Is Ultimately Good?', Broome acknowledges
that climate change raises this question—'in particular the question
if nature—species, ecosystems, wildernesses, landscapes—has value in
itself'. But that question, he decides, is 'too big' for his book—and yet
he still proceeds to offer these thoughts on the value of nature:

[76] Fazlur Rahman, *Major Themes of the Qur'an* (Chicago: University of
Chicago Press, 2009, 2nd ed.), pp. 12–13.

[77] Rahman, *Major Themes*, p. 13.

[78] An interesting text claiming—from a mixture of Hindu and Buddhist
perspectives—a special relationship between man and God is Rabindranath
Tagore's 1930 Oxford Hibbert Lectures published as *The Religion of Man*
(1931) in which Tagore showed an awareness of a Hindu theological position
that conceived of God as indifferent to human affairs but rejected it in favour
of a Buddhist understanding of infinity that 'was not the idea of an unbounded
cosmic activity but the infinite whose meaning is in the positive ideals of goodness and love, which cannot be otherwise than human'. Rabindranath Tagore,
'Crisis in Civilization', in *The English Writings of Rabindranath Tagore*, ed. Sisir
Kumar Das, vol. 3 (Delhi: Sahitya Akademi, 1999), p. 111.

[79] Cited in Ernst Partridge, 'Nature as a Moral Resource', *Environmental
Ethics* 6 (Summer 1984): 103.

Nature is undoubtedly valuable because it is good for people. It provides material goods and services. The river brings us our clean water and takes away our dirty water. Wild plants provide many of our medicines,... Nature also brings emotional good to people. But the significant question raised by climate change is whether nature has value in itself.... This question is too big for this book. I shall concentrate on the good of the people.[80]

Here, then, is my third rift. The literature on climate change reconfigures an older debate on anthropocentrism and so-called non-anthropocentrism that has long exercised philosophers and scholars interested in environmental ethics: do we value the non-human for its own sake or because it is good for us?[81] Non-anthropocentrism, however, may indeed be a chimera for, as the Chinese scholar Feng Han points out in a different context, 'human values will always be from a human point of view'.[82] Ecologically minded philosophers in the 1980s used to distinguish between 'weak' and 'strong' versions of anthropocentrism, and support the weak ones. Strong anthropocentrism had to do with unreflexive and instinctive use or exploitation of nature for purely human preferences; weak anthropocentrism was seen as a position arrived at through rational reflections on why the non-human was important for human flourishing.[83] James Lovelock's work

[80] Broome, *Climate Matters*, pp. 112–13.

[81] See, for instance, Lawrence Buell, *Writing for an Endangered World: Literature, Culture, and Environment in the U.S. and Beyond* (Cambridge, MA: The Belknap Press of Harvard University Press, 2001), Chapter 7, 'The Misery of Beasts and Humans: Nonanthropocentric Ethics versus Environmental Justice', pp. 224–42.

[82] Feng Han, 'The Chinese View of Nature: Tourism in China's Scenic and Historic-Interest Areas', PhD thesis, School of Design, Faculty of Built Environment and Engineering, Queensland University of Technology, Australia, 2006, pp. 22–3. I am grateful to Professor Ken Taylor for drawing my attention to this thesis. Han, of course, is echoing Eugene Hargrove; see the latter's essay 'Weak Anthropocentric Intrinsic Value', *The Monist* 75, no. 2 (1992): 183–207 cited in Karyn Lai, 'Environmental Concern: Can Humans Avoid Being Partial? Epistemological Awareness in the *Zhuangzi*', in *Nature, Environment and Culture in East Asia: The Challenge of Climate Change*, ed. Carmen Meinert (Leiden, Boston: Brill, 2013), p. 79.

[83] See, for example, Bryan G. Norton, 'Environmental Ethics and Weak Anthropocentrism', *Environmental Ethics* 6 (Summer 1984): 131–48. Norton was the first to propose the idea of 'weak anthropocentrism' that has since been taken up by many.

on climate change, however, produces a third position, urged on by his sense of a looming emergency. He packs it into a pithy proposition that works almost as the motto of his book *The Vanishing Face of Gaia*, and it is: 'To consider the health of the Earth without the constraint that the welfare of humankind comes first.'[84] The proposition is not as neglectful of humans as it might seem on first sight. For, as Lovelock explains in the sentence that immediately follows, it is in interest of long-term survival of our species that humans must not blindly put human welfare first: 'I see the health of the planet as primary, for we are utterly dependent upon a healthy planet for survival.'[85] In the same way as we speak of 'enlightened self-interest', we may call it a form of 'enlightened anthropocentrism'.

Coda

Scientific knowledge and analysis of climate change as such do not persuade us to act. And this is where a gap opens up between cognition and action in the context of climate change. While some of this inability to act is due no doubt to the self-interested work of those privileged individuals and institutions whose material interests are threatened by action on the emission of greenhouse gases, some of it is also owing to the problems of scale that this crisis involves.

For the first time in their history, humans are faced with the question of their being actors over two completely different scales of time, scales that have been described, respectively, as human and inhuman. The structures we inhabit, regimes of probability that govern our everyday lives, and the habits of thought that go with them are all made for scales that are human. Some of these habits are probably even of evolutionary origins. Take, for instance, the widely noticed phenomenon that when asked about global warming—but not just about global warming—individuals often place their trust more in anecdotal or experiential evidence than in the reasoning of science. Sunstein notices this in his discussion of risks and classifies it under something called 'availability heuristics', heuristics that are psychologically available to people in everyday life. Lovelock discusses the same problem—'why

---

84 Lovelock, *The Vanishing Face of Gaia*, pp. 35–6.
85 Lovelock, *The Vanishing Face of Gaia*, p. 36.

thinking anecdotally comes naturally but thinking scientifically does not'—and gives us an evolutionary explanation: 'Our intelligence is not something transcendental but a property that evolved to fit us into our niche, like the tough beak of a woodpecker evolved to fit into its world where the food supply is tree-bark bugs.'[86] Thinking anecdotally or trusting experience must have been crucial to human survival. Responding to climate change, therefore, will not be an easy matter of leaping out of our habits of thought. Yet, cognitively, we know that we also now collectively act on scales at which the mind truly boggles. This is why I used the word 'rift' to refer to openings, breaches, in the usual and habitual landscape of thoughts. A rift means we walk on both sides of it or keep jumping across from one side to the other. It is a bit like constantly having to shift gears, mentally.

Reading paleo-climatologists who are necessarily aware of the problem of scale and yet want to close the gap between cognition and action points to an interesting area of convergence between science and the humanities. Consider the following two very different rhetorical moves by two climate scientists cited before—Raymond T. Pierrehumbert and David Archer, colleagues at the University of Chicago—each dealing with human implications of anthropogenic global warming. Pierrehumbert, writing a 'how-to' book for students intending to take technical courses on planetary climates, writes in the following terms of how today's climate change may seem to future humans or some other intelligent species—his tone is calm, dispassionate, self-possessed, and does not at all sound like a call to action, for the vastness of scale here is a spur to disciplinary imagination:

> As seen by paleoclimatologists 10 million years in the future, whatever species they may be, the present era of catastrophic release of fossil fuel carbon will appear as an enigmatic event which will have a name of its own, much as paleoclimatologists today refer to the PETM [55 million years ago] or the K-T [66 million years ago] boundary event. The fossil carbon release event will show up in ^{13}C proxies of the carbon cycle,... through mass extinctions arising from rapid warming, and through the moraine record left by retreating mountain glaciers and land-based ice sheets. As an event, it is unlikely to permanently destroy the habitability of our planet.... Still a hundred generations or more of our descendants

---

[86] Sunstein, *Risk and Reason*, pp. 33–4 and Lovelock, *Vanishing Face of Gaia*, p. 80.

will be condemned to live in a planetary climate far different from that which nurtured humanity.... [87]

Compare this with the move with which David Archer opens his book *The Long Thaw*, aimed at communicating to a general reading public the urgency of action needed on climate change. Archer directly confronts questions of intergenerational ethics that straddle and illustrate the problem of temporal scale. If indeed our greenhouse gas emissions are changing the climate of the planet for the next 100,000 years, as Archer shows, how many generations beyond us should we—or even can we—really care for?[88] Our capacity to thus care, something that has evolved over a long period of time, may not be unlimited. Trying to explain as why we 'mere mortals' *should* 'worry about altering climate 100,000 years from now', Archer has to step beyond the limits of his science and ask his reader a moral–historical question: 'How would it feel if the ancient Greeks ... had taken advantage of some lucrative business opportunities for a few centuries, aware of potential costs, such as, say a stormier world, or the loss of 10% of agricultural production to rising sea levels—that could persist to this day?'[89]

Archer's rhetorical question may not persuade many, but it points up an important problem in the politics of climate change: motivating human action on global warming necessarily entails the difficult, if not impossible, task of making available to human experience a cascade of events that unfold on a non-human scale. This act of persuading humans to act brings us up against the politics of climate change. Politics means having to deal with divisions among humans. Humanity as a whole will never be a politically purposive entity, not at least for a sustainable period of time. And it is precisely because we humans are not politically one that histories of intra-human (in)justice and welfare will remain relevant and necessary to the efforts we make to cope with climate change. But we will probably have to think of these political histories that divide us for the immediate future not simply in the context of the history of capitalism but also in the much larger context of the history of life, how earth history connects to it, and where humans figure in it overall.

[87] Pierrehumbert, *Principles of Planetary Climate*, p. 66.

[88] A very significant book on the problem of intergenerational ethics in the context of climate change is Stephen M. Gardiner's *A Perfect Moral Storm*.

[89] Archer, *A Long Thaw*, pp. 9–10.

10

POSTCOLONIAL STUDIES AND THE CHALLENGE OF CLIMATE CHANGE*

For Homi K. Bhabha

However we come to the question of postcolonial studies at this historical juncture, there are two phenomena, both topics of public debate since the early 1990s, that none of us can quite escape in our personal and collective lives at present: globalization and global warming. All thinking about the present has to engage both. What I do in this chapter is to use some of the recent writings of Homi K. Bhabha to illustrate how a leading contemporary postcolonial thinker imagines the figure of the human in the era of what is often called 'neoliberal' capitalism, and then enter a brief discussion of the debate on climate change to see how postcolonial thinking may need to be stretched to adjust itself to the reality of global warming. My ultimate proposition in this chapter is simple: that the current conjuncture of globalization and global warming leaves us with the challenge of having to think of human agency over multiple and incommensurable scales at once.

* Edited from *New Literary History* 43 (2012): 25–42. A draft of this essay was presented as a lecture at the University of Virginia in December 2010. Thanks to my audience and to the anonymous readers of the journal for constructive criticisms. Special thanks are due to Rita Felski for the original invitation to write this essay and for her helpful suggestions. I am grateful to Homi K. Bhabha for making some of his recent writings available to me and for many discussions of the issues raised here.

The nineteenth century left us with some internationalist and universal ideologies, prominent among them Marxism and liberalism, both
progenies in different ways of the Enlightenment. Anti-colonial thought
was born of that lineage. The waves of the decolonization movements
of the 1950s and 1960s were followed by postcolonial criticism that
was placed, in the universities of the Anglo-American countries at
least, as brother in arms to cultural studies. Together, cultural studies and postcolonial criticism fed into the literature on globalization,
though globalization studies, as such, also drew on developments in
the cognate disciplines of sociology, economics, and anthropology.
Now we have a literature on global warming and a general sense of
an environmental crisis that is no doubt mediated by the inequities
of capitalist development, but it is a crisis that faces humanity as a
whole. In all these moves, we are left with these images of the human:
the universalist–Enlightenment view of the human as potentially the
same everywhere, the subject with capacity to bear and exercise rights;
and the postcolonial–postmodern view of the human as the same but
endowed everywhere with what some scholars call 'anthropological
difference'—differences of class, sexuality, gender, history, and so on.
This second view is what the literature on globalization underlines. And
then comes the figure of the human in the age of the Anthropocene, the
era when humans act as a geological force on the planet, changing its
climate for millennia to come. If critical commentary on globalization
focuses on issues of anthropological difference, the scientific literature
on global warming thinks of humans as constitutively one—a species, a
collectivity whose commitment to fossil fuel-based, energy-consuming
civilization is now a threat to that civilization itself. These views of the
human do not supersede one another. One cannot put them along a
continuum of progress. No one view is rendered invalid by the presence
of others. They are simply disjunctive. Any effort to contemplate the
human condition today—after colonialism, globalization, and global
warming—on political and ethical registers encounters the necessity of
thinking disjunctively about the human, through moves that in their
simultaneity appear contradictory.

   But since I come to all these questions as someone trained in the
discipline of history, allow me to approach them via this discipline and
by way of a brief historical detour. And I apologize in advance for the
slight intrusion of the autobiographical at this point, for I was also a

witness to the history I recount here. My entry into the field of post-colonial studies, quite fittingly for someone interested in the theme of belatedness, was late.[1] Postcolonial ideas, as we know, took by storm departments of English literature in the Anglo-American academe in the 1980s. Now when I look at back on it, postcolonial studies seem to have been a part, initially at least, of a cultural and critical process by which a post-imperial West adjusted itself to a long process of decolonization that perhaps is not over yet. After all, it cannot be without significance that what brought Stuart Hall, Homi Bhabha, and Isaac Julien together to read Fanon in the London of the late 1980s and the 1990s was the struggle against racism in a post-imperial Britain, a struggle sometimes given official backing by the radical Greater London Council and hosted by the Institute of Contemporary Art.[2]

The American scene with regard to postcolonial studies was admittedly somewhat different. Edward Said wrote *Orientalism* (1978) out of his sense of involvement in the Palestinian struggle and Gayatri Spivak, I assume, was responding in part to the culture wars on American campuses about opening up core curriculum (as at Stanford in the late 1980s) and redefining the literary canon when she introduced the Indian feminist writer Mahasweta Devi to academic readers in the United States. Australian developments that I personally witnessed in these years drew on both English and North American instances. I got drawn into debates about 'culture as distinction' and about the literary canon that took place in the meetings of the Arts Faculty at the University of Melbourne in the late 1980s. A leading scholar in those debates was Simon During, a pioneer in what was then emerging as the field of cultural studies.[3] The University of Essex conferences on postcolonial studies had just taken place. I was aware of During's involvement in those conferences. Lata Mani, then a graduate

[1] See Dipesh Chakrabarty, 'Belated as Possibility: Subaltern Histories, Once Again', in *The Indian Postcolonial: A Critical Reader*, ed. Elleke Boehmer and Rosinka Chaudhuri (New York: Routledge, 2011), pp. 163–76. See also Chapter 1.

[2] I discuss these developments in 'An Anti-Colonial History of the Postcolonial Turn: An Essay in Memory of Greg Dening', Second Greg Dening Memorial Lecture (Melbourne, Australia: Department of History, The University of Melbourne, 2009), pp. 11–13. See also Chapter 3.

[3] During gives his own account of these times in his 'Introduction' to *The Cultural Studies Reader*, ed. Simon During (New York: Routledge, 1993).

student with the History of Consciousness Program at the University
of California, Santa Cruz, had published a path-breaking paper on
'sati' in one of their proceedings volumes.[4] But the volumes still had
not impacted the world of historians. We began to publish Subaltern
Studies in India in 1983 without much awareness of postcolonial literary criticism. I remember Simon During returning to Melbourne in the
mid-1980s from a postcolonialism conference overseas and asking me
if I knew of the work of Homi Bhabha. I answered, with some surprise
but as any educated, newspaper-reading Indian would have answered
in those days, 'Sure, a major Indian Atomic Research Centre is named
after him. He was one of our best physicists; but why would you be
interested in him?' That was the day the *other* Homi Bhabha entered
my life, as a problem of mistaken identity, through a stand-in, as a question of difference within the identity 'Homi Bhabha' (to mimic my
dear friend who bears that name).

Subaltern Studies, the historiographical movement with which I
was associated, emerged out of anti-colonial, and not postcolonial,
thought. We were a bunch of young men (initially men) interested in
Indian history and were in some ways disillusioned with the nationalisms of our parents. The two Englishmen in the group, David Arnold
and David Hardiman, were anti-imperial in their political outlook
and rejected the predominant pro-imperial historiography that came
out of England. The Indian members of the group were disappointed
and angry about the Indian nation's failure to deliver the social justice
that anti-colonial nationalism had promised. Our historiographical
rebellion raised many interesting methodological issues for Indian
history and for history in general. Ranajit Guha, our mentor, could
easily be seen as one of the pioneers of the so-called linguistic turn in
the discipline of history though, it has to be acknowledged, Hayden
White had already raised many of the most pertinent issues in the
1970s.[5] Our analyses of subaltern histories were deeply influenced

---

[4] Lata Mani, 'The Production of an Official Discourse on Sati in Early Nineteenth Century Bengal', in *Europe and Its Others*, ed. Frances Barker et al., vol. 1
(Colchester: University of Essex Press, 1985), pp. 107–27. The book was published in two volumes out of a conference held at Essex in July 1984 on the
subject of 'the Sociology of Literature'.

[5] See Ranajit Guha, *Elementary Aspects of Peasant Insurgency in Colonial
India* (Delhi: Oxford University Press, 1983) and Hayden White, *Metahistory:*

by Guha's infectious enthusiasm for structuralism of the kind that was associated with Barthes, Jakobson, and Levi-Strauss, a structuralism one could also associate with Hayden White and with an early moment of cultural studies—especially in Britain where the New Accent series of publications emphasized the importance of structuralism, and where Guha was originally based. Gramsci—with a selection of his prison notebooks translated into English in 1971—had softened the Stalinist edges of our Indo-British Marxism and attuned us to the importance of the popular, and Mao—many of the historians in the group had earlier been involved in the Maoist movement that took place in India between 1967 and 1971—had helped us to think of the peasant as a modern revolutionary subject. But we did not encounter postcolonial thought until Spivak brought our group into contact with her deconstructionist variety of Marxism and feminism, and made us confront our theoretical innocence in proposing to make the subaltern the 'subject' of his or her own history. As we pondered the challenge she posed to the group and embraced its consequences, we crossed over from being merely anti-colonial historians (with incipient critiques of the nation-state form) to being a part of the intellectual landscape of postcolonial criticism.

What was the difference?, one might ask. The difference was signalled by Spivak's epochal essay 'Can the Subaltern Speak?', which she had begun to draft in response to the Subaltern Studies project and before our first meeting with her took place.[6] The human in our anti-colonial mode of thinking was a figure of sovereignty. We wanted to make the peasant or the subaltern the subject of his or her history, period. And we thought of this subject in the image of the autonomous rights-bearing person with the same access to representation in national and other histories as others from more privileged backgrounds enjoyed. A straightforward plea for social justice underlay our

---

The Historical Imagination in Nineteenth-Century Europe (Baltimore: Johns Hopkins University Press, 1973). I have tried to bring Guha and White together in my essay 'Subaltern History as Political Thought', in *Colonialism and Its Legacies*, ed. Jacob T. Levy with Marion Iris Young (Lanham, MD: Lexington Books, 2011), pp. 205–18.

[6] Gayatri Chakravorty Spivak, 'Can the Subaltern Speak?', in *Marxism and the Interpretation of Culture*, ed. Cary Nelson and Lawrence Grossberg, vol. 2 (Chicago: University of Illinois Press, 1988), pp. 271–313.

position, just as it did in a variety of Marxist, feminist, or even liberal histories. And like Fanon, we saw the subaltern classes as claiming their humanity through revolutionary upheavals. Becoming human was for us a matter of becoming a subject.[7]

This was why Spivak's exercise in 'Can the Subaltern Speak?' was so salutary. It challenged the very idea of the 'subject' that Subaltern Studies and much anti-colonial thought celebrated and invited us to write deconstructive histories of subjecthood.

This critique of the subject was not the same as that performed by Althusserian anti-humanism of the 1960s and 1970s that so riled E. P. Thompson, the great humanist historian of the last century.[8] Postcolonial critique of the subject was actually a deeper turning towards the human, a move best exemplified for me in the work of Homi Bhabha. It was a turn that both appreciated difference as a philosophical question and at the same time repudiated its essentialization by identity politics.[9] That single move—channelled not through identity politics but through difference philosophies—connected postcolonial thinking to thinking about the human condition in the age of globalization.

To appreciate the close political relations that existed between 'rights' thinking and the body of postcolonial thought that drew on the poststructuralist critique of the subject, we have to get beyond some of the fruitless debates of the 1990s. I think it was a mistake of the Left on both sides of the postmodern divide in the 1990s to think of these two different figurations of the human—the human as a rights-bearing subject and the figure of the human glimpsed through the critique of the subject—as somehow competing with each other in a do-or-die race in which only the fittest survived. The critique of the subject did not make the idea of the autonomous subject useless any more than the critique of the nation state made the institution of the nation state obsolete. What I have learnt from postcolonial thinkers is the necessity to move through contradictory figures of the human, now through a collapsing of the person and the subject as in liberal or Marxist thought,

[7] Guha's *Elementary Aspects* was the best illustration of this proposition.

[8] On all this, see E. P. Thompson, *The Poverty of Theory and Other Essays* (New York: Monthly Review Press, 1978).

[9] The *locus classicus* for this position is still Homi K. Bhabha, *The Location of Culture* (London: Routledge, 1994). See Homi K. Bhabha, 'Global Pathways' (unpublished).

and now through a separation of the two. Before I discuss what forces us to engage in such border-crossing in our thinking, let me illustrate the fleet-footed movement I am speaking of by turning to some recent writings of Homi K. Bhabha.

The Human in Postcolonial Criticism Today

Listen to Bhabha writing of the new subaltern classes of today: 'the stateless', 'migrant workers, minorities, asylum seekers, [and] refugees' who 'represent emergent, undocumented lifeworlds that break through the formal language of "protection" and "status" because'—he says, quoting Balibar—they are *'neither insiders [n]or outsiders, or (for many of us)... insiders officially considered outsiders'.*[10] Classic Bhabha, one would have thought, this turning over of the outside into the inside and vice versa. Yet it is not the 'cosmopolitan claims of global ethical equivalence' that Bhabha reads into these new subalterns of the global capitalist order. His eyes are fixed as much on the deprivation that the human condition suffers in these circumstances as they are on the question of rights:

> As insiders/outsiders they damage the cosmopolitan dream of a 'world without borders'... by opening up, *in the midst of* international polity, a complex and contradictory mode of being or surviving somewhere in between legality and incivility. It is a kind of no-man's land that, in the world of migration, shadows global success ... it substitutes cultural survival in migrant *milieux* for full civic participation.[11]

'Full civic participation'—one can see at once the normative horizons on which Bhabha has set his sights. They are indeed those that acknowledge that our recognition of the human condition in the everyday does not *eo ipso* negate questions of social justice. On the contrary, Bhabha, of course, acknowledges the fact that the politics of (cultural) survival often takes the place of 'full civic participation' in the lives of these new subalterns of the global economy. But he has to move between these poles (survival versus civic participation) to see

[10] Homi K. Bhabha, 'Notes on Globalization and Ambivalence', in *Cultural Politics in a Global Age: Uncertainty, Solidarity and Innovation*, ed. David Held, Henrietta L. Moore, and Kevin Young (Oxford: Oneworld, 2008), p. 39.

[11] Bhabha, 'Notes', pp. 39–40.

the subaltern politics of cultural survival not only as a zone of creativity and improvisation—which it is—but also as an area of privation and disenfranchisement. It will be interesting, then, to see how it is precisely this freedom that Bhabha claims for himself to think contradictorily—to think mobility (survival) and stasis (civic participation) at the same time—that allows him to turn the tables on his erstwhile critics, Michael Hardt and Antonio Negri. Hardt and Negri found in 'nomadism and miscegenation' 'figures of virtue, the first ethical practices on the terrain of Empire'. As they argued, 'circulation' or 'deterritorialization' were entirely positive steps towards the goal of global citizenship that entailed 'the struggle against the slavery of belonging to a nation, an identity and a people, and thus the desertion from sovereignty and the limits it places on subjectivity'.[12] 'Such an emancipatory ideal', writes Bhabha, 'so fixated on the flowing, borderless, global world—neglects to confront the fact that migrants, refugees, or nomads do not merely circulate'. Rather, he goes on to point out:

> They need to settle, claim asylum or nationality, demand housing and education, assert their economic and cultural rights, and seek the status of citizenship. It is salutary, then, to turn to less 'circulatory' forms of the economy like trade and tariffs, or taxes and monetary policy—much less open to postmodern metaphoric appropriation—to see how they impact on the global imaginary of diasporic cultural studies. Positive global relations depend on the protection and enhancement of these national 'territorial' resources, which should then become part of the 'global' political economy of resource redistribution and a transnational moral economy of redistributive justice.[13]

The point of these long quotations is simply to show how juxtaposed and crossed-over the two figures of the human remain in these discussions by Bhabha: the human of the everyday who illustrates the human condition as the embodiment of what Bhabha once called 'difference within'—the insider as the outsider and vice versa—the human who improvises and survives, and the human who asserts his or her

[12] Michael Hardt and Antonio Negri, *Empire* (Cambridge, MA: Harvard University Press, 2000), pp. 361–2, cited in Homi K. Bhabha, 'Our Neighbours, Ourselves: Contemporary Reflections on Survival' (unpublished), p. 3. For Hardt and Negri's critique of Bhabha and of postcolonialism generally, see Hardt and Negri, *Empire*, pp. 137–59.

[13] Bhabha, 'Our Neighbours', pp. 3–4.

cultural and economic rights in the expectation of being the sovereign figure of the citizen someday.

This constant movement between normative and onto-existential images of the human in Bhabha's prose is an index of the human predicament produced by dominant forms of globalization. Bhabha turns to Hannah Arendt to explain this predicament. Arendt had once argued that the very creation of a 'One World' through the positing of so many 'peoples' organized into nation states produced the problem of statelessness, not from 'a lack of civilization' but as 'the perverse consequence of the political and cultural conditions of modernity'.[14] Modernity created this new 'savage' condition of many human beings, the condition of being declared stateless if they could not be identified with a nation state, forcing them to fall back on the politics of survival. Today, it is not simply the arrangement of nation states that creates this condition of stateless, illegal migrants, guest workers, and asylum seekers. It is a deeper predicament produced by both the globalization of capital and the pressures of demography in poorer countries brought about by the unevenness of postcolonial development. Whether you read Mike Davis's *The Planet of Slums* or documents produced by Abahlali baseMjondolo, on the shack-dwellers' movement in Durban, South Africa, it is clear that today's capitalism feeds off a large pool of migrant, often illegal, labour that is cast aside by many as 'surplus population'—a process that deprives these groups of the enjoyment of any social goods and services, while their labour remains critical to the functioning of the service sector in both advanced and growing economies.[15] At the same time, it has to be acknowledged, refugees and asylum seekers are produced also by state failures connected to a whole series of factors: economic, political, demographic, and environmental. Together, these groups, today's subaltern classes, embody the human condition negatively, as an image of privation. No ethnography of their everyday lives can access its object positively through the figure of the citizen. Yet our normative horizons, belonging as we analysts do to one or another kind of civil society, cannot

---

[14] Bhabha paraphrasing Arendt in 'Notes', p. 38.

[15] Bhabha, 'Notes'. Mike Davis, *Planet of Slums* (London: Verso, 2006). For details on the Abahlali baseMjondolo movement, see their website http://www.abahlali.org/.

but depend on the measure of 'cultural and economic rights' and 'full
civic participation', even as any real possibility of effective citizenship
for all humans seems increasingly remote. Do not one billion human
beings already live without access to proper drinking water? When
will the illegal Bangladeshi and North African workers one encounters
on the streets of Athens, Florence, Rome, Vienna, Paris, London—not
to speak of illegal Bangladeshi labour in the informal sectors of India
and Pakistan—become full-fledged European citizens? There is one
predicament of our thinking, however, that speaks to the contradictions of our lifeworlds today. Our normative horizons, unlike those
of Marx's classical writings, say, give us no vantage point from which
we could not only judge but also describe and know these classes,
while ethnographies of what the marginal, the poor, and the excluded
actually do in order to survive yield no alternative norms for human
societies that are still in the grip of large and centralizing institutions,
corporations, and bureaucracies.[16]

This disjuncture is at its most acute now in what progressive
European theorists such as Étienne Balibar or Sandro Mezzadra write
by way of placing refugees, asylum seekers, and illegal immigrants in
European history, politics, and policy.[17] It may or may not surprise the
reader to know that Europe today is dotted with detention centres for
these unwelcome people. The number of such centres exceeds 100 and
they extend outside Europe into North Africa.[18] Europe has adopted
border protection policies that are reminiscent of those pursued by
the United States or Australia, except that in Europe the borders, if
a detention camp is indeed a border, are as much inside Europe as
outside. It is this indeterminacy of borders that has led Balibar to make

[16] I read Partha Chatterjee's *Politics of the Governed: Reflections on Popular
Politics in Most of the World* (New York: Columbia University Press, 2004) as
symptomatic of this predicament.

[17] See Manuela Bojadžijev and Isabelle Saint-Saëns, 'Borders, Citizenship,
War, Class: A Discussion with Étienne Balibar and Sandro Mezzadra', *New Formations* 58 (2006): 10–30.

[18] See the map reproduced in Rochona Majumdar, *Writing Postcolonial History* (New York: Bloomsbury Academic, 2010), p. 15. Thanks to Sandro Mezzadra for bringing these maps to my and Majumdar's attention. This data, of
course, does not take into account the enormous growth of refugee centres in
the years since 2010.

the observation that if the nineteenth century was the time when European imperialism made frontiers into borders by exporting the border-form outside Europe, we stand today on the threshold of an age when borders are becoming frontiers again.[19]

However, reading Balibar and Mezzadra on these questions makes it clear that their writing is caught in tension between two tendencies: on the one hand, they have to acknowledge the historical and current barbarisms that have in the past acted as a foundation of European 'civilization' and continue to do so to some extent even in the present; on the other hand, they have to appeal to the highest utopian ideals of their civilizational heritage in order to imagine being a vibrant European polity that not only practises the ethics of hospitality and responsibility that Derrida, Levinas, and others have written about, but that also grounds itself in a deep acceptance of the plurality of human inheritances inside its own borders.[20] It is no wonder, then, that European intellectuals, whether discussing refugees from outside Europe or internal migrants from the ex-colonies and the question of 'Eastern Europe', are increasingly debating postcolonial theory and are even producing their own readers and translations of postcolonial writings.[21] Europe today is clearly a new frontier of postcolonial studies—and not because the classical peasant-subaltern subject can be found in Europe. No, it is because the new subalterns of the global economy—refugees, asylum seekers, illegal workers—can be found all over Europe and it is by making these groups the object of his thinking that Homi Bhabha arrives at a figure of the human that is constitutionally and necessarily doubled and contradictory.

Let me now turn to the issue of global warming to consider how it challenges us to imagine the human.

---

[19] Etienne Balibar, 'Europe: An "Unimagined" Frontier of Democracy', *Diacritics* 33, no. 3–4 (2003): 36–44. Also Etienne Balibar, *We the People of Europe? Reflections on Transnational Citizenship*, trans. James Swenson (Princeton, NJ: Princeton University Press, 2004), p. 7.

[20] See Balibar, *We the People of Europe?* and note 21 below.

[21] Gerhard Stilz and Ellen Dengel-Janic, eds, *South Asian Literatures* (Trier: WVT Wissenschaftslicher Verlag, 2010); Sandro Mezzadra, *La Condizione Postcoloniale: storia e politica nel presente globale* (Verona: Ombre Corte, 2008).

The Human in the Anthropocene

If the problem of global warming or climate change had not burst in on us through the 2007 report of the Intergovernmental Panel on Climate Change (IPCC), globalization would have been perhaps the most important theme stoking our thoughts about being human. But global warming adds another challenge. It calls us to visions of the human that neither rights talk nor the critique of the subject ever contemplated. This does not, as I said before, make those earlier critiques irrelevant or redundant, for climate change will produce—and has begun to produce—its own cases of refugees and regime failures.[22] The effects of climate change are mediated by the global inequities we already have. So the two visions of the human that I have already outlined—the universalist view of global justice between human individuals imagined as having the same rights everywhere and the critique of the subject that poststructuralism once promoted—will both remain operative. In discussing issues of climate justice, we will thus necessarily go through familiar moves: criticize the self-aggrandizing tendencies of powerful and rich nations and speak of a progressive politics of differentiated responsibilities in handling debates about migration, legal or illegal. Indeed, one of the early significant tracts to be written on the problem and politics of global warming was authored by two respected Indian environmental activists who gave it the title *Global Warming in an Unequal World: A Case of Environmental Colonialism.*[23] The science and politics of climate change have not rendered these moves irrelevant or unnecessary; but they have become insufficient as analytical strategies.[24]

Consider the challenge that climate science poses to humanists. Climate scientists raise a problem of scale for the human imagination, though they do not usually think through the humanistic implications of their own claim that, unlike the changes in climate this planet has seen in the past, the current warming is anthropogenic in nature.

---

[22] See the recent documentary film *Climate Refugees* (2009) made by Michael P. Nash, available at http://www.climaterefugees.com/.

[23] Sunita Narain and Anil Agarwal, *Global Warming in an Unequal World: A Case of Environmental Colonialism* (Delhi: Centre for Science and Environment, 1991).

[24] For an elaboration of this point, see my essay 'Verändert der Klimawandel die Geschichtsschreibung?', *Transit* 41 (2011): 143–63.

Humans, collectively, now have an agency in determining the climate of the planet as a whole, a privilege reserved in the past only for very large-scale geophysical forces. This is where this crisis represents something different from what environmentalists have written about so far: the impact of humans on their immediate or regional environments. The idea of humans representing a force on a very large geological scale that impacts the whole planet is new. Some scientists, the Nobel-winning Paul J. Crutzen at the forefront, have proposed the beginning of a new geological era, an era in which human beings act as a force determining the climate of the entire planet all at once. They have suggested that we call this period 'the Anthropocene' to mark the end of the Holocene that named the geological 'now' within which recorded human history so far has unfolded.[25] But who is the 'we' of this process? How do we think of this collective human agency in the era of the Anthropocene?

Scientists who work on the physical history of the universe or on the history of the earth's climate in the past no doubt tell certain kinds of histories. But in Gadamerian or Diltheyan terms, they explain and are not required to understand the past in any humanist sense. Every individual explanation makes sense because it relates to other existing explanations. But a cognitive exercise is not 'understanding' in the Gadamerian sense, and until there is an element of the latter, we do not have history, not human history at least. Which is why, usually, a purely 'natural' history of climate over the last several million years would not be of much interest to a postcolonial historian who works on human history.

What is remarkable about the current crisis is that climate scientists are not simply doing versions of natural history. They are also giving us an account of climate change that is neither purely 'natural' nor purely 'human' history. And this is because they assign an agency to humans at the very heart of this story. According to them, current global (and

---

[25] I discuss historiographical and some philosophical implications of the Anthropocene hypothesis in my essay 'The Climate of History: Four Theses', *Critical Inquiry* 35, no. 2 (2009): 197–222, and reprinted in this volume. See also Will Steffen, Paul J. Crutzen, and John R. McNeill, 'The Anthropocene: Are Humans Now Overwhelming the Great Forces of Nature?', *Ambio* 36, no. 8 (2007): 614–21 and the special issue of *Philosophical Transactions of the Royal Society* edited by Jan Zalasiewicz, Mark Williams, Alan Haywood, and Michael Ellis, 'The Anthropocene: A New Epoch of Geological Time?' (2011): 835–41.

not regional) climate changes are largely human induced. This implies that humans are now part of the natural history of the planet. The wall of separation between natural and human histories that was erected in early modernity and reinforced in the nineteenth century as the human sciences and their disciplines consolidated themselves has some serious and long-running cracks in it.[26]

The ascription of a geological agency to humans is a comparatively recent development in climate science. One of the earliest references I could find of scientists assigning to humans a role in the geophysical process of the planet was in a paper that the University of California, San Diego, oceanographer Roger Revelle and the University of Chicago geophysicist H. E. Suess co-authored in the geophysics journal *Tellus* in 1957. 'Human beings are now carrying out a large-scale geophysical experiment of a kind that could not have happened in the past nor be reproduced in the future', they wrote. 'Within a few centuries we are returning to the atmosphere and oceans the concentrated organic carbon stored in the sedimentary rocks over hundreds of millions of years. This experiment, if adequately documented, may yield a far-reaching insight into the processes determining weather and climate.'[27] The Environmental Pollution Panel of the US President's Science Advisory Committee expressed the opinion in 1965 that 'through his worldwide industrial civilization, Man is unwittingly conducting a vast geophysical experiment. Within a few generations, he is burning fossil fuel that slowly accumulated in the earth over the past 500 million years.' They went on to warn: 'The climatic changes that may be produced by the increased CO_2 content could be deleterious from the point of view of human beings'.[28] Even as late as 1973, the Committee on Atmospheric

[26] For elaboration, see my 'Climate of History'.

[27] R. Revelle and H. E. Suess, 'Carbon Dioxide Exchange between Atmosphere and Ocean and the Question of an Increase in Atmospheric CO2 during the Past Decades', *Tellus* 9 (1957): 18–27, cited in *Weather and Climate Modification: Problems and Prospects*, vol. 1, summary and recommendations; Final Report of the Panel on Weather and Climate Modification to the Committee on Atmospheric Sciences, National Academy of Sciences, National Research Council (Washington: National Academy of Sciences, 1966), pp. 88–9.

[28] *Restoring the Quality of Our Environment (Report of the Environmental Pollution Panel, President's Science Advisory Committee)* (Washington: The White House, 1965), Appendix Y4, p. 127.

Sciences of the National Academy of Science said: 'Man clearly has no positive knowledge of the magnitude or the manner in which he is presently changing the climate of the earth. There is no real question that inadvertent modification of the atmosphere is taking place.'[29]

We can thus see a progress or inflation, if you like, in the rhetoric of climate scientists. Man was an experimenter on a geophysical scale in the 1950s; by the 1990s, he was a geophysical force himself. Silently and implicitly, climate scientists have doubled the figure of the human as the agent of anthropogenic global warming (AGW). Humans put out greenhouse gases in the atmosphere and the biosphere. Here the picture of the human is how social scientists have always imagined humans to be: a purposeful biological entity with the capacity to degrade natural environment. But what happens when we say humans are acting like a geophysical force? We then liken humans to some non-human, non-living agency. That is why I say the science of anthropogenic global warming has doubled the figure of the human—you have to think of the two figures of the human simultaneously: the human-human and the nonhuman-human. And that is where some challenges lie for the postcolonial scholar in the humanities.

The first challenge is the scale on which scientists invite us to imagine human agency. Consider the point that, collectively, we are now capable of affecting the climate of this planet and changing it, as the geophysicist David Archer says, for the next 100,000 years.[30] Such numbers usually function as operators with which we manipulate information. We do not understand them without training. Scientists are aware of this problem and do what historians do to bring vast scales within the realm of understanding: appeal to human experience. The Australian social and environmental historian Tom Griffiths recently published a splendid history of the Antarctic. But how does a social historian go about writing a *human* history of an uninhabited and unin-habitable vast expanse of snow and ice? Griffiths does what all good historians do: go to the experience that past humans have already had of such a region in order to write a human history of this place. He

[29] *[Report of the] Committee on Atmospheric Sciences*, National Research Council (Washington, DC: National Academy of Sciences, 1973), p. 160.

[30] David Archer, *The Long Thaw: How Humans Are Changing the Climate of the Planet for the Next 100,000 Years* (Princeton, NJ: Princeton University Press, 2010).

consults the private papers of historical explorers, looks at their letters to see how they experienced the place, and intercalates his reading of these documents with leaves from his own diary of travelling to the South Pole. This is how the Antarctic gets humanized. We use the metaphoric capacity of human language and visual records to bring its ice within the grasp of human experience. The Australian explorer Douglas Mawson went to the Antarctic for the years 1911–14, having just become engaged to a Paquita Delprat of Broken Hill in Western Australia. In one of her lovelorn letters to Mawson, Delprat wrote: 'Are you frozen? In heart I mean.... Am I pouring out a little of what is in my heart to an iceberg?... Can a person remain in such cold and lonely regions however beautiful and still love warmly?' Mawson reassured her that her love had warmed her 'proxy iceberg' and that 'he felt less cold this time'.[31] It is through such interleaving of experiences and through the employment of figures of speech—some telling metaphors and similes—that we make a human history of the empty vastness and ice of the South Pole.

Scientists interested in creating an informed public around the crisis of climate change make a very similar appeal to experience. For reasons of space, I will illustrate the point with an example from David Archer's book *The Long Thaw*. Archer distils out of his analysis a problem that turns around the explanation/understanding distinction I mentioned earlier. Human beings cannot really imagine beyond a couple of generations before and after their own time, he says. 'The rules of economics, which govern much of our behavior', he writes, 'tend to limit our focus to even shorter time frames', for the value of everything gets discounted in decades.[32] Archer faces the problem that humans may not care for the science he is telling us about. One hundred thousand years is too far—why should we care for people so far into the future? 'How would it feel', Archer asks, trying to translate geological units into human scales, 'if the ancient Greeks, for example, had taken advantage of some lucrative business opportunity for a few centuries, aware of potential costs, such as, say, a [much] stormier world, or the loss of... agricultural productivity to rising sea levels—that could persist

[31] Tom Griffiths, *Slicing the Silence: Voyaging to Antarctica* (Cambridge, MA: Harvard University Press, 2007), p. 200.
[32] Archer, *The Long Thaw*, p. 9.

to this day?'[33] I find it remarkable as a historian that Archer, a socially concerned paleo-climatologist, should be asking us to extend to the future the faculty of understanding that historians routinely extend to humans of the recorded past.

But this is also where we encounter a real problem of interpretation. We write of pasts through the mediation of the experience of humans of the past. We can send humans, or even artificial eyes, to outer space, the poles, the top of Mount Everest, to Mars, and the Moon and vicariously experience that which is not directly available to us. We can also—through art and fiction—extend our understanding to those who in future may suffer the impact of the geophysical force that is the human. But we cannot ever experience ourselves as a geophysical force—though we now know that this is one of the modes of our collective existence. We cannot send somebody out to experience in an unmediated manner this 'force' on our behalf (as distinct from experiencing the impact of it mediated by other direct experiences—of floods, storms, or earthquakes, for example). This non-human, force-like mode of existence of the human tells us that we are no longer simply a form of life that is endowed with a sense of ontology. Humans have a sense of ontic belonging. That is undeniable. We used that knowledge in developing both anti-colonial (Fanon) and postcolonial criticism (Bhabha). But in becoming a geophysical force on the planet, we have also developed a form of collective existence that has no ontological dimension. Our thinking about ourselves now stretches our capacity for interpretive understanding. We need non-ontological ways of thinking the human.

Bruno Latour has complained for a long time that the problem with modern political thought is the culture/nature distinction that has allowed humans to look on their relationship to 'nature' through the prism of the subject/object relationship.[34] He has called for a new idea of politics that brings together—as active partners into our arguments—both humans and non-humans. I think what I have said adds a

[33] Archer, *The Long Thaw*, pp. 9–10.

[34] Bruno Latour, *Politics of Nature: How to Bring the Sciences into Democracy*, trans. Catherine Porter (Cambridge, MA: Harvard University Press, 2004). Also see the debate between David Bloor and Bruno Latour: David Bloor, 'Anti-Latour', and Bruno Latour, 'For David Bloor ... And Beyond', *Studies in History and Philosophy of Science* 30, no. 1 (1999): 81–112 and 113–29 respectively.

wrinkle to Latour's problematic. A geophysical force—for that is what in part we are in our collective existence—is neither a subject nor an object. A force is the capacity to move things. It is a pure, nonontological agency. After all, Newton's idea of 'force' went back to medieval theories of impetus.[35]

Climate change is not a one-event problem. Nor is it amenable to a single rational solution. It may indeed be something like what Horst Rittel and Melvin Webber, planning theorists, once called a 'wicked problem', an expression they coined in 1973 in an article entitled 'Dilemmas in a General Theory of Planning' published in *Policy Sciences* 'to describe a category of public policy concern that [while susceptible to a rational diagnosis] defied rational and optimal solutions', because it impinged on too many other problems to be solved or addressed at the same time.[36] Besides, as Mike Hulme, a climate researcher, points out:

> This global solution-structure also begs a fundamental question which is rarely addressed in the respective fora where these debates and disagreements surface: What is the ultimate performance metric for the human species, what is it that we are seeking to optimise? Is it to restabilise population or to mini- mise our ecological footprint? Is it to increase life expectancy, to maximise gross domestic product, to make poverty history or to increase the sum of

[35] J. Bruce Brackenridge, *The Key to Newton's Dynamics: The Kepler Prob- lem and the Principia* (Berkeley and Los Angeles: University of California Press, 1995).

[36] Quoted in Michael Hulme, *Why We Disagree about Climate Change: Understanding Controversy, Inaction, and Opportunity* (Cambridge: Cambridge University Press, 2009), p. 334. Here is a contemporary definition of a 'wicked problem':

> A wicked problem is a complex issue that defies complete definition, for which there can be no final solution, since any resolution gener- ates further issues, and where solutions are not true or false or good or bad, but the best that can be done at the time. Such problems are not morally wicked, but diabolical in that they resist all the usual attempts to resolve them. (Valerie A. Brown, Peter M. Deane, John A Harris, and Jaqueline Y. Russell, 'Towards a Just and Sustainable Future', in *Tackling Wicked Problems: Through the Transdisciplinary Imagination*, ed. Valerie A. Brown, John A. Harris, and Jaqueline Y. Russell [London and Washington: Earthscan, 2010], p. 4.)

global happiness? Or is the ultimate performance metric for humanity simply survival?[37]

Given that it is difficult to foresee humanity arriving at a consensus on any of these questions in the short-term future, even while scientific knowledge about global warming circulates more widely, it is possible that the turn towards what Ulrich Beck calls a 'risk society' will only be intensified in the current phase of globalization and global warming. As we cope with the effects of climate change and pursue capitalist growth, we will negotiate our attachments, mediated no doubt through the inequities of capitalism, knowing fully that they are increasingly risky.[38] But this also means that there is no 'humanity' that can act as a self-aware agent. The fact that the crisis of climate change will be routed through all our 'anthropological differences' can only mean that, however anthropogenic the current global warming may be in its origins, there is no corresponding 'humanity' that in its oneness can act as a political agent. A place thus remains for struggles around questions of intra-human justice regarding the uneven impacts of climate change.

This is to underline how open the space is for what may be called the politics of climate change. Precisely because there is no single rational solution, there is the need to struggle to make our way in hitherto uncharted ways—and hence through arguments and disagreements—towards something like what Latour calls 'the progressive composition of a common world'.[39] Unlike the problem of the hole in the ozone layer, climate change is ultimately all about politics. Hence its openness as much to science and technology as to rhetoric, art, media, and arguments and conflicts conducted through a variety of means. The need then is to think the human on multiple scales and registers and as having both ontological and non-ontological modes of existence.

With regard to the climate crisis, humans now exist in two different modes. There is one in which they are still concerned with justice

---

[37] Hulme, *Why We Disagree*, p. 336.

[38] Ulrich Beck, 'The Naturalistic Misunderstanding of the Green Movement: Environmental Critique as Social Critique', in *Ecological Politics in an Age of Risk*, trans. Amos Weisz (Cambridge: Polity, 1995), pp. 36–57. See also the discussion in Ursula K. Heise, *Sense of Place and Sense of Planet: The Environmental Imagination of the Global* (New York: Oxford University Press, 2008), Chapter 4.

[39] Latour, *Politics of Nature*, p. 47.

even when they know that perfect justice is never to be had. The 'climate justice' historiography issues from this deeply human concern. Climate scientists' history reminds us, on the other hand, that we now also have a mode of existence in which we—collectively and as a geophysical force and in ways we cannot experience ourselves—are 'indifferent' or 'neutral' (I do not mean these as mental or experienced states) to questions of intra-human justice. We have run up against our own limits as it were. It is true that as beings for whom the question of 'being' is an eternal question, we will always be concerned about justice. But if we, collectively, have also become a geophysical force, then we also have a collective mode of existence that is justice-blind. Call that mode of being a 'species' or something else, but it has no ontology, it is beyond biology, and it acts as a limit to what we also are in the ontological mode.

This is why the need arises to view the human simultaneously on contradictory registers: as a geophysical force and as a political agent, as a bearer of rights and as author of actions; subject to both the stochastic forces of nature (being itself one such force collectively) and open to the contingency of individual human experience; belonging at once to differently scaled histories of the planet, of life and species, and of human societies. One could say, mimicking Fanon, that in an age when the forces of globalization intersect with those of global warming, the idea of the human needs to be stretched beyond where postcolonial thought advanced it.

In Conclusion

A little more than half a century ago, 'an earth-born object made by man'—the Sputnik—orbited the planet in outer space, 'in the proximity of the heavenly bodies as though it had been admitted tentatively to their sublime company'. The author of these words, Hannah Arendt, thought that this event foretold a fundamental change in the human condition. The earth had been 'unique in the universe in providing human beings with a habitat in which they can move and breathe without effort and without artifice', but now clearly science was catching up with a thought that 'up to then had been buried in the highly non-respectable literature of science fiction'. The Sputnik could be the first 'step toward escape from man's imprisonment to the earth'. 'Should the emancipation and the secularization of the modern age', asked Arendt, 'end with [a] ... fateful repudiation of an Earth who was the Mother of all living creatures under the sky?'[40] Still, Arendt's reading of this change in the human condition was optimistic. A critic of 'mass society', she saw the danger of such a society mainly in spiritual terms. A 'mass society' could 'threaten humanity with extinction' in spirit by rendering humans into a 'society of laborers'.[41] But it was in the same 'mass society'—'where man as a social animal rules supreme'—that 'the survival of the species could [now] be guaranteed on a world-wide scale', thought Arendt.[42] The Sputnik was the first symbol, for her, of such optimism regarding the survival of the human species.

Today, with the crisis of anthropogenic climate change coinciding with multiple other crises of planetary proportions—of resources, finance, and food, not to speak of frequent weather-related human disasters—we know that the repudiation of the earth has come in a shape Arendt could not have even imagined in the optimistic and modernizing 1950s. Humans today are not only the dominant species on the planet, they also collectively constitute—thanks to their numbers and their consumption of cheap fossil fuel-based energy to sustain their civilizations—a geological force that determines the climate of the planet much to the detriment of civilization itself. Today, it is precisely the 'survival of the species' on a 'world-wide scale' that is largely in question. All progressive political thought, including postcolonial criticism, will have to register this profound change in the human condition.

[40] Hannah Arendt, *The Human Condition*, 'Introduction' by Margaret Canovan (Chicago: University of Chicago Press, 1998 [1958], 2nd edn), pp. 1–2.
[41] Arendt, *The Human Condition*, p. 46.
[42] Arendt, *The Human Condition*, p. 46.

11

INTERVIEW
Dipesh Chakrabarty with *Actuel Marx*

Actuel Marx (A.M.): You were—with Ranajit Guha and Gayatri Spivak in particular—one of the initiator of postcolonial studies at the end of the 1990s. Yet, since your article 'The Climate of History: Four Theses' (2009), it seems that your interest has turned towards environmental history. Can you explain the reason for this trajectory?

Dipesh Chakrabarty (D.C.): There were both autobiographical and intellectual reasons for this apparent shift. I will not disavow the autobiographical. In work in the humanities, the two sets of reasons are often intertwined but the accidents of the autobiographical often have to yield place to the 'rational' presentations of the intellect. I have my 'rational' reasons too, but let me at least give the autobiographical its due. And this autobiographical story belongs to the history of the globalization of the Indian middle classes.

I was born in the city of Calcutta and grew up through the 1950s and 1960s to be a member of its student and academic left until I left the city at the end of 1976 to begin my doctoral studies in Canberra, Australia. The educated and literary-minded sections of the Bengali middle class to which I belonged loved depictions of nature—rivers, trees, lakes, ponds, mountains, forests, flowers, birds, animals, the sky, the rain, the sun, the moon, and the zillion stars—in literature, music, and on the screen while the city became increasingly bereft of 'nature' after its population grew and a process of economic decline set in in the years following Independence. This decline and a certain nostalgia for the 'nature' of an idealized countryside influenced our Marxism, creating, I think, a receptive ground for theories of the left that often promised a return to a mythical 'golden Bengal' that was visualized as, in essence, rural. This image was a gift of the anti-colonial nationalist movement but the Bengali Left took it over during the peasant movements of the 1940s and made it its own. It remained a powerful emotive tool in the cultural repertoire of the Bengali Left even in the 1960s and the 1970s, both in the Indian province of West Bengal and the part of the neighbouring Bengali-speaking country that became, in 1971, Bangladesh.

However, my discovery of 'real nature' and the outdoors—that is, 'nature' beyond the printed word and the silver screen—came after I went to Canberra and slowly fell in love with the Australian 'bush' that runs through and embraces that picturesque city. I visit Canberra every year and love its 'natural' beauty. Yet in one sad year, I lost all the nature spots I loved around Canberra when a horrible firestorm swept through the city in 2003 and destroyed over 300 houses. In grief, I tried to read the literature that explained the history of bushfires in Australia, and the more I read, the more this phenomenon of 'anthropogenic climate change' floated into view. All the educated commentators said that this was not a fire caused by the 'ordinary' cycle of droughts that this dry continent suffered every so often. This was a 'natural' drought, but one that was exacerbated by human-induced climate change. I got curious about what 'anthropogenic climate change' was, and when I began to read into what climate scientists were writing for the layperson, my world view received a jolt! The intellectual part of that experience is expressed in the very first essay I wrote on 'climate change': 'The Climate of History: Four Theses', which came out in *Critical Inquiry* in 2009.

For me, 'the shock of the Anthropocene' was this: as someone who supported various kinds of rights for human beings, who valued the idea of 'freedom' in its different connotations, who dreamed of emancipatory futures for humans, and whose sense of history was imbued with this idea of freedom, it was a shock to discover that what gave this theme of 'freedom' its materiality was human access to cheap and plentiful energy! And, needless to say, most of that energy came from fossil fuels, first coal and then oil and gas. Not only that. Without the use of fossil fuels, it would have been hard for humans, even poor humans, to live longer than was possible in the past. Fossil fuels, in their use in agriculture, irrigation, medicine, transport, and in technology were also what enabled us to sustain human numbers at a level unimaginable before the industrial revolution.

Let me, besides, repeat a point that historian John McNeill in particular has often made. Without fossil fuels—that is to say, without access to cheap and plentiful energy—humans would still need to make use of massive forced or 'unfree' labour to build huge structures like the Sears Tower in Chicago or the Empire State Building in New York. The history of 'free labour', in other words, cannot be written without factoring fossil fuels into the story.

As someone who ponders the ironies of human history, I was immediately struck by the ironical role of fossil fuel in the story of human 'advancement'. The same fossil fuels that gave us modern 'freedoms' were now imperilling our 'civilization' and threatening us with the gravest of ecological crises: global warming, rising sea levels, acidification of the seas leading to loss of marine biodiversity, and the possibility of a sixth great extinction of species with dire consequences to humans. This was no ordinary environmental crisis—such as particulate pollution in cities—the effects of which could be mitigated by further development of technology and economies. Anthropogenic climate change was driven by fossil fuel-based 'development' itself. There was no Kuznets's curve in climate change.

You may say that my work since has been an exploration of the human meanings of this profound 'irony' that fossil fuels represented in human progress: they are both its main enablers of this 'progress' and the reason for its own undoing.

A.M.: In what sense can we say that the 'Anthropocene'—understood as a new geological period during which humanity became a geological force—upset the classical way of writing history? What became of nature and history in this new epistemology?

D.C.: We need to be clear about what is being claimed here. Life, through its various forms, acts a geological force. Recall the role of bacteria in making the atmosphere oxygen-rich or the way oxygen-dependent life makes for a mineral-rich planet. If one takes the word 'geological' in its literal sense—relating to soil or earth—humans have been geological for probably as long as they have existed (as was claimed by George Perkin Marsh in the nineteenth century). The claim about humanity having become a geophysical force ushering in the Anthropocene is a more specific claim. Our emissions of greenhouse gases have, for instance, now interfered with the glacial–interglacial cycle of the planet. This cycle depends, in turn, on axial tilts, orbital eccentricity, precession, and so on (called the Milankovitch effect after the Yugoslav scientist who hypothesized it and whose calculations were confirmed in the 1970s). Such huge forces that, let us say, determine something like the climate system of the *whole* planet were, until recently, simply beyond the reach of human capability. These forces provided the background against which the drama of human history unfolded. Human history ran into earth history through occasional disasters, such as in the case of the eruption of a volcano or an earthquake. But now our actions appear to be determining earth history itself. Indeed, this is also the claim of the Anthropocene Working Group of the International Stratigraphy Commission in London: that the impact of human activity has now left enough stratigraphic evidence in rocks for geologists to be able to say that we have crossed the threshold of the Holocene period and pushed earth history—or earth system history—into a new geological epoch, the Anthropocene. That is to say, human institutions and practices (including their inequalities) now make humans into a geophysical force on an unprecedented scale. This is a force that can affect the planet as a whole.

Two implications follow for students of human history. The discipline of history, as it emerged in the late eighteenth and early nineteenth centuries and received an academic shape with the rise of social science as the latter century progressed, was based, intellectually, on a separation of natural and human histories. Nobody expressed this understanding better than the Oxford philosopher R. G. Collingwood (a student of Vico and Croce) who said that while the natural functions of the human body were to be studied by the biological scientist, it was only their social consequences that mattered to the historian. Natural processes included change but nature had no history in the sense that humans could have history: humans could imaginatively peer into the psychological motivations of other humans, even humans of the past, but nature had no such inner life. Even economic historians who may write about institutions and statistics, it could be said, worked with a motivational model of the human being, the *homo economicus*. In the mid-twentieth century when the Annales school began to portray 'nature' as an active background to human history, the natural was treated as either cyclical in its dynamics or a powerful, unpredictable factor that could erupt into and change the course of human history in particular regions of the world. The environmental historians of the 1970s made this interactive model more powerful: humans and their environments impacted each other. Thanks to them, we knew about the role that European expansion played in transferring species from one part of the world to another and in thus changing environments all through the globe. But even in this history, the idea of 'agency' of humans remained similar to that in other branches of history: individual humans and their motivations mattered (with some humans such as Alexander von Humboldt as heroes) as did the institutions that humans built.

Global warming changes or supplements this story in unforeseen ways. Humans are not just a force that interacts with something called 'nature'; they are an integral part of the geophysics of the planet with a potential to change the history of life on this planet by inducing the sixth great extinction. Here the human/nature binary breaks down completely and humanity becomes a controlling element of earth system sciences. This is, sure as hell, a certain kind of agency on the part of humans, but of what kind? Not one we could gauge based on motivational models of the human being. Not a form of agency to which individuals could have phenomenological access.

Second, to understand this newfound role of humans requires us to engage with the deep histories of both the planet and of life on it. Otherwise we do not know what the subject of 'earth system science' could be; nor do we follow how human actions could be interfering with the conditions of complex life that were set up hundreds of millions of years ago in the geological history of the planet. We thus feel the need to place the usual story of human history—of the last 500 or at most the last 6,000 years, say (the history of human civilization)—on a much larger canvas of time. But of this, I will have more to say in response to some of your other questions.

A.M.: You argue that the climate crisis is a major discovery of the 1980s–90s. Yet there is, as many environmental historians have shown, a long history of different traditions—especially in the colonial context—of environmentalism. Does the *longue durée* of environmentalism invalidate the great narrative of occidental modernity?

D.C.: Just as there are histories of humans destroying their environment, there are also stories of humans caring for their environment. These are indeed long histories. Both industrial civilization and modern colonial rule involved many environmental experiments and disasters—this is also true. Additionally, since at least the environmental movement of the 1960s and 1970s, we have been more aware of the environmentally destructive effects of livestock farming and other large-scale institutions. All this I do not dispute. My point was about dating the science concerning the phenomenon of 'anthropogenic global warming' that the IPCC has been reporting on. This science has old roots going back to the nineteenth century but in its modern form is of relatively recent post–Cold War vintage. As you perhaps know, it was after the Second World War that the United States government began to regularly monitor the state of the planet's atmosphere in part to keep an eye on the radioactive fallout of testing nuclear bombs, in part to keep up its position in the Cold War competition in space, and in part out of an interest in weaponizing 'weather' (the capacity to cause droughts and floods in enemy territory). As James Lovelock's experience in Carl Sagan's unit at NASA in the mid-1960s shows, it was in the context of the question of colonizing Mars for human habitation that the bigger issue of what made a planet friendly to continuous existence of complex life came up, leading to Lovelock's formulation of his Gaia theory. You also have to remember that the godfather of modern climate science in the United States, James Hansen, used to study planetary warming on Venus before he turned his attention to *this* planet. NASA set up the first Earth System Science Subcommittee in or around 1983. Besides, the exact formulation of the current 'global warming' could come about only after the gathering of some big data numbers that came from satellite observations, the digging of ice-core samples, and so on—things that would have been impossible without the scientific advancements of the post–Second World War years, spurred on to no small degree by the military and technological competition in space. So, yes, while there is no denying the longer genealogy of climate science beginning in the nineteenth century, the climate science that the IPCC uses is of a more recent origin—not exactly in the 1980s and the 1990s, but from the 1960s onwards. Much of it belongs to American 'big science' of the late twentieth century.

Does environmentalism make the great narrative of Western modernity invalid? Clearly no, not in the eyes of millions of Indian and Chinese middle-class people and their leaders who aspire to the consumerist ideals of the energy-guzzling societies of the West. But there have been environmentalist critiques of this modernity for a very long time but they have often not won the arguments of the day. Think of India. The place gave birth to an astonishingly great—great in spite of all his human failures—character in the person of someone named Mahatma Gandhi. The man was one of biggest twentieth-century critics of industrial civilization. What did Indian leaders do as the nation neared its independence? They put Gandhi gently aside and looked to the Soviet model of accumulation and industrialization to modernize the country. We have to ask a deeper question: Why did Western modernity and modernization appeal even to countries that were never formally colonized by Western powers—such as Japan and Thailand? Unless we understand the nature of modernity as an object of desire, we will not understand why it seems valid in spite of all of its obvious problems. I will come back to this issue in my response to your last question.

A.M.: One of the central purposes of the Subaltern Studies group—which you developed in *Provincializing Europe*—was to elaborate a new epistemology of historical knowledge based on the tension between the universal logic of capital (globalization), on one hand, and the multiplicity and heterogeneity of irreducible cultural experiences on the other. But your works on environmental history tend to re-use categories such as 'humanity' or 'negative universal history', which were profoundly criticized in your previous work. How can you define the necessity of the return to universalism and humanism? Is there not a contradiction here?

D.C.: The contradiction is only an apparent one. First of all, you have to realize that *Provincializing Europe* belonged to the discussion on globalization, the literature on which was generally blind to the problem of global warming. Second, my argument in *Provincializing Europe* was never opposed to universalism as such; it was not, for instance, an argument in support of nativism or cultural relativism. *Provincializing Europe* accepted both the universal logic (that is, tendency) of capital—something I called History 1—and of a universal human phenomenology in my reading of Heidegger. The argument was precisely, as you have said, about a tension between History 1 and the heterogeneity of human pasts (I named the site of this tension History 2). I resisted a certain transition narrative that saw the logic of capital as one homogenizing all human pasts and producing (and thus domesticating) 'difference' only as the expression of so many different preferences of the consumer. This argument of mine I think still holds, especially to the extent to which one positions oneself with a narrative of transition to the capitalist mode of production and, yes, within that problematic, the History 1/History 2 distinction applies to all human histories including those of Europeans. I argued that the universal is a form that becomes visible when its place is usurped by a particular claiming to embody the universal. Within that postcolonial framework, one is legitimately suspicious of universal categories such as 'humanity' that claims to be empirically true as a ruse of power. There is no politically operative agent called 'humanity'; whoever acts in the name of such an agent acts in the interests of some powerful bloc. This is one reason why I had to recourse to Adorno's 'negative universal history' in my first essay on climate.

The problem I faced in thinking and writing about the climate crisis was different from the one *Provincializing Europe* analysed. While the role of capitalist accumulation in precipitating the climate crisis is something I will turn to in a moment, it was clear to me that this was a crisis that could not be fully explained by or reduced to the 500-year-old history of global capitalism; this crisis conjured up a sense of human commonness even if that commonness could not be translated into an operative political agency (and one should be suspicious of any attempt at such translation). It was this figure of the common that was being called a 'geophysical force', or sometimes referred to as the 'human species' as in the discussion of the possibility of the sixth great extinction. Since this issue takes me directly into the problem raised by your last question, let me carry over this discussion into what I say later.

A.M.: Other words or concepts have been elaborated to describe the new geological era. For example, the concept of Capitalocene (elaborated by Jason W. Moore) which insisted on the fact that it is not humanity as such that provoked this revolution but the capitalist mode of production. The interest of this concept is to show that environmentalism is crossed by class struggle. According to you, should such a concept be abandoned in the new way of writing history you advocate?

D.C.: With all due respect to the parties involved (and to Jason Moore in particular, since I only admire his—and others'—efforts to generate an ecologically sensitive Marxism), this debate leaves me a little mystified. First of all, the name 'Anthropocene' and the expression 'anthropogenic climate change', as used by climate scientists or geologists, do not carry the implication that a 'humanity as such' (or an undifferentiated humanity) is responsible for the climate crisis that we now face. I say this because several of these scientists whom I have read have also remarked on global figures for per capita emissions that have been available for more than two decades now and that clearly showed—at least initially, since Chinese figures have really moved upwards since—that the emissions culprits were mainly the developed nations of the world. So, in spirit, the expression 'the Anthropocene' was never intended to carry the connotation of an undifferentiated humanity or an 'undifferentiated species' (as some social scientists complained, forgetting that a biological species is always assumed to be internally differentiated as otherwise natural selection would not work).

So the debate, really, has been among and on the side of the scholars on the left who took the expression 'anthropogenic' literally and wanted to show, for good political reasons, that it was capitalist institutions and practices—or the 'capitalist mode of production', as you say—that brought us to the brink of this planetary environmental crisis. Now, let us leave aside three questions to make this debate a simpler one: (i) whether there could be one compelling definition of 'capitalism' acceptable to one and all; (ii) whether some other mode of modernization of the world based on the cheap and plentiful energy produced by fossil fuels could have also engendered a similar crisis; and (iii) whether the age of global capitalism is 500 years or 200 years or about 70 years (the period that has been called the period of 'the great acceleration'). Let us simply assume that we fully understand the word 'capitalism' (which is much less precise than the expression 'capitalist mode of production' or Marx's historico-philosophical category of 'capital') and that it designates an industrial civilization that is resource extractive and that depends on strategies for accumulation of wealth that necessarily produce inequalities of various kinds between humans. Given this understanding, it is indisputable that capitalism has had a lot to do with environmental crises of various kinds including that called 'global warming'. It is, therefore, also indisputable that environmental problems are 'crossed by class struggles' that capitalists have, on the whole, won so far (since the total volume of global 'wealth' produced by capitalist procedures has increased over the centuries).

But did capitalism, in spite of all its inherent inequalities, allow humanity as a whole (not *as such*, not a humanity-in-itself) to flourish as a biological species? The answer, at least for the last 150 years, would have to be 'yes'. For two reasons, neither of which denies any inequality or class struggle: (*i*) our numbers have increased (in my lifetime the Indian population has grown more than four times), and (*ii*) even the poor have longer lives, maybe not better lives but certainly longer lives. The size of the global, consuming class today is much larger than it has ever been, and there are many populations waiting in the wings to join the feeding frenzy. As a species, humans have never had it so good and our flourishing—including the longer lives of the poor—has had a telltale effect on the lives of non-human animals. Humans—and the animals we keep or eat—claim more and more of what the biosphere produces. Many biologists seriously argue that we have already entered the first phase of what may turn out to be, in a few hundred years, a human-induced sixth great extinction of species. Most scholars on the left—there are some honourable exceptions—do not want to deal with the population question or want to see it mainly as a problem of unequal distribution of resources. The point is that our numbers—and the related issue, our growing life expectancy—count. The issue of the size of human population, as I have argued elsewhere, belongs at once to two histories: the history of industrial modernization and to our shared, collective history as a biological species.

There is thus no huge contradiction between speaking of the role of capitalism in creating the current environmental crises and speaking of humans as biological species that we also are. It is a matter of perspective or at what level of resolution you want to tell the human story. A lens of finer resolution will show you what some humans have done to other humans in order to produce and accumulate more and more wealth (and this would have been impossible without access to cheap and abundant energy that fossil fuels made available). But if you looked from afar at this 'blue marble', and could look for timescales that embraced many, many generations of humans, then humans would look like a biological species among many that used its big-brained 'intelligence' and eventually adopted politico-economic strategies that not only resulted in large-scale human inequalities but also enabled the species to populate and flourish like never before in its history. These strategies at first produced challenges for ecosystems surrounding us—many varieties of birds, animals, plants, and marine creatures have had a tough time adjusting to our runaway success. But now we have created unforeseen conditions that challenge our own survival. The two stories—of class struggle and of our flourishing as a species—can both be told simultaneously, for they operate at different levels of abstraction. The contradiction here, too, as I have said, is only apparent.

12

INTERVIEW
Dipesh Chakrabarty with Katrin Klingan

Katrin Klingan (K.K.): I would like to begin with the conceptual distinctions and somehow to see the Anthropocene idea as a diagnosis of the times in which we find ourselves. The idea suggests that humanity is the driving force behind planetary transformation. It seems, over the last century, that humankind has put processes in motion that have led to developments for which we no longer have any standards by which to explain or alter them. With the traditional methods of knowledge acquisition—the natural sciences on the one side and the humanities on the other—humankind seems to have reached a limit. Therefore, I would like to ask you what type of diagnosis of our contemporaneity unfolds with the idea of the Anthropocene and what new perspectives, new frameworks, from the position in which we find ourselves now, does the Anthropocene proposition imply? In your work 'Climate and Capital: On Conjoined Histories', you state that there is a collision of three perspectives of history that become obvious today: the history of the earth system, the history of life, and the history of industrial civilization. Could you talk a bit about the collision of these three perspectives?

Dipesh Chakrabarty (D.C.): I should make it clear at the beginning that I use the word 'collision' in two senses. First, there is a collision in our thinking, by this I mean that previously in our thinking we kept those histories—evolutionary history and human history—separate, but now they collide in our thoughts as we consider them. Second, it relates to an actual collision in reality; in other words, the small-scale things that human beings do that can now trigger large-scale changes in evolutionary and geological histories. When we think of human history alone, we depend on two kinds of explanation: one type of explanation that works, particularly for long-term events but also for institutions, are functional explanations. You may ask, say, why did Europe industrialize before the Asian countries when some regions of Europe and Asia may have been on a par in the pre-industrialized world? The answers to these sorts of questions would be functional because you would have to reply that Europeans were probably the first to make use of coal and the first to take other peoples' lands and exploit them as resources. From that position you would explain that maybe all developed countries in the pre-industrial world had reached a bottleneck with deforestation, with how much forests could produce, with wood as the main fuel. One might argue that Europe could break through that bottleneck, however, because of the discovery of coal and then the discovery of the New World, the creation of the new living spaces for Europeans. That is a functional explanation.

When history became a discipline, particularly in the early nineteenth century with Leopold von Ranke and others, it became much more dependent on documentary and textual evidence. It also became a discipline that explained human history in terms of peoples' motivations, their inner and subjective experience of the world, emotions, ethics, how they felt about something, and how they understood or misunderstood something. Now, when we write history in a humanist vein, we give space not only to the functionalist explanation but also focus on the motivational explanation. These are explanations based on human beings' experiences, and in those sorts of histories, we normally take the geological for granted. For example, if you wrote an Indian history in the seventeenth or eighteenth century, you would take the Himalayas for granted—the mountains would be there in the background supplying the rivers. One would take both geology and geography as the backdrop against which the human drama unfolded.

It is in this sense that we mentally separated geology and geography from history; while we knew that human beings had evolved and did not think of evolution in the biblical way, we also knew that geology existed. But now, when we talk about the Anthropocene or climate change, and we talk about human beings' use of fossil fuels, there is a collision: analytically, in our thinking, these different histories come together; histories that happened on different scales, at different places, suddenly come together. For example, the production of fossil fuels was a geological process taking millions of years while their exploitation by humans has developed in a very short time. The collision is happening in the outside world, where small human actions, which so far have put carbon dioxide at 400 parts per million, at 0.04 per cent of the atmosphere, are causing huge changes at a planetary level. Thus, the collision is happening at two levels: in our thinking and outside in the world.

K.K.: With respect to the collision of our perspectives, could you discuss what this means for the sciences and the humanities?

D.C.: Most social science disciplines—such as anthropology, history, politics, and economics—grew up in the late eighteenth and nineteenth centuries and have all developed to tell the drama of human progress through the use of natural resources. In economics, for example, we think of issues of the environment mainly as externalities. For instance, even when Marx published *Capital*, in 1867, he began the first chapter by saying that air and water could not be commodities—it was not necessary to put a price on them—because not only were they naturally available but were also plentiful. Many disciplines have grown up assuming climatic stability and environmental stability, particularly the social sciences. I think now, as we go forward, we have to rethink some of these assumptions. So maybe when Bruno Latour asks when economics will meet ecology, he still believes, and I think correctly, that they are two different subjects. However, if economics does indeed meet ecology, it will also mean that we will have to rethink history, sociology, and so on, especially when one considers that it was in the nineteenth century that a clear category emerged for society that was seen as increasingly different from nature. I see what is happening as evidence that we are getting more and more of a sense of how embedded human activities are in what we call natural processes. We will have to learn that if we create institutions and practices that interfere too much with these processes, then we do so at our own peril.

K.K.: You have already started to elaborate a bit on the distinction between the global and the planetary. Can I ask you to explain this distinction, and, from your perspective, point out the impacts and consequences of the collision of the planetary and global, as well as the global and local, as characteristics of the Anthropocene? Can you also explain the origins of these developments?

D.C.: Think of the history of the global and our capacity to see this planet as roughly spherical, like a sphere; clearly a lot of this goes back a long way into intellectual history. However, it also began to become part of the initial European experience when Europeans began circumnavigating the globe by ship. As the Europeans explored, they discovered the New World and experienced the proposition that the world was indeed spherical. The world came together, as Europe, capitalism, and trade expanded, so that gradually, by the end of the nineteenth century, the European empires had connected the world. However, a lot of that connection came about, not just through trade, but also through technology, for example, the introduction of the telegraph in the mid-nineteenth century, telephones, and then eventually satellites and today's mobile-phone network.

There is a tradition of German thought, which goes back at least to Kant, of thinking on behalf of the whole of humanity, speaking for all human beings. In the twentieth century, one recalls Martin Heidegger, Karl Jaspers, and Hans-Georg Gadamer. At this time, up to Carl Schmitt, there was among many of these thinkers both an acknowledgement that the world was coming together and a fear that what was bringing the world together rapidly was technology, not cultural understanding between different parts of the world. Thus, there was an apprehension among German thinkers that technology would make the world uniform and that it would ride roughshod over cultural differences and so on. Gadamer, for instance, was expressing these fears as late as the 1980s. In many ways, one could say that—and I think here of postcolonial writers such as Salman Rushdie or theorists such as Homi Bhabha—a lot of postcolonial thinking was addressing this German anxiety. It was saying that even if the world was coming together through technology, the German thinkers should not worry because the postcolonial nations (including the formerly imperial ones) would continue with the politics of cultural difference. In a way, therefore, either consciously or unconsciously, a lot of postcolonial thinking was in conversation with this line of German thought.

There is thus one tradition of thinking the globe and the planet, where the globe and the planet become the same. This is a very homocentric, human-centric story. However, if you look to the origins of the science of global warming, you see that it lies within the period of the Cold War, at a time when the Americans were actively thinking of space as a military resource, and the Soviets were too. At that time, there were discussions about whether climate, or more specifically the weather, could be deployed militarily, whether it was possible to cause floods or droughts in your enemy's territory, things like that. The so-called superpowers were also thinking about the possibilities of colonizing space as a way of gaining military superiority.

Much of global warming science comes out of the experiments that NASA began to perform, which were looking at whether or not it was possible to make Mars habitable. James Lovelock comes out of those experiments of the 1960s and so does the major climate scientist James Hansen but in a later period. With Lovelock looking at Mars and Hansen looking at Venus, scientists were trying to understand why Venus was so hot and Mars was so cold. When scientists realized that Venus's atmosphere was rich in carbon dioxide and Mars had lost its atmospheric carbon dioxide, the human question surfaced: why do some planets become hot and certain other planets become cold. This then fuelled the problem of what we might call planetary warming, and it was then that Hansen wondered if a similar type of warming was happening on planet earth, and shifted his interests to studying this planet. Global warming is a subset of a larger problem called planetary warming, and, therefore, here in our language, the expression 'the globe' meaning the earth and word 'planet' do not coincide. Planetary warming can happen without humans and mostly happens without humans, as has happened in the past of this planet.

These questions led to questions about the habitability of our planet, about why atmospheres form, which kinds of atmospheres evolve to become friendly to life, which kinds of atmospheres become unfriendly to life, and why so? This is how we became interested in the question of planetary processes: what is it that maintains oxygen at a certain level and keeps our planet friendly to life? I am not saying that Lovelock's answer to this question has been a universally accepted one, because it has not, but I am just noting that the question came up. Therefore, if I came to the word 'planet' through the globalization literature, I would *not* have to think about Venus and Mars, because globalization is a human story. Furthermore, the notion of a planet would be the same as what the globe has become, which is a connected globe. However, if I came to the global warming story through climate science my vista would expand to include other planets. Therefore, just as when you read about theories of evolution and you realize how late on in the story of evolution human beings enter it; similarly, you realize that the Anthropocene is not just an invitation to see ourselves in deep time as part of the history of the planet. It is that too, but the Anthropocene opens up the vista and humbles us even more profoundly. We become humbled when we realize that not only are we not biologically special but also that we arrived late in the planet's history. Actually, we become even more humbled, and life seems even more precious with the realization of what global warming is: it is a subset of a problem of planetary warming that has happened on other planets. It is then that we begin to realize how widespread and how deep, geologically speaking, these are, and how constitutive of the universe what we call earth processes are. For example, by asking what forms rocks, what forms water, you realize that all of those things are processes with which we can interfere (for this planet and more), which we can store as technology, as numbers, or in our imagination. Therefore, the question is how do we change our perspective? How do we persuade humans to read the situation differently? The challenge is whether the human story can any longer remain only about humans and whether the problem itself lies in our homocentrism.

K.K.: You have already elaborated on the human being as a life form, as a co-actor in the current crisis, in order to describe the processes of belonging to the deeper history of the earth; but what kind of understanding of the human being may emerge, would you say, from the variety of perspectives that you have suggested?

D.C.: There are two aspects to the human problem, which is to say that as human beings, and thinking of human history, one faces a two-sided problem. I often think of it as a problem of having a large brain, because the large brain is both an advantage and a disadvantage; actually, it creates two different worlds for us. As you know, in human evolution, the brain grew and there is a point in our evolution where the brain becomes large as we began to eat more protein. Obviously, this relates to histories of our skills in killing animals. One interesting fact reported about humans—and discussed by Noah Yuval Harari—is that their earliest tools were stone tools used to break bones. They would break bones to get to the bone marrow. Why? The reason for this innovation was that human beings were not at the top of the food chain. They could only eat after the lions had eaten, and then only when the hyenas and then the foxes had taken their shares. Once all those animals had taken away the meat, fat, and everything, only the bones would be lying there. With stone tools, human beings were able to break the bones to get to the bone marrow.

If you think of the relationship between lions and their food, let us say deer, you can see that, as lions moved to the top of the food chain, the deer evolved to be able to run faster. This meant that the lions could keep on eating deer without creating havoc. Humankind, on the other hand, has moved too fast (from the point of view of others) to the top of the food chain, and have done so through institutional changes and not through evolutionary developments. This is because, thanks to eating protein, our big brain has allowed us to create symbolic systems; symbolic systems allow us to cooperate on much larger scales than chimpanzees can, for instance. By cooperating, therefore, we could kill animals and rise to the top of the food chain; we now eat more food than wild animals. What has happened is that the rest of nature has not had time to adjust to our rapid rise to the top of the food chain. That is why fish, for example, cannot reproduce fast enough compared to our technologies.

On the one hand, the big brain allowed us, in addition to creating symbolic systems, a quite rich, detailed, and differentiated internal subjective experience of the world. This is why we can fall in love, write music, and why when we breed babies, all of whom mostly repeat the actions of all previous babies and yet each newly born baby remains fresh to us. On the other hand, the big brain also gives us cognitive faculties so that we can comprehend very large-scale phenomena, which we do not experience as part of the human story but which we comprehend intellectually. This is how we can construct problems intellectually such as climate change, black holes, or whether the universe is receding, collapsing, or expanding.

The problem with having a big brain is that you can cognitively see the problems you are creating, while at the same time the individual human life span—my own story from my birth to death, your story from birth to death—remains an enormously significant story for our own lifetimes. For example, I know much about climate change, but when I think of my pension, I do not think about climate change. There is a disconnect, because my interests lie in whether these investments will give me enough of a return, and that concern means that I continue with the human story. This is true in whichever institution we find ourselves, capitalism or no capitalism. Intellectually, therefore, global warming tells us that homocentrism is a problem; we need to expand the vision and the vista, but our inner consciousness, our sense of inner time, is not in concordance.

So while we understand cognitively that homocentrism is a problem, this does not mean that we can immediately escape our inner subjectivity and simply become part of the big story. This is why I believe that whatever the big history is, it will be channelled through more human-scale histories, because the people who will act on this planet, who will take action and do something on this planet, are the living. The dead and the unborn will not act! So when we act, both in evolutionary and social terms, we calculate over our human life span.

K.K.: I would now like to move to aspects of the Anthropocene with respect to its connection with postcolonial thinking and ask you about questions of power, justice, freedom and validity, as well as the role of capitalism.

D.C.: Postcolonial thinkers—anti-imperial or Marxist thinkers—make us more aware of two things: one is on the impact side of the climate crisis, that it will actually hurt the poor more, even though the privileged have taken the bigger role in causing the crisis. Therefore, they also point to the connection between capitalism, capitalist globalization, and the consumption of fossil fuels and crises around resources, and then the connection with the climate crisis itself. There are two problems here: one is that the Marxist story and the postcolonial story have so far both been homocentric stories, so they have not seriously taken into account how the planetary forces and evolutionary forces are co-actors. In other words, Marxists sometimes take a novel position of arguing: we (that is, Marxists) could not have described the climate crisis because we did not have climate science to define the problem; but we can nevertheless explain it better than scientists because we can explain how capitalism caused it! To me, this is a funny position to take whereby on the one hand you claim that you have a form of knowledge that cannot define a problem while at the same time claiming to be able to explain or even solve it (by abolishing capitalism)! In the end, while the Marxists can explain a part of the problem they cannot explain all of it, so to me this is a problem that at least in its definitional structure is something like Marxism-plus, a Marxism-plus climate science. However, when you bring climate science into the argument, the difficulty is clear, and this is because the basis of Marxism lies in the story of exploitation of humans by humans, but now there are co-actors in the mix and the human story alone cannot work. I find that these conundrums give us some insight into questions of justice, questions of capitalist globalization, and the burgeoning need for consumption. However, there is a difficulty Marxists have explaining why even the so-called victims of capitalism want capitalism (without invoking some variety of false consciousness or misrecognition on the part of the victims). For instance, if the capitalist development model is so discredited then why is it that India and China want to follow the same model? The Marxist model does not explain what creates this desire, because the desire actually relates to our homocentrism. If one group of human beings sees another group of humans living quite well, naturally, they will want to live like that as well, for we are a species whose members learn from one another. The fact is that capitalism or industrialization did allow a part of humanity to live quite well and it enriched their lives. With consumer capitalism, we have actually made the world quite exciting even for individual humans. Look at how much people enjoy having a smartphone.

In a way, therefore, what capitalism has done has been to promote precisely what we humans have created, which is to create more and more ways of being stimulated to the point where we are overstimulated. Normal political–economic explanations fail to take these sorts of issues into account, because they connect neither with phenomenology nor climate change. In some ways, therefore, they remain homocentric without reflecting adequately on the problem of homocentrism. This lack of insight has actually affected the politics of climate change because when climate scientists first said that humans are creating a problem they did not differentiate the category human beings, for the simple fact that they were not political economists. It was actually the environmental activists of the Third World who began to argue from the perspective of per capita emissions, lifestyle differences, and so on, out of which—from Rio de Janeiro to Kyoto in around 1991 to 1997—the formula emerged that there was 'common but differentiated responsibility' for global warming.

'Differentiated responsibility' is the story of capitalism and its inequalities; and the word 'common' in my view was a lazy one in this usage, thrown hastily into the mix to satisfy the Americans, so that when the principle of 'common but differentiated responsibility' was stated, the meaning of the word 'common' remained unclear. Now even a child on the Third World street knows that Western nations are bad nations, self-interested and aggressive. It is only when we turn to the question of homocentrism we realize that with the desirability of the internet and all of these things, the appeal of capitalism applies to everybody. Then we begin to realize what is at stake for human beings in this technology, in this story, in the condemned and yet desirable fossil fuels. We all, in different ways, differentially, found these things desirable. When I look back at Indian history, it strikes me that Mahatma Gandhi did not want industrialization, but India rejected Gandhi and wanted industrialization. No one imposed this on India; Indian leaders genuinely wanted industrialization, in the name of development, in the name of progress.

Through capitalism, humans have created a world that they would love if the climate crisis were not the reality. We would have gone on imagining that everybody eventually would have a smartphone, an SUV car—everyone would be taking transatlantic flights. You see, this was the vision of unending growth, but this vision speaks profoundly to our homocentric concerns, which means therefore that the connection between capitalism and our desires is far deeper than either the Marxists or left-wing historians generally acknowledge.

K.K.: One thing we have still to discuss is the validity of human universals, where, while confronted with new belongings and responsibilities towards other agents today, the Anthropocene confronts humans with another distinction created by the humanist Enlightenment project that established morality as a solid, rational base, putting the human being first. Could you talk a bit about the 'clash' of these distinctions?

D.C.: First, as I have said, creating the common is very difficult, because our subjectivity differentiates us. Therefore, just as we can cognitively understand that there is something called humanity (that is, cognitively we know there are seven billion human beings living on the planet and nobody would dispute that), if someone speaks on behalf of humanity we will be suspicious that they are actually trying to camouflage some very partisan interests. That is also part of our subjectivity, so while we can symbolically create bigger systems, these are processed through our very subjective perceptions of conflicts and interests—who wins and who loses, and those sorts of concerns. Whatever happens about climate change this will be so—unless we think of dictatorial arrangements, which will not work, because if some powerful nations want to go down the path of geo-engineering, for instance, it will probably increase conflict in the world because it will not help all the wealthy nations equally.

The democratic option, therefore, is to create that sense of the common we have talked about—not to give up on the differentiated—but to work alongside it, with the realization that it is everybody's problem. In my first article on climate change, for example, I wrote a sentence where I actually acknowledged that global warming would accentuate inequities; but then I also said that unlike the crisis of capital this is a crisis for everybody, as even the rich do not have lifeboats. Many on the left opposed that sentence, saying Chakrabarty is wrong, because, of course, the rich have lifeboats. First, I would argue that they read what I wrote literally. Second, I would then remind them that if global warming really assumed runaway proportions, if temperatures did start to rise above four degrees to five, six, seven degrees, I think we would then witness many collapses of our socio-economic systems, and capitalism, as we currently know it, may no longer function. In this case, the rich will also suffer, and in that sense, there will be no lifeboats.

There is a reason why I wrote that sentence: I was in Australia before the 2007 elections when I saw climate change become a top electoral issue resulting in the demand that Australia should sign the Kyoto Protocol. Before 2007, Australia had experienced a potentially catastrophic ten-year-long drought, which had seen rivers drying up, crops shrinking, and water levels sinking. There were severe water restrictions, the whole of Australian society was panicking, and there was real concern among Australians that they would have to become a water-importing nation. If you have concerns about becoming a water-importing nation then you immediately feel insecure, because you begin to worry that if there is a conflict situation your enemies will just starve you of water, and then you are finished. There were all sorts of fantasies, whether Australians would have to emigrate and settle in other countries, a collective panic, which made climate change a political matter of the highest priority for the time being. This is why

I believe that we cannot compose, in the sense of Bruno Latour, a sense of the human 'we' and sustain it for all time. However, I do think crises, such as the fear of nuclear aggression, from time to time, will create larger identities.

Another issue I believe worth considering relates to another people problem, when we cognitively realize that this is a story that involves other life forms; other species are involved in the human story. This is a story that acknowledges that humans institutions have grown faster than other species have naturally grown through evolution. Some people raise the question of whether we can act as a responsible species. My thought about that is we could act as a responsible species—by which I do not mean as do-gooders—but only if we had a multispecies government. But we have a human government, we only have the domination by this species on the planet. We face several problems therefore, one of which is that the governments of the world are human beings. It is not enough—though I welcome the gesture—to extend (human) rights to non-humans.

In the past, people have asked me why is it that if one can answer to an abstract word like 'labour'—that is, I can say that I am a labourer—that one cannot also make one's species the basis of politics. My reply is that labour is a governmental category: we have the department of labour, the labour association, labour laws, and so on. But species is not a governmental category, it is still a biological category. If it were a governmental category then, sure, one could be charged to act as a species, but the government would have to be a multispecies one. This brings us back to the Latourian problem of how difficult it is to compose what he calls the parliament of things and species.

There are these huge problems: the Anthropocene is still a huge intellectual challenge from which, probably, institutional responses will have to follow. For now, however, we are still in a world where, in many countries, climate change is still not a big issue. In India, for instance, climate change is not a big issue in the public sphere. Globalization is, but global warming is not. India wants to use more coal, thus development is an issue, and environmental pollution and corruption are issues, but not global warming, that is, planetary global warming. Climate change is still not a central issue even in the West; when teaching courses on global warming in America, or even when I get questions from well-educated Indian friends, I witness the lack of real understanding around the issues. A political science lecturer in India, for instance, after the April 2015 earthquake in Nepal wrote to me asking: do you still believe that humans have a geological agency? Evidently, he does not understand the sense in which people talk about the issues. He is just thinking that there has been an earthquake, which is of geological proportions, and we are so puny. Of course, we are puny, but his attitude illustrates the ignorance around these issues.

K.K.: Definitely, I agree. I think this brings us to the last question. Do you feel we have the right tools and means for this contemporary sense on which you have already elaborated, which I see as also triggering our future imaginary? Do you think that there is also a problem about how to narrate these stories; does the language fall short of what we require to narrate the issues?

D.C.: Yes, definitely, the language falls short of what we require. The Anthropocene is something that functions both as a name and a concept, but remains contested as both. Therefore, when you use it as a proper noun people argue that it should be renamed Capitalocene or Econocene, and all sorts of other labels. As a concept, people are still arguing about when to date it from, so Jan Zalasiewicz and other people take one sort of position, dating its beginning from the detonation of the first atom bomb, while Simon Lewis and Mark Maslin's recent paper argues that the Anthropocene starts in 1610, with the Spanish in South America and the death of a large number of American Indians.[1] This suggests to me that although Maslin is a geographer he is still involved with the politics of the concept, saying that if we date it from the Spanish in South America then we tell the story of European exploitation and so on. Others ask whether we should begin the Anthropocene from the time of the atom bomb, but Maslin and Lewis fear that that turns the story into a technological one, rendering the social story irrelevant. These debates are still ongoing. For me, whether you date it from 1610 or 1945, through all of this there is an invitation in the literature to think of human beings in the context of deep, geological, and evolutionary time. While the problems I have outlined about the big brain will always remain because we are born with it, at least if we learn to acknowledge our place in deep, geological,

---

[1] Simon L. Lewis and Mark A. Maslin, 'Defining the Anthropocene', *Nature* 519 (12 March 2015): 171–80.

and evolutionary time, at every step, then we will begin to connect our local problems with some larger ones.

I do see some incremental changes, for example with my students, who if they get the larger perspective do begin to see the world in a new way. For example, a young female PhD student, working on Indian literature, recently enrolled on my course of climate change. She came to see me one day and said that she had been looking up to the sky and noticed the trail of smoke, known as contrails, emitted from an airplane. Previously, the clouds in the sky probably would have perhaps only reminded her of the classical Indian poet Kalidasa! Therefore, although this young woman was not a typical candidate for my course, suddenly, for her, the plane and the contrails had a meaning in terms of what she was learning about the climate. This means, or at least one hopes, that the more we spread the perspective, the more people will begin to make these connections. This is to be optimistic about the future, but at present we are still at the beginning of an intellectual transition, which I think will intensify one day.

SELECT BIBLIOGRAPHY OF
PUBLISHED WORKS

A World on the Move: A History of Colonialism and Nationalism in Asia and North Africa from the Turn of the Century to the Bandung Conference. English text prepared by James S. Holmes and A. Van Marle. Amsterdam: Djambaten, 1956.

Abdulgani, Roeslan. *The Bandung Connection: The Asia–Africa Conference in Bandung in 1955.* Singapore: Gunung Agung, 1981.

Alatas, Syed Hussain. *The Myth of the Lazy Native: A Study of the Image of the Malays, Filipinos, and Javanese from the 16th to the 20th Century and Its Function in the Ideology of Colonial Capitalism.* London: Frank Cass, 1977.

Appadorai, A. *The Bandung Conference.* New Delhi: The Indian Council of World Affairs, 1955 (reprinted from *India Quarterly*).

Appadurai, Arjun. *Modernity at Large: Cultural Dimensions of Globalization.* Minneapolis: University of Minnesota Press, 1996.

Archer, David. *Global Warming: Understanding the Forecast.* Malden, MA: Blackwell, 2007.

Arendt, Hannah. *The Human Condition.* Chicago: University of Chicago Press, 1998 [1958].

Arrighi, Giovanni. *The Long Twentieth Century: Money, Power, and the Origins of Our Times.* London: Verso, 2006 [1994].

———. *Adam Smith in Beijing: Lineages of the Twenty-First Century* (London: Verso, 2007).

Asian Relations: Report of the Proceedings and Documentation of the First Asian Relations Conference, New Delhi, March–April, 1947. Introduced by Professor D. Gopal. Delhi: Authorspress, 2003.

Assayag, Jackie and Veronique Benei, eds. *At Home in Diaspora: South Asian Scholars and the West.* Bloomington: Indiana University Press, 2003.

Banerjee, Sumanta. *India's Simmering Revolution: The Naxalite Uprising.* London: Zed Books, 1984.

Bayly, C. A. *The Birth of the Modern World, 1780–1914: Global Connections and Comparisons.* Malden, MA: Blackwell, 2004.

Bhabha, Homi K. *The Location of Culture.* London and New York: Routledge, 1994.

Bolin, Bert. *A History of the Science and Politics of Climate Change: The Role of the Intergovernmental Panel on Climate Change.* Cambridge: Cambridge University Press, 2007.

Bowden, Brett. *The Empire of Civilization: The Evolution of an Imperial Idea.* Chicago: University of Chicago Press, 2009.

Braudel, Fernand. *The Mediterranean and the Mediterranean World in the Age of Philip II.* Translated by Siân Reynolds, 2 vols. London: Harper Collins, 1972 [1949].

Burke, Marie Louise. *Swami Vivekananda in the West: New Discoveries—His Prophetic Mission*, vol. 1. Calcutta: Advaita Ashram, 1998 [1958].

Burke, Peter. *The French Historical Revolution: The 'Annales' School, 1929–89.* Stanford, CA: Stanford University Press, 1990.

Calvin, William H. *Global Fever: How to Treat Climate Change.* Chicago: University of Chicago Press, 2008.

Césaire, Aimé. *Discourse on Colonialism.* Translated by Joan Pinkham. London: Monthly Review Press, 2001.

———. *Non-Vicious Circle: Twenty Poems of Aimé Césaire.* Translated and introduced by Gregson Davis. Stanford, CA: Stanford University Press, 1984.

Chakrabarty, Dipesh. 'Belatedness as Possibility: Subaltern Histories, Once More'. In *The Indian Postcolonial: A Critical Reader*, edited by Elleke Boehmer and Rosinka Chaudhuri, pp. 163–76. London: Routledge, 2011.

———. 'Can Political Economy Be Postcolonial? A Note'. In *Postcolonial Economies*, edited by Jane Pollard, Cheryl McEwan, and Alex Hughes, pp. 23–35. London: Zed Books, 2011.

———. *The Calling of History: Sir Jadunath Sarkar and His Empire of Truth.* Chicago: University of Chicago Press, 2015.

———. 'The Climate of History: Four Theses', *Critical Inquiry* 35, no. 2 (Winter 2009): 197–222.

———. 'From Civilization to Globalization: The "West" as a Shifting Signifier in Indian Modernity. *Inter-Asia Cultural Studies* 13, no. 1 (2012): 138–52.

———. *Habitations of Modernity: Essays in the Wake of Subaltern Studies.* Chicago: University of Chicago Press, 2002.

———. *Itihaser janajibon o onyanyo probondho.* Calcutta: Ananda, 2011.

———. *L'Humanisme en Una Era Global* (Humanism in an Age of Globalization). Barcelona: Center for Contemporary Culture, 2008. Reprinted in *Alltag,*

Erfahrung, Eigensinn: Historisch-anthropologische Erkundungen. Edited by Belinda Davis, Thomas Lindenberger, and Michael Wildt, pp. 74–90. Frankfurt, New York: Campus Verlag, 2008.

Chakrabarty, Dipesh. 'Place and Displaced Categories, Or How We Translate Ourselves into Global Histories of the Modern'. In *The Trans/national Study of Culture: A Translational Perspective,* edited by Doris Bachmann-Medick, pp. 53–68. Berlin: De Gruyter, 2014.

———. 'Postcoloniality and the Artifice of History: Who Speaks for "Indian" Pasts?' *Representations,* no. 37 (Winter 1992): 1–26.

———. *Provincializing Europe: Postcolonial Thought and Historical Difference.* Princeton, NJ: Princeton University Press, 2000 [2007].

———. *Rethinking Working-Class History: Bengal 1890–1940.* Princeton, NJ: Princeton University Press, 1989.

———. 'Romantic Archives: Literature and the Politics of Identity in Bengal'. *Critical Inquiry* 30, no. 2 (Spring 2004): 654–82

Chatterjee, Partha. *The Politics of the Governed: Reflections on Popular Politics in Most of the World.* New York: Columbia University Press, 2004.

———. 'Reflections on "Can the Subaltern Speak"'. In *Can the Subaltern Speak? Reflections on the History of an Idea,* edited by R. C. Morris, pp. 81–6. New York: Columbia University Press, 2010.

Chaturvedi, Vinayak. *Peasant Pasts: History and Memory in Western India.* Berkeley: The University of California Press, 2007.

Childe, V. Gordon. *Man Makes Himself.* London: Watts, 1941.

Clarke, John, Chris Critcher, and R. Johnson, eds. *Working-Class Culture: Studies in Theory and History.* New York: St Martin's Press, 1979.

Collingwood, R. G. *The Idea of History.* New York: Oxford University Press, 1976 [1946].

Croce, Benedetto. *The Philosophy of Giambattista Vico.* Translated by R. G. Collingwood. New Brunswick, NJ: Transaction Publishers, 2002 [1913].

Crosby, Jr, Alfred W. *The Columbian Exchange: Biological and Cultural Consequences of 1492.* Westport, CT: Praeger, 2003 [1972].

Das Gupta, Harendra Mohan. *Studies in Western Influence on Nineteenth-Century Bengali Poetry, 1857–1887.* Calcutta: Semushi, 1969 [1935].

Datta, Pradip Kumar. *Carving Blocs: Communal Ideology in Early Twentieth-Century Bengal.* New Delhi: Oxford University Press, 1999.

Deleuze, Gilles. *Difference and Repetition.* Translated by Paul Patton. New York: Columbia University Press, 1994.

Dening, Greg. *Beach-Crossings: Voyages Across Times, Cultures, and Self.* Philadelphia: University of Pennsylvania Press, 2004.

———. *The Death of William Gooch: History's Anthropology.* Lanham, MD: University Press of America, 1988 [1995], second edition.

Dening, Greg. *Islands and Beaches: Discussions on a Silent Land–Marquesas, 1774–1880*. Honolulu: University of Hawaii Press, 1980.

———. *Performances*. Chicago: University of Chicago Press, 1996.

Dodds, Walter K. *Humanity's Footprint: Momentum, Impact, and Our Global Environment*. New York: Columbia University Press, 2008.

Fanon, Frantz. *Black Skin, White Masks*. Translated by Charles Lam Markmann. London: Paladin, 1970 [1952].

———. *The Wretched of the Earth*. Translated by Constance Farrington. New York: Grove Press, 1963.

Farred, Grant. 'Out of Context: Rethinking Cultural Studies Diasporically'. *Cultural Studies Review* 15, no. 1 (March 2009): 130–50.

Ferguson, Niall. *Empire: How Britain Made the Modern World*. London: Penguin, 2003.

Foucault, Michel. *'Society Must Be Defended': Lectures at Collège de France*. Translated by David Macey. New York: Picador, 2003.

Gadamer, Hans-Georg. *Truth and Method*. Translated by Joel Weinsheimer and Donald G. Marshall. London: Continuum, 1988 [1975; 1979], second edition.

Gandhi, Leela. *Affective Communities: Anti-Colonial Thought, Fin-de-Siècle Radicalism, and the Politics of Friendship*. Durham, NC: Duke University Press, 2006.

Gandhi, M. K. *Hind Swaraj and Other Writings*. Edited by Anthony J. Parel. Cambridge: Cambridge University Press, 2007 [1997].

Gerschenkron, Alexander. *Economic Backwardness in Historical Perspective–A Book of Essays*. Cambridge, MA: Belknap Harvard, 1962.

Gibson-Graham, J. K. *A Postcapitalist Politics*. Minneapolis: University of Minnesota Press, 2006.

Gibson-Graham, J. K. and Gerda Roelvink. 'An Economic Ethics for the Anthropocene'. *Antipode: A Radical Journal of Geography* 41, Supplement 1 (2010): 320–46.

Gibson-Graham, J. K., S. Resnick, and R. D. Wolff, eds. *Re/presenting Class: Essays in Postmodern Marxism*. Durham, NC: Duke University Press, 2001.

Gidwani, Vinay. *Capital, Interrupted: Agrarian Development and the Politics of Work in India*. Minneapolis: University of Minnesota Press, 2008.

Guha, Ranajit. *Elementary Aspects of Peasant Insurgency in Colonial India*. Delhi: Oxford University Press, 1983.

Guha, Ranajit and Gayatri Chakravorty Spivak, eds. *Selected Subaltern Studies*. New York: Oxford University Press, 1988.

Hall, Stuart. 'A Sense of Classlessness'. *Universities and Left Review* (Autumn 1958): pp. 26–32.

Hall, Stuart, Chris Critcher, Tony Jefferson, John Clarke, and Brian Roberts, eds. *Policing the Crisis: Mugging, the State, and Law and Order*. London: Macmillan, 1978.

Hardt, Michael and Antonio Negri. *Empire*. Cambridge, MA: Harvard University Press, 2000.

Harvey, David. *The Condition of Postmodernity*. Oxford: Blackwell, 2000.

Heidegger, Martin. 'A Dialogue on Language'. In *On the Way to Language*, translated by Peter D. Hertz. New York: Harper and Row, 1982.

Hoggart, Richard. *The Uses of Literacy*. London: Chatto and Windus, 1957.

Hountondji, Paulin J. *African Philosophy: Myth and Reality*. Translated by Henri Evans and Jonathan Rée. Bloomington: Indiana University Press, 1983 [1976].

Jasimuddin. *Smaraner sharani bahi*. Calcutta: Antara, 1976.

Khilnani, Sunil. *The Idea of India*. New York: Farrar, Strauss, Giroux, 1998.

Kotelawala, John. *An Asian Prime Minister's Story*. London: George G. Harrap & Co., 1956.

Lake, Marilyn and Henry Reynolds. *Drawing the Global Color Line: White Men's Countries and the International Challenge of Racial Equality*. New York: Cambridge University Press, 2008.

Latour, Bruno. *Politics of Nature: How to Bring the Sciences into Democracy*. Translated by Catherine Porter. Cambridge, MA: Harvard University Press, 2004 [1999].

Lynas, Mark. *Six Degrees: Our Future on a Hotter Planet*. Washington, DC: National Geographic, 2008.

Macey, David. *Frantz Fanon: A Biography*. New York: Picador, 2000.

Majumdar, Rochona. *Writing Postcolonial History*. London: Bloomsbury, 2010.

Martin, Kingsley. *Harold Laski (1893–1950): A Biographical Memoir*. New York: Viking, 1953.

Marx, Karl. 'The Eighteenth Brumaire of Louis Bonaparte'. In *Selected Works*, edited by Karl Marx and Frederick Engels, vol. 1. Moscow: Progress Publishers, 1969.

Maslin, Mark. *Global Warming: A Very Short Introduction*. Oxford: Oxford University Press, 2004.

McGuire, Bill. *Waking the Giant: How a Changing Climate Triggers Earthquakes, Tsunamis, and Volcanoes*. New York and Oxford: Oxford University Press, 2012.

McKibben, Bill. *The End of Nature*. New York: Random House, 2006 [1989].

Miller, Cecilia. *Giambattista Vico: Imagination and Historical Knowledge*. Basingstoke: Palgrave Macmillan, 1993.

Monroe, Harriet. *A Poet's Life: Seventy Years in a Changing World*. New York: McMillan, 1938.

Morley, David and Kuan-Hsing Chen, eds. *Stuart Hall: Critical Dialogue and Cultural Studies*. London and New York: Routledge, 1996.

Nandy, Ashis. *The Intimate Enemy: Loss and Recovery of Self under Colonialism*. Delhi: Oxford University Press, 1983.

Nehru, Jawaharlal. 'Letter to Gandhi, 9 October 1945'. In *Hind Swaraj and Other Writings*, edited by Anthony J. Parel, pp. 152–3. Cambridge: Cambridge University Press, 2007 [1997].

———. *Selected Works of Jawaharlal Nehru*, second series, vols 27–29. Delhi: Jawaharlal Nehru Memorial Fund, 2000–2001.

Ngũgĩ wa Thiong'o. *Decolonising the Mind: The Politics of Language in African Literature*. London: James Curry, 1986.

Nyerere, Julius K. *Freedom and Unity*. London: Oxford University Press, 1967.

Oreskes, Naomi. 'The Scientific Consensus on Climate Change: How Do We Know We're Not Wrong?' In *Climate Change: What It Means for Us, Our Children, and Our Grandchildren*, edited by Joseph F. C. Dimento and Pamela Doughman. Cambridge, MA: MIT Press, 2007.

Orsini, Francesca. 'The Hindi Public Sphere and Political Discourse in the Twentieth Century', unpublished paper presented at the conference 'The Sites of the Political in South Asia', Berlin, October 2003.

———. *The Hindi Public Sphere: Language and Literature in the Age of Nationalism*. New Delhi: Oxford University Press, 2002.

Orwin, Clifford. 'Citizenship and Civility as Components of Liberal Democracy'. In *Civility and Citizenship*, edited by Edward C. Banfield, pp. 75–94. St Paul, MN: Professors of the World Peace Academy, 1992.

Pearson, Charles S. *Economics and the Challenge of Global Warming*. Cambridge: Cambridge University Press, 2011.

Perelman, M. *The Invention of Capitalism: Classical Political Economy and the Secret History of Primitive Accumulation*. Durham, NC: Duke University Press, 2000.

Pomeranz, Kenneth. *The Great Divergence: China, Europe, and the Making of the Modern World Economy*. Princeton, NJ: Princeton University Press, 2000.

Posner, Eric A. and David Wisebach. *Climate Change Justice*. Princeton, NJ: Princeton University Press, 2010.

Raychaudhuri, Debkumar. *Dwijendralal: Jibon*. Calcutta: Basudhara Prakashani, 1965.

Read, Alan, ed. *The Fact of Blackness: Frantz Fanon and Visual Representation*. Seattle: Bay Press, 1996.

Reynolds, Henry. *Fate of a Free People*. Ringwood, Victoria: Penguin, 1995.

Roberts, David D. *Benedetto Croce and the Uses of Historicism*. Berkeley: University of California Press, 1987.

Romulo, Carlos P. *The Meaning of Bandung*. Chapel Hill: University of North Carolina Press, 1956.

Rossi, Paolo. *The Dark Abyss of Time: The History of the Earth and the History of Nations from Hooke to Vico*. Translated by Lydia G. Cochrane. Chicago: University of Chicago Press, 1984 [1979].

Ruthven, Kenneth, ed. *Beyond the Disciplines: The New Humanities*. Canberra: Australian Academy of Humanities, 1992.

Sarkar, Sumit. *The Swadeshi Movement in Bengal, 1903–1908*. Delhi: People's Publishing House, 1973.

de Saussure, Ferdinand. *Course in General Linguistics*. Edited by Charles Bally and Albert Sechehaye. Translated by Wade Baskin. New York: McGraw Hill, 1966.

Seely, Clinton. *A Poet Apart: A Literary Biography of the Bengali Poet Jibananada Das (1889–1954)*. Newark: University of Delaware Press, 1990.

Selected Documents of the Bandung Conference. New York: Institute of Pacific Relations, 1955.

Sen, Dinesh Chandra. *Bangabhasha o shahitya*. Edited by Asitkumar Bandyopadhyay, 2 vols. Calcutta: West Bengal State Book Board, 1991 [1st edition, 1896; 2nd edition, 1901; 6th edition, 1926].

———. *Banglar puronari*. Calcutta: Jijnasa, 1939.

———. *Gharer katha o jugashahitya*. Calcutta: Jijnasa, 1969 [1922].

———. *Brihat banga*. Calcutta: Dey's, 1993 [1935].

———. *History of Bengali Language and Literature*. Calcutta: University of Calcutta, 1911.

Senghor, Léopold Sédar. *Prose and Poetry*. Selected and translated by John Reed and Clive Wake. London: Oxford University Press, 1965.

Shils, Edward. 'Civility and Civil Society'. In *Civility and Citizenship*, edited by Edward C. Banfield, pp. 1–15. St Paul, MN: Professors of the World Peace Academy, 1992.

Smail, Daniel Lord. *On Deep History and the Brain*. Berkeley: University of California Press, 2008.

Smith, William Edgett. *We Must Run While They Walk: A Portrait of Africa's Julius Nyerere*. New York: Random House, 1971.

Solomon, Susan et al., eds. *Climate Change 2007: The Physical Science Basis* (Contribution to the Working Group I to the Fourth Assessment Report of the Intergovernmental Panel on Climate Change). Cambridge: Cambridge University Press, 2009 [2007].

Spivak, Gayatri. 'Can the Subaltern Speak?' In *Can the Subaltern Speak? Reflections on the History of an Idea*, edited by R. C. Morris, pp. 21–78. New York: Columbia University Press, 2010 [1988].

Srivastava, Gita. *Mazzini and His Impact on the Indian Nationalist Movement*. Allahabad: Chugh Publications, 1982.

Stargardt, A. W. 'The Emergence of the Asian Systems of Power'. *Modern Asian Studies* 23, no. 3 (1989): 561–95.

Stephens, Julie. *Anti-Disciplinary Politics: Sixties Radicalism and Postmodernism.* Cambridge: Cambridge University Press, 1998.

Stern, Nicholas. *The Economics of Climate Change: The 'Stern Review'.* Cambridge: Cambridge University Press, 2007.

Sunstein, Cass R. *Risk and Reason: Safety, Law, and the Environment.* Cambridge: Cambridge University Press, 2002.

Tagore, Rabindranath. 'Bangabhasha o shahitya' (1902). In *Rabindrarachabali: Janmashatabarshik shongskoron.* Calcutta: Government of West Bengal, 1961.

———. 'Change of Times' [Kalantar]. In *The Collected Works of Rabindranath: Change of Times [Rabindrarachanabali: Kalantar].* Calcutta: Government of West Bengal, 1968.

———. 'Crisis in Civilization'. In *The English Writings of Rabindranath Tagore,* vol. 3, edited by Sisir Kumar Das, pp. 724–6. Delhi: Sahitya Akademi, 1999.

———. 'The Crisis of Civilization' [Sabhyatar Shankat]. In *The Collected Works of Rabindranath [Rabindrarachanabali],* vol. 13, p. 407. Calcutta: Government of West Bengal, 1961, centenary edition.

———. 'East and West'. In *The English Writings of Rabindranath Tagore,* vol. 3, edited by Sisir Kumar Das. Delhi: Sahitya Akademi, 1999.

Tate, Merze. 'Review of Richard Wright'. *The Color Curtain. The Journal of Negro History* 41, no. 3 (July 1956): 263–5.

Thompson, E. P. *Whigs and Hunters: The Origin of the Black Act.* London: Allen Lane, 1975.

———. *The Making of the English Working Class.* Harmondsworth: Penguin, 1963.

Tudge, Colin. *Neanderthals, Bandits, and Farmers: How Agriculture Really Began.* New Haven, CT: Yale University Press, 1999.

Viswanathan, Gauri. *Masks of Conquest: Literary Studies and British Rule in India.* New York: Columbia University Press, 1989.

Vivekananda. *The Complete Works of Swami Vivekananda,* vol. 5, pp. 79–80. Calcutta: Advaita Ashram, 1995, Mayavati Memorial edition.

Vivekananda. 'Letter to Alasinga Perumal, 20 August 1893'. In *The Complete Works of Swami Vivekananda,* vol. 5, pp. 18–20. Calcutta: Advaita Ashram, 1995, Mayavati Memorial edition.

Walicki, Andrzej. *The Controversy over Capitalism: Studies in the Social Philosophy of the Russian Populists.* Notre Dame, IN: University of Notre Dame Press, 1989.

Weisman, Alan. *The World without Us.* New York: Thomas Dunne/St Martin's Press, 2007.

Wilson, Edward O. *The Future of Life.* New York: Alfred A. Knopf, 2002.

———. *In Search of Nature.* Washington, DC: Island, 1996.

Wright, Richard. *The Color Curtain: A Report on the Bandung Conference.* Cleveland: The World Publishing Company, 1956.

INDEX

ABOUT THE AUTHOR

Dipesh Chakrabarty is Lawrence A. Kimpton Distinguished Service Professor in History and South Asian Languages and Civilizations at the University of Chicago, USA. His books include *Rethinking Working-Class History: Bengal 1890–1940* (1989), *Provincializing Europe: Postcolonial Thought and Historical Difference* (2000), and *The Calling of History: Sir Jadunath Sarkar and His Empire of Truth* (2015).

He is a founding member of the editorial collective Subaltern Studies and a consulting editor of *Critical Inquiry*. He also holds an honorary DLitt degree (2010) from the University of London, UK and an honorary doctorate degree (2011) from the University of Antwerp, Belgium. He received the 2014 Toynbee Prize for his contributions to global history and delivered the Tanner Lectures in Human Values at Yale in 2015.